THE
PRAIRIE STATE

THE
PRAIRIE STATE

A DOCUMENTARY HISTORY OF ILLINOIS
Civil War to the Present

Edited by

Robert P. Sutton

Director of Local and Regional Collections,
Western Illinois University Libraries

William B. Eerdmans Publishing Company

977.3
Sut
Pb
Vol. 2
Cop 1

Copyright © 1976 by Wm. B. Eerdmans Publ. Co.
255 Jefferson Ave. SE; Grand Rapids, Mich. 49502

Printed in the United States of America

Library of Congress Cataloging in Publication Data
Main entry under title:

The Prairie State.

  CONTENTS: v. 2.
Civil War to the present.
    1. Illinois—History—Sources. 2. Illinois—
History—Addresses, essays, lectures. I. Sutton,
Robert P.
F536.P7   977.3   76-21805
ISBN 0-8028-1652-5

To Christopher, Rebecca, and Abigail—my children.

"There is little that is more important for an American to know than the history and traditions of his country. Without such knowledge, he stands uncertain and defenseless before the world."

—John F. Kennedy

Acknowledgments

A documentary of the chronological scope of these volumes is the product of many individuals' assistance in the identification and collection of material. I am particularly indebted to Donna A. Goehner, Periodicals Librarian, Lois P. Mills, Documents and Legal Reference Librarian, and the entire staff of Memorial Library, Western Illinois University. Indispensable to the completion of *The Prairie State* was the assistance given to me by William K. Alderfer, State Historian, and Ellen M. Whitney, editor of the *Journal of the Illinois State Historical Society*. John J. Hartnett, a graduate assistant in the History Department of Western Illinois University, toiled diligently with me almost daily during the past year and thereby relieved me of hours of work. A special thanks goes to my wife, Alice, for her encouragement and for her careful reading of the manuscript. Finally, had it not been for the support of Reinder Van Til, Editor of the American History Series at Eerdmans, this documentary history might never have appeared in print.

Contents

List of Illustrations

Preface

It would seem that nature had intended Illinois to be the key-stone state of the Republic, though that name was first claimed by one of the original eastern commonwealths. Illinois's lush prairie soil and varied growing seasons were to yield the most productive grain farms on the North American continent, and under the surface lay the nation's largest deposits of bituminous coal. Bounded on the west by the Mississippi River, on the south by the Ohio, on the east by the Wabash, and on the northeast by Lake Michigan—with the addition of inland waterways—the state's geographical location has helped make it the transportation heart of the country; all the major commercial arteries enter and leave it. Illinois's population has been formed from the widely varying peoples who claimed America as their home: the Illiniwek Indians and French *coureurs de bois,* the English land settlers, the Southern frontiersmen and Yankee farmers, the nineteenth-century European emigrants, and the black freedmen. The state's contributions to American arts and culture have surpassed those of every state but New York; and, of course, it has produced many giants of American politics.

Until the publication of Robert Howard's *Illinois: A History of the Prairie State,* much of the focus of Illinois history had been on politics and wars, particularly Lincoln and the Civil War. But history—especially that of the Prairie State—goes far beyond the so-called drum-and-trumpet story. The processes that shaped Illinois find their sources not in the regimental chronicles and political speeches but in contemporaneous perceptions and original accounts of events that moved the territory and state, within a span of four generations, from a sparsely inhabited prairie to the "third state and second city" of the land by 1890, and then into the twentieth century.

Volume Two of this documentary history is organized into two chronological units: "The Gilded Age, 1860-1919," and "Modern Illinois, 1920-1975." These chronological units are divided into topical chapters. "The Gilded Age" deals with the Civil War period, the organization of farmers, industrialization and labor ferment, and progressive reforms. "Modern Illinois" chronicles the prohibition era, the Great Depression and New Deal, and the post-World War II period. Each chapter consists of special accounts (interpretive essays and selections from scholarly historical works intended to highlight important events of that era) followed by a section of original narratives, which include letters, diaries, speeches, travelogues, eyewitness reports, and reminiscences.

Part I

THE GILDED AGE, 1860-1919

Introduction

The story of Illinois in the Gilded Age is introduced by the tragic preface of the Civil War. In 1861, almost 260,000 young men answered the call to fight for the Union. Largely unequipped and untrained during the first years of the war, 34,834 were eventually listed as casualties—two-thirds of which resulted from deplorable standards of medicine and sanitation. However, the handicaps were surmounted, and under the command of Brigadier General Ulysses S. Grant, Illinois troops scored the first major Union victory against the Confederacy at Belmont and Fort Donelson. Illinoisans went on to participate with distinction at Vicksburg, Port Hudson, Atlanta, and, finally, in the siege of Richmond.

However, in the southern tip of the state sentiment against the Union ran high. The Southern sympathizers, labeled "Copperheads," organized vigilante bands such as the Sons of Liberty or the Knights of the Golden Circle to oppose the war—in the newspapers, through the ballot, and frequently by violence. In 1864, a group of the Sons of Liberty plotted a rebellion to free Confederate prisoners, capture railroads, and ultimately establish a separate government in the Northwest. In reaction to such intrigues, patriotic Unionists—often soldiers home on leave—responded with an equal share of rowdyism and violence, which sometimes resulted in pitched battles between the two groups. For example, both civilians and soldiers were killed in the Charleston riot of 1864. Partially in response to the troubles on the home front, President Lincoln suspended habeas corpus by executive order in 1862 and allowed civilians to be placed within the jurisdiction of courts-martial. This presidential action only exacerbated the division between those who supported and those who opposed the war.

Despite the internal dissension, many citizens of the state prospered from the war. In order to meet the unprecedented demands of raising, equipping, and supplying the Northern army, those at home revolutionized the economic plant of the state. Improved means of agricultural output, which had already been advanced by

John Deere's steel plow and the McCormick factory system of machine production, appeared throughout Illinois. Mass production techniques were used in towns and cities, and factories multiplied to provide the necessities of warfare. Chicago became the warehouse of the western theater of operations and, because of its strategic location as a distributing center for the Midwest, the hub of the western railroad system.

The changes brought about by war created new peacetime problems. Illinois politicians ignored the farmer in favor of business interests, whose increasing influence on the legislature during the war paralleled their increasing economic power. Farmers' pleas for help against mortgage foreclosures, high taxes, and exploitation by the railroads went unheard. In frustration the farmers organized the Grange, which under the leadership of Willard C. Flagg pushed through the legislature regulatory statutes that ultimately effected the landmark opinion of the United States Supreme Court in *Munn vs. Illinois:* that railroads could be controlled by a legislature.

Harder hit than the farmer by the emerging industrial revolution were the urban workers. Ironically, progress brought overcrowding and poverty. Returning veterans faced widespread unemployment, and slum conditions worsened with the arrival of unskilled immigrant labor. For those who had work, the Panic of 1873 and the ensuing depression meant the cutback of wages—often by 50 percent—and widespread layoffs and furloughs. In Chicago, which was barely recovering from the fire of 1871, an estimated 37 per cent of the work force was unemployed. Rioting broke out in that city, and strikers shut down railroads at Decatur, Peoria, Galesburg, and East St. Louis. On orders from Governor Cullom, the state militia, assisted by federal troops, broke the back of the strikes. But labor unrest persisted, and subsequent governors also resorted to force to maintain order. Allan Pinkerton, head of the federal Secret Service during the Civil War, even organized a detective service to repress labor organizations.

The tragedy at Haymarket Square occurred in the spring of 1886. Trouble had been brewing in Chicago for over a decade, since it had become the center of militant labor activity under the leadership of a group of German-born socialists. A meeting was called for the evening of May 4 at Haymarket Square on Randolph Street to protest a massive lockout by McCormick Works, an event which threatened the jobs of 80,000 employees. Toward the end of the gathering, police rode in on horseback to disperse 200 participants, remaining from an estimated crowd of 3,000. A bomb was thrown; seven policemen were killed and others were wounded. The uninjured officers fired on the crowd of workers, killing one of them. In the days that followed, the Pinkertons aided in apprehending a large number of suspects. A grand jury indicted 31 men, and eight known anarchists were tried for conspiracy to commit murder. Of these eight men—only one of whom was ever established to have been at Haymarket that night—seven were sentenced to death and one to 15 years imprisonment. Four anarchists were hanged, one committed suicide, and two had their death sentences commuted to life imprisonment by Governor Oglesby. In 1893, another governor, John P. Altgeld, pardoned the three remaining prisoners in a written message that was accompanied by a scathing attack on the entire trial proceedings.

The Haymarket events had scarcely receded from public attention when another outbreak of labor violence occurred. The Panic of 1893 and the accompanying depression precipitated a strike at the Pullman's workers' town because of Pullman's decision to cut pay by 25 per cent yet maintain rent and utility rates on factory housing at their pre-depression level. On May 11, 1894, the workers, led by Eugene V. Debs and the American Railway Union, walked out. The strike spread to 27 states when the union ordered its membership not to handle any trains containing Pullman sleeping cars. The railroads, faced with the calamity of a general strike, acted through the General Managers' Association to ask President Cleveland for the help of federal troops to break the strike. The necessity for federal military action, the managers said, was to keep the mail cars moving, even though Governor Altgeld had already dispatched state troops to aid in keeping order. At the same time the managers got a federal court to issue an injunction against Debs to stop the strike. Debs, in turn, defied the injunction and on July 10 was arrested on contempt charges and sentenced to six months in the Woodstock jail. Confronted by federal troops and the court, the workers returned to work and the strike subsided.

For a generation the plight of the farmer and worker had gone largely unheeded by the politicians who had taken Illinois through the war and into the industrial revolution. However, by the turn of the century a mounting demand for reform, at first focused on corruption in politics, began to take shape. The state legislature, with prodding from Governor Charles S. Deneen, enacted a statute that substituted the primary election for the boss-controlled convention as the method of gaining the party nomination for political office. Next, Illinois progressives attacked the spoils system by holding municipalities accountable to civil service laws. By 1911, approximately 80 per cent of the state's employees had been placed under the coverage of a law that guaranteed civil service coverage and restricted the reasons for worker dismissal to incompetence or other demonstrable good cause. Then the voters overwhelmingly approved a referendum on direct election of United States Senators. In the labor movement, the Illinois Federation of Labor became one of the strongest in the nation. With the close cooperation of progressive reformers such as Jane Addams of Hull House, labor, by the beginning of World War I, had succeeded in getting legislation on child labor, ten-hour days for workers in factories and laundries, workmen's compensation, safety regulations, factory inspection, and state funds for the care of dependent children.

1: Boys in Blue

This section of special accounts opens with Victor Hicken's vivid account of the Civil War engagement at Fort Donelson, where Illinois troops first "came against the real specter of war." The wounded and the dying lay unattended in their freezing blood throughout the night of February 15, 1862, and the next morning rescue workers had to hack them free of the frozen battlefield. *Illinois in the Civil War* (Urbana, 1966) was awarded, among other honors, the prize for the best work in state history in 1966 by the American Association for State and Local History. Hicken, currently President of the Illinois State Historical Society, has also written *The American Fighting Man* (1969) and numerous articles on Illinois history. Despite the ugly realities of combat, Illinoisans responded enthusiastically to calls for volunteers, as Arthur C. Cole points out in a selection from *The Era of the Civil War, 1848-1870* (Chicago, 1919). The exception, Cole notes, was the recruiting of black troops; failure by the Union army to give them the same pay and bounty as white soldiers dimmed the enlistment enthusiasm of most blacks in Illinois. For a full statement regarding the historical literature about Illinois during the Civil War, consult Victor Hicken's comprehensive bibliography in *Illinois in the Civil War* (pp. 372-384). A modern work of special interest is V. Jacque Voegeli, *Free but Not Equal: The Midwest and the Negro During the Civil War* (Chicago, 1967), a monograph which deals at length with blacks and state politics. The internal opposition to the Union cause is handled—but not impartially—by Frank W. Klement in *The Copperheads in the Middle West* (Chicago, 1960). The author sympathizes with their ideological objections to the war. A more critical account of the subversive activity is found in Wood Gray, *The Hidden Civil War: The Story of the Copperheads* (New York, 1964).

The Blooding of the Armies

VICTOR HICKEN

In the months of the war between the Union defeat at Bull Run in July, 1861, and the end of January, 1862, regiments raised in Illinois were forwarded to two principal areas. The most important was Cairo, where the bulk of Illinois troops were concentrated in order to defend that city and to carry out offensive movements into Missouri and Kentucky. Most of these regiments would later follow Grant to Vicksburg, and then Sherman to Atlanta and the sea. The other regiments, fewer in number, were sent into central and northern Missouri. They were to fight there until the enemy threat appeared to be erased. Following this, many were sent into Kentucky and Tennessee, where some became part of the Army of the Mississippi or the Army of the Ohio.

This was all in the making, however. The months before January, 1862, saw little but probing and searching by the Union armies of the West—with occasional and almost accidental fighting with the enemy. Now, at the end of January, the face of the future began to form. The Union forces in Missouri made preparations for a move against the Confederate army. At Cairo, the scouting expeditions into Kentucky and the Confederate buildup had convinced Grant and others of the need for vigorous action. Furthermore, western governors and western newspapers called for it. The desire for a movement against the principal Confederate forts of Henry on the Tennessee and Donelson on the Cumberland found further expression down through the various ranks of Illinois soldiers who waited at Cairo. "I am urging that as soon as we get a couple more Regts," wrote one Illinois officer stationed in that city, "we float up the Cumberland some night and take the 2 forts for breakfast."

Grant, continuing to press Halleck for a decision on his plan for the taking of Fort Henry, wrote to the department commander: "With permission, I will take Fort Henry on the Tennessee, and establish and hold a large camp there." Knowing his superior and his tendency for procrastination only too well, Grant was aided by Andrew H. Foote, the ranking naval officer at Cairo, in pressure upon Halleck. Foote, not a man to phrase his message to allow for a

From Victor Hicken, *Illinois in the Civil War* (Urbana, 1966), pp. 27-29, 36-43. Reprinted by permission of the University of Illinois Press. Copyright © 1966 by the Board of Trustees of the University of Illinois. Footnotes in the original have been omitted.

qualified reply, wrote: "Have we the authority to move for that purpose when ready."

In defense of Halleck, in command far away in St. Louis, one may write that he had his reasons for delaying his decision. This early in the war, when any military strike seemed to be a hazardous one, a move against Fort Henry appeared quite risky. Furthermore, who really knew how many troops the Confederacy had in west Tennessee, or how many enemy regiments were on the way? All of these factors had their impact upon Halleck's naturally cautious character. On January 30 he sent Grant what may have been one of the more important messages of the war. The commander at Cairo was ordered "to take and hold Fort Henry." Later, more explicit instructions were sent out from St. Louis. Grant was to use all of the troops available to prevent Fort Henry from possible reinforcement, and to forestall any Confederate movements from the Cumberland River to the east, or from the enemy stronghold at Columbus. Two comparatively new individuals became important at this time. General Charles F. Smith was a tough, straight-backed old soldier who had taught Grant at West Point and whom, sadly for the Union, the fates would take out of the war just before the battle of Shiloh. He was brought into the picture by Halleck's instructions to Grant for the utilization of all available troops in the area. The second, Lieutenant Colonel James B. McPherson, was Halleck's chief engineering officer, sent down to Cairo in order to lend any assistance Grant might need. . . .

As the twilight of February 3 wasted away in a cold drizzle and darkness, Foote's steamers were well on their way up the Tennessee River with Grant and his 23 regiments aboard. In the early dawn of the following day, McClernand, who was to lead the movement upon Fort Henry, placed his division ashore at Itra Landing, eight or nine miles below the enemy fort. It was a poor spot for disembarkation, and Grant ordered the troops reloaded. This time Grant chose the landing location, a spot only three miles below the Confederate stronghold.

The plan for the expedition upon Fort Henry was simple. In order to prevent enemy reinforcement from the west, Smith, who commanded one division, occupied the river bank opposite the enemy at Fort Heiman. The two brigades of McClernand's division were to move inland from the landing to a position astride the Fort Donelson-Dover road. This was to prevent the enemy from making any attempt to aid the beleaguered forts from the east. Troops moved ashore on February 4, and supplies and ordnance followed on the next day. While the officers and men struggled to land their equipment at the landing, which McClernand had hastily named

Civil War soldiers relaxing in camp

"Camp Halleck," Grant, McClernand, and Smith met in council aboard the flagship of the small fleet, the *Cincinnati.*

On February 6 McClernand deployed his two brigades under Oglesby and W. H. L. Wallace toward the Dover road. Most of the Confederate troops who had occupied Fort Henry were already fleeing down that very road, however, and only Colonel Lyle Dickey's 4th Illinois Cavalry managed to tag the enemy rear guard.

. . . .

On February 14 Foote's gunboats appeared on the Cumberland below [Fort Donelson]. After discharging reinforcements for Grant's army in the morning, the boats moved upriver in order to engage the heavy batteries of the stronghold; they hoped to achieve the same kind of victory which had been accomplished earlier at Fort Henry. The *St. Louis,* the *Louisville,* the *Carondelet,* and the *Pittsburg,* all ironclads, quickly closed the distance to the enemy Columbiads. This time, however, the results were not so fortunate. Staying tenaciously at their guns, the Confederates blew away the pilot house of the *St. Louis,* and wrecked the steering mechanism of the *Louisville.* The *Pittsburg* and the *Carondelet* took a frightful beating. The Cumberland swept the boats downstream and helped prevent further damage to the Union fleet.

The night of February 14 was bitter cold, and Union troops in the line which stretched in a long arc in front of the enemy rifle pits slept very little. Inside the fort important decisions were being made. Cognizant of the growing strength of the besieging force, the Confederate generals planned a counterattack on the following day. The attack, to be directed by General Gideon Pillow, would strike the Union right held by McClernand's thin line. The plan was to open the road, which ran through the camps of the 8th and the 18th Illinois, for an escape to Charlotte, Tennessee, and the South. Buckner's division, which would support the assault, was to fight the rear-guard action, should the movement be successful.

At exactly 5:45 Colonel William E. Baldwin's brigade of Mississippi troops filed out of the embrasures of the rifle pits in line of battle. The Illinois troops stood up immediately, and reached into their cartridge boxes to load for firing. Pillow's troops continued to pour out of their trenches, moving forward as quickly as they formed. Thus it was that the 26th Mississippi and the 26th Tennessee, aiming directly for the Forge road, came in contact with the 8th and 18th Illinois.

Fighting spread quickly down the line. W. H. L. Wallace's brigade was hit viciously by a Confederate charge, which, when repulsed, was followed quickly by another. This, too, was sent reeling. McArthur, on the far right, gave support to Oglesby and Wallace by throwing his brigade, led by the 9th Illinois, to the forefront. Soon his whole command was "hotly engaged."

The brunt of the Confederate attack fell upon Oglesby's men, who found difficulty in spotting the butternut uniforms in the thick underbrush. Slowly the Federal line began to give way. Buckner increased the pressure by throwing his regiments against Lew Wallace's brigade. By ten o'clock Oglesby's regiments were in a bad way. The cartridge boxes of the 8th and 18th Illinois, both regiments vital to the defense of the Forge road, were empty. Both Lawler, the commanding officer of the 18th, and his replacement were taken off the field wounded. Reluctantly, Oglesby gave the order to retire.

Now it was Logan, with his 31st Illinois, who grimly held the hinge of the Union right near the Forge road. Soon Logan was wounded, however, and the regiment, also out of ammunition, gave way. The burden now fell upon the 11th Illinois, under Ransom. Coolly directing his troops, Ransom threw off the Confederate attacks, but it appeared to be too late. The Forge road was open; Floyd could now move his garrison into open country.

It was hardly possible for the Confederate forces to have picked a better time for their assault upon the Union right. After the failure of the gunboats on the previous day, Grant had left his command to consult with Foote, who had been wounded. On the morning of February 15, Union troops fought without their commander. One may suppose that it was because of the capacity of the western soldier to improvise in such an emergency that a catastrophic defeat was forestalled. McClernand courageously made decisions which carried with them a terrible responsibility. McArthur's early forward movement, done principally of his own volition, gave Oglesby a needed moment to prepare for the storm. Lew Wallace's decision to strip his own command to send reinforcements to the right wing was brave and vital. There was surprisingly little confusion. The 25th Kentucky, sent forward to relieve the staggering 8th Illinois, became flustered and fired into the ranks of the latter regiment, causing some casualties. This was understandable, in view of the dense underbrush through which the fighting took place. Even Oglesby, riding up and down his shattered line, became lost. By chance, he blundered upon the regiments of McArthur's brigade on the far right. "Excuse me . . .," he shouted with needless courtesy, "I believe I am out of my brigade."

For the first time, Illinois troops came against the real specter of war. Belmont had been child's play. Some of the men were not up to it at all, and fled to the rear claiming injury; others simply disappeared, not to report until days later. One officer of an Illinois regiment rode down the Union line in panic, shouting: "We are cut to pieces." Yet bravery was a commodity commonly found. Logan, fighting hard to hold his 31st in the line, was knocked from his horse by an enemy bullet. Picking himself up, with blood streaming from his left arm and thigh, he rallied his men to continue the fight. T. E. G. Ransom, handling Wallace's 11th Illinois, seemed to be everywhere; he was a man truly in his element. McClernand, who had also come to fight, courageously exposed himself to enemy fire in order to inspire his troops. After the war almost every man in his command remembered that general's role in the battle with great feeling. Lew Wallace recalled later that McClernand's eyes, because of the "snow light," took on a severe squint. Sitting far back in his saddle, wearing an abominable wool hat which was hooked up at one side, he presented a memorable picture.

The ordinary private soldier took the brunt of the fighting, however. To stand in line against a surging enemy rush with an empty cartridge box required great courage. Private William H. Tebbetts of the 45th Illinois, holding the line along the Wynn's Ferry road, was later to describe some of the aspects of that day, writing: "I have seen trees a foot and a half through cut off entirely by the cannon balls and I have had balls strike the trees at full force not more than a foot from my head. . . ." Tebbetts concluded that "the Lord still has more work for me to do." Less than a month later, Tebbetts was killed at Shiloh.

The forced retirement of the Union right wing gave the Confederate army its great chance to escape. Ransom's 11th Illinois, its colors tattered shreds on a shattered staff, was beginning to collapse under the weight of Pillow's attack. General Lew Wallace, in answer to urgent messages from McClernand, brought up his last remaining brigade at this point of the fight. That general later recalled meeting W. H. L. Wallace just as he retired with the remnants of his command. The colonel appeared "perfectly cool, and looked like a farmer from a hard day's plowing." Greetings were casually exchanged, after which General Wallace asked: "Are they pursuing you?" His subordinate replied in the affirmative, and indicated the closeness of the pursuit. "You will have about time to form line of battle right here," said the colonel. "Thank you," was the reply. "Good day." One might suspect that an Illinois officer had perfect justification for writing the following concerning Lew Wallace: "I don't think him much of a hand for words or jokes. Think there is blood in him. . . . I like his style except his profanity. He is prompt ready and exact-brief."

[Gen.] Wallace's last brigade, under Colonel John M. Thayer, having, among other regiments, the 32nd and 58th Illinois, moved immediately to the forefront of the fight. Time was of the essence, and time was what Wallace's arrival gave to the hard-pressed Union right. W. H. L. Wallace and Oglesby reformed their men behind Thayer's brigade, replenished their cartridge boxes, and stood at rest awaiting their next command.

At this point, with the outcome still in the balance, General Grant returned to the field. Riding to where McClernand and Wallace were deep in conversation behind Thayer's brigade, he asked both subordinates for their estimates on the condition of the Union line. His face flushed with embarrassment at being absent from his command during a most crucial time, he reached a quick decision. "Gentlemen, the position on the right must be retaken," he ordered. If one is to believe both Grant and Wallace in their recollections of the incident, McClernand demurred, claiming that his troops were in no condition for another engagement. Grant insisted, however, and Federal troops moved to the offensive at that end of the line. The Confederates, after some confusion, returned to their defensive position, having failed to break out.

Grant himself carried an order for Smith to make an assault on the Union left. That division, led by their general shouting "This way, boys; come on," hit the enemy hard. The 7th Illinois and 14th Iowa managed to climb over the escarpment and into the outer rim of rifle pits. When they got there, they found the redoubtable Smith already turning a captured cannon upon the retreating Confederates. When the dim winter twilight of the long day faded, the Union line was not only back to where it had been at dawn, but beyond it on the left. With Union troops now inside their barricades, the Confederate situation was desperate.

The night of February 15 was fearful. The wounded lay throughout the battle area, their blood freezing them to the ground in the terrible cold. The Confederate command inside the fort came to some important decisions. It was Buckner's judgment that to continue the fight would be virtual suicide. Though Floyd and Pillow agreed, neither one wished to fall into Union hands. Leaving the command of the army with Buckner, Floyd marched most of his own brigade aboard two steamers which had just arrived and sailed away. Pillow managed to escape upon a flatboat. Forrest led his command through the icy backwater of a nearby creek. Only Buckner and Bushrod Johnson were left.

On the following morning Buckner sent Grant a request for terms of surrender. Grant replied: "No terms except an unconditional surrender can be accepted. I propose to move immediately upon your works." These words thrilled the nation and Grant's name became a household word. For Buckner they offered no alternative;

he surrendered. The Confederate general may have felt Grant's reply to be "ungenerous and unchivalrous," but it certainly was effective.

Shortly after daybreak on February 16, as Union soldiers along the Wynn's Ferry road were beginning to warm their morning coffee, news of the enemy surrender passed along the line. To the left of the McClernand's division, where the 45th Illinois was encamped, orderlies from the various headquarters rode pell-mell through the troops "swinging their caps and proclaiming the news. . . ." The North had won a battle. A soldier of the 45th wrote later: "Did we shout? Well, if we didn't use our lungs then we never did. Hip! Hip! Hurrah! from every man in blue." Not long afterward, the triumphant soldiers marched into the fort. "It was a grand sight," wrote an Illinois soldier, "as regiment after regiment poured in with their flags floating gayly in the wind, and the brass bands playing . . . in such style as the gazing captives had never heard in the palmy days of peace."

The defeated, numbering between 12,000 and 15,000 troops, did not seem to impress the victors as much now as they had in the previous days. "If they are the 'flower of the youth' of Miss.," wrote an Illinois officer, "I can hardly conjecture what the *leaves* must be. . . ." So overcome were the winners that they failed to notice Bushrod Johnson, who would later tear the lines of Illinois regiments to shreds at Chickamauga, calmly walking off the battlefield without so much as a salute from a sentry. The feat must have been as much a shock to Johnson as it was to the Federal forces.

Besides the prisoners taken in the fort, Grant was able to report to Halleck that he had taken "20,000 stand of arms, 48 pieces of artillery, 17 heavy guns, from 2,000 to 4,000 horses, and large quantities of commissary stores." In exchange, the price had been high. The 11th Illinois, a northern Illinois regiment, lost 339 in killed, wounded, and missing. Oglesby's 8th, from eastern Illinois, lost 242. Lawler's 18th tabulated 228 casualties; the 9th, from southwestern Illinois, reported 210; and Logan's 31st had 176. An Iowa regiment suffered 197 casualties, the highest reported by a non-Illinois regiment.

Sights about the battlefield on the day following the battle were grisly. Many of the wounded had to be chopped from the frozen ground. Mary Bickerdyke made five trips to the field in order to find wounded men. One night, shortly after the battle, an Illinois officer observed a flickering light moving about the field of conflict. An orderly, sent out to ascertain the cause of it, found Mrs. Bickerdyke, lantern in hand, moving slowly among the dead. "Stooping down, and turning their cold faces towards her," Mary

Livermore was later to write, "she scrutinized them searchingly, uneasy lest some might be left to die uncared for."

Mrs. Bickerdyke's experience must have been frightful. A month after the battle, James A. Connolly of Charleston, Illinois, visited the scene and described it as follows:

> A great many horses were lying on the field, just where they fell, scattered all over the field, singly, by twos, threes and fours. Frozen pools of blood were visible on every hand, and I picked up over twenty hats with bullet holes in them and pieces of skull, hair and blood sticking to them inside.
>
> The ground was strewn with hats, caps, coats, pants, canteens, cartridge boxes, bayonet scabbards, knapsacks, rebel haversacks, filled with biscuits of their own making . . . pieces of exploded shells, six and twelve-pound balls, and indeed all sorts of things that are found in the army. . . . You can form no conception of what a battlefield looks like. No pen and ink description can give you anything like a true idea of it. The dead were buried from two to two and a half feet deep; the rebels didn't bury that deep and some had their feet protruding from the graves.

The Union victory at Donelson had an electrifying effect on the North. In Chicago, the bells were rung incessantly and cannon were fired until the city itself sounded like a battleground. Flags flew from almost every window, and men clapped each other on the back, embraced, wept, and shouted. Public schools displayed new flags, and students were allowed to give patriotic speeches and to sing national airs. Bonfires burned late that night.

. . . .

Recruiting Ground

ARTHUR C. COLE

The heavy enlistments of the late summer of 1862 may be accounted for largely on the basis of the choice that was to be offered between volunteering or being conscripted. In the weeks

From Arthur C. Cole, *The Era of the Civil War, 1848-1870* (Chicago, 1919), pp. 275-282. Footnotes in the original have been omitted.

following August 23, an enrollment of the entire militia force of the state was made in case a draft to fill up old regiments should be required. Meantime the republicans of Illinois supported the stand taken by Senator Trumbull in favor of federal conscription. He pressed the bill in congress against the opposition of the more timid and was rewarded by witnessing its enactment on March 3, 1863. The provost marshals and their assistants were soon at work preparing the rolls and making arrangements for the drawing. It was generally expected that the process of drafting would commence promptly, but hundreds of companies were sworn into service, and Illinois with volunteers far in excess of its quota was relieved from the operation of the draft.

The same goal of keeping ahead of her quota was adopted by Illinois in the succeeding years of the war. Enlistment, with reënlistment of veteran regiments, was sufficiently heavy to delay the necessity of conscription. With a surplus of 8,151 under the draft quota, with an additional credit of 10,947 for volunteers discovered in a reëxamination of the rolls, and a net credit of 4,373 from the 6,032 Illinois citizens enrolled in Missouri regiments, recruiting placed Illinois on January 1, 1864, far in excess of the total quota under all calls of 145,100.

Preparations were again made in 1864 for heavy drafts. The people of Illinois, flattered by previous reports, immediately set out to maintain this record, spurred on at times by warnings of the danger of conscription. In this way enlistments kept well ahead of quotas, reaching an excess of nearly 35,000 in the summer of 1864. This was a noble record; Governor Yates took just pride in the response to his energetic efforts to have Illinois take her full part in fighting the battles of the union. When finally the south was crushed and the war record of Illinois was surveyed, it was found that the state had furnished under various periods of service over one-quarter of a million men.

. . . .

The great spur to enlistment, however, was the desire to avoid the enforcement of the draft. This whip was held over the able-bodied men of the state, and arrangements were made repeatedly for the application of the law. In the summer of 1862 the draft seemed so near at hand that a rush for Canada was only checked by the requirement that traveling could be done only under passes issued by deputy marshals. The democrats condemned the conscription law and challenged its constitutionality; they found special fault with the provision making possible exemption for those paying a fee of $300. The *Chicago Tribune,* which had originally

Courtesy of the Illinois State Historical Library

Richard Yates, Civil War Governor

defended this section as one essentially making for democracy, came to admit that "if the $300 clause is the *poor* man's fund we don't think *they* see it." From the winter of 1863-1864 to the end of the war it seemed that the lottery of life and death would be drawn at almost any time; draft protection associations were organized in almost every community to raise funds to procure substitutes for members who might be drafted. The draft was actually ordered and the wheel set in motion in the fourth and tenth districts in October, 1864, and in most districts in March, 1865, when the order arrived in April to stop the draft and recruiting in Illinois. Thus it happened that recruiting in Illinois involved a quota of only 3,538 draft men.

Strangely enough, the most satisfactory response to appeals for enlistment came from the democratic counties in southern Illinois. True, there had at first prevailed a disposition to regard the contest as an aggressive war on the part of a new president and therefore a corresponding reluctance to take up arms; but, the war having become a reality, the feeling grew among the people of Egypt that they had to "see the thing through." Even under the first call, the

Cairo district in the extreme southern end of the state offered more companies than could be received. When in the summer of 1861 John A. Logan, "the little Egyptian giant," tendered his services to the stars and stripes, following the lead of John A. McClernand, who had already become a brigadier general, the tide was turned in favor of the union; the response to Logan's call for a regiment to follow him was immediate. Henceforth, Egypt, following the advice of the lamented Douglas, was tendering troops not by companies but by regiments; it not only filled its quotas but usually piled up a surplus. On the first of October, 1863, the ten extreme southern counties were officially credited with an excess of nearly fifty per cent. Old democratic strongholds charged with copperheadism, offered recruits with a generosity that shamed their opponents.

. . . .

The adopted citizens in Illinois made an important contribution toward winning the battles of the Civil War. The Germans around Belleville responded enthusiastically from the start; a company was immediately organized by Augustus Mersy, a veteran officer of the Baden army of the German revolution of 1848, who promptly became lieutenant colonel. Friedrich Hecker, who had at first enlisted in Franz Sigel's Missouri regiment as a private, was given authority to raise an independent regiment, so that the Twenty-fourth Illinois infantry became known as the "Hecker regiment." With the return of the three months men in July, Koerner offered to raise two German regiments, officered by men of experience. After considerable delay Governor Yates gave Koerner the necessary authority to raise one independent regiment, which was recruited in a few weeks and placed under the command of Colonel Julius Raith. This was the Forty-third infantry, or "Koerner regiment." Many German recruits of that region joined Missouri German regiments, because of the failure of their leaders to secure prompt organization for exclusive German regiments. Companies were also organized in Springfield, Ottawa, and elsewhere, while the Chicago Jaegers, the Turner Cadets, and the Lincoln Rifles were ready from the start for incorporation in the union army. The Thirteenth cavalry regiment was the "German guides," organized at Chicago in December, 1861. Within a sixmonth, it was estimated that 6,000 Germans from Illinois were in the federal army. This stream kept up during the war; it was possible as late as 1864 to recruit a German regiment in Chicago and vicinity. The Irish were not to be outdone. In a week's time they organized in Chicago the Twenty-third Illinois, otherwise called the Irish brigade, which was accepted as an independent regiment under Colonel James A. Mulligan. Irish companies from Springfield and Rockford also tendered their services. The following year the "Cameron guards" were recruited at the capital, while the "Ryan guards" from Galena and other companies were being organized for a Chicago regiment. The "Irish Legion," the Nineteenth infantry, was mustered into service at Chicago in the late summer of 1862. During the first two years of the war two so-called "Scotch regiments," the Twelfth and Sixty-fifth, were organized. Even the Israelites of Chicago were aroused; in 1862 within forty-eight hours they raised a company together with a fund of several thousand dollars to put it in the field. The Portuguese in Springfield and in Morgan county enrolled large numbers in the companies recruited in those regions.

The idea of using Negro troops had long been urged upon the national administration by Governor Yates and Senator Trumbull, and in the fall of 1863 the first Illinois regiment of Negro soldiers was finally authorized by the war department. Before this a colored company had been started in Galesburg, and recruits had been secured from Illinois for Rhode Island and Massachusetts organizations; a state-wide canvass was now inaugurated which brought together five hundred recruits at Quincy in February, 1864. But failure to give them the same pay and bounty that was paid to white soldiers prevented Negro enthusiasm from developing; as a result less than two thousand colored troops were mustered into service and these naturally played little part in the fighting of this war.

. . . .

Original Narratives

At the time William H. Russell visited the United States in 1861, he was something of a celebrity in England because of his vivid reporting of the Crimean War for *The Times* of London. He was given an audience with President Lincoln and met with Secretary of State William Seward and the commanding general of the Union army, Winfield Scott. That spring he toured the South, arriving in Illinois in June. The following narrative begins as Russell leaves Cairo enroute to Chicago by train. Note the contrast he saw between the southern and northern parts of the state in terms of physical characteristics and sentiment concerning the Confederacy.

From Cairo to Chicago by Train

WILLIAM H. RUSSELL

June 23d [1861] . . . At four o'clock in the evening I started by the train on the famous Central Illinois line from Cairo to Chicago.

The carriages were tolerably well filled with soldiers, and in addition to them there were a few unfortunate women, undergoing deportation to some less moral neighbourhood. Neither the look, language, nor manners of my fellow passengers inspired me with an exalted notion of the intelligence, comfort and respectability of the people which are so much vaunted by Mr. Seward and American journals, and which, though truly attributed, no doubt, to the people of the New England states, cannot be affirmed with equal justice to belong to all the other components of the Union.

. . . .

Leaving the shanties, which face the levees, and some poor wooden houses with a short vista of cross streets partially flooded at right angles to them, the rail suddenly plunges into an unmistakeable swamp, where a forest of dead trees wave their ghastly, leafless arms over their buried trunks, like plumes over a hearse—a cheerless, miserable place, sacred to the ague and fever. This occurs close to the cleared space on which the city is to stand,—when it is finished—and the rail, which runs on the top of the embankment or levee, here takes to the trestle, and is borne over the water on the usual timber frame work.

"Mound City," which is the first station, is composed of a mere heap of earth, like a ruined brick-kiln, which rises to some height and is covered with fine white oaks, beneath which are a few log huts and hovels, giving the place its proud name. Tents were pitched on the mound side, from which wild-looking banditti sort of men, with arms, emerged as the train stopped. "I've been pretty well over Europe," said a meditative voice beside me, "and I've seen the despotic armies of the old world but I don't think they equal that set of boys." The question was not worth arguing—the boys were in fact very "weedy," "splinter-shinned chaps," as another critic insisted.

There were some settlers in the woods around Mound City, and a jolly-looking, corpulent man, who introduced himself as one of the officers of the land department of the Central Illinois railroad,

From William H. Russell, *My Diary North and South* (London, 1863), pp. 334-342.

described them as awful warnings to the emigrants not to stick in
the south part of Illinois. It was suggestive to find that a very
genuine John Bull, "located," as they say in the States for many
years, had as much aversion to the principles of the abolitionists as
if he had been born a Southern planter. Another countryman of his
and mine, steward on board the steamer to Cairo, eagerly asked me
what I thought of the quarrel, and which side I would back. I
declined to say more than I thought the North possessed very great
superiority of means if the conflict were to be fought on the same
terms. Whereupon my Saxon friend exclaimed, "all the Northern
States and all the power of the world can't beat the South; and
why?—because the South has got cotton, and cotton is king."

The Central Illinois officer did not suggest the propriety of
purchasing lots but he did intimate I would be doing service if I
informed the world at large, they could get excellent land, at sums
varying from ten to twenty-five dollars an acre. . . .

It sounds very well to an Irish tenant farmer, an English cottier,
or a cultivator in the Lothians, to hear that he can get land at the
rate of from £2 to £5 per acre, to be his for ever, liable only to state
taxes; but when he comes to see a parallelogram marked upon the
map as "good soil, of unfathomable richness," and finds in effect
that he must cut down trees, eradicate stumps, drain off water,
build a house, struggle for high-priced labour, and contend with
imperfect roads, the want of many things to which he has been
accustomed in the old country, the land may not appear to him
such a bargain. In the wooded districts he has, indeed, a sufficiency
of fuel as long as trees and stumps last, but they are, of course,
great impediments to tillage. If he goes to the prairie he finds that
fuel is scarce and water by no means wholesome.

When we left this swamp and forest, and came out after a run of
many miles on the clear lands which abut upon the prairie, large
fields of corn lay around us, which bore a peculiarly blighted and
harassed look. These fields were suffering from the ravages of an
insect called the "army worm," almost as destructive to corn and
crops as the locust-like hordes of North and South, which are vying
with each other in laying waste the fields of Virginia. Night was
falling as the train rattled out into the wild, flat sea of waving grass,
dotted by patch-like Indian corn enclosures; but halts at such places
as Jonesburgh and Cobden, enabled us to see that these settlements
in Illinois were neither very flourishing nor very civilised.

. . . .

The towns of Jonesburgh and Cobden have their little teapot-
looking churches and meeting houses, their lager-bier saloons, their

restaurants, their small libraries, institutes, and reading rooms, and no doubt they have also their political cliques, social distinctions and favouritisms; but it requires, nevertheless, little sagacity to perceive that the highest of the bourgeois who leads the mass at meeting and prayer, has but little to distinguish him from the very lowest member of the same body politic. Cobden, for example, has no less than four drinking saloons, all on the line of rail, and no doubt the highest citizen in the place frequents some one or other of them, and meets there the worst rowdy in the place. . . .

A considerable number of towns, formed by accretions of small stores and drinking places, called magazines, round the original shed wherein live the station master and his assistants, mark the course of the railway. Some are important enough to possess a bank, which is generally represented by a wooden hut, with a large board nailed in front, bearing the names of the president and cashier, and announcing the success and liberality of the management. The stores are also decorated with large signs, recommending the names of the owners to the attention of the public, and over all of them is to be seen the significant announcement, "Cash for produce."

At Carbondale there was no coal at all to be found, but several miles farther to the north, at a place called Dugoine, a field of bituminous deposit crops out, which is sold at the pit's mouth for one dollar twenty-five cents, or about 5s. 2d. a-ton. Darkness and night fell as I was noting such meagre particulars of the new district as could be learned out of the window of a railway carriage; and finally with a delicious sensation of cool night air creeping in through the windows, the first I had experienced for many a long day, we made ourselves up for repose, and were borne steadily, if not rapidly, through the great prairie, having halted for tea at the comfortable refreshment rooms of Centralia.

There were no physical signs to mark the transition from the land of the Secessionist to Union-loving soil. Until the troops were quartered there, Cairo was for Secession, and Southern Illinois is supposed to be deeply tainted with disaffection to Mr. Lincoln. Placards on which were printed the words, "Vote for Lincoln and Hamlin, for Union and Freedom," and the old battle-cry of the last election, still cling to the wooden walls of the groceries often accompanied by bitter words or offensive additions.

. . . .

Next morning, just at dawn, I woke up and got out on the platform of the carriage, which is the favourite resort of smokers and their antithetics, those who love pure fresh air, notwithstanding the printed caution "It is dangerous to stand on the platform"; and under the eye of early morn saw spread around a flat sea-like expanse not yet warmed into colour and life by the sun. The line was no longer guarded from daring Secessionists by soldiers' outposts, and small camps had disappeared. The train sped through the centre of the great verdant circle as a ship through the sea, leaving the rigid iron wake behind it tapering to a point at the horizon, and as the light spread over it the surface of the crisping corn waved in broad undulations beneath the breeze from east to west. This is the prairie indeed. Hereabouts it is covered with the finest crops, some already cut and stacked. Looking around one could see church spires rising in the distance from the white patches of houses, and by degrees the tracks across the fertile waste became apparent, and then carts and horses were seen toiling through the rich soil.

A large species of partridge or grouse appeared very abundant, and rose in flocks from the long grass at the side of the rail or from the rich carpet of flowers on the margin of the corn fields. They sat on the fence almost unmoved by the rushing engine, and literally swarmed along the line. These are called "prairie chickens" by the people, and afford excellent sport. Another bird about the size of a thrush, with a yellow breast and a harsh cry, I learned was "the sky-lark", and *apropos* of the unmusical creature, I was very briskly attacked by a young lady patriot for finding fault with the sharp noise it made. "Oh, my! And you not to know that your Shelley loved it above all things! Didn't he write some verses—quite beautiful, too, they are—to the sky-lark." And so "the Britisher was dried up," as I read in a paper afterwards of a similar occurrence.

At the little stations which occur at every few miles—there are some forty of them, at each of which the train stops, in 365 miles between Cairo and Chicago—the Union flag floated in the air; but we had left all the circumstance of this inglorious war behind us, and the train rattled boldly over the bridges across the rare streams, no longer in danger from Secession hatchets. The swamp had given place to the corn field. No black faces were turned up from the mowing and free white labour was at work, and the type of the labourers was German and Irish.

The Yorkshireman expatiated on the fertility of the land, and on the advantages it held out to the emigrant. But I observed all the lots by the side of the rail, and apparently as far as the eye could reach, were occupied. "Some of the very best land lies beyond on each side," said he. "Out over there in the fat places is where we put our Englishmen." By digging deep enough good water is always to be had, and coal can be carried from the rail, where it costs only 7s. or 8s. a ton. Wood there is little or none in the prairies, and it was rarely indeed a clump of trees could be detected, or anything higher than some scrub brushwood. These little communities which we passed were but the growth of a few years, and as we approached the Northern portion of the line we could see, as it were, the village swelling into the town, and the town spreading out to the dimensions of the city.

. . . .

The scene now began to change gradually as we approached Chicago, the prairie subsided into swampy land, and thick belts of trees fringed the horizon; on our right glimpses of the sea could be caught through openings in the wood—the inland sea on which stands the Queen of the Lakes. Michigan looks broad and blue as the Mediterranean. Large farmhouses stud the country, and houses which must be the retreat of merchants and citizens of means; and when the train, leaving the land altogether, dashes out on a pier and causeway built along the borders of the lake, we see lines of noble houses, a fine boulevard, a forest of masts, huge isolated piles of masonry, the famed grain elevators by which so many have been hoisted to fortune, churches and public edifices, and the apparatus of a great city; and just at nine o'clock the train gives its last steam shout and comes to a standstill in the spacious station of the Central Illinois Company, and in half-an-hour more I am in comfortable quarters at the Richmond House, where I find letters waiting for me, by which it appears that the necessity for my being in Washington in all haste, no longer exists. The wary General [Scott] who commands the army is aware that the advance to Richmond, for which so many journals are clamouring, would be attended with serious risk at present, and the politicians must be content to wait a little longer.

. . . .

Carol Benson Pye, editor of the following letters, is the great-grand-daughter of Louisa Jane Phifer. A graduate of Oberlin College with an M.A. from Lehigh University, she has taught history in both Maryland and Pennsylvania, where she now lives.

Letters from an Illinois Farm, 1864-1865

LOUISA JANE PHIFER

INTRODUCTION BY CAROL BENSON PYE

The letters of Louisa Jane Phifer to her husband, George Brown Phifer, a corporal in the Union Army, shed light on an important but neglected aspect of Civil War history—the day-to-day life of a family headed by a woman. From October, 1864, to September, 1865, Louisa and her seven young children managed the family farm near Vandalia, Fayette County. The letters reveal her resourcefulness and her optimism for the future.

Both Louisa and George came from immigrant families of predominantly German background. Louisa was the daughter of George C. and Margaret Selvey Heisler. She was born on June 3, 1825, near Gettysburg, Pennsylvania, and moved with her family sometime thereafter to Ohio. George was born in Knox County, Ohio, on March 18, 1823. His grandfather, Jacob Phifer, had emigrated from Strausberg, Germany, in 1818 and settled in Jelloway, Ohio.

Louisa and George were married on March 20, 1845, in Richland County, Ohio. Five of their children—George Aurelius, Louisa Ulrica, Simon Bolivar, Washington Irving, and Margaret Rosilia—were born in that state. Some time between 1854 and July, 1857, the family moved to Michigan, and another child, Sarah Lucinda, was born there. They left Michigan and purchased a farm in Otego Township near Vandalia in 1859. In addition to working the farm, Phifer taught school, as he had in Michigan. The two youngest Phifer children, Charles Lincoln and Atlanta Sherman, were born after 1859.

In the early days of the Civil War, the number of Illinois volunteers more than filled the state quotas set by the army. By 1864, enlistments were insufficient, and Phifer, at the age of forty-one, was drafted. He was mustered into Company F of the Thirty-second Illinois Volunteer Infantry on October 18, 1864. His brother Jacob, who is mentioned in the letters, entered service at the same time as a substitute. The two men joined the Thirty-second at Chattanooga, Tennessee, and from there set out to meet the army of General William T. Sherman. George did not

From *Journal of the Illinois State Historical Society*, LXVI (1973), 387-395, 401-402.
Used by permission. All but three footnotes in the original have been omitted.

complete the march. He became ill with pneumonia and was sent to a hospital in Nashville.

A total of twenty-three letters exchanged by George and Louisa Phifer are now in the Illinois State Historical Library. . . .

The first of Louisa's letters is addressed to her husband at Nashville. Throughout these letters Louisa has not marked the ends of sentences with periods. Terminal punctuation has therefore been inserted, and first letters of words beginning new sentences have been capitalized. Other punctuation and spelling irregularities appear as on the original. . . .

Vandalia Sunday Evening Dec the 4 (64)

Dear Husband and Father

We seat our selves this evening to answer your verry kind letter which stated that you was gaining verry fast. We are all well hoping this may find you getting better. The time draws near I suppose when you Will have to leave there (if you do not get a place in the hospital) Which will be so hard for more than likely then We will not get to hear from you for 2 or three Weke at a time and how will We stand that not knowing whether you are sick or Well or how you are getting along and for that Reason and to Save your self. We want you to try every way you know if you have to spend some of your money to get on the good side of the doctor to get in a Situation in the hospital or in the Commissarry Department or some place else.

Father We had to tend a sad burying the other day. Poor George Tinker is dead. He took sick last Sunday Evening and died the next Wednesday night at eleven O Clock and was buried thursday. The disease Was Congestion of the Brain. How quick people are Carried in to Eternity.

Well father we are getting along first rate with our work. We have about all the Corn husked but what is in the dry. The Corn Crib is full even with the door of the best kind of Corn. Corn is from 75 to 80 cts per bushel. We have the Sheep stable finished. We have put alittle manure around all the apple trees. We have paid Tom pilcher his 5.00 Dollars and Hickerson his Corn. The Wheat looks Just as good as it Could Look the early and late sewing. This has been the best fall on Wheat that I ever saw being warm and Wet. The Old mare and Colt looks well and so do the Ewes. The hogs fatten fast and look nice.

George you have spoken several times in your letters telling us to eat apples for you. George it is poor satisfaction to do so. O if you only could be here to eat for yourself. O how glad I should be. But knowing that it is impossible We shall hope that you Will get back next fall to eat your Share of what we may have.

George We got aletter from Lutitia and Sam last night. They have almost give up coming out here this fall on account of Sams Mother and Brother Visiting them this fall although they may come between this and spring. We wrote to them when you took sick and she Says she wants you to write to them so they will know how to direct to you. They said in their letter that Pap and Mam and George Was Rank Copperheads. Now George When you write to Sam give the Copperheads a fair history of how things stands and where they are Wrong so that they Can show it to pap & George. But for all the world do not let on that you know they are Copperheads for Tacy said they would Judge who wrote to us about them and she said she Wanted to live in peace she said. Uncle Manuels Puelenas man was Drafted and he paid $800 and 50 dollars for a substitute. Sams two Brothers was Drafted and in the Township they live in they made up Nineteen thousand Dollars to clear the Township.* Father I will mention in this letter that in our last We sent you $6.00 Dollars. When you write let us know whether you Received it all Right or not. There has been a good deal of sickness here this fall but as far as I know all the Neighbors are Well now. Aunt Rachel and Hickersons Folks are all Well. Our School Miss boards at Hickersons and so does the Over-Cup Teacher.

Ulrica & Washington started to school A Week ago to morrow. Me and Simon will not start till a week from to morrow. simon Simon will board at Rachels and go to Over Cup. I read A letter from the Prisoners that Was took from the 32nd Reg. One of them Wrote it and all the rest signed it. They all ask for some thing to be sent to them as they are all verry needy. They are at Florence South Carolina. Sam Smith and Dingle and Carter are With them. There is a dozen Signed the letter. George this may be the last letter that we can write to you there. Now if We have done any thing that you do not like I want you to forgive me for We intend to take as good care of the things as is possible till you get back. George if there is any thing you want done that We have not done Write and let us know what it is, for We want to do the things as you want them done. Now if you have to go away down there I want you to get in as Cook or something else. George I know you don't like to Cook but I want you to get in to some thing so that you will not have to expose your self by being out of nights.

George when you get down there We want you to Write as often as you can for that will be our main trouble not hearing from you

*The money demanded by substitutes soared dramatically when the $300 commutation charge was abolished after Feb. 1864; substitutes frequently received as much as $1,200.

for so long. When you do write be sure and give us the Right Direction so that we can write as often as possible and let you know how things are going at home as I know you will like to hear from us as we do from you.

Father I forgot to tell you Mary Bail I dont suppose will live many Days. She is verry Sick.

George when you get down to the Regiment and any of them that went from here tries to get in to office for the purpose of making money I do not want you to give your influence any more than you can help to look Right for it will make certain people feel prety large. George do not think hard in the way I am writing. Do not think there is any hardness for there is not. Now George We have not much more to write. Olny write as soon and often as possible. Do not if you go to your Reg push in to any danger one inch but try and take care of your self as good as you can. George when you get this letter maybe it would be as well for you to destroy it as Jacob might See it and think hard of what we are writing. Well George We have not got much more to Write. Only take the best Care of your self you can. So I will stop.

From Louisa J. Phifer & Children

To George B Phifer

Vandalia
Saturday morning Dec 17th AD (64)

To Our Respected and Much Thought of Husband and Father

We seat our selves to answer your verry verry kind letter of the 11 which found us all well and hoping most earnestly for your welfare. Your letter Removed the fear partially that we had for your safty. We had heard that hood* had taken Nashville and we were afraid that you was taken prisoner. You said nothing of it in your letter and so we felt a considerably releived in having aletter from you.

. . . .

George you said we had done every thing right except the wheat. We have plenty to do us. Now George you wrote for me to get me a side saddle. I would not ride if I had one. I dont want you to think hard of me but I dont want to get a side saddle. We will keep the Old Mare well till you get back and then I want you to get you a saddle. And then I want to learn to ride behind you. You wrote for

*John Bell Hood stormed Nashville on Dec. 2 and was in retreat by Dec. 16.

me to visit my Neighbors and take all the satisfaction that I can. I will visit my neighbors and have them visit me but now loved One we could take more satisfaction in having you here to talk to us one night after we get our work done than to visit all Winter. We live in hopes that we can see that time Once More. The Circuit Riders name is something like Rice. We have almost forgotten. He is a splendid preacher and is well liked. He speaks of you every time he comes. We like him first Rate. We mentioned in one of our letters About buying Rachals white mare. Since that she has lost an eye and her Colt. Rachal says she will take 45 Dollars. When you write let us know whether you think 40 Dollars will be cheap enough or not. Hickerson says he would not give more than that. Suzie begin to look like she would have a colt pretty early. She is fat. We think we will kill our hogs between christmas & newyears for corn is likely to be a good price and we are to stingy of it. The hogs will be fat by that time.

. . . .

From all that we can hear hood is making great preparations and throwing up breast works for a great Battle. Now George Do not be taken Prisoner. Rather run than that for you know that I never could never stand to have that News come to me now for all the World. Be careful on mine and your own account George Do. I would Rather you would do any thing than to stand and be taken Prisoner. George the time is getting so long to see you that I cannot hardly put over the time when you are well and if any thing should happen to you how would I get along.

The Breeding Sow has 3 beautiful piggs. The other Mary Sow will have pigs before long. Wince and Starr will have Calves about the first of February. Doctor Ingles Wife is buried to Day. As soon as you get this letter write immediately and let us know whether there is any Danger there at all or not.

Well father we came to town to Day and got Our likenisses taken. Enclosed you will find them. They are prety good. We will have to stop as we are in a hurry so no more from your Family.

to George B Phifer
Write Soon

                                                    Vandalia Fayette Ills
                                            Wednesday Evening Dec 21 1864
Much Beloved Husband and Parent

We seat our selves this evening to answer your verry verry kind letter of the 16 which came to hand this morning. It found us all well. It brought fresh trouble to us on your account. Oh you can not tell how much we feel for you in your awful Task. George my trouble is so much on your account that I dont know hardly how to bear it much longer. I would Just say that every thing looks well and we are doing the best we can. Now George you told us to write oftener. There certainly is something the matter with the Mail. You do not get 1/3 of our letters for we write Twice or three times A Week. Oh how we wish that you could get our letters. We have wrote as much as 16 since you started. We have got 17 from you. We have wrote all about how we payed for the Place how much it took and all about the whole matter. When you write let us know whether you have got that letter yet.

Oh my George it must be an awful awful place where you are where you can hear the cries of the wounded and the hum of battle. It is awful. Oh the terrible Suffering that war must cause from your letter.

I am verry thankful that you have friends there to comfort you Some. George I cant think what you meant by Saying you wanted 5 dollars and that you would tell us what it was for when you saw us and that there was nothing the matter that there was Docters there. We want you to have the Money and as much more as you want but I am verry afraid there is some thing the matter that you are sick or something else. If there is any chance see the Doctor and if you can buy a discharge if it costs 25 Dollars or more. If you can let us know and we will forward you what you want father. Mother is awfully discouraged about you and we are all afraid that you have a hard task before you and that you will overdo yourself and like as not if you aint careful never get home. So for our sakes and that of your own be careful. Give up if you see that the work is too hard for you.

Now George you wrote to have us send you our likenesses. We did so. They were Ambrotypes and cost $1.00 apiece. They were they the cheapest we could get. They are pretty fair pictures. We got your likeness cased for 75 cts so that it would not injure.

Enclosed We will send you ten Dollars. You said you owed five Dollars and we thought you might need a little for yourself. Aunt Rachel and the Neighbors are all well. But Jim Morton he is no better and that is pretty bad. Father every thing Ranges verry high here. Corn is from 85 to 100 per bushel. Pork from 9 to 13 per pound and other things in proportion but that is nothing to what it is where you are I suppose. It has been Snowing all Day and it is pretty Cold. Now the snow is about 4 or 5 inches deep.

George we will have to Close as it is late bed time. Hoping for your welfare and that you may only get through safe to Return home so that we can take some comfort together. We hope you will not have to stay up much more of nights for you cant stand it. May God keep you safe. We Remain your Family till Death.

From LJP & Family

To George B Phifer

. . . .

Vandalia Ills
Monday Evening April 17th (65)

Dear Husband & Parent

Again we seat our selves to write you ashort letter to let you know that we are all Very Well & harty & we do hope these few lines may find you Still gaining in health. Father we I have just finished getting my Oats in to day & if it dont rain I want to Commence plowing for Corn in the Morning. But I think it will rain for it is thundering & lightning all around. People are very backward with their work this Spring on account of the great amount of rain that has fell here. There is very few has their Oats in yet. George some time back you wrote for me to get Some Meadow to Cut of Solomon Campbell. I went to See him & he Said him & Austin was going to get a Mower if they could. He said they had so much stock that they would have to try & Cut all their Meadow themselves. But Solomon said if they did not get a mower he would let me have one of the Meadows to Cut. Mortons have heard that Samuel Morton was killed at the Battle of Bentonville. N.C. Neither of the Mares has Colts yet but the gray Mare (Nell) is making a very nice bag & I think She will have a Colt in the course of a week at the farthest. Turk is gaining some now. He is shedding fast & the lice is leaving him. The wheat looks fine. Hickerson says we will have 300 bushel. Father there is Awful bad News here now. It was reported Saturday & Confirmed to day that A. Lincoln the President of the U.S. is assassinated & Seward nearly so. That is the worst news that we have heard since the Rebelion. Copperheads & all seem to take it very hard & think it was entirely out of All Reason. We have wrote but very little but it is getting late and we canot think of much to write. So we will have to draw our poor letter to a Close. We would like to see you oh so very much & we would like to have you come home on a furlow as soon as possible for we all would like to see you so well. Let us know as nearly as possible when you think you will be home. We will have to close by wishing for your health & happiness.

Yours in Love
L J Phifer & Children

to G.B. Phifer

We have not got a letter from you for a week or more & we are getting uneasy

Write Soon*

. . . .

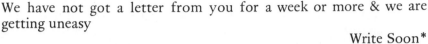

Orville H. Browning was born in Kentucky in 1806, the second son of a prosperous Virginia pioneer. In 1831 he moved to the small village of Quincy, Illinois, a newly settled community located on the bluffs of the Mississippi River. Browning served in the state senate and general assembly as a member of the conservative wing of the Whig party. He later became a United States Senator and head of the Department of Interior under President Andrew Johnson. A long-time acquaintance of Lincoln, he was instrumental in gaining the presidential nomination for his friend at the Republican Convention of 1860, even though Lincoln had initially been Browning's second choice for the office. As a practicing attorney, Browning vigorously defended the railroads against state regulation both before the Civil War and during the 1870s, when he participated on behalf of the Chicago, Burlington, & Quincy Railroad in one of the famous Granger cases. The only biography of Browning is Maurice G. Baxter's *Orville H. Browning, Lincoln's Friend and Critic* (Bloomington, Ind., 1957). His "Diary," published in two volumes by the Illinois State Historical Library, was written between 1850 and 1881, the year of his death. In the selections reprinted here he comments on events at Decatur, Springfield, and his hometown of Quincy.

Diary

ORVILLE BROWNING

Tuesday Nov 11, 1862 At 9 A M left Bluff City. I kept on to Decatur to visit Genl. Oglesby who was badly wounded at the battle

From Orville Browning, "Diary, November 1862," *Collections of the Illinois State Historical Library*, XX (1927), 583-585, 680-683. Reprinted by permission of the Illinois State Historical Society.

*George rejoined his regiment in mid-May. The men of the Thirty-second attended the "Grand Review" in Washington on May 24 and 25. On June 7 the regiment set out for Fort Leavenworth, Kansas, and in July it was detailed to Fort Kearny in Nebraska. Soon thereafter the unit was ordered to return to Fort Leavenworth for mustering out. Phifer was mustered out on Sept. 16, 1865.

of Corinth. I reached his house between 1 & 2 P. M. dined with him and remained with an hour, busily engaged in conversation

He said he had never met 20 men in the army who were in favor of arming the negro—The soldiers cared nothing about the negro, or party politics—They wished to put down the rebellion, restore the Union, and restore the authority of the constitution and laws, and let all other questions alone. He said great injustice had been done Genl Grant by the charge of drunkenness—that he once had been dissipated and sometimes drank a little now, but did not get drunk—that he was personally brave, and anxious to discharge his duties as a soldier, but was not a very able Genl—that he never informed himself of the topography of a Country in which he was to operate, and that he had no capacity for combining his forces, and when combined he did not know how to separate them for action on different points at the same time—that if he had 40,000 in battle, and found it necessary to use 10,000 upon given point he would not know what to do with the other 30,000 in the mean time, but would leave them to go in pell-mell if they chose to do so.

Genl Rosencranz* he said in these particulars was perfect. That he kept all his staff at work for him, and wherever he was would have exact maps of all the Country for ten miles round, on which every road, and path, and hill and ravine would be accurately marked, and that he could also handle his men well in the field. He further said that the Genls he had met with did not seem to have any feeling about the war, or to care how long it lasted, but seemed only desirous to acquit themselves honorably and faithfully of the duties imposed upon them.

After remaining with him an hour I took the cars and returned to Springfield where I arrived at 5 P. M. and stopped at the American House—Went over to State House, and had a long talk with Hatch. Afterwards Philips U S Marshal, Weldon U S atty Jack Smith & others called to see me at the Hotel

Wednesday Nov 12, 1862 Had a conversation with Butler this morning in which he told me that during the battles in Virginia under Popes command Genls Fitz Jno Porter and Griffing sent a courier to Genl McClelland with a despatch signed by them saying "hold on, dont send reinforcements, and we have Pope where we can ruin him", and that the despatch fell into the Presidents hands and he now had it.

I asked him how the paper got into the Presidents' hands, and he said the President was notified that such a despatch had been sent,

*Brigadier General William S. Rosecrans, 1819-1898. Replaced Buell as commander of the Army of the Cumberland in 1862; conducted the operations against Bragg until relieved after the battle of Chickamauga in 1863.

and that he had the courier watched for, seized and the note taken from him I asked him if this was true how it was possible the President could permit either Porter or Griffing to remain in Command a day, and why he did not have them arrested, tried and shot. He answered that he did not know unless he was afraid to have them arrested.

Had a conversation with Hon Jno: T. Stuart. He is warmly for prosecuting the war with all possible vigor until the rebellion is put down, the Union restored, and all rebels compelled to submit to the authority of the Government. He does not believe there can be any compromise. He thinks the Presidents emancipation and Habeas Corpus proclamations were most unfortunate, and but for them that the democrats would steadily and earnestly have supported the administration.

. . . .

Thursday Sept 1, 1864 Mr Palmer & family dined with us—
Friday Sept 2 Walked out to my new house after dinner
Saturday Sept 3. This and the two preceding days have, I believe, been the hottest of the season Intelligence of the capture of Atlanta by Genl Sherman reached us this morning, & in the afternoon Col Lockwood & Mr Brooker called on me to say there was to be a meeting in Washington Square, at night, to celebrate the victory, and to invite me to attend and address the meeting, which I consented to do. At 8 P. M. I went down—found a large crowd in attendance waiting for me—I spoke ¾ of an hour—Congratulated them that standing as we were upon the eve of a Presidential election which promised to be one of more than usual animation, if not excitement, that an occasion was now presented upon which all patriots of all political parties could unite without asperity, to rejoice over the triumphs of our arms. After a eulogy upon Genl Sherman, and his gallant army, I proceeded to say that the most ardent desire of my heart was to see this desolating war at an end, and peace, fraternity and happiness restored to the land, but that we could have no permanent peace which would give us prosperity except upon the basis of the Union, and that we could have no union until the great masses of the people in rebellion were brought to consent to return to the old government and to submit to its laws, for there could be no union with an unwilling people. To accomplish this we must break the power of the rebel armies, and separate the people from their wicked and ambitious leaders, by assuring them that whenever they laid down their arms, and returned to their allegiance, they should be restored to their rights, and receive the protection of the government in person and prop-

erty—that we could not treat millions of people as traitors and punish them as traitors, and the effect of attempting to do it would be to keep them in revolt—that no great rebellion was ever happily terminated without a general amnesty to the masses, and without it we could not restore the union, but we hoped to be able to make examples of the leaders &c That the people of the South were deluded, and believed that the old government was their enemy and that they were to be disfranchised and stripped of their property whenever they submitted to its authority—that we must dispel this delusion, and assure them that our only purpose in prosecuting the war was to suppress the rebellion, restore the union and re establish the authority of the constitution and laws, and that when this end was attained the war should cease, and that whenever they ceased resistance and returned to their allegiance they should be restored to the enjoyment of all their rights.

The meeting was composed of men of all parties, and I carefully avoided subjects of a merely partizan character, and made no allusion to the Presidential candidates. I did say, however, that I thought the rebellion the most causeless and atrocious piece of political wickedness the world ever saw, and that it must be put down at whatever cost, and that more men must yet be raised for that object. My remarks were received with every demonstration of approval, and I had reason to believe were acceptable to all, but Genl B M Prentiss took the stand, and was almost denunciatory in his dissent.

He called God to witness that he would never consent that any man who had borne arms against this government should ever enjoy the rights of citizenship again—that he did not recognize the Southern people as his erring brethren, and would never agree to live under the same government with them—that he was for emancipation, confiscation and every other measure that could be adopted against them—yet strange inconsistency he announced, in the same speech, his belief that hundreds of thousands of men in the rebel army were as loyal as he was. He had much to say in praise of Prest: Lincoln and Genl Grant, and in abuse of the democratic party &c.

When he concluded Jack Grimshaw took the stand. He was drunk, and as coarse and vulgar as drunk. He raved and fumed—denounced our "erring Southern brethren"—not one of them should ever enjoy the rights of citizenship again—their Country should be given to the negroes, and if they did n't like to live among negroes they could leave &c He had a brother in the army who had been shot thro the arm—his law partner Williams had a brother in law who had been in Libby prison, and he was not willing that the Southern people should ever have rights under this government again.

He defended arbitrary arrests, and found fault that more of them had not been made, and said that when a man was arrested and put in prison he should never be permitted to see the light of day again till the war was over. He was fierce in his abuse of the democratic party and copperheads &c.

Both he and Prentiss were loudly cheered, but by only a small part of the audience—I think not more than fifty or sixty.

· ·

Henry Clay Bear, whose letters to his wife Lucetta (whom he called "Duck") are excerpted here, was born in 1838 in Cumberland County, Pennsylvania. In 1857 he came with his family to Macon County, Illinois, where his father started a brickyard. He married Lucetta in 1857 and worked a small rented farm near the town of Oakley. When the war began, Bear enlisted in Company A of the 116th Illinois Volunteers. The letters reprinted below describe events in the fall of 1862, as the troops are preparing for the move against Vicksburg. Bear saw action at Chickasaw Bluffs, was wounded at Vicksburg, and served under General Sherman at Missionary Ridge, Lookout Mountain, Atlanta, and across Georgia to the ocean. He was one of the 339 veterans of the original 980 men of the 116th to return to Illinois in 1865. After the war Bear became a prosperous grain merchant and was active in local civic and political affairs until his death in 1927. Wayne C. Temple, the editor of Bear's letters, is director of the Department of Lincolniana, Lincoln Memorial University.

The 116th Illinois on Bivouac

HENRY C. BEAR

[Memphis, Tennessee]
November the 25 [1862]

My Dear Jane

Another day is past and the brick house stands yet but a great many houses and stables had to suffer last night. Our camp is out a

From Wayne C. Temple, ed., *The Civil War Letters of Henry C. Bear* (Harrogate, Tenn., 1961), pp. 5-9. Reprinted by permission of the Lincoln Memorial University Press.

little way from town. 300 yds from camp there was two buildings burnt last night—our stable with two horses and a cow. There was fires burning all over town last [night.]

John Rogers will stay here in the hospitle. The doctor says he is not able to march with us. I hear that the Cololnel says we have to unpack our coats and take them with us. They say we will Cramp enough of wagons to carry the extra load. They have taken in quite a number of wagons allready. We are all in high spirits. You my little woman must not fret about me to[o] much for I am bound to go through allright. Good by my little wife. We will all soon be home again.

H. C. Bear

DIARY NUMBER ONE

A Camp near Abb[e]ville
state of Mississippi
Dec. 7, 1862

My Dear and affectionate wife,

I once more will try to let you know that I am in the land amongst the living. I have taken a very bad cold which anoys me considerable. Standing out in the rain and snow storm [as] we did day before yesterday is enough to give an ox a bad cold. Yesterday and this morning it frose tollerable hard. We are going to stay here till we eat every thing up we can get from the sesesesh around here then we will go farther.

This is a nice clear sunday morning. We, that is our whole Company, was out on picket yesterday. We had a good time. We killed a couple of hogs and confiscated several bush[els] of sweet potatoes.

The nigers says the reble army fled in an awful hury from the breast works when they found out we were so near them. They had a large force. They are now on full retreat. The news came in that Grant had captured 6,000 of [Sterling] Prices force about forty miles from here. We soldiers dont know any thing that is going on in any other Department. We dont get any news. We dont know much that is going on in this department. You up home talk of the South starving. It is not the case though. They have but very little salt and coffee but plenty of hogs and sweet potatoes, plenty of sugar and molasses and some corn, some wheat and if we leave them have the slaves they allways will have plenty, but when the first of January comes the slaves will be like the Duchmans flea: when they think they have them they wont be there. I never thought I could relish a chunk of cold corn bread like I did last night. It was deliscious sure. We have not been on full rations for several days but the teems have arrived and we will get our hard crackers. We breakfasted on sweet potatoes, coffee and fresh pork this morning.

My little woman, I intend to fill this book up with things that take place, that is evry day occurrances. I then intend to send it to you in an envelope as a letter.

The Captain, Brown, was out cramping to day. He brought in three quarters of a barell of sugar. We, that is our Company, will go out forageing tomorrow. We intend to take four or five wagons with us. I will tell you tomorrow evening how we make out, so good night my duck.

Monday morning [December] the 8th
[1862]

We will not get to go a forageing this morning as we supposed we would. We will have to go on Skirmish drill in half an hour. I Still have a bad Cold. It was very cold last night so that I did not sleep very well. It frose ice half an inch thick. It is warm through the day and Cold at night. Yesterday was my birthday. The boys cuffed me around Considerably. I have not heard from John for some time.

Two O'clock, P. M.

The colonel give our first Lieut fits to day after drill about (Kate). She goes in mens clothes. She has been with the Regt ever since we left Memphis. She used to be an occupant of the Brick. There is a few in our Company that would like to have such rips as her in camp, and on account of them our lieutenant was talked to as was some of the rest. You could hardly tell her from a man. I did not notice her till in camp on [the] Tallahachee and then I would not [have] if some one had not showed her to me. I could not find out why John [B. Purdew] was reprimanded without it was because she was out on picket when he was in command of the Company.

Tuesday [December 9, 1862] ten O'Clock

We are ordered back to Memphis to start at 12 o clock. It is all bustle and hurry in camp now. I suppose most of the force will leave for Memphis. I feel some better with my cold this morning.

Wednesday morning [December] the 10
[1862]

We marched back to the Tallahachee river yesterday. We have orders to start this morning at 7 O'Ck. toward Memphis. We are to

make it in three days. I am not very well this morning. I am
reported sick this morning.

Two hours later

I am now setting along the road about a mile from where we
encamped. I got part of my load hauled. [George] Wilson, [George
Alexander] Jones and I went on a head. The whole army is halted
in consequence of two Regts taking the wrong road, but now the
bugle sounds forward and I must go.

12 O'C.

I just five minutes ago passed by an ambulance that was labeled
Small Pox. I read it and then looked in and seen a man of the (55
Regt) just broke out with the Small Pox. You better believe I went
away quick. I am still ahead of our Regt. We have come about 8 ms.
We are within 12 miles of Holl[y] Springs. There is several cases of
the Small Pox in this Division. When we get to Memphis they are
going to vaccinate all that is not vaccinated. I stood marching this
morning very well.

7 O'Clock Evening

We did not go to holly Springs. We took another road and
encamped on a stream called pigeon roost, 19 ms from Tallahachee.

6 O'Clock, A. M. Thursday [December]
the 11th [1862]

We are to march at 9 O Clock and go 15 ms.

5 O'Clo[ck] Evening

We have marched the 15 miles. We are encamped on a stream
called Cold water. I stood marching very well excepting my left
foot got sore.

Friday December the 12 [1862]
5 O Clock A. M.

We will not start till ten O clock. We are within 22 ms of
Memphis. We will hav today and tomorrow to make it in. A great
many of the Boys have bad colds. George Wilson took morphine
yesterday morning and it came near killing him. He could not walk
to the ambulance. He is a little better now. I am writing by the light
of the fire. It gives poor light so I will quit. All the boys from our
neighborhood stands marching well. I though Da[n] Miller would
get home sick but he dont. He gets along as well as any of us. He is

as hardy as a buck. Dan Bowen is fat and harty. Bill Hickman is in our mess and is more Develish than ever.

A lead pencil is a poor thing to write with but you must try and figer it out.

Eight O'Clock, P. M.

We are encamped for the night on what is called Clear lake, six miles from Memphis. We came Sixteen ms today. We all stood it well excepting our feet. This is the first time my feet swelled or got sore. It rained today occasionaly. They say we will stay in the camp till we go on board a boat to some point on the river. I'll bet I will send my overcoat home when I get to town. I left it on the road, it was picked up and I got it again. I hope we will get the mail in the morning. You must write often for it does one good to hear from home. You dont know how we long to hear from home. When you write tell evry thing that takes place. Be sure to write often. The boys are full of life. Dan Bowen and Dan Miller is just now scuffeling in the ten[t] at my feet. I must stop writing for I am setting on Georg[e] Wilsons bed and he wants to go to bead, so good night.

"Riding the rail," military discipline at Camp Douglas

Courtesy of the Illinois State Historical Library

Dec. the 13 [1862] A. M. Saturday

It is raining this morning. We just finished our breakfast. I had to cough considerable last night.

Dec. 13th [1862] Saturday
2 O'Clock P. M.
Camp at Memphis

We have arrived here at last. We had a hard march this morning. I never was so near give out as when we arrived in camp today and so was all the rest. I carried all my load. It rained most of the time. The roads was slipery. We certainly had a hot march.

But our sorrow is all forgotten. Our Company, as did all the rest, drawed a bucket full of Whiskey and each mess got a quart, and it revived us up sure. It was the first we drawed. And it made me feel tipsy sure as it did some of the rest. You know it takes but little to make me feel funny. We have a nice camp here, within two hundred yards of our old camping ground. I do not know how long we will stay here. There is more troops here now, a great deal [more,] than when we started on this march.

I have not heard from John since we left Tallahachee. David St[a]pp came from Holly Springs to Tallahachee and he saw him there. He was not fit to stand marching then. He would of like[d] to come along but had to stay at the Hospital there. John give out when we ware near Holly Springs and was taken there. Balch staid here when we started on this march but John and some of the rest that was under the weather would not.

I have not seen Balch since we arrived. John and Father Wilson will soon be discharged. I think Wilson could get one if he would take it. I suppose he will now. We all hope the war will soon be over. I am not home sick by a great ways but I would not care if the war would end tomorrow. One does not know how sweet home is till he goes through the roughs of a Soldiers life. You must not think I am despondent for I aint, for I would not take a discharge if one was give to me.

I studied the cost and measured the way before I enlisted and I intend to stick it throug manfuly. You must try and bear your lot Heroically for this war cant certainly last long. I hate marching above all things. I hope the next trip we take will be on board a steam Boat. I am going to send my Gum blanket and Overcoat home sure for they are too heavy to cary on a march.

Two hours later

I have just told you we ware having a good time Over our whiskey But O! Sweet time nothing compared to receiving three letters at once from you. You ought to have been here to see how eager we was to get our letters when the Captain brought our letters to Camp. Some of the boys got as high as twelve letters. It has been along time since we received any mail. This Regt got about two bushel of letters. The Captain got his arms full for this Company.

I received your three letters; the dates are Nov 26, Nov 30 and Dec the 3[rd.] We still have the same guns. There is but little talk when we will be paid off. I still have a $5.00 greenback and a quarter in silver. I am surely glad and nothing pleases me better than to hear that you and the rest gets along in peace. It would be hard to hear that you all could not live in without quarreling. If you ever get in a quarrel think of me and quit.

You see the edges of this book is colored. It is colored by my swet. When we stoped here there was not a dry sti[t]ch on my shirt. I had it in my shirt pocket and it was perfectly wet when I took it out.

You must be cheerful for I will take good care of my self sure. I am glad to hear that Mother is a little better but sorry to hear that William Morris is poorly. Tell Ross I would like to be up there to take a hunt with him. I believe I could beat him killing a turkey. You can tell him he would have give out if he had to march with as big a load as we had to. Tell him to be sure to keep his gun clean for I will be home before long.

Sunday morning [December] the 14th
[1862]

The Sergeant came to me just as I was going to bed last night and told me I had to go on guard. I did not like to do it but had to. My shirt was not dry this morning yet from the swet yesterday. I took more cold, had to be reported sick. The doctor gave me two blue mass pills. I would not take them I made hoarhound sure.

[Memphis, Tennessee, December 15,
1862]

This morning I feel a good bit better now which is about noon. At Camp near Abb[e]ville is where I commenced writing this letter dated Dec the 7. I tell you this so as to tell wher to commence reading this letter. I thought when I commenced this letter I would fill the front part up with some thing else.

Tell Ross if he wants to marry and wants to get a good looking wife never to go South for I have not seen a good looking girl since I have landed in dixie. There may be some but I have not seen them. Once in a while we see some of the sesesh boys. They always look sneaking. On our march every house we Stopped at they wanted to be protected because they said they ware widows. There was a good many white flags stuck up and two of the Stars and Stripes. You better believe we gave them three good Cheers. We hear since we come back to Memphis that our Regt was all cut up. That it was so reported in a Chicago paper. What a lie. There was not a Shot fired at us yet and dont expect there will be.

I suppose if you have heard the Regt are all killed but ten men as was reported, you was considerable troubled. What lies are gotten up and such unnatural lies too. I hear to[o] that we are most starved and hat to sleep with only our blanket to cover us, which is not so. We fare as well as soldiers generally could expect. Some times we run short but only for a while, then we have plenty. Bill and I sleep together. We each have a blanket, also a gum one to sleep on and two to cover over and our two overcoats yet. It is not cold here like up ther. I can stand it with one gum and one wollen blanket when two sleep togeather. I suffer more carrying so much load than I do with the cold. What will you think when I tell you I have not had my pants off since I took them off when you and I slept together last. I changed shirts once and done my own washing. I got them tole[r]able clean for a raw hand. I give the Captains Niger one of my check shirts on the March and Charley Rundles, my shoes. I would not care if I had a good pair of boots. Mine run crooked on the march but is good otherways. I notice that my lead pencil writing will be hard to read in consequence of it rubing out. Mayb[e] you can make it out. What I write to you Duck is the same as writing to Father and Mother. You should allway[s] show it to them. It will save sending two letters and answer the same purpose.

Tell Uncle Ephrim that I am in for tetotal Subjugation rather than Compromise with the rebles. I would rather see the whole South peopled with nigers rather than to end the war Dishonorable to the government of the United States. I would like to be home but not till the last dog lays down his gun, which they soon will have to do I think.

You may tell evry man of Doubtful Loyalty for me, up ther in the north, that he is meaner than any son of a bitch in hell. I would rather shoot one of them a great [d]eal than one living here. There is no comparison between the two. There may be some excuse for the one but not for the other. One could allways tell them by there finding fault with the President or with the government some way and thats just the way we tell them here. There is some Ohio regt here. May be there is some that is acquainted with the Hills. I will try to find out and I will let you know.

Tell John I will write to him tollerable soon. Tell him to write to me whether I write or not. He has got a better place and chance to write than I have. It is no fun to set humped up in our little low tents writing sure but I am surely anxious to get letters from home. So whether I write or not, write to me. I suppose you would like to get this letter, Duck, for it is a kind of history of our march: so with this I will end.

I Remain as ever your true and affectionate husband

Henry C. Bear

[P. S.] I was glad to get those stamps. I was plume out and they are hard to get sure. I will end by asking you to give my love and best respects to all the folks.

Your Hen

[P. P. S.] I will tear the Back off this book before I put it in an envelope.

. . . .

Unfortunately, all that is known of Henry H. Eby is that he was born in Mendota, Illinois, in 1841, enlisted in the 7th Illinois Volunteers in April 1861, was discharged in the fall of 1864, and died sometime after he published his own war recollections in 1910. One is struck in the following reminiscence with the contrast between the frivolities and high spirits of departure for war and early camp life, and the later grim scenes of life in the Confederate prison at Belle Island, Virginia. A similarly gruesome picture of prison life is found in Ray Meredith, ed., *This Was Andersonville: The True Story of Andersonville Military Prison as Told in the Personal Recollections of John McElroy* (New York, 1957). See also William B. Hesseltine, *Civil War Prisons: A Study in Psychology* (Columbus, Ohio, 1930).

Battle, Camp and Prisons, '61-'65

HENRY H. EBY

I was now 19 years of age, and considered it my duty to help defend the flag.

From Henry H. Eby, *Observations of an Illinois Boy in Battle, Camp and Prisons—1861-1865* (Mendota, Ill., 1910), pp. 16-28, 198-205.

By the latter part of April a company of about 100 was organized in Mendota, with Capt. Rust as commander. We were drilled here for a few days before leaving for Springfield. We were all rather green in regard to military affairs and it was laughable to see the performance. There was about as much awkwardness shown as there would be in breaking a pair of young oxen. In a few days we started for Springfield, Ill. On the day of our departure, which was April 19, 1861, the excitement in Mendota was beyond description. It was probably as intense as when McClellan's army left Washington for the capture of Richmond. People came flocking into town from all the surrounding country and villages, with flags flying, to see the soldiers start off for the war. The streets were crowded with people who came to bid us the last good-bye. Flags were unfurled and speeches made in honor of our departure.

About 11 o'clock all who had enlisted were formed in two ranks in front of the Illinois Central freight house, facing toward it, when a Miss Davis, who stood upon a raised platform at the northwest corner of the building, delivered an appropriate address, presenting us with an elegant flag in behalf of the citizens of Mendota. This was responded to in a happy manner in behalf of the company by L. B. Crooker, a chubby farmer boy about 20 years of age, who had drifted to Mendota for the purpose of studying law, and who had also enlisted.

. . . .

About 12 o'clock we marched to the depot, and an immense crowd of people gathered around us, bade us good-bye, and we boarded the train and were soon on our way to Springfield, where we arrived the following morning and met a number of companies from different parts of the State. A few days after our arrival we were organized into a regiment, which required ten companies. The Mendota company was made Co. B, and the regiment the 12th Illinois Infantry, with Col. McArthur in command, who was subsequently commissioned Major General.

The Mendota company contained more than the required number of men. Among the surplus bone and sinew who found no place in the home company were L. B. Crooker, James W. Larabee, William Eckert, George C. Loomis, S. P. Whitmore and myself, who all determined to stick together and stay in service. We immediately began looking about for an opening large enough to hold these six husky farmer boys, and it was at last accomplished by entering Co. H of the same regiment. This was from Tiskilwa, and was commanded by Capt. Swain, who subsequently lost his life at Shiloh. We remained together in the same mess until discharged at the end of three months.

It was now imagined that we were going south to crush the Rebellion at once, but, alas, we failed to realize what was before us. Little did we think it would require four long years to end the great Rebellion. We remained here several weeks, passing the time in drilling and running about town. On May 25 we were transferred to Caseyville, Ill., about ten miles east of St. Louis, where we remained a month or more. While here we received a good many instructions in military tactics, and soon considered ourselves equal to Napoleon or any other great general.

The guns we received were of the old kicking variety, and could kick equal to a mule. I can well remember having a very lame shoulder from the effects of discharging one of these firearms. . . .

The latter part of June the 12th was transferred to Cairo, Ill. We marched across the country from Caseyville to East St. Louis, then got on board a steamer and went down the Mississippi, arriving at our destination on the following day. The only excitement occurring on the way down the river was caused by a man on the Missouri shore waving a rebel flag at us while passing. We went into camp at Cairo on the river bottom behind the levee, our camp being about ten or fifteen feet below high water mark in the river. The levee was constructed for the purpose of keeping high water in the river from overflowing the city. This camp proved to be worse than any experienced during all our subsequent three years' service. While here we received a visit from Gen. McClellan, who addressed us.

We remained here during the balance of the three months' term, and nearly all of us were sick, caused by the malaria of the river bottoms and other causes. After the expiration of the three months' term of service I enlisted for three years in Co. C, 7th Illinois Cavalry.

. . . .

Beginning of Three Years' Service.—Camp Butler and Bird's Point

The three months' service ended in August, 1861, and I enlisted for three years in Sept., 1861. Was discharged Oct. 15, 1864, serving in all three years and about four months. The 7th was organized at Camp Butler, near Springfield, Ill., in the fall of 1861, where it was partly drilled. . . .

The army has settled down to weeks of forced inaction, and the men make themselves as comfortable as the means at hand will allow. They have shown wonderful thrift and industry in housing themselves. The tent in the foreground shows this. Its builders have made a pen of logs neatly chinked with chunks and clay to keep out the wind. They have built a fireplace of clay and used an old plow

From Henry H. Eby, *In Battle, Camp and Prisons, '61-'65* (1910)

A scene in winter quarters

on top of the chimney to assist the draft. The roof is made of pieces of shelter tents and ponchos and at the entrance has been laid a pavement of pork-barrel staves to keep mud from being carried into the sleeping apartment. The other tents in the distance show similar devices. The whole is as accurate a picture of a winter camp as the camera could make.

The veteran in the foreground is a man whose love of music is so strong as to be irrepressible. He has constructed a fiddle out of a cigar box and such other material as he could lay his hands on. It shows as much ingenuity as his tent. Probably the tail of the Colonel's horse has suffered to furnish hair for the bow. The music made is far from that which could be drawn from a high-priced instrument, but he and his boy listener enjoy it a hundredfold more than the most cultivated listener ever did high-priced strains. And he plays the tune that always went most directly to the soldier's heart, "Home, Sweet Home."

While at Bird's Point the 7th performed the ordinary camp and picket duties, occasionally going out on a scouting expedition, making a visit to the vicinity of the enemy. Every morning about daybreak four men from the cavalry were sent out on the road leading from the camp outside of the picket line for the purpose preventing a surprise by the enemy. One morning, some time after they had gone out as usual, the four horses returned to camp riderless and with blood-stained saddles. A force of the boys was immediately sent out to investigate. After they had passed some distance beyond the picket lines, the bodies of the four men were found lying in the road dead, and almost riddled with buckshot, supposed to have been fired from shotguns. It was evidently the work of bushwhackers, as there was a large log lying within a few feet of the road and parallel with it, and behind this in the soft ground were seen tracks made by a number of men, and the conclusion was reached that these bushwhackers had concealed themselves behind the log and awaited the approach of the four men until they were very near. They then fired upon them, probably killing them instantly.

. . . .

Soon after our arrival here we began the construction of barracks for winter quarters, which were built of logs in log house fashion. Co. C's building was a long, one-story structure, with bunks for beds, which contained straw and made very comfortable sleeping places.

About Christmas time nearly all were supplied with good things from home. I can never forget the luxuries we received. They were just delicious. I received a box containing a roast turkey, a number of pies, cakes, and other things too numerous to mention. We had just moved into our new barracks, and stored away our delicacies for safe keeping until wanted. Late one afternoon, when nearly all of us had gone to water our horses, one who remained in camp lit a candle and placed it under the bunk to aid him in searching for something he had lost. The lighted candle immediately set fire to the straw in the bunk and in a few minutes the whole building was in a blaze. When we returned our good things had nearly all been destroyed by the fire. Scarcely anything was saved, and thus our anticipations of grand feasts and dinners were dashed away. We were obliged to be content with hard-tack, bean soup, and bacon.

The event of the day was falling in for soup, prepared by the cook on detail for the day, in his open-air studio. It was an article that would not pass muster at a fashionable restaurant, but it was hot, there was usually plenty of it, the beans were abundant and as good as Michigan or New England soil could produce, the pork was the finest product of the Illinois pork raisers, and if the cook had been mindful of his duty, had cooked the soup long enough, and stirred it diligently to prevent its burning, it was very appetizing, went right to the spot, and built fine locomotive apparatus for the future marching and battling. If on the other hand he had been careless and lazy, there was likely to be a summary court-martial, and he was lucky if he escaped with nothing worse than being tossed in a blanket. When one looks on the steaming pot, the words of the old refrain rise at once to mind.

"Beans for breakfast,
Beans for dinner,
Beans for supper,
Beans, beans, beans."

. . . .

My Second Entrance into Belle Island Prison Pen, Feb. 13, 1864.

The day that I entered the island the second time, Feb. 13, a Confederate preacher delivered a very long sermon to us, and tried to convert us to the Southern Confederacy cause, but with poor success.

We could not be converted to an institution that tried to freeze us and starve us. He was listened to attentively for a long time when he remarked before closing that he didn't know as he was doing any good talking to us, it was like casting pearls before swine, and he would close his remarks. One of our boys told him that he might have stopped long ago if he had wanted to, as we would have had no objections whatever.

On entering the prison pen on the island, for the second time, my spirits sank to zero, for the prospect before me was certainly a gloomy one. This was a low and barren island, over which the cold February winds swept from up and down the James River, making it very uncomfortable for us, exposed as we were to the elements of the weather. I could now see a great change in the appearance of the prisoners since my short stay of six days here, in October, 1863, and not for the better, but very much worse. Many were nearly destitute of clothing, and had been so starved and exposed to the severe weather that they were mere skeletons, slowly moving about. Some of them were being fairly eaten alive by graybacks. From lack of proper means of keeping clean, and only the icy river water in which to wash, many were nearly as black as negroes. Some indeed were too weak to keep themselves clean, and too discouraged to care. I was informed that there were about 8,000 of us on the island at this time, and a large number, perhaps several thousand, including Herrick and myself, were without shelter of any kind, although we were more fortunate than some of them. During our stay here we received no fuel for fires. I saw a few sticks of wood, which were being whittled into splinters and small fires made with them, around which hovered the poor, shivering, almost lifeless human forms, sitting upon the frozen ground. This wood being pitch pine, produced very black smoke, which blackened the faces of the poor fellows who tried to warm over the little fires and caused them to appear still more hideous. Those of the prisoners who were without shelter contrived different ways to keep from freezing at night, while trying to sleep. I slept in a shallow rounding ditch in the ground, in which I lay also in the daytime, when becoming tired of walking about, standing or sitting on the frozen ground. This protected me to some extent from the cold, piercing winds which blew over the island, but it was very uncomfortable during a rainstorm, of which we experienced several during our confinement there. During a rainstorm the sand and ground about me would become saturated with water, and keep my clothing wet for days, and I would become so chilled and numbed that I would be scarcely able to get up. One cold night, while trying to sleep, my toes were frozen so that the skin peeled off sometime after. While we were here in this condition the water in the river froze over nearly the whole of its surface. I saw ice over three inches in thickness.

A day seemed to me as long as a month. Rations were very small, consisting almost entirely of unsifted cornmeal, stirred up with water, and often without salt, as salt was a scarce article with the Confederacy. This was baked in cakes about the size of a brick, only about one and one-half inches thick. One-half a cake of this size was given each man for a day's ration, and nothing else with it, with the exception that two or three times while on the island we received beans or meat. This was generally entirely devoured at once, leaving nothing for the other two meals, and yet we remained nearly as hungry as before eating. Our drink consisted of icy river water, which did not warm a person very much, thoroughly chilled as we were.

Days and weeks passed slowly on, with nothing to cheer us, but everything to depress our spirits. Cold, hungry, and discouraged with the sight of so much misery all about us, little wonder that some lost their reason. Our main topic of conversation was the comforts of home, and the subject of something to eat, especially as this was most forcibly impressed upon our minds. I well remember receiving as a part of one day's rations some small beans (called here cow beans). Some were red and others black. I placed them in my left hand and counted them, and found that there were just fifteen. These were all the beans that I received while on the island, and as I had no means of cooking them I ate them raw.

At another time I received a piece of boiled beef, about the size of a black walnut, which was all the meat I had to eat while on the island. After a short stay in this place I began to fail rapidly. On arising in the morning I would ache all over, and could scarcely

A prisoner being shot crossing the "dead line" in the military stockade at Andersonville, Georgia

straighten up, and it appeared to me that even the marrow in my bones was chilled. Occasionally I would take a walk down to the water's edge, in order to start circulation and get a little warmth into my shivering body, in which I generally failed. In order to get to the water we were obliged to pass down through a narrow lane, fenced on each side with a tight high board fence, and plenty of guards on all sides. Through this we passed to procure water, and to wash our hands and faces if we washed at all. We were not supplied with washbasins, and therefore when washing would use the river as a basin, which did not improve the water for drinking purposes, where several thousand men washed within a space of 30 or 40 feet in length. The closet was also located very near where we obtained our drinking water. This was at the lower end of the island where there was no current to carry away the filthy water.

Our clothes could not be washed because the weather was too cold. We were in the same predicament as the man who possessed only one suit and was obliged to go to bed while his garments were being washed. But we were not so fortunate as he because we had no beds to go to and not even what a person would call a suit.

During some of these walks I saw most horrid sights as I walked through the camp. I remember one day of seeing several boys or young men who had become so weakened and emaciated by their treatment here that they were unable to stand erect while walking but were obliged to bend over like old men of eighty. Their clothing on the outside, under their arms, was white with graybacks and nits, and as I stood looking at the poor boys I wondered what must be the condition on the inside of their garments. But I was helpless as far as giving them relief. They were only a sample of hundreds of similar cases. As I stated in a previous chapter, we who were able would take off our shirts, turn them inside out, and kill (between our only weapons of defense our thumb-nails) all the graybacks we could find. During this operation we would keep our coats (when we possessed any) closely buttoned around our shivering bodies. But many poor fellows had become unable to do even this much toward their own comfort, and there were hundreds and thousands in the same wretched condition. At other times, when passing through the prison, I saw squads of prisoners who were such objects of pity that I am utterly incapable of describing them. The memory of them will remain fresh in my mind as long as I live. Some were mere skeletons, scarcely able to move, barefooted, pants worn off halfway to their knees, shirt or coat sleeves worn off nearly to the elbow, their long matted hair and whiskers which had not been cut for months hanging over their dirty, emaciated faces. Add to this, in many instances, perhaps sore and frozen feet. They were objects calculated to enkindle pity in the heart of a tyrant. Again, I saw some who were unable to walk, lying on the ground with no better clothing than those I have just described, and no other protection from the bitter cold.

To these death soon came as a welcome relief. Nearly every morning a number of dead were carried out to some burial place. All these scenes did not have an inspiring effect on us. The craving for meat had become so intense that one day as Lieut. Boisseux, commander of the guards, came strolling through the prison pen with his pet dog following him, the dog was enticed into a tent by some of the prisoners. They caught him, cut his throat, dressed him and prepared the meat for cooking, which was soon done, and he was devoured by the hungry men. I did not see any of this transaction, but learned of it through other prisoners. One day I met one of the prisoners who possessed a small brass kettle. He showed it to me and said, "This is the kettle in which we cooked the dog." I wondered where they could procure fuel enough to cook a dog, as it was a very scarce article on the island. . . .

2: Farmers Organize

Illinois farmers, like their counterparts in the upper Mississippi Valley, responded to the difficult times of the postwar depression by organizing into clubs. Basing their activity in the socio-economic organization called the Grange, whose laws—interestingly enough—forbade political activity, they mounted a well-defined political program calling for legislative regulation of railroads and grain elevators. Illinois led the way, enacting regulatory statutes which culminated in the landmark court case of *Munn v. Illinois.* In this 1876 case the Supreme Court upheld the right of states to bring railroads to accountability. Interest and membership in the Grange had peaked by the time of the Munn decision, and where it left off the Farmers' Alliance took over. Stressing the need for laws against price-fixing and monopoly on basic farm machinery like the plow, they laid the groundwork for the political reform movement known as Populism. In his standard study *The Farmer's Last Frontier, 1860-1897* (New York, 1945), Fred Shannon briefly discusses these events. Shannon earned his Ph.D. in 1924 at the University of Iowa working under the late Arthur Schlesinger. Until his death in 1961 he was a member of the history department at the University of Illinois. His many books include *The Organization and Administration of the Union Army* (Gloucester, Mass., 1928) and *The American Farmers' Movements* (Princeton, 1957). The present selection was published as a part of the Rinehart Economic History of the United States. For more recent monographs on the agrarian situation after the war, see Carl C. Taylor's *The Farmers' Movement, 1820-1920* (New York, 1953) and Solon J. Buck's *The Granger Movement* (Lincoln, Nebraska, 1965).

The Agrarian Uprising

FRED SHANNON

As soon as depression began to settle down on the farm, after the Civil War, farmers' clubs began to appear in many states of the Middle West and South. Some of them had existed for many years earlier, but now they multiplied in number and became more political in their aims. Then came the Grange in 1867 with its elaborate secret ritual and all-round program of social, cultural, and economic uplift for farmers. The constitution of the Grange prohibited political action, but there was no restriction on individual participation in third-party movements. When a local grange adjourned from its regular meeting, it often resumed activities in the same place as a unit of a farmers' political party. Though many kinds of political and economic reforms were agitated, the chief objective of these third-party organizations was railroad regulation. Many farmers resented the secrecy of the Grange as well as its opposition to developing into a political party. So farmers' independent clubs grew up in the same areas as the Grange, and in some ways in opposition to it. Yet, the members all voted together in the Independent, Reform, Anti-Monopoly, and Farmers' parties which were active in eleven states by 1874. In Illinois, Wisconsin, Iowa, and Minnesota the Grangers had a numerical superiority over their rivals, and the Granger name was given to the legislation that ensued.

The Grange itself reached an estimated membership of some 1,500,000 by the spring of 1874, and it continued to grow till early in 1875, after which the numbers dropped to about 759,000 by the first of October. . . .

Farmers' clubs in Illinois inaugurated a movement for railroad regulation, some years before the Grange became prominent in that state. In 1867, they got a Warehouse Act adopted to compel railroad companies to handle grain from independent elevators. In 1870, they got a constitutional amendment permitting state control of the railroads, and in 1871 the legislature fixed a scale of maximum freight and passenger rates. The carriers refused to abide by

From Fred Shannon, *The Farmer's Last Frontier, 1860-1897* (New York, 1945), pp. 309-317. Copyright © 1945 by Fred Shannon.

these regulations, and ejected passengers who insisted on paying only the legal fares. In 1873, the state supreme court overruled the rate law, after which it was re-enacted along more cautious lines, and remained long in effect. In 1871, Minnesota adopted rate regulation, followed by Iowa and Wisconsin in 1874, but these acts were all repealed a few years later. After fighting such legislation from the political stump to the state courts, the railroads carried appeals to the United States Supreme Court. Meanwhile, they made use of loopholes in the laws to make the acts unpopular with their patrons. For example, the train service in Wisconsin was reduced until the law of that state was repealed. Then in October, 1876, the Supreme Court gave opinions favorable to the farmers' contentions in eight cases originating in laws of the four regulating states. In the fundamental case of Munn vs. Illinois the right to regulate was established, and in succeeding decisions, notably Peik vs. Chicago and Northwestern Railroad, it was declared that a state might regulate rates even for interstate traffic, on shipments entering or leaving the state.

Thus was the first battle won in the efforts at railroad regulation. Though some of the legislation was repealed, though the courts later limited state rate-fixing powers, at least a precedent was set. Truly effective regulation was not to come till the next century, but . . . drastic downward rates began in the period of Granger agitation, and continued afterward. Perhaps other factors, even more important, affected this change, but the fear of even more rigorous legislation seems to have been ever present. Incidentally, it is now generally held that the Granger laws were eminently fair to the carriers, as well as to the public. . . .

The Beginnings of the Farmers' Alliances

Though the Grange dropped out of sight as a political force after the late 1870's, farmers' clubs continued their activities and tended to coalesce into alliances.

. . . .

The National Farmers' Alliance, commonly called the Northwestern Alliance, may have had some generic connection with an alliance of Grangers in New York, uniting for political purposes, in 1877. The latter may have got the idea from a Settlers' Protective Association started in Kansas in 1874, to help squatters in their fight against the railroad land monopolies. Such are the claims, though slightly overwrought. But it was Milton George of Chicago, editor of the *Western Rural*, who in 1880 established the alliance

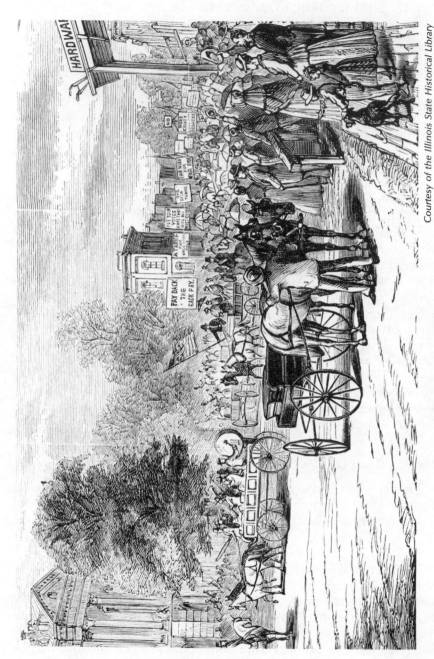

A procession and mass meeting of the Grange

that, within two years, was to claim 2,000 local groups with 100,000 members. This organization followed on the heels of two or three years of hard times in the Prairie states. As conditions improved, in 1883 and 1884, interest lagged. Then, following low wheat prices in 1884-1885, membership picked up in all the wheat states of the Northwest, and by 1887 the Northwestern Alliance was beginning to demand such things as federal competition with railroads and the revival of free coinage of silver. In the Minneapolis convention of that year, there was some tendency to cooperate with the Knights of Labor. By 1890, the Midwest farmers were thoroughly class conscious. Kansas claimed 130,000 alliance members, while Nebraska, the Dakotas, and Minnesota were close rivals. The organization had already spread through fifteen states, and was reaching out for more.

There was ample reason for the great outburst of farmer unrest as exemplified in the rapid growth of the alliances in the late 1880's. . . . In the West, while Eastern capital continued to flow in, the farmers merely grumbled at middlemen, trusts, and the railroads. . . . After the collapse of the land bubble in the West, in 1887, the mortgage companies clamped down. Where interest rates of 8, 10, or 12 per cent had prevailed, the charge now was from 18 to 24 and sometimes as high as 40. . . . Price fixing, trusts, and monopolies were already gaining headway. A Missouri editor noted in 1888 that as soon as the plow trust was organized the price of plows was doubled. There was, at the same time, a belated realization of the consequences of installment selling by the harvester trust, continual debt being the outcome. Also, it was noted, land taxes of farmers could not be evaded like those on intangible property, but the railroads were lightly assessed. The carriers even escaped the tax on their huge railroad land grants by postponing the taking out of final patents till the land could be sold.

. . . .

While demands were pouring upon the farmers for more money for taxes and interest, for installments on their mortgages and farm machinery, and for monopoly-fixed prices on many of their necessities, they could easily feel that an increase in the nation's stock of money was a likely solution of the difficulty. When the most money in hand was needed—in crop-moving time—credit was always scarce. Later, when the crops had been dumped on the market at low prices to meet urgent obligations, credit became plentiful and the speculators reaped the profits. It seemed that money and credit were being manipulated by the creditors for their own further enrichment. Farmers out of debt could stand the money and credit situation. They made very little, but they did not pay out much. In the West and South, however, there were few debt-free farmers, and interest, commissions, and the like seldom totaled less than 20 or 25 per cent. It was easy for them to believe that the creditors also had conspired to enact and perpetuate the "Crime of '73," the Resumption Act of 1875, and other measures that restricted the nation's supply of money.

. . . .

To supplement this cry for greenbacks, strength was gradually added to the demand for a renewal of the free and unlimited coinage of silver at the time-honored ratio of approximately sixteen to one with gold. In 1873, following a tendency already under way in Europe, the American Congress had adopted a law stopping the coinage of silver for domestic circulation, and giving only a limited legal-tender value to silver coins already in existence. . . .

Orthodox economists immediately declared that remonetization would demonstrate Gresham's law. Gold would go out of circulation. The United States would revert to a purely silver basis, absorbing all the cheap silver of the world that did not flow to Asia or Latin America. . . .

The Bland-Allison Act of 1878, which was offered as a sop and compromise to the silver interests, fell far short of the demands. The Secretary of the Treasury was to buy not less than $2,000,000 and not more than $4,000,000 worth of silver bullion each month and have it coined into dollars of full-legal-tender value. . . . During the twelve years that the act was in force, each of the five Presidents was a gold-standard man, and never more than the minimum amount of silver was bought. Some $378,000,000 were put in circulation from silver that cost the Treasury about $300,000,000, the profit going to the government instead of to the mining companies. But, during these same years, $100,000,000 were withheld from circulation as a reserve to protect the value of greenbacks. From a virtually empty Treasury in 1878, the surplus above reserves against paper money grew to over $220,000,000 in 1890, while the volume of national bank notes declined from nearly $359,000,000 in 1882 to $186,000,000 in 1890. They had stood at $325,000,000 in 1873. Here was nearly $460,000,000 taken out of circulation to offset any additions of silver and gold coin. Had not the stock of gold increased from $213,000,000 to $696,000,000 there would have been less money to circulate among the people in 1890 than in 1878; and a reversal in trade balances was soon to drain some of this gold out of the country again. By 1893, the stock had dwindled to $598,000,000. There was nothing in the slight gold inflation of the period to gladden the hearts of indebted farmers. The continuing fall in the price of silver, till the dollar in 1889 was worth only 72 cents, showed the silver interests also that the Bland-Allison Act was not enough for them.

. . . .

Original Narratives

J. B. Loudon was born in Scotland and was living in Coventry, England before embarking on a journey to Illinois. Loudon typifies the numerous English and Scots visitors to Illinois after the Civil War; they provide valuable descriptions of life in the Prairie State outside the city of Chicago.

The Fox River Towns

J. B. LOUDON

The first town I visited after leaving Chicago, was Aurora. This place is very pleasantly situated on the banks of the Fox River, 35 miles from Chicago, and as the land on each side of the river rises with a gentle slope, it gives the town a very picturesque appearance. The houses, which were formerly constructed of wood, are gradually giving way to very noble cream-coloured brick buildings. Aurora has a population of over 12,000. It seems to be a very prosperous little town, and has several very important trades in it. All the Pullman cars are built here, and here are many other railway works of great size. After leaving Aurora, I followed the course of the Fox River, and soon found myself in Geneva, Kane County. This certainly is the most charming little town I have ever visited. Here the Fox River is about a quarter of a mile wide, and, as at Aurora, the banks upon each side of the river slope for about a quarter of a mile down to the river's edge, the banks being completely covered with trees of various coloured foliage; while tower-

From J. B. Loudon, *A Tour through Canada and the United States of America* (Coventry, 1879), pp. 72-79.

ing above the trees may be seen some very beautiful villas, and as I
stand upon the bridge, taking in the whole scene, it looks as perfect
a little paradise as it is possible for the eye to gaze upon. I often felt
sorry while lingering amongst such scenery, and feeling all the
poetic influences such sights called up in my nature, at my utter
inability to fully convey to the mind of the reader the beauties of
the scene in such language that might, as it were, re-produce a
correct picture before the minds of my readers. I hope, however,
that they may be able to so draw upon their imagination that they
may fully realise the grandeur of the scenery on the banks of the
Fox River as seen at Geneva. I was so charmed with the scenery
that I made it my home for several days, visiting the various places
of interest, and mixing with the villagers in both their joys and their
sorrows. . . .

From Geneva I travelled along the Fox River to St. Charles. This,
too, is a very sweet little town, similarly situated to Geneva, on
either side of the Fox River. It has a population of about 2,000. It
is far-famed for its cheese and butter making establishments (they
tell me there is a great deal of Cheshire cheese made here). I visited
several cheese factories, and was very kindly shown the various
processes. One of these places makes on an average 50 cheeses per
day, and 420 lbs. of butter. The milk and cream is sent to them
fresh from the neighbouring farmers every morning. There are also
two or three paper mills for making paper from straw, sent to them
from the same persons; so that the farmers round here form a very
prosperous community. This is the little town where Dr. Thomas
resided, well-known both in England and Scotland as an eminent
writer and lecturer on prophetic literature. . . . St. Charles is also
noted for its mineral springs, which I visited, and drank from the
flowing stream; but with this kind of water my thirst is very soon
quenched. I then left St. Charles for Elgin, which is ten miles drive,
all the way along the banks of the Fox River; and the morning
being fine, the drive was one of immense pleasure, the river gradually widening in some places to nearly one mile, and as every bend
of the river presents a different view, with little islands here and
there covered with trees, the whole scene was one of surpassing
beauty. As we neared Elgin the land was very hilly, gradually rising
until quite near to the town. Elgin is a very thriving little town, and
viewed from the top of the hill, with the Fox River flowing gently
through its centre, it looks quite a charming little city. It has several
very fine streets, and some very large business establishments. The
inhabitants, too, look happy and contented. This place has a very
large watch manufactory employing 700 hands, which I also visited.
It forms two immense blocks of buildings, one in rear of the other,

but connected in the centre, and open at each end. It stands on several acres of land, which is beautifully laid out, and in splendid condition, looking more like the pleasure grounds in front of a nobleman's mansion, than grounds in front of a manufactory. The front entrance to the manufactory is also very spacious, and quite equal to the entrance into a first class American hotel. Being anxious to have a run through an American watch manufactory, I announced myself to the manager, but was doomed to disappointment, as no visitors are now allowed admittance without an order from the President of the Company, who resides in Chicago. . . . I contented myself by having a chat with two or three Coventry workmen I met with at the factory, and very pleased they were to see me. I had many pressing invitations to stay amongst them for a few days. The Coventry men say they are very busy, and are doing very well, but amidst all their prosperity they still retain very warm recollections of their native city, and said how much they would have liked to have returned home with me. It is their opinion, however, that unless Coventry and the other watch-making towns in England bestir themselves by the introduction of machinery, America will very soon run us out of every market in the world. The machine made American watches give general satisfaction, both as to price and quality.

Leaving Elgin, I drove a few miles into the country, and spent a very enjoyable day amongst the farmers, some of whom were friends of my youth in Edinburgh; they are now well-to-do farmers. At one farm they were busy threshing wheat, and getting 50 bushels to the acre. Altogether the farmers all through the State of Illinois present a very pleasing picture of comfort and contentment. They nearly all possess beautiful orchards, and this year there is an abundance of fruit, and being so near to Chicago, they get a ready market for all their produce.

. . . .

Albert Britt, former president of Knox College, Galesburg, Illinois, has published, among other works, *Abraham Lincoln—For Boys and Girls* (New York, 1925), *The Great Biographers* (New York, 1936), *Great Indian Chiefs* (New York, 1938), and *Toward the Western Ocean: The Story of the Men Who Bridged the Continent, 1803-1869* (Barre, Mass., 1963).

Life on an Illinois Farm

ALBERT BRITT

It is a favorite American thesis that the frontier was the abode of such sturdy virtues as industry, thrift, rough and ready justice, all the cardinal essentials to right living. It was a time and place where men were men—and presumably—women were women. On the latter point there can be no doubt. Ours was not the frontier, only a fading echo of it, but the manness of men and the womanness of women were marked in both work and play.

Horses were in the man's half of the world. I knew only two or three girls who learned to ride, one of them my sister Molly, after she became a country school-teacher. They rode only from necessity, never for pleasure. Sidesaddles and long, cumbersome skirts were mandatory and a girl in riding breeches riding astride would have been a social pariah. We were aware that women had legs and our curiosity about them was at least normal, but women's legs were never mentioned in mixed company and for the owner of the legs to reveal them deliberately would have been cause for horrified or leering gossip. Clearly such a one was no better than she should be and that wasn't nearly good enough. Bathing suits offered no problem because women never swam. I doubt if there was a farm woman or girl in the whole county who knew how.

Women might drive a stolid old horse hitched to a top buggy, but I have no recollection of seeing a woman drive a team, certainly not in the field. Of course they never worked in the field, with or without horses, although wielding a hoe in the garden was permissible, in some cases necessary, if there was to be a garden. Women were not supposed to have any knowledge of the care of horses beyond the simple acts of harnessing and unharnessing, and that only when there was no man available. The concept of woman had no place for horsemanship.

There were similar dividing lines in play. Boys and girls played together in recess time at school, but only in the earlier years. Adolescence drew a sharp line and beyond this point the girls disappeared from the ball games and the boisterous pum-pum-pull-away. One husky Irish girl got herself talked about around the district by playing baseball at the age of sixteen, and her offense was the greater because she was a better player than most of the boys. Clearly she could come to no good end. If she still lives she is undoubtedly several times a grandmother and probably critical of the unwomanly behavior of the modern girl.

Of course, we knew about sex. A boy on the farm learned the facts of life early. It was impossible to live in the midst of domestic animals without becoming aware of the basic biological urge. The breeding of animals was a commonplace necessity if the flock or herd was to be replenished. Roadside trees and fence posts carried posters announcing that a pure-bred Percheron or Norman stallion was available at a certain farm and at a stated fee for service. "Standing" was the country term for it. But the breeding of stock was matter for the talk of men only. In mixed company the subject was never referred to.

There were curious avoidances of words when a definite designation of sex was necessary. "Bull" was barely permissible, but I have heard a bull called a "male cow," which is some sort of record in prudery. Such words as "stud" and "boar" were barred and "bitch" was unthinkable, but "rooster" was a matter of course. The convention required that only the most oblique and veiled reference be made to an expected baby. Pregnancy was such a guilty secret that the word was never mentioned.

It was the natural corollary of this morbid prudishness that the conversation of men was flavored with coarse allusions to sex, but this was seldom a fault with the older and more settled men of the community. Itinerant farm workers were the worst offenders. These gentry seemed to take a particular delight in shocking a sensitive boy with bawdy yarns that were without point or humor. One young man of the neighborhood had a collection of such tales which he would unfold with or without provocation. Later on he became a pillar of the church and censor of local morals, a not illogical transition.

I recall no instance of an older man talking seriously with a youngster about the nature and pitfalls of sex. The most careful and understanding explanation by a teacher as a legitimate part of the process of education would have brought instant dismissal. The natural result of this system of avoidance on the one hand and leering allusion on the other was to stimulate a boy's curiosity without warning him of the dangers ahead. We learned about sex in the worst way possible. Harm was done, and the fact that it was not greater can be credited to our native timidity and perhaps an innate sense of decency. Even so the atmosphere surrounding sex was unhealthy when it might so easily have been clean and decent. Those who object to adequate teaching of the facts of life as a smirching of the innocence of youth are talking about something that didn't exist in our neighborhood. Whatever else we were, we were not innocent on this point at least.

In principle the code of virtue was high and permitted no exceptions. Illegitimacy was neither forgiven nor forgotten. Even though the identity of the father was rather more than suspect, it was on the mother and the child that the penalty fell of course.

How well did this sort of social policing control the relations of the young before marriage? No one knows. When a young couple had reached the stage that we called "going together" there were occasional sly allusions to top buggies standing long on secluded side roads on summer evenings.

The ratio of domestic fidelity was high. Separations were infrequent and divorce practically unknown. The cost of such an extreme step was enough to discourage thought of it. Even today real farmers or farmers' wives are strangers to Reno. It should not be concluded that all marriages were happy ones, but in spite of frequent minor jangles home life was placid, though undemonstrative. Open expressions of affection were not common. Within the family circle kissing was for babies or the brief period of courtship. Our life was as sparing of praise as of money. Undoubtedly parents liked to hear their children praised, but the common response was deprecatory. Compliments were likely to make a child "bigheaded." Also there was a lingering fear that praise of children to their faces was likely to attract the jealous attention of a bad-tempered God. One of my teachers incautiously in my presence told Mother that I was doing good work in school. The prompt reply was calculated to put me in my place: "He ought to. He's lazy enough at home." It didn't take us long to discover that this was a mere formality, part of a masquerade, not to be taken seriously. Like the whippings it was for our good, and like the whippings it had little effect.

. . . .

The code that governed the personal relations of grown men was casual and tacit. Boys fought for any reason, or none at all. A spark of temper might turn a good-natured scuffle into a brawl with a wild flurry of futile blows. My first battle occurred before my conscious memory had begun to record events, so I have only family rumor to rely on. My opponent was one Freddy Richardson, otherwise unknown to me. I had been ordered to conduct Freddy to the strawberry bed and there to help him pick some berries to take home to his mother. A reference by the visitor to the fact that the berries were for him aroused my wrath, and we fell to in the midst of the berries, to the indignant shame of my mother and the vast amusement of Freddy's father.

With grown men there were a few words that called for instant action. The lie direct was not to be overlooked. Terms that demanded prompt physical retort were "bastard" and "son of a bitch." These were not to be used lightly or condoned if used.

. . . .

The line between city and country people was sharply drawn. The easy speech and the good clothes of the city men who came among us was reason enough for fearing the worst. The villain was easily identified in the melodrama of that day. He wore a silk hat, a frock coat, and sharp-toed patent leather shoes, and he smoked cigarettes. Give him a cane to swing nonchalantly, and the simple country maiden in a gingham dress hadn't a chance in the world.

Our clannishness in the presence of outsiders was a frontier heritage. In spite of the growth of population and the steady flowing of the American people westward for new land and another chance, there were backwaters like ours where time seemed to stand still. We were hundred per cent Americans, if there have been any, and we instinctively shied away from strange faces and new things. Our physical environment of woods and hills strengthened the illusion of permanence. Such youthful hoodlumism as we exhibited was possible because there were woods to roam in and hills to hedge us about. A dark night, country roads, and horses to ride stirred the pulse and called us to mischief. It was seldom malicious and it had no sinister meaning for the future. The boys who had fancied themselves as night riders soon settled down to respectable matrimony and hard work.

Many of the real bad men of the Old West were town products. Billy the Kid was born on the East Side in New York, and Wild Bill Hickok came from a small town along the Illinois. Most of his killing had warrant of law. Wyatt Earp and his brothers who tamed the killers in the corral fight in Tombstone grew up in Monmouth, our county seat town. They also were town marshals and deputy sheriffs, agents of law and order. The line between law enforcement and law breaking was a vague one. We may sometimes have seemed to flout the law, but our offenses were products of the time and place, with little significance except as the overflowings of youth and high spirits.

In spite of farm duties and long hours of work, there was no lack of social life. At the core of it was neighborly visitation, with Sunday dinner as an important feature. This was something of a feast, especially if the visiting wife was known to be a star in her own kitchen. If there was china and silver that could be described as "best," it was brought forth for such occasions. Children were included as a matter of course, and there was a nice question of age involved in determining the exact point at which this inclusion ceased to be automatic. Summer was preferred for these affairs. There was plenty of room out of doors for the young fry, although noisy play was frowned upon.

The sedate elders generally adjourned to the sitting room, commonly called the Best Room, after the hearty dinner had been duly dealt with. If the weather was bad, these Sunday afternoons were ordeals for the young, unless a roomy barn offered large opportunity for play. With the elders, talk drifted idly along obvious channels: the condition of crops, the price of hogs, the latest report from neighborhood invalids—with much shaking of gloomy heads —politics always, if it was campaign time with party lines to attack or defend, religion sometimes, although this was a dangerous theme calculated to lead to violent dogmatic differences. The women discussed children and recipes and exchanged patterns for clothes or quilts. The family photograph album was good for half an hour or more any time. The routine of viewing the album never varied. "That's Roy when he was two. Wasn't he cute? Here's Aunt Martha when she was little. Would you ever believe it?"

. . . .

A social event of considerable magnitude was the county fair, usually in early September. That was the week when rain was a catastrophe, however much it might be needed. The fair was a combination livestock show and exhibition of farm machinery and farm products, fruit, vegetables, grain, jams, jellies, preserves, pickles, rows of canned fruits from farm kitchens. Blue, red, and white ribbons, emblems of awards, were proudly displayed by exultant winners. There were side shows too, the fat, tattooed, or bearded lady, a snake charmer with a sluggish serpent twined around her, the Streets of Cairo with the barker making tactful allusion to the daring dances performed inside, the grisly bones unearthed in a cellar somewhere, record of a mysterious murder. In the afternoon there were running and trotting races, without benefit of pari-mutuel.

One popular feature was the balloon ascension. This always drew a crowd, from the building of the fire that heated the air for the inflation of the big bag to the moment when the daring aeronaut cut loose with his parachute and floated down, usually to land in the middle of a cornfield half a mile away. Hot-air balloons had low ceilings so we had a good view of whatever happened.

For country people the fair was another and bigger picnic with fried chicken, lemon pie, and endless visiting. Farmers from all over the county met and gossiped around the pens of fat Chester Whites or prize-winning Shorthorns, and women made envious comment on the blue-ribbon peaches or the excellence of a patchwork quilt that the judges had ignored. There were exhibits of work done in country schools. One year our district walked off with some kind of ribbon. The reason for our achievement is forgotten, but it is certain that samples of my penmanship were not included in the exhibit.

Picnics and baseball games were public affairs, open to all comers. All that was needed was a festival mood and a basket of lunch, and there were few who could not meet these simple requirements. "Parties" were more exclusive. Invitations, though usually verbal, were necessary. Houses were small and space was limited, so party crashing was looked upon with great disfavor. For entertainment we played parlor games, charades, post office, forfeits, mild substitutes for the forbidden dance. Some of the games were hard to distinguish from dancing, "Skip-cum-a-loo" for example, with its chanted refrain, "I've got another girl, prettier than you, Skip-cum-a-loo, my darling."

Many of them were kissing games. In post office the charge for the delivery of a letter was a kiss. In forfeits the phrase ran, "Heavy, heavy, what hangs over your head?" The victim must inquire, "Fine or superfine?" "Fine" was for a man, "superfine" for a girl. If the hidden article was loaned by a man, a favorite penalty was "Speak to the prettiest, bow to the wittiest, and kiss the one you love best." Applause was always loudest for the gallant youth who paid the tribute of the word, the bow, and the kiss to the same girl. One quick-witted boy with many girl friends raised a storm of protest by selecting his good-looking young mother. He probably dodged a lot of trouble too.

One game, name forgotten, called for the putting of a man's hat on a girl's head to this refrain:

> So take this hat on your head,
> Keep your head warm,
> And take a sweet kiss,
> It will do you no harm,

suiting the action to the words. To see my favorite schoolteacher of the moment meekly accept this salute from a young man whom I held in particular dislike was almost more than I could bear.

The reason for widespread objection to dancing and bland approval of kissing games closely resembling a country dance is for social psychologists to think about. We did not bar the fiddle as a musical instrument because of its association with the dance. Win Terpening, with an endless repertoire of old dances for his fiddle, was in demand as a complete entertainment in himself. I heard them all, "Money Musk," "Irish Washerwoman," "Arkansaw Traveler," "Buffalo Gals, Are You Comin' Out Tonight?" "Oh, Susannah," and many more, over and over, times beyond memory, and I never heard Win criticized for playing or myself reproved for listening.

The sin of dancing was not in the fiddle. I have heard country people call waltzing "hugging to music." But we enjoyed music, at least our kind, and I know of no Illinois Blue Law against hugging, with or without music. The American frontier danced all the way from Virginia to Oregon, but it did not waltz. Perhaps it was the waltz that introduced sin. When I first saw waltzing it seemed to me a dull and spiritless way of wasting time, not to be compared with rabbit hunting or lying on one's back in the shade and dreaming. If waltzing was a sin, then sin was not as interesting as had been represented. It was all very bewildering.

. . . .

We read little and our knowledge of literature was slight, but that did not deter us from organizing Literary and Debating societies. That was the twilight of the old Lyceum, and if it hadn't been, we were beneath the notice—and price—of the famous figures of the platform. As with so many things, if we wanted intellectual entertainment we must provide it ourselves. So we debated. Some of the questions that come down to me are alluring with their naive hints of philosophic entanglement. "Resolved, That the pen is mightier than the sword," was one. Another was, "Resolved, That the love of money is the root of all evil." I have a dim impression that I took part in the latter, but I have no recollection whether I was for money or against it. Prohibition was a favorite theme, the judges invariably finding against the demon rum, whatever the merits of the argument. Nevertheless, the saloon business in nearby Galesburg and Monmouth continued profitable.

We seemed never to debate contemporary problems, tariff, civil service reform, the waste of public lands, railroad rates, and dwindling farm incomes. These were all important issues, but we expressed no views and reached no decision, indicating that we had not become politically awake and articulate in national affairs. The storm decade of the nineties was still to come.

Our opportunities to sit at the feet of oratorical greatness were limited, but our appreciation of the power of the spoken word was real. No Websters, or Lincolns came our way, but thin and shadowy as the local equivalents were, we listened and admired. A candidate for Congress was by right and of necessity an orator and a candidate for the state legislature was assumed to be worth hearing, whatever his politics. If a candidate was weak on evidence and argument, there was always the fall of Rome and the greatness of America to fall back on. English tyranny was always a sound play, to the great annoyance of Father and Uncle Jim.

Campaign speeches were infrequent and only mildly entertaining, but our social life we had with us always. A favorite pastime on summer evenings was the Ice Cream Sociable, highly regarded as a means of making money for church or Sunday School or similar worthy causes. Most of the real fun was in the preparation. Japanese lanterns were strung from trees and posts, tables were improvised with rough boards, tickets were printed by hand, and there remained only to provide the ice cream and cake that were the standard fare. If there had been a good strawberry season an extra ten cents could be tacked on the usual charge of a quarter.

Usually some farmer not too far away had an icehouse filled with cakes cut from an artificial pond and stored against the coming heat. We made the ice cream ourselves, spelling each other in the long turning of the freezer, also borrowed from the owner of the icehouse. As night approached the weather became the burning question. If clouds gathered in the southwest, heralding a thunderstorm, spirits sank as the afternoon wore away. Would the wind shift and give the rain to someone in less need of clear skies and dry grass? Our prayers were not always effective, but rain or no rain, the sociable was held at the appointed time. Even small houses had possibilities on such nights.

The real crisis came with the counting of the receipts. Our scale of operations and also our estimate of possible profit was modest. Because most of our expense was our own labor and time, we usually came out with a perpendicular balance. And if there was a deficit, what of it? Win or lose, we had had a good time.

Small boys who lived not too far from each other occasionally exchanged visits, sometimes overnight. Three, sometimes four, in a bed was not too many. Kicking each other out of bed was good fun, but it had its hazards if it became too noisy. Leavetaking at the end of a daytime visit had its own variation with us, different from the lingering farewell at the door of the older ones. With boys the protocol required the host of the moment to walk part of the homeward way with the visitor. This was "going piece ways." For the host to decline would have been a serious affront.

It has become a fixed belief in America that the old-fashioned farmer was the perfect individualist. Maybe so, but he was also gregarious. Even a funeral gave opportunity for neighborly chat, in a reverently subdued tone of course. Every crossroads store was a social center and the most casual meeting an occasion for the exchange of local news. The farmer who lived the life of a hermit usually had something wrong with him.

How Did We Talk?

The numbers of people, men and women, old and young, involved in our westward movement can only be estimated roughly by noting the rate of growth of the Western States. The figures for California are eloquent, slightly over ninety thousand in 1850, today crowding twenty million, mostly native born but not in California. Our immigration statistics are more illuminating; beginning with 1820 approximately forty-two million from overseas have been added to our total count. Naturally in such a tremendous shifting of human beings many things were changed, our dress, our occupations, our speech. In general, we thought of ourselves as English somewhere back, but what does that mean? The speech of Sussex is not the speech of Northumberland and the accent of the London Cockney differs from both. In our small countryside could be heard traces of the broad A of Massachusetts and the soft drawl of Virginia. The process of change continued to work as we moved westward with new experiences and associations adding new elements to the conglomerate of our speech to change us still further. Some of the elements so added had historical backgrounds of their own. Jerry Hawkins had come among us from somewhere in eastern Kentucky, our only hillbilly. When Jerry said: "Do you want me to *hope* you with your threshin'?" we thought of it as only another of Jerry's many oddities. Much later when I explored the *Canterbury Tales* in college I learned that the unlettered hillbilly was speaking an English older than Shakespeare, Chaucer, and beyond: "That hem hath *holpen* whan that thy were siecke." Jerry was old-English.

Another contribution was "Friday week" as a definite date, meaning a week from Friday. This at first confused then annoyed me. Why not say what he meant and be done with it? For all my annoyance Jerry continued his confusing habit until the day he died, and he lived to be over ninety.

For most of us the words of greeting were obvious and commonplace, "Good morning," "How do you do?" "How are you?" frequently contracted to "Har you?"—but not with "Uncle" Robert Adcock with Virginia in his near background. With him the word was "Howdy," and when he spoke it to a small boy the effect was curiously that of a benediction endowing the boy with an individuality not often conceded by his elders. Somewhere along the way I encountered the phrase "What's the good word?" I never knew the proper response to that one. A few Missourians had drifted upriver to us, bringing a locution that puzzled me for a long time. For most of us evening was the time between supper and bedtime, but evidently in Missouri evening began right after midday dinner; there was no afternoon, even for lotus eaters.

. . . .

Mother used aphorisms that hinted at the past. "Waste not, want not" was one of these and it was applied rigorously in the household operations. Akin to this was a warning often leveled at me when I was caught taking more than I needed of some article on the table, sugar probably. That was a sign that a day would come when I would go hungry for that particular thing. Of a young man who had married a girl with what Mother regarded as toplofty social ambitions, she foretold drily: "He'll come to hard work before he dies." And he did. Of course we used phrases that were native products. Many years later I asked a brother about a man we had both known as a boy in country school. "Is he working?" I inquired idly. My brother's answer was in eloquent vernacular: "He don't aim to!" There was no need of further light.

Such phrases as "Hit the nail on the head," "Hew to the line" were redolent of pioneer beginnings, as was "Calling a spade a spade." "Set your sights" required no translation to anyone familiar with the function of the rear sight of the old long-barreled rifle. "Take care of the pennies and the pounds will take care of themselves" was obvious wisdom in an economy that sent more pennies than pounds our way. "Hoe out your row" came from a primitive past before the horse-drawn cultivator had supplanted the humble hoe, but the variant "Hoe your own row" was an oblique way of suggesting that the other fellow mind his own business. "Tend to your knitting" was a progenitor of the modern "keep your eye on the ball." "Early to bed and early to rise makes a man healthy, wealthy, and wise" was misplaced in a time when all men went to bed early and got up with the sun or earlier. In that pre-electric time, darkness was the time for sleeping, but only a favored few achieved wealth or wisdom.

Courtship and marriage had their techniques and ceremonials of course, but I recall no talk of engagement and I was grown and in college before I heard anyone speak of his "fiancee" as of an obvious relationship. "Going together" was the proper term with us and the equity thus established was generally recognized by rival swains. Today's teenagers call it "going steady." Of the boy who betrayed his state of mind by an air of helpless enslavement it might be said that he was "sitting up to her like a sick kitten to a hot brick."

Weddings were generally held in the bride's home; at least I recall no church ceremonies. Neither do I recall wedding "breakfasts," although the word "infare" comes to me vaguely, defined by Webster as wedding reception or "housewarming." The first night after the ceremony was usually spent at the bride's home and the second at the groom's. Then the happy couple settled in their new home, wherever it might be. Honeymoons shone only in romantic novels.

A feature of a wedding was a "shivaree" that usually took place the first evening. (I was a proud boy when I found the proper spelling was "charivari.") However it was spelled or pronounced, the institution remained the same, a discordant concert of horns, tin pans, shotguns fired in the air, horse fiddles, anything to make a noise. It was usually mercifully brief, then the door opened and the makers of noise trooped into the house to be treated to cigars by the provident groom. My dictionary states solemnly that this cele-bration was aimed only at an unpopular pair and was intended as an insult. It was not so with us.

The cryptic slang of the day filtered through to us in due course, and we said "Skiddoo!" "Twenty-three," and "You know it" as glibly and with as little sense as did the town boys. There were other phrases that were closer to the grass roots. The sound of distant thunder was "the devil's potato wagon crossing a bridge," and "like a bat out of hell" connoted great speed. "Like hell abeatin' tanbark" also suggested speed or vigor. "Taking a fall out of him" was not a wrestling term but a serious affair with bare knuckles. When two boys on the playground stood toe to toe to test which would first back away, they were "chugging," not boxing, and a similar test with hazel switches instead of fists was "lick jacket." "Mad as a wet hen" was the ultimate in anger. Those who have seen a wet hen will understand.

When a man was suspected of a feeling of superiority, he thought he was "a somebody." Undue individualism was to be "independent as a hog on ice." For some reason, beans entered rather largely into our common speech. One who "didn't know beans" was plain stupid, and one who knew "how many beans make five" was smart beyond the average. Poor soil "wouldn't grow white beans."

We had no colored families in our neighborhood, so there was no hint of an Uncle Remus influence in our talk or our ideas, but we picked up bits of Swedish words and phrases, some of them probably improper. Some words of common use were beginning to have a tinge of vulgarity. Such a one was "puke." To us all Missourians were pukes as all Illinoisans were suckers. Why? Don't ask me. The people of Iowa were Hawkeyes, of Indiana, Hoosiers, of Ohio, Buckeyes. Today an old-time Oklahoman is a Sooner, reminiscent of the opening of the Cherokee Strip in 1893.

By the time I was a senior in college, I regarded myself as a purist in speech, only to be called sharply to account by my favorite professor John P. Cushing for saying "I didn't get to go" when he asked me if I had heard a certain visiting lecturer. "Young man," he said, "if you intend to live in New York or anywhere in the East 'get to go' will mark you as a provincial." But I wondered; to me it suggested a definite interference with my plan to attend. John P. found our Illinois speech sometimes quaint, as when a student said of his sheepskin coat "It turns the wind." Another Easterner was vastly amused by our common statement "The dog wants out"—or in. We said "down cellar" because that was where the cellar was, but we didn't say "Up attic" as New Englanders do—probably because we had no attics. Participles bothered us, especially when we were trying to speak correctly, when something like this might emerge "I seen him yesterday but I ain't saw him today."

From the same prairie sod that nurtured the political talent of Abraham Lincoln came the literary genius of Edgar Lee Masters. Indeed, Masters' boyhood home, Petersburg, is only a couple of miles from Lincoln's first Illinois home at New Salem. Masters gained a national reputation as a member of the so-called Chicago Literary Renaissance, a movement that included poets such as Carl Sandburg and Vachel Lindsay. Although his career as a writer began after he had spent twenty-five years as a successful Chicago attorney, Masters' total output amounted to thirty volumes. In this selection from his autobiographical *Across Spoon River* he displays his poetic gift of bringing to the commonplace of life the vividness and insight of art. Masters' works as a whole reflect his rejection of rural life; nevertheless, here a note of nostalgia rather than bitterness prevails. The best studies of the "Renaissance" are Bernard I. Duffey, *The Chicago Renaissance in American Letters: A Critical History* (East Lansing, 1954), Dale Kramer, *Chicago Renaissance: The Literary Life of the Midwest, 1900-1930* (New York, 1966), and Michael Yatron, *America's Literary Revolt* (Freeport, N.Y., 1959).

Across Spoon River

EDGAR LEE MASTERS

My father failed in Kansas in the sense that there was nothing there with which he could have succeeded. What do we see in people's lives so salient as the taking of the wrong path or the marrying of the wrong person? These mistakes can be traced into the blood, into the myopia or overfarsightedness of physical and spiritual eyes. So come to pass the sorrows and the long after effects of human lives. However, my father returned to Illinois. He longed, no doubt, for Petersburg; he hungered, I know, for his mother's home and for her never-exhausted cheerfulness and affection. Back at the Masters homestead my father resumed his boyhood life of helping with the farmwork; my mother, annoyed by her dependence, and not in agreeable association with my father's sisters nor with my grandmother, lived unhappy days.

· ·

With one thing and another, it was not possible for my father and mother to live at the homestead. And so my grandfather rented a farm for him on the Shipley Hill, about a mile from his own house. And here my father felt the pinch of hard life. In addition to

From Edgar Lee Masters, *Across Spoon River* (New York, 1936), pp. 12-18, 23-25, 50-53, 139-141. Copyright © 1936 by Edgar Lee Masters. Reprinted by permission of Farrar, Straus & Giroux, Inc.

farming he taught a district school two miles away, to which he walked through the bitter winter. Before setting forth he got his own breakfast and chopped enough wood for the day. My mother was ill, and about to bear another child; and she had not yet learned how to cook and keep a house. On returning from school my father had to take care of his horses; he had to milk the cow and chop wood for the night, and help with the supper, and wash the dishes. He was paying heavily for any inattention to school and any neglect of opportunities. All the while he was thinking of getting into Petersburg where he could practice law. But his father was holding him down, with the advantage that he controlled the purse and could remind him of past failures. Then my sister was born in this log house, and was named Madeline by Aunt Mary Masters, who in her invalidism of seven years read Shelley and Tennyson, while being patiently nursed by my grandmother.

The Shipley Hill farm was a poor makeshift for a living, I am sure. But my grandfather was determined that my father should be a farmer. He feared that at the county seat my father would run wild with that great vitality which was his, and that evil companions would work his ruin. The village of Atterberry, where the farmers took their products for shipment, was four miles from the Masters house; and near Atterberry was a farm which my grandfather had been looking at. He finally said that he would buy it for my father if he would stay on it and settle down to farming, and my father in his plight promised to do this. The farm was about 160 acres with a common house on it, sheds and a barn; the land was very fertile. So when I was about three years old and my sister was about one we moved to the Atterberry farm. And here my memory begins.

One is likely to confuse what one has been told with what one remembers from his own experience. It seems to me that I remember when the veil was lifted from my face and when my grandmother's dancing eyes and her laugh shone upon me like sunshine. But this is doubtless impossible. However, I have no doubt that I remember the Atterberry farm. I cannot visualize the house. I only see it as standing quite a distance back from the front fence, by which stood a great tree. I remember an occasion when an uncle, Beth Vincent, and Aunt Minerva visited us, and this uncle whittled for me a windmill as we all sat under the tree. I have a kind of memory of a spacious back yard with its paths worn hard and smooth. And I recall vividly an occasion when one of my cousins, a youth about fourteen who was living with us at the time, tried to get me to drink some lye from a saucer. My mother was making soft soap, and this lye, obtained by pouring water in a barrel of wood ashes and letting the water percolate through them, was put in a

Courtesy of the Illinois State Historical Library

Edgar Lee Masters

kettle and boiled with refuse grease thrown into it. The lye looked like dark tea, and I was about to drink it when my mother rushed forth and knocked the saucer from my hand.

At that time the ground was cleared for planting corn by first breaking down the old stalks with a break; then they were raked into long windrows and burned. As if it were yesterday I can see my father walking along the windrows setting them afire while the field here and there flowed with the burning stalks. I was sitting in the corner of the rail fence with my mother and my sister as this work was being done. The country here was as level as a table, rimmed far off with strips of forest. The rail or worm fence divided the land. The raking and burning of stalks was done in late March or early April when the balmy winds began to blow and the frogs were setting up their liquid chorus in the meadow pools.

There were days when my grandfather and grandmother came to see us, driving up in the closed carriage with its rear oval window and blue silk curtain. My grandfather was always dressed in black broadcloth and a silk hat, when going forth to see his friends, and with buckskin gloves to protect his hands against the lines and the handling of the horses. My grandmother on these occasions wore her black silk dress and her bonnet with silk ribbons and a jet ornament. There was great shouting on my part when they arrived; for they were always laughing and calling to me and my sister, and my mother who ran out of the house. And they never failed to bring us something. It might be apples, or peaches, or stick candy, or a wonderful condiment which my grandmother made, called peach-leather. And we went frequently to the old homestead, often for Sunday dinner. So gradually the house emerged to my eyes, and became a place of enchanting charm. My own home very early, really from the first, seemed a poor and barren place compared with the house of my grandparents. There were a thousand reasons for this, chief of which might be mentioned the many objects of wonder, the books and curios that my grandparents had gathered and cherished; the grindstone in the yard which could be driven by a pedal; the tools in the carpenter's shop; my grandmother's canaries and redbird; the fascinating pictures on the walls; the wonderful parlor with its piano, and much else. But there was such order, such comfort at that old house. The meals were always on time—and the table was filled with delicious things. My grandmother was always laughing; my grandfather always singing, or saying quaint things; and both of them were so full of affection for me, and so indulgent toward me. Soon this old house became a very heaven to my imagination; while in point of fact it was not much of a house, and not to be compared with some of the other farmhouses around it, a number of which were of brick and much larger.

It was only a story and a half high, and had but nine rooms. But it was built of walnut and hickory timbers set upon a brick foundation. Its weather boarding was of walnut, for in 1850 when the house was built, the woods abounded in walnut trees, which the farmers ruthlessly cut down to make rails for fences, or logs for hogpens, or what not. There was a board fence painted white in front of the house; and a brick walk leading from the gate to the front door. My grandmother had planted red and yellow roses under the windows of the living room; and she had flower beds of tulips and phlox; and she had lilac bushes. The ubiquitous pine trees adorned either side of the walk; and to one side were fine maples under which we used to sit on hot days. Entering the front door one came into a hallway from which ascended a stairway with a walnut banister. To the left of this was the parlor, a room where my aunt's Mathushek piano was. At the windows were lace curtains held back by cords fastened around large glass knobs. The couch was upholstered in horsehair, as were some of the chairs. There were two mahogany tables, one lyre shaped. There was a large ornate lamp with a glazed-glass shade on one of these tables. There were two paintings on the wall, of country scenes, paintings of the sort which are done by copyists and can be bought anywhere for a small price. There was a wood stove of Russian iron, always in a high state of polish; and back of it a wood box papered with wallpaper. Back of the parlor was the spare bedroom, always smelling musty and rarely really aired. In it was a walnut bedstead heavily built up with quilts of my grandmother's making. At one side was a stand holding a bowl and pitcher.

At the end of the hallway was a door leading to the dining room. To the right was the living room where my grandfather and grandmother spent nearly all of their time, and where they slept. There was a lounge in the room where my aunt Mary lay for those long years of illness; and a mahogany bureau. In one corner was an old mahogany chest which Rebecca Wasson had brought from North Carolina to Illinois, and which she had given my grandmother. On this chest was a walnut case for books. The chest had two drawers, one used by my grandfather for his awl, needles, flax and wax for harness mending. The other drawer was my grandmother's where she kept her daguerreotypes, and the watch of a beloved son who was drowned in the Platte River in 1862; besides sticks of cinnamon and trinkets of various sorts. In the east wall of the room was a huge fireplace, in which cordwood could be burned; and the mantel over it had a clock with weights, and a bell which rang loudly when the clock struck. In one corner was my grandmother's trunk; and in a closet near by she kept her shoes and dresses, her hats and apparel.

The dining room was a long room running east and west the full width of the house except for a small dark room at the west end which was used as a spare bedroom. Between the dining room and the separate building containing the kitchen and the hired man's room there was a long porch, with a shelf against the kitchen wall where were hung old gloves, turkey wings, or what not; and on one end of which was a water tank supplied with ice in summer. For my grandfather was one of the few farmers about who had an icehouse. Outside this porch was the workhouse, so called, where saws and augers and other tools were kept on a workbench, or hung over it. This was one of my delights from the time that I could saw a board or bore a hole, when I made windmills for myself.

The upper rooms were sleeping chambers, one of them being occupied by my uncle who was nine years my senior. Back of the chambers was a place under the roof, called the Dark Ages, where old trunks were stored, containing, as it turned out, many books which became my delight as the years passed.

But my favorite room was the living room, where as a child and long after I sat with my grandparents before the fireplace: the big burning logs cast a light about the room and on the ceiling. The heat made sizzling sounds in the frozen apples which had been brought from the cellar and placed there to thaw out. Meanwhile the wind whistled from above the prairies and the snow beat at the windows. Here I listened to my grandmother tell about the buffalo grass that overgrew all the country about when she first saw Menard County, and about the days that they lived in the log house on the lower lot when my father was a baby, and until the *new* house was built, that being this house just described. Later I learned that when the wagons from Morgan County, from which they were moving, came up bearing their possessions, and my grandmother got out of one to see where she had come to and what the country was, she broke into tears. The pioneer women were not always enduring uncomplainingly, nor always hiding their disappointments.

Mrs. Anno, whose husband had sold my grandfather this farm, came from the log house, and comforted my grandmother by saying that the country was a good one, and that my grandmother would like it after a time. There were Indians about, and for several years after 1847. They were beggars for the most part, going from farmhouse to farmhouse asking for food. One frightened my grandmother very badly one day.

And then my grandfather with a hearty laugh would tell tales of Tennessee: about the possum hunts there, and the feasts which the negroes had when they got a possum; about the little niggers that danced and tumbled and laughed and smeared their faces with the possum sop; about the fiddlers; about the brook which ran across his father's farm into which he put pebbles to be rolled over by the water until they were made into round marbles. He told me about the Blackhawk War, and stories out of the Old Testament. He never touched upon Jesus or the New Testament wonders; for these constituted the mystical miracle of salvation. But he recounted with great gusto the fight between David and Goliath, and put the fear of holy men into me by telling me about Elisha, the mocking boys and the bears. And as time went on I heard from him about his days in Morgan County: how he hauled the brick to build one of the buildings of Illinois College; and how a lawsuit arose out of the purchase of the farm from Anno in which my grandfather had Lincoln for his lawyer, and lost the case.

Now the other room of my delight in this house was the kitchen, where for many months of the year—in autumn after the heat of summer, in the cold winter, and in the raw spring—the long table was kept set, spread with a red tablecloth and full of delectable food when we sat down to eat. I loved the fragrance and the taste of the sassafras tea which my grandmother made. The kitchen stove kept the room warm; and it was a great delight to run from my cold room to this kitchen, and there find my grandmother laughing and frying cakes, or baking corn bread. Back of this kitchen was the hired man's room; and this functionary was always sitting by the stove when the meal was about to be served, or if he was in his room I could run in there to see his treasures, like his harmonica and nickel cigars perfumed with cinnamon.

This was the house and these the rooms that emerged into my imagination and my comprehension of my world. It was full of magic. And when on Sundays we set off from the Atterberry farm to have dinner with my grandparents my heart leaped up, my happiness knew no bounds. All their long lives, Uncle Beth Vincent and Aunt Minerva showered presents on me and my sister; as they had given my uncle Will a great many books wonderfully illustrated, such as *The Babes in the Wood,* Grimm's *Fairy Tales,* besides wonderful tops and toys, field glasses, cabinets of tools, and much else that delights a boy. There were these things for me to see; besides my grandmother's trinkets, her illustrated books, and the like. And then there was the dinner.

That long table was filled with wonderful food: fried chicken and boiled ham, and mashed potatoes and turnips, and watermelon pickles and peach pickles, stuck with cloves; and in season fresh strawberries and cream or blackberries, and sponge or jelly cake. All this was enough to fascinate any boy, particularly if his own home was not run on a scale of such plenty and variety, such order and punctuality.

Outside of such memories the days at the Atterberry farm are all a mist. . . .

Chapter II

At this time Petersburg was a town of about three thousand people. It was surveyed and platted in 1832; but in 1836 Lincoln resurveyed it, being at the time a deputy surveyor of Sangamon County, and then residing at New Salem less than two miles up the Sangamon River from Petersburg. Two men at New Salem, Peter Lukins and George Warburton, who had laid out the town first, played a game of seven-up with the understanding that if Lukins won the game the town should be called Petersburg; if Warburton won the game, it should be called Georgetown. Lukins won the game.

About 1837 Lincoln left New Salem to take up the practice of law at Springfield, the new capital of Illinois; and with one thing and another New Salem began to disintegrate. Many New Salem families moved to Petersburg, sometimes bringing with them their log houses, which were set up again about the square or at one side of it. In 1839, Menard County was formed by slicing off a part of Sangamon County; and in the spring of that year New Market, Miller's Ferry, and Huron, a town also surveyed by Lincoln, contested with Petersburg for the honor of being the capital of the new county. Petersburg won the fight. In 1843, a courthouse was built at a cost of $6,640; to which Lincoln often came to try cases. He did this up to the time that he was elected president. This was the courthouse which I knew as a boy, and in which my father had his office as state's attorney. It was a small two-story brick building with an observatory in the roof. When political rallies were held stands were built against its walls, on which men like Douglas addressed the people. On one occasion when my father was perhaps twelve years old he was taken by my grandfather to meet Douglas; and as my father stood beside the great man he was very proud to see that he was as tall as Douglas.

At the time that we moved to Petersburg the town had two railroads, several coal mines, a woolen mill, several grist mills, some factories, a small brewery, and a winery. People had come there from Maryland, Virginia, Kentucky, Tennessee, New Jersey. And the Germans in town and about the country gave a liberal character to the inhabitants. The Americans were a lively people, full of the joy of living and of great hospitality. The Mexican War had given several majors and the like to the town, and with bankers and merchants, lawyers and politicians, it was a center of many activities. The courthouse mentioned stood in a square of trees where men gathered to talk, or loafers lay and slept.

The town had been built on a circle of hills with the business part lying in a level between their feet and the shores of the twisting Sangamon. Driving out of Petersburg to the east, to the north, to the West, one must climb hills. But going along the New Salem and Springfield road one skirts the river and the wooded slopes above it. From the heights of the New Salem Hill one looks down a valley of luxuriant forestry, with the river winding between its heavy green-eries. From this elevation the Sangamon River is picturesque, yel-low and muddy as its waters are when closely seen. From the beginning the people built houses on the crest of this circle of hills; and when we moved there many of these houses of brick and frame seemed to me like great mansions. They looked so to me for many years. At any rate they had a certain distinction; and as time went on some very good houses of attractive architecture looked down upon the courthouse and the square; and the square itself acquired business blocks of marble fronts, and blocks of pressed brick, all unusual for a town of this size. To the west of Petersburg lies the rich and level country of great farms; and to the north the equally fertile lands which stretch to the Masters farm, and beyond it to the Mason County Hills.

The town has been improved a little since I was a boy there, but it has not essentially changed. The old courthouse was supplanted by a new one about 1896; and new hotels have been built, and new houses along the crest of the hills. The old schoolhouse, where I started my schooling, gave way to a modern high school; and the like. But the flagstones about the square, and many of its buildings remain to this day. And when I go back I can revisualize Mentor Graham or William H. Herndon, who used to be familiars there when I was a boy. By that time Mentor Graham was a very old man, irascible and always in litigation; while Herndon in his middle fifties was practically burnt out. I don't remember how either of these men looked. Mentor Graham passes through my memory as an old man stamping around the square; Herndon as a man with a beard, who was often with my father.

We went to live in a common house a few blocks east of the square. A switch of the railroad ran by the fence so close that when the engine paused, I could climb on the fence and shake the hand of the engineer. This is one of my memories. The river was not far away; and one spring it overflowed, and came around our house and as far to the west as the square itself. Men were going about in boats on their business errands, and there was much sickness. A little boy, the son of the jeweler who lived a few doors from us, died of diphtheria. That was my first acquaintance with death, for I had played with this boy. His name was Lee too, and he was about my age. One day the houses across the street from us took fire. Flames enveloped the roof and the occupants were throwing ticks and bedding from the windows. Something about fire or water makes ineradicable pictures on the mind.

. . . .

In the early winter of 1880 my father resigned his office as state's attorney and went on to Lewistown and took up the practice of law. We were to come on later. By this time there was another son, who was named Thomas after my great-grandfather Masters; and we were living in the house on the Braham Hill much as we had before. My mother, who had the greatest trouble in getting and keeping a maid, had taken into the house an orphan named Mary, who had been partly raised by a Petersburg family. She had come to my mother complaining that she had been badly abused in this other household; and my mother, who all her life was taking orphans and oppressed souls to her bosom, took this Mary as a maid. And she was going to Lewistown with us.

In time my father sold the house which his father had given him. My mother would not sign the deed until he promised her that he would give her enough of the purchase money to travel back to Marlboro, New Hampshire, to visit her mother whom she had not seen since she came west in 1867. That being settled the deed passed, and very soon the purchaser, his wife and his children were coming and entering; while carpenters in behalf of the new owner were taking measurements with reference to changes in the house, and the building of a porch. This man had bought one of the grist mills in Petersburg, as well as our house, and was handling everything with a large hand, as though he had plenty of money.

. . . .

For some reason my sister went out to the farm in June. She was never attached to it as I was; but my grandfather was fond of her. He used to saddle one of the gentle horses, and lifting my sister into the saddle, would lead the horse around the lot for the good part of an hour. It was still the era of cyclones, and one night in the latter part of this June a cyclone swept down upon the farm-house, and the buildings around it, wreaking curious destruction. It happened about eight o'clock in the evening.

My uncle happened to be in Petersburg that night, or he would have lost his life. After paying a call upon his lady friend he came to our dismantled house and stayed for the night. Petersburg was not touched by this cyclone, and was not even aware that there was one near. But the next morning rumors came to us; and my uncle bestrode his horse and galloped out to the farm. I followed him soon on my pony, making the distance of five and a half miles in half an hour, or so.

And what a spectacle greeted my eyes! The fences were torn away; the walls of the barn lay flat, with the hay bulging from the dislocated roof. The corn crib and sheds were demolished. The kitchen was swept clear away. The main house was wrenched from its foundation, and the walls at the corners torn apart. A great apple tree was lying on the roof, the roots sticking in a great mass of earth which had been lifted as the tree was snatched up by the storm. In the yard under one of the maple trees stood my grandmother cooking on an old stove which had been set up in this emergency. She was laughing and talking, and when she saw me she frowned and said that I should not have come. I had gone to a store and bought an apron for her for a present. This I now gave her, and she relented with a laugh, but went on to say that she had more aprons than she needed. And so, with other things ended, the farm was gone, at least until the buildings could be restored. But would the carpenter shop be made like the old one? Would the new kitchen be as full of charm as the old one?

This cyclone announced itself with a sound such as can be made by blowing one's breath over the mouth of a jug. My grandfather and grandmother were in bed, and my sister was lying on the lounge in the room. Suddenly things began to crash. The clock fell striking from the mantel. The lightning was terrific, and rain poured into the room through the parted corners and the broken roof. All this was followed by terrible darkness as the cyclone swept on its way toward the Houghton woods. My grandmother got up and finally found a candle. Her first thought was of her son Will, whose room was upstairs. When she got to the hallway she found it filled with debris, and got upstairs with difficulty only to find the door of her son's room jammed so that it could not be opened. The apple tree on the roof had mashed down the timbers so that the whole room was twisted out of shape. And thinking that her son had been killed she descended the stairs, croaking and crying, to take care of my sister. She heard now the voice of the hired man. He was praying as loud as he could. The kitchen walls had been thrown down around his bed, but he was not hurt. And no one was even scratched. The horses in the barn stood at their stalls with the timbers lying about them. The cows in the sheds escaped injury. But strange things were done to the chickens. They were stripped of their feathers, and these feathers were blown with such velocity that the quills stuck deeply into the boards of the house, as if shot there by a bow. Rails from the fences were picked up and carried into the fields and there driven so far into the ground that only a team of horses could have pulled them out. One rail was sent through the west wall of the house as if it had been a javelin thrown from a catapult.

Thus there was confusion all about in the labor of restoring living conditions. My grandmother did not want me; she had work enough on her hands. And the presence of my sister excluded me from staying. So I went back to town on my pony.

This year the Fourth of July fell on Sunday and the celebration was being held on Saturday, the third. On Friday we started for Lewistown. Our possessions had been loaded in a freight car to be taken to Lewistown by way of Peoria, as there was no direct line from Petersburg. So we took the morning train, after being bidden farewell by many people. In a minute we passed the house we had first lived in in Petersburg. At my right I could see the brewery and the Sangamon River; at my left the schoolhouse where I had been whipped with the pointer; then soon the hill up which I had gone so often when riding to the Masters farm. We passed within sight of the Atterberry farm, and then through the village where I gazed upon the country store where my uncle and I had so often come when out riding. Next was Oakford, almost as familiar to me as Atterberry. Then the country was not so well known. I had never seen Salt Creek, though I had heard of it always. My grandmother sang some verses about it. Now we crossed it. Then we got into sandy Mason County, all strange to me. I was sad now. I could see that I was really going away. But my father was in high spirits, and my mother, though partly infected with them, was in meditation, holding in her arms my brother Thomas then three years old.

At Havana we went to the hotel, one of the largest I had ever seen; and at mealtime into the dining room, where waitresses scurried about taking care of the guests. There was the Illinois River about a block away. I walked to look at it, and saw steamboats for the first time in my life; I had seen none in Leavenworth. We stayed overnight in Havana. Next morning, amid the firing of cannon and firecrackers, we took the stage for Lewistown, crossing the long bridge over the Illinois River, then driving by the side of Spoon River, and so on until we reached the uplands on which Lewistown was situated.

For more than five miles the road from Havana to Lewistown runs through the Spoon River bottoms, one of the most forbidding pieces of country that I know anything about. Jungle weeds crowd the banks of the river, overshadowed by huge cottonwood trees. The land about is fertile, but is much flooded, or was then. The farmhouses for the most part were ramshackle, some of them mere log houses. As it turned out, the people who lived here were wretchedly poor and drunken, some of them vicious and criminal. My mother found all this out to her great disgust. And as we drove along she took in the scene amid exclamations of distaste. It was July and very hot. The black flies bit the stage horses, and smells of dank weeds, dead fish, and the green scum of drying pools smote our nostrils. At Duncan's Mills, a place of one store and a post office, we crossed Spoon River on a covered wooden bridge, and ascending a long hill a mile beyond reached the uplands that surround Lewistown. Here the country is truly beautiful. The farms are well kept, and were at the time; the houses, freshly painted, were surrounded by yards with lilac bushes and roses. There were rims of forest about. A mile away I saw the spire of the church amid trees. The horses trotted along, and after crossing the Burlington tracks we drove north in Main Street to the hotel, which was larger than anything in Petersburg. The cannon boomed around us, and drunken men whooped and guns were fired. It was Independence Day, but not for us, not for me. A curious crowd of boys and men drew around the stage to see the newcomers, and passing among them we entered the Standard House. A new day set in, far more new than I imagined or my father had any idea of.

. . . .

Chapter VII

The heat in Havana was unspeakable. The fish flies swarmed about the street lights as I walked along changing that heavy satchel from hand to hand to relieve my fatigue. The sweat poured down my face; my tall stiff collar, as shiny as celluloid from the hands of Yee Bow at Lewistown, wilted. My white vest crumpled; but on I walked gazing across the Illinois River into the jungles fed by the fat mud of the shore, which stank of dead fish and decaying weeds. I could have gone to the Taylor House, where I knew the amiable clerk and had had some happy days with my father or when I went to Havana on business for him. And there were those acquaintances in Havana, but our friendship had declined as I have already told. However, I did not want to see anyone. I wanted to get to Chicago as soon as possible; and I was hoping that it would be many days before I saw this country again.

There was a lonely agent at the station of the Red Express. He was walking back and forth behind the grating of the ticket window, whistling at times in a nervous way. We were the only two persons there for hours, and perhaps until about traintime. I knew the exact minute when the Express was scheduled to arrive, yet I asked him its time, and then took up the long wait of about five hours for the train. I began to go out on the platform and to return to the waiting room. Finally an agent spoke to me, perhaps asking me where I was going. Gradually he began to tell me something about himself and his state of mind. He confessed to anxiety and depression. Under my questioning he told me that he had a girl who was driving him to distraction by her mystifying ways. No one came in to interrupt us, and a long conversation ensued, in which I gave him advice out of *Mademoiselle de Maupin, Anna Karenina* and other books I had read. He looked at me in wonder, not realizing that out of my own experience I knew nothing about the perplexity he was in or how to counsel him about it. But that long talk with this man whose name I never knew filled me with reflections all the night and stayed with me the next day as a strange mood, as if I had dreamed what was said between us.

The agent was still talking about his girl when the Red Express rolled in. In the sudden whirl of the exciting moment I parted from him, and never saw him again. I took a seat in the chair-car, as I had no money for a sleeper. Anyway I wanted to see the country from the window; I did not want to sleep. I wanted to think. Above all I had made up my mind to see the first traces of Chicago, to see how and where it began. So all night long I sat looking out at the prairie, an expanse of blurs and darkness, and at the stars which looked like splotches of running grease in the hot sky. When the sun came up like a fireman who has slept, all refreshed for more stoking, we were still many miles from Chicago. There were hours ahead of enduring the stifling atmosphere of the car impregnated with the hot breaths of sleeping men, women and children slumped down in the seats.

Going to Minneapolis I have traveled along the Mississippi River, and suddenly came into the middle of the town. I was wondering what Chicago would look like, how it would begin. It turned out that it didn't exactly begin. It was difficult to tell when we left the prairie, where the Illinois and Michigan Canal ceased, where it was that we first bumped over the tracks of the outlying belt lines, where there was still farming country and widely separated houses. Then came the truck gardens of the city with houses closer together along half-made streets which stretched into vanishing distances of flat country. Then there were the new subdivisions springing up all around, with newly built and half-finished apartment buildings and houses, all in anticipation of the World's Fair, along plowed strips soon to be streets or boulevards, and already half curbed, where newly planted trees were making a desperate effort to grow. Factories, lumberyards, coalyards, grain elevators, tugs, sailing vessels, steamboats on the river and the canal swam into view as we rattled over the switch tracks; and all around was the increasing density of the illimitable city, formed of miles of frame houses, lying cooked by the July sun and smothered in smoke and gas and smell, and in exhalations from the breweries, and in reeks from the stockyards. This was not Minneapolis with its flouring mills and its comparative quiet by the shores of the Mississippi. Now there were noises from a thousand engines, the crash of switching trains, the yells of laborers, and now and then the dull thunder of dynamite; for already the Drainage Canal was being dug to connect Chicago with the Gulf, and thus purify the drinking water of the city. Chicago thus began for me as a mist rising from the sea, in a sense without a beginning. Already Havana and my talk with the station agent seemed far away.

In these last few minutes of the journey two card sharpers, who had boarded the train at Joliet, tried to engage me in a game of poker. They were obviously confidence men who took me for the greenhorn that I was, and probably overestimated the amount of money I had. I have never had the slightest inclination toward gambling and little toward games; and these two fellows saw at once that they could do nothing with me. Just as the train began to slow its speed they dropped off the car and sped through the switch tracks. And the train drew under the dark shed of the Polk Street station, and there was Uncle Henry, who had come to meet me. From photographs and from memory of him I should have known him, but he was visibly older. He was now about sixty, and somewhat shaky for that age. He was a silent man, a sad-looking man. He smiled a weary cordiality upon me, and off we started to take the Cottage Grove Avenue cable to 22nd Street and Michigan Avenue, dodging through insistent cabmen and porters who wanted to take my satchel.

I took my first glances of Chicago now, noting the countless saloons, and near at hand a whole street which looked suspiciously wanton, like streets I had seen in Peoria, and which turned out to be one of the brothel sections of Chicago. North along Dearborn Street, as we hurried on, I could see the city of the Loop district, not then called the Loop. The Monadnock Block, the Owings Building and some other sixteen-story structures were then standing in that street. Crossing State Street at Polk we were in the midst of saloons, dives, flophouses, cheap hotels, sordid places of assignation. The streets swarmed with people of every clime: Chinese, Poles, negroes, and at doorways the ubiquitous Jew was selling clothes. The great trucks made the cobblestones rattle. The air was suffocating with smoke and gas. And the heat! It seemed to me I had never before experienced anything like it.

My white vest soon looked as though it had been dragged through the dirt. I was thirsty, I ached from sitting all night in the train, I was sleepy from the long wide-awake hours of the night. At Wabash Avenue we boarded the cable, and swept down that feculent thoroughfare, turning at 22nd Street until we came to patrician Michigan Avenue where the jingle of harness and the Glockenspiel of the docked horses trotting upon the pavement gave a very different impression of what Chicago was after all. Here stood the new Lexington Hotel, finer by far than anything I had ever seen. It was soon to play a part in my fate. Two blocks south in plain view was the dignified elegance of the Metropole with the spire of a great church sticking above it. Uncle Henry's house was one of the three stories and basement brick houses which lined Michigan Avenue.

. . . .

3: Industrialization

Bringing rural life into the industrial age, Ernest L. Bogart and Charles M. Thompson portray various aspects of the common people's social life during the 1870s. A selection taken from *The Industrial State, 1870-1893* (Chicago, 1920) touches on amusements, problems in education, and the temperance movement. In the metropolitan industrial areas of East Saint Louis and Chicago life was anything but bucolic. Bogart received his doctorate from the University of Halle, Germany, in 1897. From 1909 he taught at the University of Illinois and during World War I was active as an economic advisor to the federal government. Among his many publications are: *Economic History of American Agriculture* (Wilmington, 1923), *Economic History of the American People* (New York, 1947), and *Financial History of Ohio* (Urbana, 1912). Thompson, also an economist, was a Harvard Ph.D. (1913) and taught in the College of Commerce and Business Administration of the University of Illinois. He has written *Economic Development of the United States* (New York, 1939), *Library of American Lives* (Hopkinsville, Ky., 1950), and *The Illinois Whigs Before 1846* (Urbana, 1915). Dorothy Culp points out that conditions surrounding the labor movement in Chicago worsened as time passed. Like the nation as a whole, Chicago experienced an enormous increase in population in the 1870s and 1880s, a good deal of it foreign-born. Conditions then, Culp notes, were such to exaggerate and intensify the plight of the worker. And in reaction, the labor movement there took on an anticapitalistic—what was called "anarchistic"—tone, which led eventually to the tragedy of the Haymarket incident. Miss Culp worked in the 1920s as an assistant to Bessie Louise Pierce in researching material for *A History of Chicago* (New York, 1937). Her paper on the labor movement was prepared for a session of the 1937 Annual Meeting of the Illinois State Historical Society. An interesting but little-known aspect of urbanization was the strong reaction to the appearance of the urban department store. Professor Joel Tarr, in an article in the *Journal of the Illinois State Historical Society* of 1971, explores the background and effect of one such crusade occurring in Chicago in the late 1890s. Tarr, a Rutgers University Ph.D., specializes in urban history and currently teaches at Carnegie-Mellon University, Pittsburgh.

The Industrial State

ERNEST L. BOGART AND CHARLES M. THOMPSON

The diversions of rural life changed but little during the seventies. Exorbitant railroad rates still largely forbade traveling, so that occasional visits to the neighboring town to see Barnum and Company's circus or to attend the county fair were the only trips that took the average farmer and his family out of their accustomed environment. A pioneer mail order firm offered its customers only croquet, playing cards, dominoes, chess, and cribbage boards, though occasionally an agricultural paper would advertise "Chivalrie, The New Lawn Game."

For reading matter, in addition to the family Bible, which in most homes was the only book the house afforded, there was sometimes a community or metropolitan newspaper, but for mental stimulus the entire family depended upon the agricultural paper, which found its way into almost every home. Within its few pages was combined a wide variety of matter; political news of interest to farmers; progress of the state granges; scientific and popular articles on agriculture and its new developments; labor-saving devices on the farm and in the home; fiction and poetry for children; occasional love stories or extracts from diaries of farm women; poetry, puzzles, anagrams, enigmas—these were a few of the varied items to be found in a typical agricultural paper of the day.

If rural life afforded little in the way of formal amusement, it was growing richer in organized social life. The serious business of fighting the railroads had led to the formation of farmers' clubs, and of local and state granges. Women were admitted on an equal footing with men, and consequently when business was over the session took on the air of a festive gathering. Local granges often provided for picnics and excursions; and delegates to grange conventions listened to programs where poetry as well as papers on cheaper transportation played a part.

. . . .

The question of admitting Negroes to common schools roused great political and sectional bitterness. It was urged that the admis-

From Ernest L. Bogart and Charles M. Thompson, *The Industrial State, 1870-1893* (Chicago, 1920), pp. 34-47. All but two footnotes in the original have been omitted.

The city of Chicago, site of the Republican national nominating convention, May 16, 1860

sion of Negro pupils was unwarranted, unconstitutional, unnecessary; that it exposed Negro children to ridicule; that to have Negro children thrust into the schools was unfair to white pupils. Springfield was the seat of a decidedly heated controversy over the so-called "public school outrage." The *Illinois Journal* claimed that the fourteenth amendment practically bound them to open schools to Negro children, that it was the constitution and the law which were to blame, if the members of the school board opened the schools to Negroes in a conscientious discharge of their duty. The *State Register* answered that the fourteenth amendment "is not violated by the establishment of separate schools for colored children. . . . If the negro race were the equal or even the superior of the white race, we should still be opposed to the mixing of white and black children in our public schools for the reason that such intermixing of children tends to establish social intimacies, which will result in intermarriage and amalgamation." Many of those who opposed admission of Negro children began to look about them for private and other schools in which to place their children. On October 20, 1873, "eighteen negro children" of Springfield "were admitted to the Fourth ward school"; the following day several prominent protestants began to arrange "with the Christian Brothers of the Roman Catholic church for the establishment . . . of a school embracing the various grades for boys."

Chicago supplied a bone of contention for educators when by the action of the school board a unanimous vote dropped Bible reading and the Lord's Prayer from school programs. Protest and commendation at once greeted this action. The resolutions of a public mass meeting condemned the action of the school board; the Chicago presbytery strongly deprecated it, while Methodist ministers petitioned for the rescinding of the action. Other members of the clergy, however, indorsed the change; the Reverend E. F. Williams, a congregational minister, thought it "unwise to insist upon Bible-reading as an exercise in the public schools," believing it to be "a violation of the conscientious convictions of many good citizens, and in this way a species of tyranny and oppression which ought not be countenanced by a Government professing to be republican in form." Dr. Samuel Fallows, a Reformed Episcopal rector, argued for the entire separation of church and state, while the Reverend C. L. Thompson, a Presbyterian clergyman, claimed that since schools were supported by taxation from all, it was unfair to compel "children of Romanists and Jews to engage in a form of worship which they do not believe."*

---

*The school board took the latter stand, and by a vote of ten to three refused to rescind their action. *Chicago Tribune*, October 4, November 13, 1875.

The impartial spirit that led such men to a stand which would probably have been impossible to ministers of the foregoing generation was significant of the general broadening that was coming over the religious world. That it was an age of transition was obvious to all; the awakening scientific attitude was affecting the life of the spirit. In some pulpits fear of the new dispensation took the form of a puritanical reaction against any form of current amusements. The Methodists expressed officially their "cause for apprehension concerning another growing evil,—the fondness of social and public amusements. . . . We do not refer to the theatre, the circus, the ball room, or the wine-party. These confessedly lead to spiritual death." They frowned upon the practice of laymen reading Sunday papers, pronounced against Sunday trains, and denounced the Sunday meat market, though such restrictions were laughed down by many laymen.*

. . . .

The new social consciousness which was influencing education and religion in the seventies found in the temperance movement a concrete issue upon which it could lavish its energy. The temperance question was by no means a new one in the politics of the prairie state. In *ante bellum* days it had been a force to be reckoned with; and after suffering an eclipse it had again appeared in church resolutions and on the banners of "radical reformers;" once more it became a subject of heated discussion on the debating forum and was thundered forth from lecture platforms. When temperance men, not content with mere agitation, insisted upon entering practical politics with their own candidates in the field, old-time politicians looked askance. Republicans were at first inclined to assure "an educated, practical people, Germans and Americans, composing the republican party," that the republican candidate was "as good a Champion of Temperance Principles As Any Man Can Desire." One wing of the republican party, however, soon came out openly for temperance, but the democrats steadfastly refused to temporize with the issue. When the *Bloomington Democrat* heard that not only a temperance candidate was in the field but that the republican nominee had taken a temperance stand, it ejaculated: "If both these candidates are *monomaniacs* on this subject, which is a

---

Ibid., January 1, 12, 1875. When resolutions embodying such pronunciamentos were passed by the Rock river conference the *Chicago Tribune* scoffingly remarked that when such measures could be passed "in this good and centennial year of grace, railroads, telegraphs . . . [it] must give us cause sufficient to rub our eyes and see if there is not some old woman hanging from the telegraph pole or some erring brother branded with a scarlet letter for eating unsanctified beans for his Sunday dinner." *Chicago Tribune*, October 19, 1876.

PROHIBITION HEADQUARTERS

IT'S UP TO YOU!

VOTE FOR

X ORLEY. E. LAIRD

AND

LAW ENFORCEMENT

HOME PROTECTION

Courtesy of the Illinois State Historical Library

Monroe Street prohibition headquarters in the 1890s

thread-bare hobby, we trust the congressional democratic convention . . . will bring out a man whom all sensible people can and will
support." This attitude the democrats consistently maintained, and
it began to worry republicans somewhat; when John V. Farwell was
nominated for congressman-at-large by the prohibitionists, he declined, declaring, "I am a Republican in my political convictions,
and I can see no practical result to follow the nomination of a
temperance ticket at the present time but the weakening of the
Republican party for the advantage and benefit of the Democratic
party. I cannot be an instrument in producing such a result."

The definite goal at which the temperance forces were aiming
was the enactment of a law which would adequately express their
attitude toward the liquor traffic and which would "provide against
the evils resulting from the sale of intoxicating liquors in the State
of Illinois." They formulated a measure which required a licensee to
give bond for $3,000, with two good sureties, conditioned that he
would "pay all damages to any person or persons which may be
inflicted upon them, either in person or property, or means of
support, by reason of the person so obtaining the license." More-

over, members of the family who had been injured in person or property or means of support by an intoxicated person could require damages, conjointly from him who sold or gave the intoxicating liquor and from him who owned the property from which the liquor was dispensed. Other stringent provisions regarding Sunday closing and further indictments and penalties insured the fiercest opposition to the most dogmatic championship of the proposed bill. Before the opposition forces fully realized how strong the temperance wave had become, however, their agitation, meetings, pleas, and persuasion culminated in the passage of the temperance bill of 1872. It was approved by Governor Palmer on January 13, 1872, but, since it was not to go into effect until July 1, the intervening months gave opportunity for a sharp battle.

The forces backing the temperance bill claimed to have all the elements of morality, decency, and honesty arrayed with them. The churches, indeed, had taken a decided stand in favor of temperance. In Chicago, during the first weeks after adoption, enthusiastic meetings were held in many churches. At one meeting early in February, hundreds were turned away. When the Reverend Dr. Fowler spoke on the new temperance law, he praised the law as the best that could be obtained and wanted it enforced "even at the point of the bayonet." In opposition to such support the *Ottawa Republican* listed three classes—"the keepers of low groggeries, the owners of hotels in which these groggeries are kept, and that despicable class of small politicians who court and depend upon the influence of the groggery element."

The opposition did not expend their energies in vain invective, but immediately after the passing of the bill organized themselves to bring about its repeal or defeat its execution. In Chicago, and indeed wherever there was a large body of German citizens who felt their personal liberty to be endangered by this development, opposition was particularly spirited. Early in February, meetings of protest were held by Germans to oppose the law in so far as it applied to the sale of beer and wines. At Quincy, on January 29, a huge mass meeting of Germans gathered together at which prominent citizens denounced the law as unconstitutional and illiberal and as intended to operate especially against the foreign population. At Peoria, on February 12, the "antis" organized to prevent the law's enforcement. On the ninth of March, the Chicago Wholesale Liquor Dealers' Association decided to make a concerted effort to secure the repeal of the law. Finally, "in consequence of action in the central part of the state," on the fourteenth of March the opposition called an antitemperance law convention at Springfield. It was heavily attended by Cook county and downstate Germans, who were, for the most part, brewers and liquor dealers. After effecting a permanent organization under the imposing title of "state association for the protection of personal liberty," resolutions were adopted, which, claiming to "abhor habitual drunkenness and the habitual drunkard as much as any so-called temperance men," opposed "the so-called temperance law because, while it hypocritically affects to be in the interests of an advanced morality, it is only a species of class legislation in behalf of the wealthy and against the poorer, but equally worthy citizens; giving the former power to poison, (as alleged), while the same is refused to the latter." Pro-temperance advocates seemed little impressed by this move of the opposition; they were inclined to dismiss the whole convention as a "demonstration of the bummers, saloonkeepers, and balance of power parties," where "the low groggery element largely predominates."

In the end, the temperance forces were triumphant in preventing the repeal of the law, and on July 1, 1872, it went into effect. It was another matter, however, to enforce it. Opposition on the part of the German element made it especially difficult to enforce the measure in Chicago and in other of the larger cities. From the first, republican leaders were doubtful as to the attitude of this group toward prohibition. When, on October 10, 1872, the mayor of Chicago "issued an order to the Police Commissioners for the closing of all saloons, public bars, and other places where intoxicating liquors are sold on Sunday," the *Chicago Tribune* raised the question "whether lager-beer comes under the designation of 'intoxicating drinks,'" arguing that since lager beer does not produce intoxication, "though it may, if taken in sufficient quantities, produce stupefaction," an exception might logically be made in favor of that beverage. The mayor's orders were enforced, however, and "there was a grim feeling among the Germans." Again the *Tribune* made the pleas in behalf of the disgruntled element that "Beer is the national beverage of the German. He has drunk it daily from youth up. It is the bread and meat of the peasant, and as indispensable to him as water to the American laborer. . . . The enforcement of the law in such a manner as to stop the German from drinking beer is not only foolish as invading his personal rights . . . but it is foolish, also, because it threatens the public with new dangers and serious disturbances of the peace. It will tend to provoke riots, and perhaps bloodshed." In spite of anything the *Tribune* could say, now that enforcement of the law was bringing disagreeable results, the fact remained that the republican party had stood back of the measure in the first place; many Germans began to show serious disgruntlement with the party to which they had long given full allegiance. This fact and the anxiety of republican leaders, the democrats gleefully seized upon. "The action of the Germans and others who oppose the law," commented the *State Register*, "has quite taken these political gentlemen by surprize, for they were quite sure nothing would induce the Germans to leave the Republican party." Where now was the assurance of a republican leader who declared that "the Dutch couldn't be kicked out of the republican party?"

German opposition finally went so far that the *Illinois Staats-Zeitung* urged its readers to vote for no man, irrespective of party affiliation, who was not pledged to vote for the repeal of the existing temperance and Sunday law. Whereupon the *Chicago Tribune*, alarmed at such independence, solemnly declared that the *Zeitung* had come "very near overstepping the line which separates a truly loyal paper from a traitorous Copperhead sheet." But the break had now become real, and during the next two years there was a marked exodus of Germans from the republican party.

. . . .

The Radical Labor Movement, 1873-1895

DOROTHY CULP

Chicago, in the last quarter of the nineteenth century, was the scene of a radical labor movement interesting not only from the local point of view, but also from the national, which it epitomized. Against the dramatic background of a city rising, in fifty years, from a frontier town to the center of a great commercial empire, the problems of the working men were brought into sharp relief. It was no accident that the three great crises of the labor history of the late nineteenth century centered in Chicago—the railroad riots of 1877, the Haymarket riot of 1886, and the Pullman strike of 1894.

From Dorothy Culp, "The Radical Labor Movement, 1873-1895," *Papers in Illinois History*, **XLIV** (1937), 92-99. All but one footnote in the original have been omitted. Used by permission.

What was this Chicago which was to be the scene of a movement which attracted national attention? In 1871 much of the city had been destroyed by fire, and many people believed that the day of Chicago had passed, that some other middle western city would become the capital of the great prairie section which had looked to Chicago for leadership. But the fire, terrible catastrophe though it was, proved but an impetus to a development even more spectacular than the previous twenty years had witnessed. In size Chicago grew, in the years between the fire and the World's Fair of 1893, from thirty-five to over two hundred square miles. Her population increased, in these two decades, from a little under three hundred thousand to more than a million people. Such an increase would in itself have caused vexatious problems, but other factors made the situation even more serious. To a certain extent the growth in population was due to natural increase; a part resulted from expansion from more established communities of the United States; but a large part resulted from immigration into the United States. During the twenty years under consideration, the two main strains of the immigrant influx into Chicago were German and Irish, and these two racial groups alone accounted for over half of the city's population.

Under any circumstances the adjustment of the immigrants to the new society would have been difficult, but the situation in Chicago only added to the complexity of the problem. Chicago had become by 1871 the commercial capital of the Middle West and was beginning to establish factories which were to make her a manufacturing center of equal importance. In this maelstrom of commercial and industrial activity, the immigrants found it difficult to adjust to the ethics and basic idealism of the dominant middle class, whose will for power and quest for profit set the tone for urban American civilization. In spite of the difficulties involved, the vast majority of the newcomers soon accepted the ideology of nineteenth century America—believing that within their reach or that of their children lay the possibility of attaining the comfort, security and power of the middle class.

There were those, however, who could not accept the "great American dream," who could find no hope for themselves or their kind in the system they found in America. These men, largely German, espoused various of the anticapitalist theories current at the time and attempted to spread the teachings of these various schools of thought. There had been a socialist movement in Chicago even before the fire, but it remained for the panic of 1873 and the terrible distress which lasted for several years afterwards and found violent outlet in the railroad riots of 1877 to give the movement a

Courtesy of the Illinois State Historical Library

A backyard scene in Chicago's tenement slums

degree of cohesion and the powerful motivating force of what Mr. Louis Adamic, with characteristic lack of delicacy but amazing aptness, calls "an underdog, belly-hunger movement."

The first organization of anticapitalist thinkers among Chicago workingmen was that of the Universal German Workingmen's Association, whose members, affiliated with the International, were followers of the doctrines of Lassalle. In 1874 another organization of Lassalleans was begun under the name of the Labor Party of Illinois. Both of these organizations emphasized political action with but little success, and in 1875, discouraged by their failure to gain converts, they joined forces and turned their energies to trade union action. Meanwhile, another organization was growing up which, after several vicissitudes typical of radical organizations, emerged as the Socialistic Labor Party, and adopted a program of political action which had as its goal "to place the means of labor into the hands of the whole people, and thus establish a system of cooperative industry, by abolishing the present wage system." By 1880, two diverse factions had grown up inside the Socialistic Labor Party, and the following year the trade union faction split off from the political socialists. The new party formed by the trade union group came to be known as the International Workingmen's Association, and was thus described: "For a year and a half the character of this movement was very vague. There was loose talk of violence, dynamite, and assassination, but the party as a whole dangled self-consciously between Marxism and Nihilism, between theory and action."* The Chicago members of the group scoffed at the possibility of reorganizing society by political action, but they were perfectly willing to use this means of propagandizing their faith.

At the same time that a small but vehement group in Chicago was becoming convinced that anarchism was the ideal system to replace the capitalistic chaos, another more widespread change was making itself felt. It seems characteristic of the American labor movement that there be periodic swings from a belief in the efficacy of political action to a dependence upon direct action. Such a change was visible in the Chicago labor movement in the eighties. It was partly due to the fiery criticism of political action by the anarchist

---

*Adamic, *Dynamite, The Story of Class Violence in America* (New York, 1931), p. 45. The national convention of the International Workingmen's Association in 1883 announced its belief in the destruction of class rule by "energetic, relentless, revolutionary and international action, the establishment of a free society based upon cooperative organization of productions without commerce and profit mongery; the organization of education on a popular, scientific and equal basis for both sexes; equal rights for all without distinction of sex or race, and the regulation of public affairs by free contracts between autonomous communes and associations resting on a federalistic basis." Nathan J. Ware, *The Labor Movement in the United States* (New York, 1929), p. 308.

leaders, August Spies, Albert Parsons and others, for there were many who, although they were unwilling to accept the anarchist system, were still ready to believe with the anarchist that the vote offered no solution to their problems. And the anarchists could in this case back their criticism with facts. It had for years been apparent that the working classes could hope for little from either of the major parties. Nor had the attempts to form special workers' parties been particularly successful. Their greatest strength came in 1879 when they cast over 10,000 votes in the Chicago mayoralty election. Generally they were unable to compete with the older established parties for important offices, and were successful only in securing the election of one or two aldermen, who found themselves impotent against the organized party machines. The climax came, to the discontent of the radical workers for political action, with a particularly blatant action by which the Democratic machine in 1880 was able to prevent the socialist member of the council from taking his place in that body for almost the entire term for which he had been elected. After this time the number of votes cast for socialist candidates in Chicago steadily dwindled, until in 1884 they polled only some six or seven hundred votes. This falling off was, of course, partly caused by the disgust of certain socialist groups with the possibility of attaining their goal by political action, and was partly due to the fact that with the return of comparative prosperity many workers who had previously voted socialist as a protest and not as a means of indicating their belief in the constructive program of that group, now returned to their old-line affiliations.

By 1885, anticapitalist thought in Chicago's labor circles was fairly well-advanced and divided into two schools: the old-line socialist and the anarchist. The Socialistic Labor Party and the Amalgamated Trades and Labor Assembly represented the former, and the International Workingmen's Association, the Progressive Central Labor Union and the *Lehr* and *Wehr Verein,* which were armed German drill organizations, represented the latter.

Already, however, just as the anarchist faction was establishing itself and gaining strength, the movement was beginning which was to result in the complete silencing of the anarchist movement in Chicago. It is a curious anomaly that the eight-hour movement, which resulted in the Haymarket incident and the ruthless suppression of the anarchists, was adopted only after hesitation by the anarchist leaders. Late in 1885 the Central Labor Union, organization of the anarchist faction, adopted the program of agitation for the eight-hour day. An eight-hour league was formed in which this Union coöperated with the Socialistic Labor Party and the Knights of Labor. Agitation was carried on by means of mass meetings and May 1, 1886 was set for the inauguration of the campaign. May day passed without serious trouble, much to the surprise of the worthies of the city who felt sure that revolution and murder were imminent. But on May 3, after a meeting near the McCormick Reaper works, where the men were out on strike, there was a serious encounter with the police, in which six men were killed. Angered by what they considered an unjustified assault upon a workers' meeting, the anarchist leaders determined to hold a large meeting in the Haymarket which was to be at once a protest meeting against the McCormick outrage and a demonstration in favor of the eight-hour day. Of the events of that tragic evening, but little need be said. Parsons, Fielden and Spies addressed the crowd, giving speeches not unlike those that they had been giving for the past several years, advocating the overthrow of capitalism and the achievement of social justice. As the crowd was beginning to disperse, over-zealous policemen appeared on the scene and ordered the meeting to disperse. Immediately after the order was given, a bomb was thrown into the ranks of the police, killing several and wounding many others. Within the next few weeks, August Spies, Michael Schwab, Samuel Fielden, Adolph Fischer, George Engel, Oscar Neebe, Louis Lingg and Albert Parsons were arrested and charged with the murder of Matthias Degan, one of the policemen who had been almost instantly killed by the explosion. In an atmosphere of animosity which was almost hysterical, the trial of these men took place. One commentator expressed it: "There is not a shred of evidence to connect these men with the Haymarket bomb throwing. They were anarchists and had talked wildly of violence and revolution at one time or another, and on these grounds they were found guilty. It was a case of Society against Anarchy with revenge as the motive." Viewed as a murder trial the case was a tragic travesty upon justice. It emerges as a more understandable event when we realize that in the eyes of the middle-class America the anarchists had—whether by deed or word is unimportant—destroyed the symbol of authority upon which their civilization rested. It was not to be expected that with the defense attorneys men of little experience, with both judge and jury at least predisposed in favor of guilt and with the added force of a hysterical public opinion, these men would be acquitted. Finally they were found guilty, one being sentenced to life imprisonment and the others to death. The sentences of Fielden and Schwab were commuted to life, and that of Oscar Neebe to fifteen years; Louis Lingg committed suicide in prison and the others were hanged.

The hysteria which the Haymarket incident caused among sub-

Courtesy of the Illinois State Historical Library

The Haymarket bombing of 1886

stantial citizens did not soon die away. Prominent businessmen of the city raised a fund of several hundred thousand dollars to convict the anarchists and to wipe out whatever survived of the anarchist movement. When Governor Altgeld pardoned the three surviving defendants, a storm of protest was unleashed against him, equalled only by the applause that came from those whom time had permitted to see the affair more objectively.

The incident had several important effects. It did undoubtedly silence the anarchists. Their great leaders, the ones who had believed sincerely in the constructive theory of anarchism, were imprisoned or hanged. But it would be a mistake to think that the labor movement as a whole was so affected. On the contrary it emerged from the 1886 hysteria in many respects stronger than it had been before that time. The diverse elements of labor, and the different organizations and nationalities were all drawn together by the realization that their common cause was more important than factional differences and theoretical disagreements among themselves. Furthermore, the labor movement really gained in practical strength with the removal of the radical intellectuals.

It was not until 1894 that labor in Chicago was faced with another such crisis as the one of 1886 which had been climaxed by the throwing of the Haymarket bomb. By this time the panic of 1893 had caused a serious amount of unemployment, wage cuts were being made and whole industrial plants were being shut down. The trouble this time centered about the Pullman Palace Car Company works. The paternalist system of Mr. Pullman's town, excellent though it may have been in theory, caused great dissatisfaction among his workers. Consequently, they welcomed the opportunity to join the American Railway Union which had been organized in Chicago in 1893 under the leadership of Eugene V. Debs. Dissatisfaction caused by the refusal of the company to recognize the union came to a climax in May, 1894, when the company announced a wage cut. The men walked out, and the company retaliated by closing the plant—a step it was not at all averse to taking, since conditions made operation at a profit difficult. It is unnecessary to discuss the details of the Pullman strike, already so familiar to modern American historians. Eugene V. Debs emerged as the leader of the labor forces, and directed the strike until the employer groups made use of the formidable weapon of the injunction, and Debs and his lieutenants were arrested and the strike broken.

These, then, are the highlights of the radical labor movement in Chicago in the years from 1873 to 1894. The period was one in which the organization of labor went forward at a rapid rate, when trade unions were increasing in numbers as well as in strength. At the same time a numerically small but vocal group was espousing anticapitalist theories, and in this group, too, there was a period of organization and of definition. The course of the development is indicated by the mention of the great names of the labor movement of this period in the city—Parsons and Spies at the beginning and Debs at the end. As epitomized by these men, the socialist labor movement had changed from a thing of eloquent theorizing and idealism impossible of realization to the idea of evolutionary revolutionary socialism which Debs represented.

The Chicago Anti-Department Store Crusade of 1897

JOEL A. TARR

A common feature of the expanding city in late nineteenth-century America was the development of a downtown central business area. These downtown sections usually contained retail and wholesale establishments, office buildings, and banks and financial houses. Invariably by the 1880's they also contained a retailing innovation called the department store.

The department store differed from other retail institutions in a number of ways. It was located in a central urban shopping center; it catered primarily to women; it carried a wide variety of merchandise under one roof; and it depended upon a large volume of business. John Wanamaker, Philadelphia mercantile king, noted that the department store was a "natural product," made possible by "cheaper capital, better transportation, [and] more rapid communications." Indeed, the development of the department store would have been impossible without the technological innovations that stimulated the growth of large cities in the second half of the nineteenth century. Most important were transportation improvements: the successive urban adoption of the omnibus, the horsecar, the cablecar, and finally the electric street railway. Construction

From Joel A. Tarr, "The Chicago Anti-Department Store Crusade of 1897: A Case Study in Urban Commercial Development," *Journal of the Illinois State Historical Society*, LXIV (1971), 161-172. Footnotes in the original have been omitted. Reprinted by permission of the author and the Illinois State Historical Society.

developments such as the iron and steel frame made it possible to build large open stores conducive to the favorable display of merchandise. Central heating plants made the buildings comfortable in winter. And mechanical elevators enabled customers to move easily from floor to floor for the various kinds of merchandise. The rise of the daily mass-circulation newspaper also played a key role in department store growth, for the big stores were among the first to use wide-scale advertising to attract customers.

Although thousands of shoppers hailed the convenience of being able to purchase a variety of goods under one roof, there was widespread opposition to the department store. It came primarily from three groups: small and middle-sized retail merchants located outside the central business districts, real estate men with holdings in the outlying areas, and some labor unions that objected to department store labor policies. These critics of the big stores charged them with fraudulent advertising, monopolistic practices, driving the small man out of business, and pauperizing labor. In state after state, organizations of retail merchants pressured legislatures and city councils to enact punitive legislation against their competitors.

The movement against the department store was particularly intensive in Chicago, where a number of department stores had appeared during the 1880's and 1890's. Some, such as Marshall Field and Company, Carson, Pirie, Scott and Company, and Mandel Brothers, were the result of the expansion of stores formerly specializing in dry goods. Carson, Pirie, Scott, for instance, had originally featured imported dress goods and linens but expanded to begin selling shoes in 1881; Marshall Field introduced furniture in 1896; and Mandel Brothers opened an art department in 1883. Huge variety stores, such as the Fair Department Store and Siegel, Cooper and Company, which sold goods ranging from children's toys and kitchen equipment to fancy groceries and baby carriages, also began to appear in the downtown section in the 1890's.

As streetcar lines spread throughout the city, these downtown stores expanded their operations and volume of business. Correspondingly, there was a decline in retail business in other sections of the city, especially on Clark Street, Madison Street, Milwaukee Avenue, Blue Island Avenue, and on Cottage Grove Avenue north of Thirty-ninth Street. From 1877 to 1896, land values in these areas decreased steadily while those in the central business area rose 700 percent.

In the depression of 1893-1897 the outlying retail businesses were hurt even further by department store competition. More than half the state's depression business failures were mercantile and commercial enterprises. The number doubled from 1892 to 1893. The peak year was 1896, when 817 Illinois trading and commercial firms went into bankruptcy (there were fewer failures among manufacturing concerns). The large Chicago department stores, however, continued to prosper. Significantly, many new urban transportation lines were built between 1894 and 1898, a development which undoubtedly bore a relationship to the growth of department store business.

Sorely affected by the depression and resenting continued department store prosperity, retail merchants and their associations were bitter about the big stores, which they held responsible for the high rate of failure among small retail businesses. "Department stores are slowly but steadily driving us out of business," complained one hardware dealer. "Making all allowance for trade depression, there is still a big scarcity of customers that we can trace directly to the department stores." Other complaints related to the advertising practices of department stores. Testifying before the Illinois Industrial Commission in 1900, S. W. Roth, secretary of the Cook County Retail Dealers Association, blamed the decline in

Marshall Field and Company in the 1890s

Courtesy of the Illinois State Historical Library

retail trade on "fraudulent advertising" by department stores. D. R. Goudie, proprietor of a Chicago confectionary—cigar store, called department stores the "worst trusts," and noted that their "bargain" advertising had a serious "indirect effect" on small retail businessmen by making customers believe that the owner was making an inflated profit.

To obtain relief from the ruinous competition of the department store, merchants throughout the city began forming associations to push for punitive and regulatory legislation. In February of 1897, forty organizations formed the Cook County Businessmen's Association. C. F. Gillman, head of the West Side business group, was elected president. The Chicago Federation of Labor agreed to work with the association because of the anti-union stance of the department stores and their employment of child labor. Several real estate men, including Marvin Farr, president of the Chicago Real Estate Board, also participated.

From the beginning, the organized agitation against department stores was political; the retail business organizations sought protection for themselves through punitive legislation against their large competitors. The chief proponent of such legislation was Congressman William Lorimer, Cook County Republican boss. Some of the loudest complaints about unfair department store competition came from the West Side, Lorimer's main bailiwick. It was significant that a machine politician, rather than a municipal reform organization, adopted the issue. The reform-oriented Civic Federation talked about appointing a committee to investigate the problem but never acted. Lorimer's willingness to become involved in the matter reflects the local and particularistic base of the urban political machine, which rested upon ward and precinct institutions. Small retail merchants often ran for municipal office under machine auspices, while many others benefited from connections with the ward organization.

Municipal reformers had a very different orientation and were concerned with eliminating the local and particularistic forces that supported the machine. They wanted to reorganize urban life, using as their model the rationalized and systematized business corporation with a vertical administrative decision-making structure. The department store, with its great variety of goods, its ability to draw people from throughout the city, and its efficient organization of work force and departments, was undoubtedly attractive to the reformers and corresponded to their ideal for the city. It should not be surprising that among those active in the Municipal Voters' League, Chicago's chief reform organization at the turn of the century, were Henry G. Selfridge, second in line at Marshall Field and Company, and John V. Farwell, Jr., one of the city's leading dry goods merchants. It is also significant that the Municipal Voters' League consistently endorsed representatives of large businesses, rather than small ones, for seats on the city council.

In February, 1897, legislation providing for the regulation of department stores was introduced in the Illinois General Assembly. The legislation called for the classification of trade and commerce into seventy-five categories and the licensing of any establishment that sold goods from more than one category. Delegates to the Republican city convention endorsed the legislation and passed a resolution that decried "the destruction of the profits of the small shopkeepers by the competition of the department stores, which, by the use of labor grossly underpaid, have succeeded in largely driving out of business the many smaller shopkeepers throughout the city." "We believe," continued the resolution, "that the theory of the Republican party in favor of protection goes to the extent that the local business of every neighborhood . . . should be transacted in that neighborhood, and we favor . . . the wiping out of the present system of big department stores."

Department store owners fought back, defending their policies in full-page advertisements in the Sunday newspapers. The Fair Department Store stated, for instance, "There is no secret about the success of this business—Chicago consumers have simply bought where they could save the most money—the more we sell, the cheaper we sell." A. M. Rothschild and Company maintained that "no one has a right to object to our underselling if you, the consumer, do not. No bright woman is going to pay double at other stores for articles she can get here for half." The spokesman for Carson, Pirie, Scott and Company said that while his firm did not approve of the department store bill in general, it welcomed the clause calling for honest advertising—every shopper had a right to expect this.

In spite of opposition from the department stores, the Illinois Senate passed the anti-department store bill on March 24 by a vote of 39 to 4. Hundreds of small businessmen were on hand for the occasion. Lorimer's lieutenant Thomas N. "Doc" Jamieson pushed for the passage of a similar measure in the lower house. Realizing the popular appeal of the issue, both Chicago mayoralty candidates, Republican Nathaniel C. Sears and Democrat Carter H. Harrison, sent telegrams to assemblymen asking their support of the legislation.

During the next two months, however, legislative interest in the anti-department store issue declined markedly as politicians and the press became involved in the struggle over controversial traction bills. Downstate opposition to the department store bills also began to develop. Although Cook County assemblymen from both parties supported the measure, downstate members were suspicious of any legislation emanating from Chicago. As the Chicago *Dry Goods Reporter* noted, "In no other city of Illinois does the department store exist as it is in Chicago, and nowhere else does the small merchant so severely feel its competition. Until this evil ... becomes more widespread, it is not probable that many State legislatures will take it into serious consideration."

Public opposition to the bill also appeared. "The great consuming public has no quarrel with an institution which it believes to have been instrumental in reducing the cost of living," commented the *Dry Goods Reporter.* Furthermore, the charges made against the department stores concerning mistreatment of labor, fraudulent advertising, and false pricing were also applicable to the smaller retail specialty shops. And, finally, rural legislators realized that in many ways the department store was merely a larger version of the country general store. Legislation that hit at one because of its variety of goods might conceivably be used against the other, unless mere size be made the determining point for condemnation, a point of doubtful constitutionality.

On April 8, 1897, the anti-department store bill failed in the house by a vote of 63 to 77, with the bulk of nays coming from downstate representatives. State legislatures in Minnesota and New York defeated similar measures that spring. In Chicago the leader of the Businessmen's Association blamed the defeat of the bill on bribery. A more pertinent reason was given by one department store owner: "It is no crime to sell dry goods and shoes under one roof, and the department stores stand vindicated." People would go where they found the "better values for their money."

An English newspaper reporter observed that legislation like the Illinois anti-department store bill reflected "the widespread tendency of the American people to appeal to the legislatures to protect them from the economic changes of the times." In their attempts to ward off the adverse effects of economic alterations, small businessmen turned naturally to the local political machine instead of to municipal reform organizations, for the machine rather than the reformer best represented the economic and social institutions of the community. In this case, however, the forces of localism were unable to block the centralizing tendencies at work in the modern American city. Downtown central business areas and department stores continued to grow, or at least to hold their own, until after World War II, when suburban residential dispersal, spurred by the automobile, was accompanied by suburban eco-

Courtesy of the Illinois State Historical Library

Chicago's Fair Building under construction

nomic and commercial dispersal. Thus, the forces responsible for the decline of the downtown store were demographic and technological—the same kinds of forces that had originally caused the department store to grow.

. . . .

Original Narratives

The following document is a firsthand account of the Chicago Fire of October 1871. It was published within two months of the tragedy by the C. F. Vent company of Chicago! Other eyewitness accounts are: Mabel McIlvaine, *Reminiscences of Chicago During the Great Fire* (Chicago, 1915); James W. Sheahan and George P. Upton, *The Great Conflagration of Chicago: Its Past, Present and Future* (Chicago, 1871); and *The Great Chicago Fire*, published by the Chicago Historical Society in 1946. Sheahan and Upton were associate editors of *The Chicago Daily Tribune* at the time of the fire. The historical society's book, with an introduction by Paul M. Angle, is a reprint of seven letters of individuals who experienced the catastrophe. A more recent account of the fire is found in Robert Cromie, *The Great Chicago Fire* (New York, 1958). Chicago's remarkable recovery is dealt with by Bessie Louise Pierce in *A History of Chicago* (New York, 1940, 1957) and Wyatt Winton Belcher, *The Economic Rivalry Between St. Louis and Chicago, 1850-1880* (New York, 1947).

A Night of Terror

ELIAS COLBERT AND EVERETT CHAMBERLIN

The fire broke out in the densely-populated section of the city somewhat after midnight, as we have seen. The people of the quarter through which it first passed were of a class the most likely to be careless in the extreme. In that quarter were the low brothels of Griswold, Quincy, Jackson, and Wells Streets, as well as the more showy haunts of vice on more respectable streets, and the rooms of kept mistresses in the upper stories of business blocks. The rest of the population living in this quarter were people used to excitements and alarms, and not likely to be disturbed, especially on a Sunday night, by any fidgeting about fire. Among such the panic,

From Elias Colbert and Everett Chamberlin, *Chicago and the Great Conflagration* (1871, Viking Press facsimile edition, 1971), pp. 214-225.

Courtesy of the Illinois State Historical Library

The Lake Street area before the Fire

when at length aroused by the close presence of danger, would naturally be the most intense. Awakened from their slumbers, or aroused from their orgies by the near approach of the flames, which traveled almost like lightning from house to house and from street to street, the denizens of that inflammable quarter had barely time to escape—half-clad, for the most part—and rush, pell-mell, through the streets—whither, they knew not. Nearly everybody brought along something—a few articles of clothing—a pet bird or animal— perhaps a trunk—whatever their various impulses prompted them to seize upon in their hasty flight. A few were fortunate enough to secure a wagon or a carriage, at the fabulous prices charged for such accommodations. These filled and clogged the streets, and dashed down those on foot—for the sidewalks would by no means hold the crowds that surged, swearing, shouting, jostling, this way and that. The sidewalks, too, were occupied with men saving (that is, trying to save) and pillaging from the shops along the way. Stores were thrown open, and the people were told to help themselves to what they liked—it must all go. Saloons, too, were opened, and bottles

Courtesy of the Illinois State Historical Library

Burnt-out Chicago streets

and taps passed from mouth to mouth among the crowd. Many rough, transient fellows, who had nothing to save, or who came by thousands from distant parts of the city, attracted by curiosity or worse motives, drank deep potations and became wild and dangerous. Among these, to make the scene more revolting, were many boys.

The scene at this point of the conflagration's progress is thus graphically and for the most part correctly described by a local writer:

"The people were mad. Despite the police—indeed the police were powerless—they crowded upon frail coigns of vantage, as fences and high sidewalks propped on rotten piles, which fell beneath their weight, and hurled them, bruised and bleeding, into the dust. They stumbled over broken furniture and fell, and were trampled under foot. Seized with wild and causeless panics, they surged together backward and forward in the narrow streets, cursing, threatening, imploring, fighting to get free. Liquor flowed like water, for the saloons were broken open and despoiled, and men on all sides were to be seen frenzied with drink. Fourth Avenue and Griswold Street had emptied their denizens into the throng. Ill-omened and obscene birds of night were they. Villainous, haggard with debauch and pinched with misery, flitting through the crowd, collarless, ragged, dirty, unkempt, were negroes with stolid faces and white men who fatten on the wages of shame; gliding through the mass like vultures in search of prey. They smashed windows, reckless of the severe wounds inflicted on their naked hands, and with bloody fingers rifled impartially, till, shelf, and cellar, fighting viciously for the spoils of their forays. Women, hollow-eyed and brazen-faced, with foul drapery tied over their heads, their dresses half-torn from their skinny bosoms, and their feet thrust into trodden-down slippers, moved here and there, stealing, scolding shrilly, and laughing with one another at some particularly "splen-did" gush of flame or "beautiful" falling-in of a roof. One woman on Adams Street was drawn out of a burning house three times, and rushed back wildly into the blazing ruin each time, insane for the moment. Everywhere dust, smoke, flame, heat, thunder of falling walls, crackle of fire, hissing of water, panting of engines, shouts, braying of trumpets, roar of wind, tumult, confusion, and uproar.

"From the roof of a tall stable and warehouse, to which the writer clambered, the sight was one of unparalleled sublimity and terror. He was above almost the whole fire, for the buildings in the locality were all small wooden structures. The crowds directly under him could not be distinguished, because of the curling vol-umes of crimson smoke through which an occasional scarlet lift could be seen. He could feel the heat and smoke and hear the maddened Babel of sounds, and it required little imagination to believe one's self looking over the adamantine bulwarks of hell into the bottomless pit. On the left, where two tall buildings were in a blaze, the flame piled up high over our heads, making a lurid background, against which were limned in strong relief the people on the roofs between. Fire was a strong painter and dealt in weird effects, using only black and red, and laying them boldly on. We could note the very smallest actions of these figures—a branchman wiping the sweat from his brow with his cuff and resetting his helmet, a spectator shading his eyes with his hand to peer into the fiery sea. Another gesticulating wildly with clenched fist brought down on the palm of his hand, as he pointed toward some unseen thing. To the right the faces of the crowd in the street could be seen, but not their bodies. All were white and upturned, and every feature was as strongly marked as if it had been an alabaster mask. Far away, indeed for miles around, could be seen, ringed by a circle of red light, the sea of house-tops broken by spires and tall chimneys, and the black and angry lake on which were a few pale, white sails.''

. . . .

The hotels—those immense caravansaries for which Chicago had become noted above all other cities—were filled with guests, who, having, up to two o'clock, no intimation that any danger threatened, were all soundly sleeping at that hour. There was the greatest danger—indeed one might say a certainty—that many of these would perish before they could be aroused and got out of the vast buildings in which they were imprisoned. It is now believed, however, that all the occupants of the hotels—the nine-story Palmer, the seven-story Sherman, with its mile of halls, the Tremont, Briggs, and the rest—all escaped in safety to the streets, whatever may have been their fate afterward. Undoubtedly many of them perished in trying to thread their way through the burning streets, unacquainted, as they were, with the geography of the city, and hindered by their attempts to save their luggage.

The lowest price at which a hack or cart could be obtained for this service was ten dollars; and from that figure it ranged upward, according to the ability of the owner or the degree of the hackman's devilishness. Mr. E. I. Tinkham, the cashier of one of the banks, actually paid an expressman one thousand dollars for taking a box to the railroad depot on the west side, a distance of a mile; but this was an unusual case, the box carried being full of treasure, amounting to $600,000, taken from the bank-vaults, and to be carried through walls of fire at the peril of the brave carter's life. This case is not to be reckoned among those of inhuman wretches of drivers who extorted all a poor man's means, or perhaps a helpless woman's, for taking on board a trunk containing a meager remnant of clothing, perhaps to be thrown off at the next corner, where the extorting process could be repeated upon another customer. It was in the North Division that the vulture-like qualities of the expressmen and other drivers culminated; for it was there that the distress was greatest, and the demand for vehicles most urgent. By the time the flames had reached the north side, all thought of checking its progress had long been abandoned, and the only hope of the most hopeful was to escape with their lives and a few of such valuables and clothing as they could lay hands upon in the haste of their flight. There were many carters about, but they wanted now fifty dollars for moving a load. Having found a victim, they would stop midway and assess him again, or if he refused to submit to their levies, or was unable to pay them, off went his goods into the street, to be ravaged by roughs, trampled upon by the crowd, or consumed by the flames. In more than one case, however, these unconscionable drivers were brought to a sense of their duty by a sudden declaration of martial law on the part of the owner, and the exhibition of a loaded revolver—a sort of *mandamus* fully excusable in such a strait.

The fugitives from the fire on the south side had fortunately had many avenues of egress, so that it was only those who too bravely or too rashly staid to save friends or treasures, or those who, by reason of the night's debauches, or other cause, slept too soundly in their isolated quarters, who fell prey to the raging element. Others fled in the direction which their impulse or reason suggested. They had reason to thank the flat topography and square, open plan of the city for their delivery from being roasted by thousands in the flames. Without straight broad streets, plenty of bridges across the river and its branches, and an open country on three sides of the city, the slaughter must have been terrible; for the streets would have been irremediably choked with colliding vehicles and the people cornered up and consumed by the flames. As it was, those who, instead of flying straight to a point to the south or west beyond the reach of the monster, shrank to the nearest refuge—the lake-shore—or fled northward before the whelming wave, fared the worst of all. The narrow space of unoccupied lake-shore lying between Randolph and Congress Streets, and adjoining "the basin"—a section of the lake protected by a breakwater—was crowded during the night and early morning with forlorn creatures of all classes, and strewn with every description of goods snatched from burning homes. Each fugitive had brought along some article or other—whatever was most clearly prized or could be most hastily reached; but, by and by, as the rigors of the situation increased, they had abandoned these *impedimenta,* and strove only to save what was dearest of all, their lives. As the choking heat increased and the smoke blinded their eyes, and the sparks and brands fell in thicker showers, those poor creatures shrank further and further into the chilling water of the basin. The most of them were women, and their shrieks and moans enhanced the terrors of the scene. One of these—apparently quite delicate—came bringing an immensely heavy sewing-machine; and when her place of refuge became too hot to live in, she seized her ponderous burden and bore it on southward. Poor thing! she *must* sustain it, for it is now all that is left to sustain *her!* Another young woman clutches a small bundle—probably her clothing—so tenaciously as to excite the cupidity of a ruffian, who knocks her down, seizes her precious package and makes off with it. Here is another group—two daughters supporting an invalid mother, who faints repeatedly, each time as if dead. With such scenes as these the night wears away.

By and by all chance of escape to the southward, of which the braver ones have been availing themselves hitherto, is cut off, and the shrieking fugitives are now pent up between a fiery and a watery death—the terrors of which are increased by the suffering and ruffianism around them, and the wide-spread ruin beyond, the loss of home, property, and perhaps kindred, already accomplished, and the state of poverty into which they must now emerge, if emerge they should at all.

This was the situation through nearly twelve hours, from Sunday midnight to Monday noon, at which time the flames had been subdued at the south, and the immediate terrors of the situation removed. Those terrors were eclipsed by those suffered by the denizens of the ill-fated North Division. These were, for the most part, surprised at three o'clock in the morning, and woke to find themselves *surrounded by fire.* The manner in which the conflagration spread in this part of the city has been already described. Called from their beds to witness the fire upon the south side of the river, the people of the quiet and elegant residence-quarter east of Clark and south of Superior Streets were gazing at the magnificent spectacle and uttering their exclamations of pity for the unfortunate inhabitants across the river, when they discovered, to their horror, that the flames had already been communicated to their own quarter, and that the Water-works and other buildings to the rear of them were all ablaze! The appalling significance of this discovery was soon apparent to all. It meant that their own homes were doomed, and that, before they could save any of their goods—perhaps before they could escape with their lives—they would be walled in on either side by fire.

A terrible panic ensued. There was sudden screaming and dashing about of half-clad women, gathering up such valuables as could be suddenly snatched. There was frantic rushing into the streets and shouting for vehicles. There was anxious inquiry and anon distressed cries for absent protectors—a large portion of the men being on the far side of the river, and in many cases unable to reach their homes. Then there was a pell-mell rush through the streets, some of the wild faces pushing eagerly in this direction and others quite as eagerly in the opposite; and children screaming; and shouts resounding; and brands falling in showers; and truckmen running each other down; and half-drunken, wholly desperate ruffians peering into doors and seizing valuables, and insulting women; and oaths from lips unused to them, as hot as the flames which leaped and crackled near by; and prayers from manly breasts where they had slumbered since childhood; and every other sign of turmoil and terror.

Those who had sufficient warning endeavored to escape to the northward with their best effects. Mr. Eastman, the Postmaster of

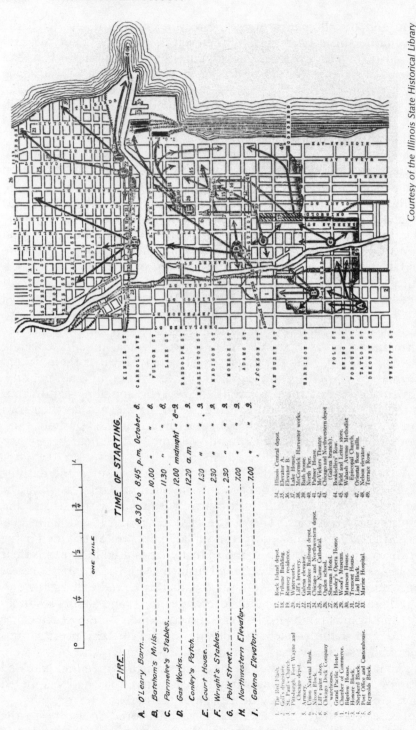

Chicago street map showing the direction and progress of the Fire

Courtesy of the Illinois State Historical Library

the city, whose house was on Erie Street, hauled out some trunks of clothing, and found a hackman whom he desired to take them on board, but the fee demanded exceeded his means, and he was obliged to drag his trunks along, with the help of a maid-servant, his wife carrying her infant in her arms. Four times they halted, exhausted, in what seemed a place of safety, and four times they were driven on by the insatiate flames.

The most natural resort of the people of the quarter mentioned, however, was the sandy beach of the lake, where there were but few houses, and those were shanties. This strip of shore, known as "the Sands," was famous, or, rather, infamous, in years agone, as the *locale* of numerous low brothels, to which "Long John" Wentworth, when Mayor of the city, gave the *coup de grace* by *allowing* them to burn up. Their place had never been fully occupied, and to the bleak, narrow area thus afforded, the terrified population shrank for refuge from the pursuing monster. Such an assemblage as there congregated, Chicago never witnessed before and probably never will witness again. It was the scene at the "basin" repeated, with more diversity. The extremes of wealth and squalor had been dwelling within a stone's throw of each other in this section of the city which had emptied itself upon this scant skirt of sand. These inequalities of societies were now leveled off as smooth as the beach itself. No, not leveled; for the landlord and aristocrat, whose many stores are burning on the other side, and his precious library and cabinet—the accumulation of a doting lifetime—has still a preferment over the boor who now jostles him; he is allowed to lose more and to suffer more, and is required to lament less. But that is all; the two must for to-night share each other's bed—the damp sand— and to morrow each other's fare—nothing but sights of horror.

Scarce a person among the thousands collected on the sands, and there pent up for thirty hours, but had lost some dear one in the confusion attending the escape from their burning houses. Whether these were alive or dead, none could know.

Here was the wife of a well-known musician, with her two children—one of them but three months old. When the flames came too close, she must retreat into the water, breast-deep, and bear them aloft. Her husband, after escaping with her from their house, had gone back to save some precious article from the fire, and had not returned to her.

Here was a distracted husband who had failed in his effort to reach his invalid wife—a cousin of the celebrated Madame Parepa Rosa, and a lady of rare gifts. (Poor woman! she died a few days afterward, a raving maniac, and one of the many victims of the conflagration.)

Here was a family of brothers and sisters, mourning a mother who had perished before their eyes. Here were sick ones, snatched from their beds, and dying of exposure.

Here was every imaginable scene of distress, and knotted threads of narrative, which, if followed, would fill this book many times over.

As the morning advanced, some of the sufferers, crawling along the shore and down upon a pier, were taken up by tugs and propellers and carried up the river or out to sea for safety. They embarked at the peril of their lives, for the docks were on fire, and more than one staunch steamer burned alongside.

Such of the north side people as did not resort to the lake betook themselves toward Lincoln Park, where a day and night of imprisonment and exposure awaited them, or (which proved the wisest course) escaped to the west side, where they found shelter with friends, or, at least, safety upon the open prairie. Chicago Avenue was the main avenue of escape, and this becoming choked with vehicles and goods, many perished in the attempt to reach the next thoroughfare to the north. Bremer and Wesson Streets, in this vicinity, were found strewn with charred corpses when the smoke cleared away.

All Monday the fire raged through the ill-fated North Division; but its progress was noted with little interest, except by the luckless people whose abodes it seized upon as it advanced; for every body had given up the whole of that quarter as lost, and there was no longer any struggle, even of hope and fear. It seemed as if those emotions had run down, as a clock, neglected by its keeper, stops for lack of winding. The index had stopped at the figure of despair!

Mary E. McDowell taught at the University of Chicago and was director of the university's Settlement House in the stockyards area in 1893.
In the early 1920s she was the city's Commissioner of Public Welfare.
This account of the women workers and labor leaders in the stockyards
after the Chicago fire is particularly interesting because most of the historical attention on the industrial revolution in Illinois has been on men's
labor movements in or near Chicago in the 1880s and 1890s. A biography of the author is Howard E. Wilson, *Mary McDowell, Neighbor*
(Chicago, 1928).

A Quarter of a Century in the Stockyards District

MARY E. MCDOWELL

I am taking for granted that twenty-seven years in an industrial
community must be of value today because the struggle of the wage
earners the world round is full of significance, and, if one could
know the meaning of their struggle in the stockyards district, then
one might get at the meaning of the universal unrest of the workers.
To understand that struggle, to get at the point of view of the wage
earners was my own reason for coming to this community, as it has
been that of so many who have thrown in their lot with the
struggling mass the existence of whose members depends upon
whether they have a job or do not have a job. That very word "job"
came into my vocabulary in '94 and has since become a sacred
word, for I have learned that it means to my neighbors, food,
clothing, shelter, and a chance to be human. It is the word first
learned by the immigrant, the children lisp it and the aged cling to
it to the end "A steady job," "no job," or "please get me a job" is
ever at the front of their minds and on the tips of all tongues.

It was in September of the eventful year of '94 just after
Chicago's World's Fair, after the Pullman strike, when the stockyards workers went out on a strike in sympathy with the railroad
men. The stockyards at that time was unorganized and therefore
undisciplined, and the strike futile and disastrous. Disorder reigned
back of the yards that autumn that I came to live on Gross Avenue,
between "Whiskey Point" and Ashland Avenue. Cars had been
burned a few blocks from this point, blood had been shed near the
corner of Gross and Ashland Avenues where the regular army had
been encamped. The people were left cowed and helpless.

The old citizens—property owners whom I learned to know—
were conservative and critical of a sympathetic strike, but were also

From *Transactions of the Illinois State State Historical Society*, **XXVII** (1920), 72-83.

Courtesy of the Illinois State Historical Library

The Chicago stockyards after they opened in 1865

bitter in their denunciation of the attitude of the public towards the railroad union men, who, these conservative citizens said, put out the fires that the hoodlums and the mob set going. This was my first touch with the real struggle of labor for industrial democracy—an experience that made me question the practicality of the sympathetic strike, for the community was disheartened and the packing house workers possessed with fear and left unorganized. In my home life I had been used to men with courage—men who had gone into battle for a conviction, and now for the first time I was meeting men who "for fear of losing a job" went and came from work with a silent protest against conditions, and a sense of justice that they were afraid to express. When in my ignorance I would inquire about organization, there would be sudden, awful stillness and the man questioned would afterwards avoid me for fear I might again touch on this forbidden topic.

For the first two years I slept in a front room so close to the sidewalk that all hours of the night I could hear the tramp of men going to or coming from work. The impressions are vivid of these first autumn mornings when I would look out on the great army of men, women, and children, as they tramped to their work through the fog and smoke. That tramp, tramp, tramp of the "mighty army of the poor" and the significance of it will be with me always as a symbol of the tread of those who shall never cease marching onward and upward through suffering, through mistakes and blunders, until some day the machine will become the servant and the brutish will become humanized.

. . . .

In these early days the Settlement home was upstairs over a Day Nursery; every morning when it was barely light in the winter, I would be wakened by the cry of the little children who wanted the mother to stay at home and not go to work. Here again for the first time in my life I saw the meaning of the job and how wage-earning women had to carry two burdens—that of the home and that of the wage-earning world. In that day there was no child-labor law and the packing industry found useful the boys and girls of eleven years of age, and men and women and children had no limit to their day's work. When I would ask why the people came from work at all hours of the day and in the evening, I was told that the killing had to go on until there were no cattle left to be cared for over night; and when in my greenness I would ask why a packing industry could not keep cattle over night when farmers did it very well, I was surprised to learn that because it cost something to feed and water them, men must butcher often sixteen hours at a stretch. It was then I learned for the first time how it happened that when in the morning these men, women, and children went out to work, large numbers could not tell whether they would return home for supper, or work from one to sixteen hours.

My social education—so slow in the beginning—was quickened by personal contact and neighborly relationship with all kinds of workers. One of my best friends was a German cattle butcher who began work at eleven years of age on the "killing floor," where he worked for twenty-five years until his right arm began to shake from the constant wielding of a huge cleaver, more like a battle axe.

This sober, intelligent and loyal worker was most unsocial—he much preferred to work by himself and to go home to his family, put on his slippers, light his pipe, and read his church and foreign papers. He was not by nature "a joiner" but was happy in studying history at the Settlement with a young university student, who is now a president of note in a Western university.

Another pleasure the Settlement offered this intelligent cattle butcher was that of meeting the university student in a genial social atmosphere and giving the working man's point of view with regard to the organization of labor. The student on purely theoretical grounds argued for the organization of labor—while the conservative cattle butcher who had gone through the eight hour strike and the sympathetic railroad strike and had seen both fail, took the opposite view. The university student needed this opportunity to meet the working man face to face and with "feet under the same table," and to give and take ideas with perfect freedom. It was the unsocial cattle butcher who held to the opinion that if men were out of work it must be their own fault. He had seen the eight hour movement fail in the yards and had gone through the disastrous railroad strike, but had kept a steady job all the way, which gave him a sense of security.

But at thirty-five years of age this loyal worker had a new experience which he could not understand. Why after going twenty-five years on a "killing bed," where he had been one of the few skilled workers, receiving forty-five cents an hour, he should be suddenly dismissed without any reason given by the boss, except that his right arm was shaking and that he was unable to keep up with the "pace maker," who was a giant. The day he was turned off, he stopped in to tell me that he had been "thrown out on the industrial scrap heap at thirty-five years of age," and with a face white with emotion he said that he could not understand that his long and loyal workmanship had not been considered by those whom he had served for twenty-five years. "I understand now," he said, "why men are not sure of a job always, and why they organize, for at thirty-five I have reached my old age limit. I shall never again receive forty-five cents an hour." And he never did, though for a quarter of a century he had been working and had given his best strength to this trade that demanded so little skill and such physical endurance. After many odd jobs he again, for a short time, got back into the packing house in another department, at less pay.

. . . .

At first, the women workers were not recognized as ready for organization. It was difficult to learn just how many worked in that square mile, where it was said thirty to forty thousand people were employed. Then, too, they had come into new departments so quickly that the men were not aroused by their inroads until they were given a knife as a tool. Only then did these "petticoat butchers" become a factor to be dealt with. The women had in the early days of this comparatively new packing industry been working in the canning department, painting and labeling the cans. When men went on a petty strike in the stuffing room, women—mostly girls—were given the men's places at much lower wages. In this way the girls entered the sausage room where they linked the sausages with their hands as tools; but it was in the trimming room that they were given a "man's tool," a knife to cut the fat from the lean, though women had used this tool in their home longer than men. In one packing house the room is kept to the freezing point and considered scientific. I visited a room colder than your ice box—a veritable cold storage box, where pork was prepared for shipping long distances. "Here nothing is wasted," the superintendent told the visitor. But the immigrant girls worked in mid-winter wrappings—while cold sweat ran down the walls of the enclosed room. As soon as they became Americanized they found a better job if they lived through the experience.

Piece-work as a method of modern industry was revealed to me for the first time by my friendship with Maggie, her sisters, and Hannah, who worked in the labeling room of one of the principal packing plants. Maggie and Hannah were born in Ireland, but came with their parents to the "Town of Lake" when they were infants. There was no child labor law when these girls were eleven years of age. The old country parents had the old country notions and were in need of money; so these young Irish girls began their industrial life in this rather new industry of packing meat. In the early days of the industry the girls painted and labeled by hand the cans filled by men and boys. There was no ten hour law to limit the day, and no child labor law; and there was no public opinion demanding light, fresh air, sunshine and fire escapes. The steam from the canning room permeated the labeling room, making the turpentine all the more pungent. This room had one row of windows and high stacks of cans obscuring the light from the middle of the room where the girls worked much of the time by artificial light. The half hour for lunch was in this same atmosphere. If they chose they could go into a dressing room, partly partitioned off from the work room and filled with the same turpentine odor. Maggie told me that while she was at work she could not eat or even drink for it all tasted of turpentine.

The fathers and brothers of these Irish girls were working in the packing houses as butchers of cattle, sheep or hogs, while the Germans and after a time the Bohemians manned the sausage departments. It was when the men and boys struck and lost their places that the girls of the new incoming immigrants, Bohemians, Poles, and at the last, Lithuanians, took the places of the young

Courtesy of the Illinois State Historical Library

An alley in Chicago's tenements in the early 1900s

men, and the boys, at one-third to one-half the wages, and did the work quite as well and with much less "fooling." For boys liked to play with knives at the risk of injury to themselves and others, while the girls took their work seriously and patiently, especially if it were piece work. Maggie represented the serious idealistic Irish type while Hannah was the social solvent of the shop, loved by all the girls, friendly with the boss and the forelady, until her sense of injustice was aroused; then she was the one inspiring to action and became for the moment a leader. Maggie had fine ambitions; Hannah had few, except to aid Maggie with her loyal admiration. Maggie wanted some things in her home that only her wages could procure. The old country father and mother could not understand Maggie's untiring, unresting ambition for a parlor with a piano, where she and her beautiful young sisters could have company. She wanted privacy—a room for herself—and comforts for the father and mother who had worked hard all their lives. Maggie had long, tapering fingers and a nervous temperament that could be keyed to a speed that was marvelous while it lasted. She could paint cans by the many thousands a week and often made $22.00 a week. Just when Maggie, the unconscious "pace maker" of the shop, would reach the goal of $22.00 a week and begin to feel that she could secure the necessities of her fine nature, a cut would come, and again she would urge herself and all her co-workers to renewed and more difficult speed, and once more she would reach the $22.00 a week mark, and again would come the cut in wages by adding a greater number of cans to be painted for a stipulated amount. It was after the third cut that the Irish girls began to see the method of the "boss," and Maggie and Hannah called a strike in the shop. All the girls laid down their tools, and when the boss was obdurate, Hannah tied a red handkerchief to her umbrella and the girls marched up and down the streets of Packing-Town, having no one to turn to in this time of distress, for they were without organization. The men had no union at that time. They had heard of some Knights of Labor and they were determined to appeal to these knights. But they received no response from the men.

At last they organized a Maud Gonne Club, in honor of the only patriot they knew. This organization took place about the sick bed of Maggie, who was found to have tuberculosis, and who pleaded with them to be as courageous and unselfish as the Irish heroine who suffered for Home Rule; for, said Maggie, "You know we must work for those who come after us." The Maud Gonne Club had a short life but the memory of it held this small group together until Michael Donnelly organized the men and the appeal for help from the girls to the Settlement brought them and Mr. Donnelly together resulting in the local which was organized with ten girls from several packing houses as charter members. This was the first Packing House Woman's Union in the Meat Cutters' organization. Maggie lived just long enough to serve as their first vice president.

I shall never forget that meeting very early in the organization when two of the young women who had worked for fifteen years in one packing house were discharged because they were discovered to be officers of the Union. But this experience, disheartening as it was to me, only inspired the Irish girls to renewed and eager efforts. The girls of the red flag demonstration had not been able to get back to work. They formed a group of so-called "black listed girls," who now began to work in earnest for the Union which they hoped would protect them from the injustice of "speeding up" followed by "cuts."

The next significant experience of this Union of "petticoat butchers" was the night of a thunderstorm when we sat, a frightened group, in the Settlement Gymnasium and discussed whether it would be harmful or helpful to march with the men on Labor Day of 1903; for the timid ones felt that all who marched would lose their jobs, as the officers had a few weeks before. The lightning and the thunder filled all with present and future fear, but at last the Irish spirit rose above the storm and it was decided that they would march but would ride in busses, sing labor songs, wear white dresses, and carry the flag of the red, white, and blue.

It was a pretty sight on Labor Day when the two "busses," filled with packing house girls in white—young, attractive, full of courage, singing of Labor, rode out of Gross Avenue to meet a procession of men who were also running a great risk that day. Perhaps they too would never go back to the job so necessary to their existence. The effect of that act on Labor Day—of the thousands marching together for collective bargaining—was magical.

. . . .

The community's interest in the struggle for two and a half cents an hour is not easily understood by outsiders. Two and a half cents an hour meant a higher standard of living that the workers were unwilling to give up—we can't live "the decent American way" they said over and over. One wonders after hearing this so often if it is not this growing standard of living that the workers call "the decent American way," one of the strongest factors in the great unrest today, this, with the uncertainty of a steady job, and the demoralization of the casual or seasonal work.

The immigrant who is intelligent enough to send his children to the public school finds a constant tug upon his lean purse by demands that were not made upon his parents. The school nurse and the medical inspector report the children need glasses, that they may see clearly; their ears must be cared for that they may hear distinctly; the teeth must be cared for and the adenoids removed so that the children may be healthy and may keep up with their grades in school.

Rents advance, yet the parents with this growing standard of living are not willing to deprive their children of the privacy needed, and will not take in lodgers as some with lower standards do to help out the lack in income. The rent must be paid and food is high.

The children, therefore, must have less nourishing food. The employer and the economist tell us that wages cannot come up to the worker's standard, as long as the many wait for jobs at the doors of the industry. Industry is so specialized that perhaps a surplus of labor is a necessity to the business, but surely it should not be a menace to the higher standard of living of the working people.

After ten weeks of waiting and arguing, after priest and politician had failed to bring together the leading representatives of both sides in the struggle and the situation was getting tense and serious—for the Union had no funds to feed the strikers, and hunger makes men desperate—a woman physician filled with the spirit of the "called of the Lord" secured audience with the packer who agreed to see the men's representative. While the twenty-two thousand waited and talked of the decent American wage ideal, a cattle butcher who waited with me for the momentous word from these two representatives, said a significant thing that I shall never forget. "You know," he said, "I think the world has to learn that Michael Donnelly represents quite as important an interest as does the representative of the packers, Mr J Ogden Armour."

After hours of waiting the word at last reached the twenty-two thousand outside that the skilled workers could return to work with the wages unchanged but the unskilled workers must be reduced two and one-half cents. When a plea was made for some recognition of this long struggle for higher wages for the 60 per cent of the workers, the answer was, "As long as there are thousands waiting for a job every morning we cannot pay a higher rate of wages." Then the plea was made for a more stable week's work in order that the casual work might be lessened, and it was urged that the industry might be so organized as to carry the needed surplus and make work steadier. Of course some recognition has to be made of the fact that this is in some sense a seasonal industry in that the supply of cattle, hogs and sheep is not a fixed or certain supply, but the packers promised to consider the proposition of steadying the work but would not consider the raising of wages. Michael Donnelly urged a labor commissioner such as the mine operators of Illinois had to deal with on matters brought up by the Union, which commissioner would make it possible to do away with shop stewards. One superintendent who had to deal with over 300 in a large packing plant, said he found the strike a rest cure from shop stewards.

The proposition to end the strike was brought at once before the members of the various Unions with the argument that the strike benefit fund was gone and that if the men did not go back to work they would not be cared for. This compelled an affirmative vote. But at one mass meeting of the unskilled I heard a Polish worker speak in four languages urging the men to hold out for the two and one-half cents for the same reasons that I had heard over and over. He spoke quietly and with ease, and was listened to with dignified attention. When he said, "You know that you can't give your children an American living; you can't send them to school and give them what they ought to have; you can't have a decent American home on fifteen and one-half cents an hour and only forty hours a week the year around." And the men who listened were ready to vote against returning to work until the officers of the Union explained the lack of funds. Then they agreed to give up, though most reluctantly, and some showed a lack of faith in those who had settled the strike.

It was Labor Day when these negotiations between packers and men were in progress.

. . . .

The power to wait is what the workers did not have. The strike ended. Most of the men and women, except the leaders, were taken back. Many never got their old places, and many of those who did were dismissed after a time. Some went away to better places. Some took to a different kind of work, while a few were demoralized; in the struggle for industrial democracy the strike, like a war, carries a long train of evils.

. . . .

Henry Christman, who introduces the following excerpts from John Peter Altgeld's executive pardon, is editor of *Progressive* magazine and editorial consultant to the Macmillan Company. His many published works include *History of Bigotry in the United States* (New York, 1960), *The Nation* (Freeport, N.Y., 1970), and *Josip Broz Tito* (New York, 1970). A standard treatment of Altgeld's courageous act is Harry Barnard, *Eagle Forgotten: The Life of John Peter Altgeld* (Indianolis, 1962). See also the analysis of Harvey Wish, "Governor Altgeld Pardons the Anarchists," *Journal of the Illinois State Historical Society*, XXXI (December 1938), 424-448.

Reasons for Pardoning Fielden, Neebe, and Schwab, the So-Called Anarchists

JOHN PETER ALTGELD

Executive pardon issued at
Springfield, June 26, 1893

INTRODUCTION BY HENRY M. CHRISTMAN

When Altgeld took office as Governor of Illinois in January of 1893, no miscarriage of American justice loomed larger than the Haymarket Riot trial. Seven years earlier, there had been great labor unrest in Chicago, climaxed by a mass meeting in the Haymarket. Although the meeting had been peaceable, and in fact had begun to disperse, a formation of almost two hundred policemen prepared to attack the speakers and spectators. A bomb was thrown, and several policemen were killed. The police then opened fire upon the unarmed spectators.

Although it was impossible to determine who had thrown the bomb, eight Chicago labor leaders were tried on the ground that they had preached labor agitation and violence, and hence had incited the bomb-throwing. All were found guilty, and seven of them—Albert Parsons, August Spies, Samuel Fielden, Michael Schwab, George Engle, Adolph Fischer, and Louis Lingg—were sentenced to death. The eighth defendant, Oscar Neebe, was given a fifteen-year penitentiary sentence.

Many questions were raised about the legality of the trial; nevertheless, all judicial appeals failed. Fielden and Schwab then appealed to executive clemency, and Governor Oglesby—who privately shared the widespread misgivings about the trial—commuted their sentences to life imprisonment. On November 11, 1887, Parsons, Spies, Engle, and Fischer were

From Henry M. Christman, ed., *The Mind and Spirit of John Peter Altgeld: Selected Writings and Addresses* (Urbana, 1960), pp. 63-65, 78-79, 85-87, 89, 103-104. Reprinted by permission of the University of Illinois Press. © 1960 by the Board of Trustees of the University of Illinois.

hanged; Lingg escaped execution by committing suicide in his cell the day before.

When Altgeld took office, public opinion seemed prepared to accept a gubernatorial pardon of the three survivors, provided the pardon be made as an "act of mercy," without questioning the propriety of the trial. In discussing the case with associates and friends, Governor Altgeld held that the question of a pardon should rest upon whether or not the men were guilty as charged.

On June 26, 1893, Governor Altgeld exercised his power of executive clemency and, on the ground that they were illegally convicted, issued an unconditional pardon for the three surviving defendants, Fielden, Neebe, and Schwab.

Statement of the Case

On the night of May 4, 1886, a public meeting was held on Haymarket Square, in Chicago; there were from 800 to 1,000 people present, nearly all being laboring men. There had been trouble, growing out of the effort to introduce an eight-hour day, resulting in some collisions with the police, in one of which several laboring people were killed, and this meeting was called as a protest against alleged police brutality.

The meeting was orderly and was attended by the mayor, who remained until the crowd began to disperse, and then went away. As soon as Capt. John Bonfield, of the Police Department, learned that the mayor had gone, he took a detachment of police and hurried to the meeting for the purpose of dispersing the few that remained, and as the police approached the place of meeting a bomb was thrown by some unknown person, which exploded and wounded many and killed several policemen, among the latter being one Mathias Degan. A number of people were arrested, and after a time August Spies, Albert R. Parsons, Louis Lingg, Michael Schwab, Samuel Fielden, George Engle, Adolph Fischer, and Oscar Neebe were indicted for the murder of Mathias Degan. The prosecution could not discover who had thrown the bomb and could not bring the really guilty man to justice, and as some of the men indicted were not at the Haymarket meeting and had nothing to do with it, the prosecution was forced to proceed on the theory that the men indicted were guilty of murder, because it was claimed they had, at various times in the past, uttered and printed incendiary and seditious language, practically advising the killing of policemen, of Pinkerton men, and others acting in that capacity, and that they were, therefore, responsible for the murder of Mathias Degan. The public was greatly excited and after a prolonged trial all of the defendants were found guilty; Oscar Neebe was sentenced to fifteen years' imprisonment and all of the other defendants were sentenced

Courtesy of the Illinois State Historical Library

Governor John Peter Altgeld

to be hanged. The case was carried to the Supreme Court and was there affirmed in the fall of 1887. Soon thereafter Lingg committed suicide. The sentence of Fielden and Schwab was commuted to imprisonment for life, and Parsons, Fischer, Engle and Spies were hanged, and the petitioners now ask to have Neebe, Fielden and Schwab set at liberty.

The several thousand merchants, bankers, judges, lawyers and other prominent citizens of Chicago, who have by petition, by letter and in other ways urged executive clemency, mostly base their appeal on the ground that, assuming the prisoners to be guilty, they have been punished enough; but a number of them who have examined the case more carefully, and are more familiar with the record and with the fact disclosed by the papers on file, base their appeal on entirely different grounds. They assert:

First—That the jury which tried the case was a packed jury selected to convict.

Second—That according to the law as laid down by the Supreme Court, both prior to and again since the trial of this case, the jurors, according to their own answers, were not competent jurors, and the trial was, therefore, not a legal trial.

Third—That the defendants were not proven to be guilty of the crime charged in the indictment.

Fourth—That as to the defendant Neebe, the State's Attorney had declared at the close of the evidence that there was no case against him, and yet he has been kept in prison all these years.

Fifth—That the trial judge was either so prejudiced against the defendants, or else so determined to win the applause of a certain class in the community, that he could not and did not grant a fair trial.

. . . .

The Twleve Who Tried the Case

The twelve jurors whom the defendants were finally forced to accept, after the challenges were exhausted, were of the same general character as the others, and a number of them stated candidly that they were so prejudiced that they could not try the case fairly, but each, when examined by the court, was finally induced to say that he believed he could try the case fairly upon the evidence that was produced in court alone. For example:

Theodore Denker, one of the twelve: "Am shipping clerk for Henry W. King & Co. I have read and talked about the Haymarket tragedy, and have formed and expressed an opinion as to the guilt or innocence of the defendants of the crime charged in the indictment. I believe what I read and heard, and still entertain that opinion."

Q. Is that opinion such as to prevent you from rendering an impartial verdict in the case, sitting as a juror, under the testimony and the law?

A. I think it is.

He was challenged for cause on the ground of prejudice. Then the State's Attorney and the court examined him and finally got him to say that he believed he could try the case fairly on the law and the evidence, and the challenge was overruled. He was then asked further questions by the defendant's counsel, and said:

"I have formed an opinion as to the guilt of the defendants and have expressed it. We conversed about the matter in the business house and I expressed my opinion there; expressed my opinion quite frequently. My mind was made up from what I read and I did not hesitate to speak about it.

Q. Would you feel yourself in any way governed or bound in listening to the testimony and determining it upon the pre-judgment of the case that you had expressed to others before?

A. Well, that is a pretty hard question to answer.

He then stated to the court that he had not expressed an opinion as to the truth of the reports he had read, and finally stated that he believed he could try the case fairly on the evidence.

John B. Greiner, another one of the twelve: "Am a clerk for the Northwestern railroad. I have heard and read about the killing of Degan, at the Haymarket, on May 4, last, and have formed an opinion as to the guilt or innocence of the defendants now on trial for that crime. It is evident that the defendants are connected with that affair from their being here."

Q. You regard that as evidence?

A. Well, I don't know exactly. Of course, I would expect that it connected them or they would not be here.

Q. So, then, the opinion that you now have has reference to the guilt or innocence of some of these men, or all of them?

A. Certainly.

Q. Now, is that opinion one that would influence your verdict if you should be selected as a juror to try the case?

A. I certainly think it would affect it to some extent; I don't see how it could be otherwise.

He further stated that there had been a strike in the freight department in the Northwestern road, which affected the department he was in. After some further examination, he stated that he thought he could try the case fairly on the evidence, and was then held to be competent.

G. W. Adams, also one of the twelve: "Am a traveling salesman; have been an employer of painters. I read and talked about the Haymarket trouble and formed an opinion as to the nature and character of the crime committed there. I conversed freely with my friends about the matter."

Q. Did you form an opinion at the time that the defendants were connected with or responsible for the commission of that crime?

A. I thought some of them were interested in it; yes.

Q. And you still think so?

A. Yes.

Q. Nothing has transpired in the interval to change your mind at all, I suppose.

A. No, sir.

. . . .

Does the Proof Show Guilt?

III. The State has never discovered who it was that threw the bomb which killed the policeman, and the evidence does not show any connection whatever between the defendants and the man who did throw it. The trial judge, in overruling the motion for a new hearing, and again, recently in a magazine article, used this language:

"The conviction has not gone on the ground that they did have actually any personal participation in the particular act which caused the death of Degan, but the conviction proceeds upon the ground that they had generally, by speech and print, advised large classes of the people, not particular individuals, but large classes, to commit murder, and had left the commission, the time and place and when, to the individual will and whim or caprice, or whatever it may be, of each individual man who listened to their advice, and that in consequence of that advice, in pursuance of that advice, and influenced by that advice, somebody not known did throw the bomb that caused Degan's death. Now, if this is not a correct principle of the law, then the defendants of course are entitled to a new trial. This case is without a precedent; there is no example in the law books of a case of this sort."

The judge certainly told the truth when he stated that this case was without a precedent, and that no example could be found in the law books to sustain the law as above laid down. For, in all the centuries during which government has been maintained among men, and crime has been punished, no judge in a civilized country has ever laid down such a rule before. The petitioners claim that it was laid down in this case simply because the prosecution, not having discovered the real criminal, would otherwise not have been able to convict anybody; that this course was then taken to appease the fury of the public, and that the judgment was allowed to stand for the same reason. I will not discuss this. But taking the law as above laid down, it was necessary under it to prove, and that beyond a reasonable doubt, that the person committing the violent deed had at least heard or read the advice given to the masses, for until he either heard or read it he did not receive it, and if he did not receive it, he did not commit the violent act in pursuance of that advice; and it is here that the case for the State fails; with all his apparent eagerness to force conviction in court, and his efforts in defending his course since the trial, the judge, speaking on this point in his magazine article, makes this statement: "It is probably true that Rudolph Schnaubelt threw the bomb," which statement is merely a surmise and is all that is known about it, and is certainly not sufficient to convict eight men on. In fact, until the State proves from whose hands the bomb came, it is impossible to show any connection between the man who threw it and these defendants.

It is further shown that the mass of matter contained in the record and quoted at length in the judge's magazine article, showing the use of seditious and incendiary language, amounts to but little when its source is considered. The two papers in which articles appeared at intervals during years, were obscure little sheets, having scarcely any circulation, and the articles themselves were written at times of great public excitement, when an element in the community claimed to have been outraged; and the same is true of the speeches made by the defendants and others; the apparently seditious utterances were such as are always heard when men imagine that they have been wronged, or are excited or partially intoxicated; and the talk of a gigantic anarchistic conspiracy is not believed by the then Chief of Police, as will be shown hereafter, and it is not entitled to serious notice, in view of the fact that, while Chicago had nearly a million inhabitants, the meetings held on the lake front on Sundays during the summer, by these agitators, rarely had fifty people present, and most of these went from mere curiosity, while the meetings held in-doors, during the winter, were still smaller. The meetings held from time to time by the masses of the laboring people, must not be confounded with the meetings above named, although in times of excitement and trouble much violent talk was indulged in by irresponsible parties; which was forgotten when the excitement was over.

Again, it is shown here that the bomb was, in all probability, thrown by some one seeking personal revenge; that a course had been pursued by the authorities which would naturally cause this; that for a number of years prior to the Haymarket affair there had been labor troubles, and in several cases a number of laboring people, guilty of no offense, had been shot down in cold blood by Pinkerton men, and none of the murderers were brought to justice. The evidence taken at coroners' inquests and presented here, shows that in at least two cases men were fired on and killed when they were running away, and there was consequently no occasion to shoot, yet nobody was punished; that in Chicago there had been a number of strikes in which some of the police not only took sides against the men, but without any authority of law invaded and broke up peaceable meetings, and in scores of cases brutally clubbed people who were guilty of no offense whatever.

. . . .

Now, it is shown . . . that peaceable meetings were invaded and broken up, and inoffensive people were clubbed; that in 1885 there was a strike at the McCormick Reaper Factory, on account of a reduction of wages, and some Pinkerton men, while on their way there, were hooted at by some people on the street, when they fired into the crowd and fatally wounded several people who had taken no part in any disturbance; that four of the Pinkerton men were indicted for this murder by the grand jury, but that the prosecuting officers apparently took no interest in the case, and allowed it to be continued a number of times, until the witnesses were sworn out, and in the end the murderers went free; that after this there was a strike on the West Division Street railway, and that some of the police, under the leadership of Capt. John Bonfield, indulged in a brutality never equalled before; that even small merchants, standing on their own doorsteps and having no interest in the strike, were clubbed then hustled into patrol wagons, and thrown into prison on no charge and not even booked; that a petition signed by about 1,000 of the leading citizens on and near West Madison street, was sent to the Mayor and City Council, praying for the dismissal of Bonfield from the force, but that, on account of his political influence, he was retained. Let me say here, that the charge of brutality does not apply to all of the policemen of Chicago. There are many able, honest and conscientious officers who do their duty quietly, thoroughly and humanely.

. . . .

Prejudice or Subserviency of Judge

V. It is further charged, with much bitterness, by those who speak for the prisoners, that the record of this case shows that the judge conducted the trial with malicious ferocity, and forced eight men to be tried together; that in cross-examining the State's witnesses, he confined counsel to the specific points touched on by the State, while in the cross-examination of the defendants' witnesses he permitted the State's Attorney to go into all manner of subjects entirely foreign to the matters on which the witnesses were examined in chief; also, that every ruling throughout the long trial on any contested point, was in favor of the State; and further, that page after page of the record contains insinuating remarks of the judge, made in the hearing of the jury, and with the evident intent of bringing the jury to his way of thinking; that these speeches, coming from the court, were much more damaging than any speeches from the State's Attorney could possibly have been; that the State's Attorney often took his cue from the judge's remarks; that the judge's magazine article recently published, although written nearly six years after the trial, is yet full of venom; that, pretending to simply review the case, he had to drag into his article a letter written by an excited woman to a newspaper after the trial was over, and which therefore had nothing to do with the case, and was put into the articles simply to create a prejudice against the woman, as well as against the dead and the living; and that, not content with this, he, in the same article, makes an insinuating attack on one of the lawyers for the defense, not for anything done at the trial, but because more than a year after the trial, when some of the defendants had been hung, he ventured to express a few kind, if erroneous, sentiments over the graves of his dead clients, whom he at least believed to be innocent. It is urged that such ferocity of subserviency is without a parallel in all history; that even Jeffries in England contented himself with hanging his victims, and did not stoop to berate them after death.

These charges are of a personal character, and while they seem to be sustained by the record of the trial and the papers before me, and tend to show the trial was not fair, I do not care to discuss this feature of the case any farther, because it is not necessary. I am convinced that it is clearly my duty to act in this case for the reasons already given, and I, therefore, grant an absolute pardon to Samuel Fielden, Oscar Neebe and Michael Schwab, this 26th day of June, 1893.

John P. Altgeld,
Governor of Illinois.

An unsympathetic perspective on the rise of organized labor appears in the following chapter from Allan Pinkerton's book *Strikers, Communists, Tramps, and Detectives* (New York, 1882). The Scots-born Pinkerton had been emotionally scarred as a boy of ten when his father was paralyzed while putting down a labor riot as a member of the Glasgow police force. A cooper by trade, Allan Pinkerton came to America in 1842 and soon established a shop at Dundee. After intermittent success in law enforcement there, he joined the Chicago police in 1850. Then he and E. G. Rucker established the world's first private detective agency, which initially devoted most of its time serving railroad corporations. During the Civil War, under former client General George B. McClellan, he organized the secret service. Pinkerton was convinced that labor unions were hurting the workingman by their radical political views and actions; so after the war he actively suppressed the unions with a force of 1600 men. Pinkerton's other works include *Criminal Reminiscences and*

Detective Sketches (Chicago, 1879), and *The Spy of the Rebellion* (Chicago, 1884). See also James D. Horan, *The Pinkertons: The Detective Dynasty That Made History* (New York, 1967).

Communism and Riot at Chicago

ALLAN PINKERTON

The surgings of trouble reached Chicago, the great inland metropolis of America, at a late date, and although they soon passed beyond, were fierce and furious while they lasted.

This city undoubtedly contains as pestilential a crew of communists as any city in the world. Its mechanics and artisans, as a rule, are among the most intelligent and advanced. Wages have always been fair; at times, exorbitant. The push, energy, and pluck for which its business men have a world-wide reputation, constantly furnish new avenues for all those business men or working men who really desire to make some advancement beyond their previous condition; but notwithstanding every opportunity offered all classes of earnest laborers, Chicago among her upwards of a half million of inhabitants, from her fame, through her disastrous fire and the subsequent marvelous rebuilding of the city, and from being the grand half-way house of public resort between the commercial East and the vast and productive West, has gradually drawn to her a floating population both vicious and unruly. Among this unhealthy element the genuine order of communists has given her authorities the most trouble, and her citizens the greatest dread. They have repeatedly marched upon her Relief and Aid Society, her City Hall and Common Council, and showed their snarling teeth in divers ways.

It was this class, and no other, that precipitated riot and bloodshed in Chicago, and it is a notable fact in connection with these communists, that their viciousness and desperation were largely caused by the rantings of a young American communist named Parsons. This fellow had many of the characteristics of the Pittsburg rattle-brained mock hero, "Boss Ammon." Parsons is a printer by trade, and just previous to the great strikes had been a compositor on the Chicago *Times.* He had also distinguished himself by running for the office of alderman, and being beaten. He seems to possess a strange nature in every respect, as he has for several years lived in Chicago with a colored woman, whom he has at least called his

From Allan Pinkerton, *Strikers, Communists, Tramps, and Detectives* (New York, 1882), pp. 387-399.

wife. He is a young man, like Ammon, of flippant tongue, and is capable of making a speech that will tingle the blood of that class of characterless rascals that are always standing ready to grasp society by the throat; and while he can excite his auditors, of this class, to the very verge of riot, has that devilish ingenuity in the use of words which has permitted himself to escape deserving punishment.

It was more through this man's baleful influence, than from any other cause, that the *conditions* were ripe in Chicago for all manner of excesses. Because they were not greater is from the fact that the authorities were prompt and vigilant, and the citizens came to the rescue of their city in such a grand outpouring as was witnessed at no other point.

On Monday, July 23d, the pay of the engineers on the Chicago and Northwestern Railway, which had been slightly reduced, was restored. From this date everything on that road was devoid of trouble, although the officers of the company took the precaution to remove the greater portion of the most valuable of rolling-stock to suburban towns along the line, in order to get it out of harm's way in case of fire and riot like that which desolated Pittsburg.

Although there had been no recent reduction of wages on the Chicago and Alton road, the moving of trains at the St. Louis end had been badly interfered with by rioters, and General Superintendent McMullen, on Monday, decided to at once discontinue the movement of all freight trains until the trainmen on his road were sufficiently over the common excitement to warrant a safe and expeditious handling of the company's business. General unrest and apprehension prevailed all over the city, but the day closed with no record of important events.

On Tuesday the strike in Chicago was fairly inaugurated and was begun by the men from the Michigan Central road, proceeding first among the Chicago, Burlington and Quincy men, whom they induced to join them, and, with this reinforcement, to the depots and shops of all other railroads centering in Chicago.

In every instance the men quietly quit work, and remained peaceably about their different resorts, while it is only a simple matter of justice to state that, in all the subsequent riot and trouble, the striking trainmen were guilty of no single act of violence.

But encouraged by the show made by trainmen, and the ease with which a general strike had been effected upon all the railroads, the communists, just before noon, rallied from the slums of the West Side, and that famous and infamous locality in the southwestern part of the city, known as "Bridgeport," and accompanied by a bevy of little boys and girls, some of them not over six years of age, but all of whom carried some sort of a stick or club, proceeded first through the manufacturing district of the West Side, compelling them to close, most of which immediately reopened the moment the ragamuffin troop were out of sight, and thence to the manufactories and wholesale business houses of the South Side, where but partial success was met with, and the crowd finally dispersed from sheer want of leaders, who were quietly nabbed by the police, or who slunk shamefacedly away when confronted by the business men of that section of the city. At night a mass-meeting, composed of about five thousand roughs and communists, was held in Market Square, in front of the office of the *Vorbote*—or *Freebooter*, translated—the organ of the communists in Chicago. The authorities saw that the temper of the meeting boded no good, and the police broke it up, dispersing its members by a very free use of their clubs.

On the next day there was one continuous scene of disorder, which, however, did not culminate in anything serious until late in the evening. Everybody was excited, and in every section of the great city there was gathering in squads by respectable citizens, and gathering in mobs by the roughs, yet with a few charges by the police, a few rushes by the rioters, the day wore on, both the authorities and the vicious elements becoming each more determined to win the fight when it should come.

Colonel Hickey, Police Superintendent, had previously given orders which resulted in the removal of all arms and ammunition from the various gun and hardware stores to places of safety, which had been both secretly and effectively done; so that the pillaging which occurred at Pittsburg could hardly have transpired. Neither was there at any time apprehension of ungovernable riot occurring in the finer business portion of the city; for every business house had promptly organized such emergency forces, that, with the near aid of the police from headquarters, and that of my own large, uniformed, and well-armed Preventive Police, any attack which might be made from across the river could have been met and repulsed with great disaster to the common enemy. Besides this, the riot and disorder seemed naturally to confine itself to the southern portion of the city, where most of the freight depots of the different roads, as well as some of the largest manufacturing establishments in the whole country, are located, and upon the West Side—particularly the southern portion of the West Side—where there are innumerable packing-houses, machine-shops, "slop-shops," or houses for the manufacture of ready-made clothing, rendering establishments, foundries, and all manner of the grosser industries that draw around them the most ignorant, as well as the most vicious and desperate, of laborers. Within an area of four square miles, covering this section of the city, all the rioting in Chicago was done. One of the chief reasons for this was found in the fact that the police forces were admirably handled, and instead of being held at headquarters to protect a trifling area, as was the case in some other cities, were separated into serviceable squads, and made to engage the communist ruffians *on their own ground,* thus rendering the most effectual protection possible to the best portions of the city, for the wild mobs were so hustled and worried in their own sections, that they had little time, or opportunity, for projecting trouble beyond.

By this time the people of Chicago had become thoroughly aroused. Its two handsome militia regiments, the First and Second, had turned out splendidly, a local battery was in fine fighting trim, and Colonel Agramonte, with the hearty co-operation of the authorities, had hastily organized a cavalry force which subsequently did most effective work in riding down the rioters. Besides this, several companies of United States troops, bronzed and war-scarred veterans from the Indian countries, had arrived, and had been received with such an ovation as had never been tendered to soldiers before, many of the swarthy fellows being carried for blocks on the heads and shoulders of jubilant citizens.

But the people of the city, as before stated, were now thoroughly aroused, and while each well-wisher for the common good had lasting faith in the eventual peaceful solution of the trouble, every man of standing and respectability had a desire to do something to give beyond question public expression to a common determination to wipe out the stain upon the city's name.

The outgrowth of all this was an almost simultaneous movement from all quarters of the city towards the mammoth Tabernacle building, the great barn erected by certain business men, primarily as an advertising scheme, and, secondarily, for the purpose of spreading physical disease through spiritual salvation as distributed by Moody and Sankey. This meeting was called for three o'clock on Wednesday afternoon, but by two o'clock from between ten and twelve thousand people had wedged themselves into the place. Fully as many more surrounded the structure, failing to gain admission, and it is certain that twenty thousand business men whose hearts and souls were with the meeting never went near it, knowing the impossibility of getting within blocks of the building. If there had been a building in Chicago which held fifty thousand people, on that day, and for the purpose named, fifty thousand earnest, determined men would have packed it full. Chicago will forever sustain the reputation of never doing things by halves.

As an illustration of the temper of this meeting I cannot resist reproducing the words of that patriotic citizen and grand man, Robert Collyer. He came forward as if in the old times, when he was the strong-armed "Yorkshire Blacksmith" of Ilkley, to drive home with the hammer of supreme earnestness the heated iron which should weld all minds into a common purpose, and said:

"This is no time for preaching; this is a time for practice!

"The wisest and bravest and best thing we can do has got to be done now. We are going to take care of our city whatever comes. We are cowed by an insignificant mob. The great wheels of commerce and trade are stopped. I cannot expect to live long in course of nature. I thought I might live twenty years—I would like to. Do you know, fellow-citizens, as God lives, and as my soul lives, I would rather die in twenty minutes in defense of order, and of our homes, against these men, than to live twenty years of as happy life as I have lived all these fifty years. My thought was this: that we should have special committees in the wards and districts of our city; that we should organize a force of twenty thousand constables; that we should subscribe one million dollars as a fund to be drawn on, to take care of these men who are acting with us, but who cannot take care of themselves. I am poor, but I am willing to give two hundred dollars to begin with. That is my speech, gentlemen!"

It was not Robert Collyer alone, but half a hundred thousand men who, like him, got at the heart of the thing without any nonsense, and the result was an organization of men who would have swept a respectable army from any field. Gray-haired man and full-blooded youth stood side by side, and were equally strong and powerful in the one great purpose.

So sudden and summary was the action of Tuesday's mob in closing up the manufactories of the southern portion of the West Side, that but a few of these places attempted to resume work on Wednesday. In the great lumber district, where at any time can be seen the largest number of planing-mills and the vastest amount of lumber at any one point in the whole world, the men gathered at their customary places of employment, only awaiting the signal from their employers before resuming their labor, but only one mill dared begin. At half-past eight o'clock fully one thousand lumber-shovers and mill-men had congregated in the vicinity, and, with a mob's freak, instead of attacking the mill which had begun work, turned its attention to the Chicago Planing Mill Company, and an adjoining distillery, which the rioters—every one of whom was armed with a piece of hard lumber from three to five feet in length, and every man's pocket bulging out with stones—favored with a lively volley of missiles, and a general clubbing of doors and windows. But suddenly they left this mill, and quickly rushed to the first which had attracted their notice, where they drove the workmen away with the utmost violence, and nearly demolished the building.

The mob then headed for the works of the United States Rolling Stock Company, McCormick's mammoth reaper factory, and similar large establishments in the neighborhood, to complete their work of the day previous, and to, if possible, destroy all those places whose proprietors had the temerity to defy their dictatorship.

Lieutenant Vesey, with all the available police at his command, made a flank movement, arriving at the Rolling Stock Company's Works in advance of the rabble, stationing his men in front of the building. The Lieutenant attempted to conciliate the mob, but it was useless. It was spoiling for a fight, and the arrest of one of its most blatant members precipitated it. They first tore down one hundred feet of the fence, and then, having received reinforcements, turned suddenly on the police in a most savage manner. The latter retaliated with their clubs, hoping that this would be sufficient, but, finding that several of their number were being struck down, drew their revolvers and advanced on their assailants, wounding many, when the mob retired sullenly, savagely contesting every inch of ground, until the crowd was suddenly assaulted in the rear by more police, under Sergeant Callahan, who had arrived at an opportune moment. Then firing ceased, and clubbing began in earnest. The mob fought back desperately, but were finally beaten, flying precipitately over the prairies in every direction.

Later in the day portions of the same mob surged back to the north, gathering force and impetus as it progressed, and made an attack upon the passenger depot of the Northwestern Railway, for the purpose of stopping all trains. They were, however, successfully resisted by the police and a *posse* of citizens, driven off with many a broken and aching bone, and their leaders dragged ignominiously to the lock-up.

But, whenever the mob dispersed at one locality, it seemed to have a strange and mysterious faculty of rising, "phoenix-like," at half a dozen different points. Manufactories were again visited in the eastern and central portion of the West Side, and closed with the ugliest of violence.

An instance worthy of record, where this brute force failed to succeed, was when a vile crowd attacked the manufactory of the Crane Bros. & Co. This company had large contracts in iron-work to be filled by August 15th. Their men were working on full time, at good wages, and would not be bullied from the place. Arming themselves with convenient pieces of iron, they defied the mob, which was most ridiculously dispersed, by showering its members with water until they were completely drenched.

Back and forth all the afternoon and into the night, small crowds of rioters pushed their way through this section of the city, carrying terror everywhere. Countless collisions with bodies of citizens and police occurred, in which the latter were always victorious, but which never had the effect of effectually quelling the devilish spirit of the infuriated ruffians, and Wednesday ended, as it had begun, with turbulence and disorder, but with a drawing nearer to the grand climax, when the riotous classes should get their fill of conflict, and when the determination of all Chicago that the city should cast off the pestilential terror which had come upon it should prevail.

On Thursday morning everything was ripe for conflict. The citizen organizations, which were mainly relied on for service, in case the business portion of the city should be invaded, had been well perfected, the militia regiments, whose loyalty had been somewhat doubted, were in full force, and ready for hard knocks; the cavalry organization was well equipped with everything necessary to do effective charging and slashing; the artillery company had been as effectively manned by old battery men as ever was a company during our late war; a large force from the postoffice, armed to the teeth with revolvers and muskets, the Veteran Reserve Corps, under old and skilled army officers, and, better than all, the United States troops, who had been increased to seven hundred men, every one of them quite as ready to meet communists as to follow Sitting Bull; while the mob elements had gathered still greater force and power, and were ready for any work which it might be possible for them to compass.

The hall was opened at ten o'clock Thursday morning by a riot at Vorwaert's Turner Hall, on West Twelfth Street, half a block east from Halsted Street. A meeting of self-styled workingmen had been called, and by nine o'clock the crowd of hoodlums that had collected ran up into thousands. At about the hour first named, a detachment of regular and special police marched across the Twelfth Street bridge on their way to Twelfth Street Station. They were on foot and numbered about thirty men. No sooner had they neared the hall, than they were attacked by the dense crowd with stones and other missiles. They were compelled to fall back, when the rioters so hotly pursued them, that, in self-defense, they were obliged to turn upon them. The police fought like tigers, and, inch by inch, forced the ugly fellows back towards the building. Fortunately, a block and a half west from the scene of conflict, near the station, and in wagons, were nearly a score of police who had been sent from the Central Station, and were awaiting orders. As soon as they were apprised of the desperate condition of their comrades, there was never a quicker charge made. At them they went like a prize crowd at Donnybrook, and clubbed and smashed anybody and everybody before them, until they had formed a junction with the other party of police, when the main crowd, with yells of pain and rage, broke and fled in all directions. Then the combined force fought their way more fiercely than ever through the dense masses wedged into the vestibule and upon the stairways, pitching men bodily out into the street, or hurling them down the stairs, until the main auditorium was reached, when a scene transpired that beggars description.

Here was found a panic-stricken mob of perhaps two hundred persons, the larger portion of whom had taken refuge within, when the attack upon them by the police in the street had become too severe. But the officers kept at them with a vigor and enthusiasm beautiful and wonderful to behold. Many rioters climbed columns, like monkeys, and hid in the galleries; others secreted themselves beneath the stage, and among the "wings" and "flies" of the scenery; others jumped from the windows at the risk of broken limbs, and still others, too hotly pressed to escape, seized chairs, converting them into weapons of defense which they handled with the power of desperation; but no mercy was shown, and the clubbing went on until the great hall was cleared, and the mob had got the first taste of what was freely distributed in Chicago throughout the entire day.

. . . .

One of the most significant leaders of organized labor in America was the head of the American Railway Union, Eugene V. Debs. He was born and raised in Terre Haute, Indiana, the son of immigrant parents from Colmar, Alsace. At the age of fifteen he quit school to work at the Terre Haute and Indianapolis Railroad, and he early became active in union affairs. While holding a number of key offices in the Brotherhood of Locomotive Firemen, he advocated organization of labor by industries rather than by crafts; and in 1893 he helped form just such an industrial union, the American Railway Union. Two years later, after serving a six-month jail sentence for a contempt charge resulting from the Pullman strike, Debs spoke passionately on the subject of liberty. The hyperbolic language of the speech is typical of his public statements. A modern appraisal of Debs is Arthur M. Schlesinger, Jr.'s introduction to *Writings and Speeches of Eugene V. Debs* (New York, 1948).

Liberty*

EUGENE V. DEBS

Manifestly the spirit of '76 still survives. The fires of liberty and noble aspirations are not yet extinguished. I greet you tonight as lovers of liberty and as despisers of despotism. I comprehend the significance of this demonstration and appreciate the honor that makes it possible for me to be your guest on such an occasion. The vindication and glorification of American principles of government, as proclaimed to the world in the Declaration of Independence, is the high purpose of this convocation.

Speaking for myself personally, I am not certain whether this is an occasion for rejoicing or lamentation. I confess to a serious doubt as to whether this day marks my deliverance from bondage to freedom or my doom from freedom to bondage. Certain it is, in the light of recent judicial proceedings, that I stand in your presence stripped of my constitutional rights as a freeman and shorn of the most sacred prerogatives of American citizenship, and what is true of myself is true of every other citizen who has the temerity to protest against corporation rule or question the absolute sway of the money power. It is not law nor the administration of law of which I complain. It is the flagrant violation of the constitution, the total abrogation of law and the usurpation of judicial and despotic power, by virtue of which my colleagues and myself were committed to jail, against which I enter my solemn protest; and any honest analysis of the proceedings must sustain the haggard truth of the indictment.

In a letter recently written by the venerable Judge Trumbull, that eminent jurist says: "The doctrine announced by the Supreme Court in the Debs case, carried to its logical conclusion, places every citizen at the mercy of any prejudiced or malicious federal judge who may think proper to imprison him." This is the deliberate

*Speech at Battery D, Chicago, on his release from Woodstock Jail, November 22, 1895. From Eugene V. Debs, *Debs: His Life, Writings and Speeches* (Girard, Kan., 1908) pp. 327-344

Courtesy of the Illinois State Historical Library

Eugene V. Debs

conclusion of one of the purest, ablest and most distinguished judges the Republic has produced. The authority of Judge Trumbull upon this question will not be impeached by anyone whose opinions are not deformed or debauched.

At this juncture I deem it proper to voice my demands for a trial by a jury of my peers. At the instigation of the railroad corporations centering here in Chicago I was indicted for conspiracy and I insist upon being tried as to my innocence or guilt. It will be remembered that the trial last winter terminated very abruptly on account of a sick juror. It was currently reported at the time that this was merely a pretext to abandon the trial and thus defeat the vindication of a favorable verdict, which seemed inevitable, and which would have been in painfully embarrassing contrast with the sentence previously pronounced by Judge Woods in substantially the same case. Whether this be true or not, I do not know. I do know, however, that I have been denied a trial, and here and now I demand a hearing of my case. I am am charged with conspiracy to commit a crime, and if guilty I should go to the penitentiary. All I ask is a fair trial and no favor. If the counsel for the government, alias the railroads, have been correctly quoted in the press, the case against me is "not to be pressed," as they "do not wish to appear in the light of persecuting the defendants." I repel with scorn their professed mercy. Simple justice is the demand. I am not disposed to shrink from the fullest responsibility for my acts. I have had time for meditation and reflection and I have no hesitancy in declaring that under the same circumstances I would pursue precisely the same policy. So far as my acts are concerned, I have neither apology nor regrets.

. . . .

Standing before you tonight re-clothed in theory at least with the prerogatives of a free man, in the midst of free men, what more natural, what more in consonance with the proprieties of the occasion than to refer to the incarceration of myself and associate officials of the American Railway Union in the county jail at Woodstock?

I have no ambition to avail myself of this occasion to be sensational, or to thrust my fellow-prisoners and myself into prominence. My theme expands to proportions which obscure the victims of judicial tyranny, and yet, regardless of reluctance, it so happens by the decree of circumstances, that personal references are unavoidable. To wish it otherwise would be to deplore the organization of the American Railway Union and every effort that great organization has made to extend a helping hand to oppressed, robbed, suffering and starving men, women and children, the victims of corporate greed and rapacity. It would be to bewail every lofty attribute of human nature, lament the existence of the golden rule and wish the world were a jungle, inhabited by beasts of prey, that the seas were peopled with sharks and devil-fish and that between the earth and the stars only vultures held winged sway.

The American Railway Union was born with a sympathetic soul. Its ears were attuned to the melodies of mercy, to catch the whispered wailings of the oppressed. It had eyes to scan the fields of labor, a tongue to denounce the wrong, hands to grasp the oppressed and a will to lift them out of the sloughs of despondency to highlands of security and prosperity.

Here and now I challenge the records, and if in all the land the American Railway Union has an enemy, one or a million, I challenge them all to stand up before the labor world and give a reason why they have maligned and persecuted the order. I am not here to assert the infallibility of the organization or its officials, or to claim exemption from error. But I am here to declare to every friend of American toilers, regardless of banner, name or craft, that if the American Railway Union has erred, it has been on the side of sympathy, mercy and humanity—zeal in a great cause, devotion to the spirit of brotherhood which knows no artificial boundaries, whose zones are mapped by lines of truth as vivid as lightning, and whose horizon is measured only by the eye of faith in man's redemption from slavery.

I hold it to have been inconceivable that an organization of workingmen, animated by such inspirations and aspirations, should have become the target for the shafts of judicial and governmental malice.

But the fact that such was the case brings into haggard prominence a condition of affairs that appeals to all thoughtful men in the ranks of organized labor and all patriotic citizens, regardless of vocation, who note the subtle invasions of the liberties of the American people by the courts, sustained by an administration that is equally dead to the guarantees of the constitution.

It is in no spirit of laudation that I aver here tonight that it has fallen to the lot of the American Railway Union to arouse workingmen to a sense of the perils that environ their liberties.

In the great Pullman strike the American Railway Union challenged the power of corporations in a way that had not previously been done, and the analysis of this fact serves to expand it to proportions that the most conservative men of the nation regard with alarm.

It must be borne in mind that the American Railway Union did not challenge the government. It threw down no gauntlet to courts or armies—it simply resisted the invasion of the rights of working-men by corporations. It challenged and defied the power of corpo-rations. Thrice armed with a just cause, the organization believed that justice would win for labor a notable victory, and the records proclaim that its confidence was not misplaced.

The corporations, left to their own resources of money, men-dacity and malice, of thugs and ex-convicts, leeches and lawyers, would have been overwhelmed with defeat and the banners of organized labor would have floated triumphant in the breeze.

This the corporations saw and believed—hence the crowning act of infamy in which the federal courts and the federal armies participated, and which culminated in the defeat of labor.

. . . .

I have said that in the great battle of labor fought in 1894 between the American Railway Union and the Corporations banded together under the name of the "General Managers' Association," victory would have perched upon the standards of labor if the battle had been left to these contending forces—and this statement, which has been verified and established beyond truthful contradic-tion, suggests the inquiry, what other resources had the corpora-tions aside from their money and the strength which their federa-tion conferred?

In replying to the question, I am far within the limits of accepted facts when I say the country stood amazed as the corporations put forth their latent powers to debauch such departments of the government as were required to defeat labor in the greatest struggle for the right that was ever chronicled in the United States.

Defeated at every point, their plans all frustrated, out-generaled in tactics and strategy, while the hopes of labor were brightening and victory was in sight, the corporations, goaded to desperation, played their last card in the game of oppression by an appeal to the federal judiciary and to the federal administration. To this appeal the response came quick as lightning from a storm cloud. It was an exhibition of the debauching power of money which the country had never before beheld.

The people had long been familiar with such expressions as "money talks," "money rules," and they had seen the effects of its power in legislatures and in Congress. They were conversant with Jay Gould's methods of gaining his legal victories by "buying a judge" in critical cases. They had tracked this money power, this behemoth beast of prey, into every corporate enterprise evolved by our modern civilization, as hunters track tigers in India jungles, but never before in the history of the country had they seen it grasp with paws and jaws the government of the United States and bend it to its will and make it a mere travesty of its pristine grandeur.

The people had seen this money power enter the church, touch the robed priest at the altar, blotch his soul, freeze his heart and make him a traitor to his consecrated vows and send him forth a Judas with a bag containing the price of his treason; or, if true to his conviction, ideas and ideals, to suffer the penalty of ostracism, to be blacklisted and to seek in vain for a sanctuary in which to expound Christ's doctrine of the brotherhood of man.

The people had seen this money power enter a university and grasp a professor and hurl him headlong into the street because every faculty of mind, redeemed by education and consecrated to truth, pointed out and illumined new pathways to the goal of human happiness and national glory.

The people had seen this money power practicing every art of duplicity, growing more arrogant and despotic as it robbed one and crushed another, building its fortifications of the bones of its victims, and its palaces out of the profits of its piracies, until purple and fine linen on the one side and rags upon the other side, defined conditions as mountain ranges and rivers define the boundaries of nations—palaces on the hills, with music and dancing and the luxuries of all climes, earth, air and sea-huts in the valley, dark and dismal, where the music is the dolorous "song of the shirt" and the luxuries, rags and crusts.

These things had been seen by the people, but it was reserved for them in the progress of the Pullman strike to see this money power, by the fiat of corporations, grasp one by one the departments of the government and compel them to do its bidding as in old plantation days the master commanded the obedience of his chattel slaves.

The corporations first attacked the judicial department of the government, a department which, according to Thomas Jefferson, has menaced the integrity of the Republic from the beginning.

They did not attack the supreme bench. A chain is no stronger than its weakest link, and the corporations knew where that was and the amount of strain it would bear. How did they attack this weakling in the judicial chain?

I am aware that innuendoes, dark intimations of venality are not regarded as courageous forms of arraignment, and yet the judicial despotism which marked every step of the proceedings by which my official associates and myself were doomed to imprisonment, was marked by infamies, supported by falsehoods and perjuries as destitute of truth as are the Arctic regions of orange blossoms.

Two men quarrelled because one had killed the other's dog with an ax. The owner of the dog inquired, "When my dog attacked you, why did you not use some less deadly weapon?" The other replied, "Why did not your dog come at me with the end that had no teeth in it?"

There is an adage which says, "fight the devil with fire." In this connection why may it not be intimated that a judge who pollutes his high office at the behest of the money power has the hinges of his knees lubricated with oil from the tank of the corporation that thrift may follow humiliating obedience to its commands?

If not this, I challenge the world to assign a reason why a judge, under the solemn obligation of an oath to obey the Constitution, should in a temple dedicated to justice, stab the Magna Charta of American liberty to death in the interest of corporations, that labor might be disrobed of its inalienable rights and those who advocated its claim to justice imprisoned as if they were felons?

. . . .

In prison my life was a busy one, and the time for meditation and to give the imagination free rein was when the daily task was over and night's sable curtains enveloped the world in darkness, relieved only by the sentinel stars and the earth's silver satellite "walking in lovely beauty to her midnight throne."

It was at such times that the "Reverend Stones" preached their sermons, sometimes rising in grandeur to the Sermon on the Mount.

It might be a question in the minds of some if this occasion warrants the indulgence of the fancy. It will be remembered that Aesop taught the world by fables and Christ by parables, but my recollection is that the old "stone preachers" were as epigrammatic as an unabridged dictionary.

I remember one old divine who, one night, selected for his text George M. Pullman, and said: "George is a bad egg—handle him with care. Should you crack his shell the odor would depopulate Chicago in an hour." All said "Amen" and the services closed. Another old sermonizer who said he had been preaching since man was a molecule, declared he had of late years studied corporations, and that they were warts on the nose of our national industries,— that they were vultures whose beaks and claws were tearing and mangling the vitals of labor and transforming workingmen's homes into caves. Another old stone said he knew more about strikes than Carroll D. Wright, and that he was present when the slaves built the pyramids; that God Himself had taught His lightning, thunderbolts, winds, waves and earthquakes to strike, and that strikes would proceed, with bullets or ballots, until workingmen, no longer deceived and cajoled by their enemies, would unify, proclaim their sovereignty and walk the earth free men.

. . . .

From such reflections I turn to the practical lessions taught by this "Liberation Day" demonstration. It means that American lovers of liberty are setting in operation forces to rescue their constitutional liberties from the grasp of monopoly and its mercenary hirelings. It means that the people are aroused in view of impending perils and that agitation, organization, and unification are to be the future battle cries of men who will not part with their birthrights and, like Patrick Henry, will have the courage to exclaim: "Give me Liberty or give me death!"

I have borne with such composure as I could command the imprisonment which deprived me of my liberty. Were I a criminal; were I guilty of crimes meriting a prison cell; had I ever lifted my hand against the life or the liberty of my fellowmen; had I ever sought to filch their good name, I would not be here. I would have fled from the haunts of civilization and taken up my residence in some cave where the voice of my kindred is never heard. But I am standing here without a self-accusation of crime or criminal intent festering in my conscience, in the sunlight once more, among my fellowmen, contributing as best I can to make this "Liberation Day" from Woodstock prison a memorial day. . . .

Gustave Kobbé was a recognized expert on the music of Richard Wagner, about whom he wrote extensively as a music critic for New York newspapers. He was born there in 1857 and studied piano in Germany. Although Kobbé received a law degree from Columbia University in 1877, he chose a career as a journalist and critic. To the exposition observers like Kobbé, the repression and squalor of the industrial revolution was all but invisible. The rapid changes in America's post-Civil War economic plant—which the World's Fair epitomized—meant only social and technological advance.

Sights at the Fair

GUSTAVE KOBBÉ

It was in the Italian section of the Liberal Arts Building, and I was looking at a fine piece of armor well set up,—helmet with vizor, breastplate, greaves, etc.,—when a woman's voice behind me exclaimed: "It's a diver. I've seen 'em. Ain't he natural looking!"

They were evidently an elderly country couple, and she had just caught sight of the armor. I wondered what the smith who had wrought with such patient art would have said could he have heard the exclamation, and have seen the couple walk on perfectly satisfied that they had seen a diver, the husband delighted with his wife's knowledge. The very resemblance which made the mistake not altogether inexcusable made it all the funnier. Doubtless amusing mistakes like this have counted up into the millions at the Fair; yet in spite of these it has not failed in its function as an educator.

It is, however, as an exposition of landscape-gardening and architecture that the Fair will most grandly fulfil this function. If there were not a picture, nor a yard of textiles, nor a ton of machinery, inside the buildings, these themselves, and their disposition about the grounds, would preach most eloquently the gospel of beauty. For this reason the location of the Fair near the geographical center was most fortunate. No unprejudiced visitor to the West can fail to admire many of its characteristics; but cheerfulness in architecture is not one of these. Somberness is rather the prevailing key in the large business blocks of most of the Western cities. In Chicago there is nothing quite so bad as the rows of brown-stone fronts with which post-bellum taste made large portions of New York hideous, but there is generally a lack of the happy and the engaging. Surely the bright, cheerful buildings of the Fair must have a gladdening effect upon the future of building in the rapidly developing West.

From *The Century Magazine*, **XLVI** (September 1893), 643-655.

Courtesy of the Illinois State Historical Library

The Illinois Building, World's Columbian Exposition, 1893

Strolling through this fairy-land of modern enterprise, I often wondered what any one of the intrepid early navigators of this "brother to the sea" would have thought, if, as he approached this shore, he could have seen the White City rising in all its beauty as if out of the lake itself. Of course he would have laid it to mirage, and, having discovered that it was real, he would have had another and perhaps greater surprise on finding out that it was all in honor of Columbus. The latter, by the way, is not very prominent at the Fair. There is a statue of him on the basin front of the Administration Building, and I presume the central figure in the fine group of statuary on the peristyle was intended for him; but as a whole what started out as the "World's Columbian Exposition" has become simply the "World's Fair."

While the Fair lasts Washington will have to yield to it the title of "City of Magnificent Distances." One does not realize how much physical exertion sight-seeing requires until one has spent a day at the Fair. You are so occupied with looking at things that your fatigue does not find a chance to make itself felt until you turn homeward. Then you begin to wonder if you have any legs left. For this reason the wheelchairs pushed by intelligent beings clad in skyblue with white piping are a boon. You can "do" the Fair comfortably and systematically, and if you happen to have the same cicerone several days in succession he is apt to become *en rapport* with you, divining your tastes, and pushing you whither these would lead you. Many of the gracious pushers are theological students, a fact which has gradually fastened upon these chairs the appellation of "gospel chariots." The late Mr. Cook, in the earlier days of his efforts to excite the migratory propensities of the human race, was wont to add to his circulars the announcement that "a number of marriages have been among the results of these tours." From what I have observed, I incline to think that several of the "gospel chariot" excursions will lead to equally felicitous results.

The sum of human happiness being to get about without any effort on your own part, other means of accomplishing this are provided in the electric launches and gondolas. Of these the latter are the more pleasurable, because, as the gondoliers—real ones from Venice—are obliged to work, you are made to feel delightfully lazy, lying back and gliding over the pretty lagoons, and imagining yourself in Venice—providing you have never been there. The illusion continues until your round trip—at an investment of twenty-five cents—brings you near the little wharf from which you started, when one of your gondoliers remarks: "Finis'! Gli gondolieri lika some beer!" Among these gondoliers I found an inveterate fisherman, who, when off duty, could be seen dropping a line in the shadow of one of the arches over the lagoon. Even on illumination nights he would scorn the fairy-like scenes, and seek the shadows of the arch. Possibly the fact that he never caught anything made him feel as if he were at home again in Venice.

If you wish to see the buildings from the lake, there are steam-launches which, passing under the arches of the peristyle, run out to the end of the long steamer-pier, and then, turning north, convey you to the pier from which you can board the brick battle-ship *Illinois.* This is probably the most complete naval exhibit ever made by any country, and it attracts great attention. But I saw one man who did not go aboard. He was not allowed. "Ephraim," exclaimed his wife, "you don't know nothing about ships. It might sink, or it might sail away with you." And Ephraim wisely adopted the advice of his better half, and sailed away with *her.* By the way, I am always struck at expositions of this kind with the fondness of mankind for implements devised for the destruction of mankind. This battle-ship, the models of war-ships in the Transportation Building, the Krupp guns, and the guns shown by our own Ordnance Department, seemed to me the most popular exhibits. The superb guns shown by our Ordnance Department must have created the impression that our forts are as well armed as those of any country. As a matter of fact, each gun exhibited was unique—the only one of its kind at the disposal of our army, except that we have a few more of the fine modern field-pieces, an example of which was shown.

Speaking of the Transportation Building reminds me of the general subject of transportation to the Fair, and suggests an incident which has a decided Gilbert-and-Sullivan flavor. The Exposition managers were from the start anxious to have the railroads make a low rate to Chicago. Accordingly they appointed a committee on transportation which consisted entirely, I believe, of railroad men whose lines come into Chicago. In their capacity as committeemen these gentlemen passed a resolution requesting their respective railroads to make reduced rates during the World's Fair months. On receiving this resolution by mail the next day at their respective offices, they, in their capacity as railroad managers, wrote letters to the transportation committee denying the request which, as members of that committee, they had made.

The Transportation Building is one of the few instances of color in architecture at the Fair. Its prevailing tone is terra-cotta, and along its frieze, done somewhat after the manner of illumination in old missals, is a line of angels. This frieze is highly artistic, yet the idea of painting angels on the outside of the Transportation Building always had a humorous aspect to me—it was so suggestive of the kind of transportation we are all anxious to avoid, yet (there was a touch of the grim in this) are perhaps most exposed to when we use modern means of transportation. The golden arch which forms the main entrance to this building is probably the architectural detail most admired by the general public.

France figures in a dual rôle at the Fair. She not only makes an exhibit, but shows the other nations of the world how to make an exhibit. After passing along the rows of sarcophagus-like show-cases in which the American textile exhibit is made,—an admirable exhibit so far as the goods are concerned,—it is a positive relief to come within view of the handsome façade with which the French have surrounded the space reserved for them in the Liberal Arts Building. Between the arches of this façade, fronting on the main avenue, are alcoves for the exhibit of furniture, costumes, and other articles requiring an interior for their most effective display. Through the main arch of the façade one enters an apartment hung with rich tapestries, and suitable mural decorations make the *entourage* of the section as artistic as the exhibits themselves. You leave the glare and heat of the rest of the building to find a subdued light and cool shade in the French section; for the French have made ceilings of cloths—some of them with borders or centers cut in lace patterns— to keep out the glare and the heat. Throughout their section they have placed comfortable settees, which are simply a boon to the weary. I have seen exhausted women throw themselves down upon these settees and fall asleep. The French section has become widely known as a place of refuge for those in need of rest. How many of those who admire the setting of this French section, and the humanity which prevails in all its arrangements, realize that it is simply the gracious expression of a national art-sense? Here was a lesson that to be great a nation need not be brutal. When I first arrived in Chicago a feeling of suppressed grief seemed to pervade the ranks of the French employees—even of the marines who stood guard in this section. I wondered what was the matter until I accidentally learned that one of the subordinate American employees in the Art Building had pasted a small label on one of Meissonier's paintings.

The Lyons silk exhibit—which has a "coast-line" of about 1000 feet of show-cases—is in the gallery. For the stairways which lead to the gallery in other parts of the building the French have substituted a broad and easy flight of steps, and the floor of the space occupied by this exhibit has been specially carpeted. The Soieries de Lyon attract a vast amount of attention from women; and, indeed, some of the silks are beautiful enough to be called woven music. This exhibit must equal in money value that of the combined textile exhibits of all the other nations. To show what a Frenchman can do with a loom, I may mention a piece of silk which represents a stretch of sea with sunset colors above it. It is not a set woven picture, like the woven copy of Gilbert Stuart's portrait of Washington, but a piece of delicate fantasy. Strange to say, the one blot on the artistic arrangement of the French section was in this Lyons exhibit. The cases had been "dressed" about as prosaically as was possible. As an expert dry-goods man said to me, they couldn't have been worse if the goods had "just been chucked in for a fire-sale." Yet so beautiful are these silks, that the men who usually rebel at the length of time they are compelled by their wives to remain among the textiles lingered willingly enough here. For myself, I prefer the small but exceedingly refined exhibit of hand-made laces made by the Compagnie des Indes down-stairs, the cheerful human toil which enters into the delicate products giving them an interest which no machine-made fabric can possess.

I happened to witness one rather funny incident in the American silk exhibit. A concern which manufactures spool silk has as a special feature a mammoth artificial silkworm. Under the case is an electric mechanical contrivance by which raw silk is made to pass into the worm at one end, and spools of silk are caused to drop out at the other. A woman, after watching this for some time, exclaimed, "Well, I can understand it all except how it manages to get the silk colored!"

In the Midway Plaisance is probably the greatest collection of "fakes" the world has ever seen. The proprietors thereof rejoice, however, in the proud title of "Concessionnaires." Whenever I grew tired of formal sight-seeing I would stroll down the Plaisance (which was so popular that everybody soon got the knack of pronouncing it correctly) to the Egyptian temple. Here was the greatest fakir of them all. I am proud to say he was an American. In Egyptian raiment he squatted in front of the temple, and delivered his speech as follows:

"This, ladies and gentlemen, is the temple of Luxor, the tomb of Rameses II. You will find his mummy about the fifth one on the right. On the left the mummy of King Solomon's father-in-law—also his sister-in-law. The sacred dances are about to begin."

To discover, after all this, that the mummies at which people were gazing so reverentially were dummies was an unmitigated joy.

One evening after the Egypto-American above mentioned had delivered his speech about the temple of Luxor and the mummy of Rameses II, a man in the crowd turned to me and asked, "Is this the German Village?"

The personnel of the Plaisance shows reminded me of Thackeray's inventory of passengers in the *White Squall*. There are innumerable Oriental dances—Turkish, Algerian, Persian, and Egyptian, the latter in a theater annexed to the "Street in Cairo." These dances are supposed to be very suggestive, but I think most people must find them simply ugly, and wonder if they really convey the Oriental idea of grace in motion.

Much more interesting is the dancing in the large Javanese village, and in the theater of the South Sea Islanders. The former is really graceful; the latter is the best dancing in the Plaisance. It makes no pretense to grossness, but is simply downright savage. There is a certain indescribable charm about the Plaisance with its varied life; and the crowd which it attracts is an added feature of interest. Not far from the Plaisance was Buffalo Bill's Wild West Show with its Deadwood Coach, "which, ladies and gentlemen, has carried more royalty, and more royalty at one time, than any other coach in the world—Colonel Cody on the box!" It costs about $30 in dimes and quarters to do the Plaisance. But the fakes, including the Beauty Show, are often seen in procession through the grounds.

Very little has been said about the music at the Fair, but it is an important "life" exhibit. I do not refer to the playing of the wind-instrument bands on the out-door stands, but to the concerts in the music and festival halls. At the head of the department of music is Theodore Thomas, who still conducts with his old-time grace and significance, and can get more music out of his orchestra with a simple wave of the hand than many conductors can with hands, arms, head, and body. He is assisted by Mr. Tomlins and Mr. George H. Wilson, the latter being in charge of the arduous duties of administration. Mr. Thomas has a permanent orchestra, which can be brought up to 150 by drawing in some of the players from the bands, who for this purpose become, temporarily, musicians. Choral and instrumental concerts, many of them free, are given nearly every day, and the results cannot fail to be far-reaching.

When I laid emphasis on the importance of the Fair as an exhibit of landscape-gardening and architecture, I had in mind the unusualness of those features as compared with the exhibits as a whole, among which there are necessarily few surprises. The great firms have done about what might reasonably have been expected of them; but those strokes of genius by which individuals hitherto unknown attain on occasions like these immediate and lasting fame are not strikingly apparent. Nor should I say that outside the Art Building and the United States Government Building, residents of our large cities see much that could not be found at home. It must be remembered that our great trade bazaars—which have come up since the Centennial—draw on nearly all industries and all parts of the world, and are really world's fairs. For this reason the location of the Fair in Chicago was fortunate. It has brought things which are familiar to us in the East, where our town and rural population often gets into the large cities, to the cognizance of the great West. Thus exhibits which, perhaps, strike the visitor from a large city as nothing more than rows of show-cases are veritable revelations to the vast majority of visitors.

I have seen many descriptions of the World's Fair, but none has quite expressed what seems to me its most valuable characteristic. That is neither its size nor its magnificence, but its gracious beauty and engaging loveliness, which linger in the memory like the remembrance of a pleasant dream. We Americans are apt to boast of the bigness of various things American; but here we have something as beautiful as it is big—nay, more beautiful. So let us for once overlook its size and let the world know that we have something that is simply beautiful.

4: Progressive Reforms

The politics of reform is the subject of the excerpt from Ernest L. Bogart's and John Mabry Mathews' *The Modern Commonwealth 1899-1918* (Chicago, 1920), another monograph in the series commemorating the state's centennial. Mathews received his doctorate from Johns Hopkins University in 1909 and taught in the Political Science Department of the University of Illinois. He contributed to many scholarly journals and encyclopedias and was the author of seven monographs on state and local government. Crucial to the beginning of the progressive movement in Illinois was the adoption of the direct primary: thus the basic political process of election to office was taken from the power brokers and returned to the people. Then the legislature adopted a form of initiative and referendum. All of this is rather standard fare in the progress of reform; what is of some debate, however, is why these changes occurred when they did in Illinois. Why not sooner? One interpretation is the so-called Hofstadter thesis: namely, that a revolution in status occurred after the Civil War, whereby the prewar elite were displaced by the vulgar rich. These Yankee Protestant classes used the cause of reform to regain their lost prestige and power. John D. Buenker closely examines this thesis as applied to Illinois and finds that it does not hold up. His revision, included in this section of special accounts, originally appeared in *Essays in Illinois History* (Carbondale, 1968), edited by Donald F. Tingley. Buenker, a member of the history department of the University of Wisconsin—Parkside, received his doctorate from Georgetown University in 1964. In recognition of his scholarship, the Illinois State Historical Society chose him for the Harry E. Pratt Award in 1971. Tingley teaches at Eastern Illinois University and specializes in American intellectual and religious history. He has also written "The 'Robin's Egg Renaissance': Chicago and the Arts, 1910-1920," *Journal of the Illinois State Historical Society*, LXIII (1970), 35-54. Another dimension of the progressive movement can be seen in those who worked for social reform outside of politics. One Illinoisan famous for her dedicated efforts toward social reform was Jane Addams of Hull House. Anne Firor Scott describes the early days there and Addams' relationship with ward boss John Powers. Scott, a Radcliff Ph.D., is professor of history at Duke University. Some of her many publications are *The Southern Lady: From Pedestal to Politics* (Chicago, 1970), *Women in American Life* (Boston, 1970), and *Democracy and Social Ethics* (Cambridge, Mass., 1964).

For recent accounts of Addams' full career as a social reformer, feminist, and pacifist, see Margaret Tims, *Jane Addams of Hull House, 1860-1935* (New York, 1961) and Cornelia Meigs, *Jane Addams: Pioneer of Social Justice* (Boston, 1970).

Special Accounts

Parties and Elections

ERNEST L. BOGART AND JOHN M. MATHEWS

The movement to subject political parties to legal regulation involved the formulation of a definition of a political party. This became especially necessary in connection with the introduction of the uniform Australian ballot, prepared and printed by the government, for the question immediately arose as to the method of determining what names should be printed on the ballot as the candidates of the several political parties. To print upon such official ballot the names of candidates in accordance with a mere certificate of nomination caused to be filed with the proper official by a convention or other body representing an association of qualified voters is in itself a recognition that such association of voters constitutes a political party. Thus, under the act of 1891 introducing the Australian ballot into Illinois elections, it was provided that "any convention of delegates, caucus or meeting representing a political party which at the general election next preceding polled at least two (2) per cent of the entire vote cast in the State or in the electoral district or division thereof, or the municipality for which the nomination is made, may for the State, or for the electoral district or division thereof or municipality for which the convention, caucus or meeting is held, as the case may be, by causing a certificate of nomination to be duly filed, make one such nomination for each office therein to be filled at the election." The two per cent rule is, of course, an arbitrary limitation, and it may happen that an association of voters having all the other essential characteristics of a political party fails to poll the required

From Ernest L. Bogart and John M. Mathews, *The Modern Commonwealth, 1899-1918* (Chicago, 1920), pp. 354-361, 365, 371, 375-377, 379-380. Footnotes in the original have been omitted.

percentage of votes. Provision is made for this case as well as for the case of a candidate of an independent group of voters by the next section of the same act, which provides that nominations of candidates for any office to be filled by the voters of the state at large may also be made by nomination papers signed for each candidate by not less than one thousand qualified voters of the state and, in the case of candidates for local offices, by a specified percentage of the voters at the next preceding general election in the given locality.

. . . .

No political party can, under ordinary conditions, expect to win success at the polls without maintaining some sort of organization. This organization consists principally of conventions and party committees of various grades and kinds. Provision is made under the direct primary election law for county, congressional, and state conventions. Formerly, the arrangements for holding the conventions, such as time and place of meeting and ratio of representation, were entirely in the hands of the party committees. Thus, in 1898, the republican state committee decided that the state convention of that party should be held at Springfield on June 14, 1898; and the ratio of representation was fixed at one delegate for each four hundred votes and major fraction thereof cast for McKinley in 1896. This ratio made a convention of 1,521 delegates, of whom 555 were from Cook county. The ratio of representation in the republican state convention of 1916 was fixed at one delegate for each four hundred votes cast for L. Y. Sherman for senator in November, 1914. In the democratic state convention of 1916, there were 1,029 delegates, of whom 343 were from Cook county. The date of holding state conventions and the method of electing delegates thereto have now come under legal regulation. Conventions are required to be held shortly after the April primaries. The county convention consists of a meeting of the members of the county central committee and is empowered to choose delegates to the congressional and state conventions of its party. The congressional convention is empowered to choose delegates to national nominating conventions and to recommend to the state convention of its party the nomination of candidates for presidential electors. Since the amendments of 1913 to the primary law, however, the delegates and alternate delegates to the national nominating conventions have been chosen by the party voters at the direct primary election. Possibly, the power of congressional conventions to choose such delegates might be operative when, for any reason, the party voters fail to choose them at the direct primary election, but the attorney-general has held that the congressional conventions have no longer any official duty to perform with reference to the selection of such delegates.

. . . .

Under the direct primary election law, it is provided that the state, senatorial, and precinct or ward committees shall be elected by the primary electors of the respective parties. State central committeemen are elected by the primary electors of each party, voting by congressional districts. The county and city central committees consist of the precinct and ward committees, if any, within their respective territorial limits, while the congressional district committees are composed of the chairmen of the county central committees of the counties composing such district. Each committee may elect a chairman from its own membership. It has sometimes happened that the real party control was not in the hands of the party committees but in those of one man or small group of men who held no official position in the party. An attempt to remedy this abuse is made in the direct primary election law by the provision that the "several committees shall not have power to delegate any of their powers or functions to any other person, officer, or committee."

The power of the party machine over the nomination of candidates for public office under the convention system was so extensive as to lead to grave abuses. The delegates to the conventions ceased to be representative of the rank and file of the party and were sometimes mere dummies acting under the domination of a small group of leaders. Of the more than seven hundred delegates to a Cook county convention which met in 1896, it is said that 265 were saloonkeepers, 148 were political employees, 84 were ex-Bridewell and jailbirds, and 43 had served terms in the penitentiary for murder, manslaughter, or burglary. It is not surprising that nominations made by such conventions were unsatisfactory to the mass of voters. In order to remedy these and other abuses, the system of nomination by direct primary elections was introduced shortly after the beginning of the twentieth century. The demand for primary legislation arose immediately out of the gubernatorial contest in the republican party in 1904. There were six candidates, five of whom made a general canvass throughout the state. At the republican state convention, there were double delegations from eleven counties. The republican state convention unseated 112 delegates, while the democratic convention unseated 241 delegates. The republican state convention, consisting of 1,502 delegates, was in session from May 12 to June 3, 1904, and took seventy-nine ballots for governor before a candidate was nominated as a result of combinations and withdrawals by some of the other aspirants for the office. During the deadlock a resolution was introduced to refer the governorship nomination directly to the republican voters of the state, to be voted upon at a special primary to be called for that purpose in all parts of the state on the same day. After some discussion, the resolution was tabled. Primary elections to choose delegates to nominating conventions had already been in existence for many years. In 1885 an act was passed prohibiting any except persons qualified to vote at regular elections from voting at primary elections or elections called to select delegates to party conventions.

The first of a long series of acts designed to regulate the whole process of the nomination of candidates by political parties was enacted in 1889 under the title, "an act to regulate primary elections of voluntary political associations, and to punish frauds therein." This was merely an optional act, to be used or not at the discretion of the party committees and has since been repealed. The first primary election act in Illinois which introduced the compulsory principle was enacted in 1898, though it was compulsory in Cook county only and was optional in other parts of the state. This law, and the amendatory act of 1901 were noteworthy as early attempts to apply to primary elections the system of regulations and safeguards already in force at general elections. None of these acts, however, provided for the nomination of candidates by direct primary election. The popular desire for the introduction of the latter system was indicated in November, 1904, when a proposition was submitted under the public policy law to the effect that the primary laws should be amended so as to provide for party primaries at which the voter would vote under the Australian ballot directly for the candidate whom he wishes nominated by his party. The proposition was approved by a decided majority of the votes cast on the proposition and also by a majority of all the votes cast at the election.

In pursuance of this popular mandate, the legislature has passed in quick succession four direct primary election acts, in 1905, 1906, 1908, and 1910.

. . . .

Most observers are agreed that the experience thus far had with the direct primary in Illinois shows it to be decidedly superior to the delegate-convention method of making nominations. It tends to reduce the control of the party machine over nominations and

Looking east on Chicago's Randolph Street, 1908

correspondingly to increase that of the rank and file of the voters. It is not, however, without defects, some of which appear to be remediable while others appear to be inherent in the system.

. . . .

By an amendment to the election law, enacted in 1899, it is provided that, whenever a constitutional amendment or other public measure is proposed to be voted upon by the people, the substance of such amendment or measure shall be printed on a separate ballot, which is handed to the voter at the polls together with the candidate ballot. Since the enactment of this provision of law, three proposed constitutional amendments have been submitted to the voters, two of which have received a majority of all votes cast at the election and the other one received a majority of all votes cast at the election for legislative candidates. It may also be noted in this connection that, under the act of 1901, questions of public policy submitted to popular vote, are also printed on separate ballots.

. . . .

In addition to the referendum there has also existed in Illinois since 1901 a public policy law which confers upon the voters a power somewhat analogous to the initiative in ordinary legislation as found in some other states. Under this law on a petition signed by twenty-five per cent of the voters of any political subdivision of the state or ten per cent of the voters of the whole state, it is the duty of the proper election officers in each case to submit any question of public policy so petitioned for to the voters of the subdivision or state respectively at any general or special election named in the petition. Not more than three propositions may be submitted at the same election. The petition must be filed not less than sixty days before the election. The purpose of the law is to make it possible to secure an expression of public opinion as a guide to the general assembly in the enactment of laws. It does not follow, however, that because public opinion, as thus expressed, favors the enactment of a particular law, such law will necessarily be passed by the general assembly. There is no legal compulsion resting upon it to do so, and no pledge taken by the members of the legislature to vote in favor of such a law, and, in practice, most of the propositions favored by public opinion as expressed under the public policy law, have not been enacted by the general assembly. It should be added, however, that several public policy votes related to proposed constitutional amendments, and consequently could not have been enacted into law by the legislature.

Among the propositions which have received the approval of public opinion, as thus expressed, but which have not been enacted into law by the general assembly, are those for the popular initiative and referendum, a corrupt practices act, and a short ballot commission. Neither the referenda mentioned above nor the power of the people under the public policy law constitute a real initiative and referendum in ordinary legislation as found in Oregon and some other states, and there has been considerable agitation in favor of introducing in this state the Oregon system of direct legislation. A proposed question of public policy embodying this system was submitted to the voters of the state in 1902 and approved by a vote of 428,000 to 88,000. The proposition was again submitted in 1910 and approved by a vote of 448,000 to 128,000. These repeated indications, however, of considerable public opinion in favor of the proposition have thus far borne no fruit in actual legislation.

A proposition was presented to the voters in 1910 under the public policy law to the effect that the next general assembly should "enact a corrupt practices act, limiting the amount a candidate and his supporters may spend in seeking office, and providing for an itemized statement under oath showing all expenditures so made, for what purposes made and from what source or sources received, thus preventing the corrupt use of money at elections." This proposition was approved by a vote of 422,000 to 122,000. The state platforms of both the leading parties have contained planks favoring the enactment of a corrupt practices law. In 1913, Governor Dunne declared that "candidates have concededly spent in election contests more than twice the salary they could collect during the whole term of their offices;" and he recommended the passage of an act "which will limit, within reasonable restrictions, the expenditure of money during a political campaign, and compel the publication of all amounts collected and expended both before and after election." The general assembly, however, has not yet passed the act suggested.

. . . .

Much of the expense of elections could be saved in other directions, such as by combining certain local or nonpartisan elections in which the issues would not be greatly different, by the introduction of a system of permanent or central registration, and by abolishing the primary in certain cases and nominating candidates by petition.

. . . .

The state as a whole, however, is interested in the efficient and orderly management of elections, especially where state officers are to be chosen. The question may, therefore, in the near future become acute whether, in all except purely local elections, the state should not assume at least part of the expense and undertake the administrative control or supervision of such elections.

. . . .

Urban Immigrant Lawmakers and Progressive Reform in Illinois

JOHN D. BUENKER

According to the prevailing interpretation of the nature of the Progressive era, the urban, immigrant masses and their representative were a decidedly unprogressive lot. Taking their cue from studies of the contributions made by middle-class reformers and intellectuals, the Status Revolution historians have excluded the urban masses and their leaders from the Progressive movement, either explicitly or by implication. George Mowry, for example, has constructed a composite progressive who is of old-American stock, probably of British origin, economically secure, well educated, middle class, and motivated by the intellectual and religious influence of New England. Even more explicit on the attitude of the New Immigrant toward progress is the view of Richard Hofstadter that "the immigrant was usually at odds with the reform aspirations of the American Progressive," and that "together with the native conservative and the politically indifferent the immigrant formed a potent mass that limited the range and achievement of Progressivism." For Hofstadter the Progressive movement was a struggle between "the ethos of the boss-immigrant-machine complex and that of the reformer-individualist-Anglo-Saxon complex."*

This Status Revolution interpretation, while it has made an extremely valuable contribution to understanding the Progressive

"Urban Immigrant Lawmakers and Progressive Reform in Illinois" by John D. Buenker, from *Essays in Illinois History in Honor of Glenn Huron Seymour* edited by Donald F. Tingley, pp. 52-61, 70-74. Copyright © 1968 by Southern Illinois University Press. Reprinted by permission of Southern Illinois University Press. Footnotes in the original have been omitted. A footnote on the Hofstadter thesis has been added for reference purposes.
*Richard Hofstadter, *The Age of Reform* (New York, 1955), pp. 182-187.

era, is clearly too restrictive. It is particularly so when matched against the attitudes of the urban, immigrant masses and their representatives in Illinois; for these lawmakers did not oppose all progressive legislation, in fact, they were actually enthusiastic supporters of much of it.

It should first be made clear just what group of lawmakers this paper is considering. They are definitely not of British or Anglo-Saxon origin. Many of them were of Irish lineage, but there were also Czechs, Poles, Italians, Danes, Norwegians, and Jews from various countries. Many of these were either immigrants themselves or, at the most, second- or third-generation Americans. In 1913, for example, the *Blue Book* listed twenty-one legislators as having been born outside the United States, and several others as the children of immigrants. Most of them had working-class backgrounds, although many had risen into other fields, usually connected with politics or in areas which required little formal preparation. Naturally the vast majority were from the polyglot city of Chicago, inasmuch as three-fourths of the city's two million residents were of non-Anglo-Saxon antecedents and two-thirds were either foreign born or second generation. Fifty-one of Chicago's eighty-four representatives and senators fit this pattern in 1913, and the major downstate cities, such as Springfield, Peoria, Bloomington, and those of the St. Louis area, occasionally produced lawmakers of similar origins who tended to be in sympathy with the Chicago delegation.

Moreover, it is unlikely that these gentlemen could have been influenced in any significant way by the intellectual and religious influence of New England. The great majority were Roman Catholics, educated in parochial schools where Calvinism was something to be attacked rather than emulated. The remainder were Lutheran, Jewish, or Bohemian Free Thinkers, not likely to be much attuned to the voice of Yankee Protestantism. The majority were Democrats and composed what was commonly called the Chicago districts who were Republicans, Progressives, or Socialists, but they were exceptions. Indeed it would not be too much to say that the Democratic party in Illinois was the main organ for the aspirations of the New Immigrants, and the ethnic and religious differences between it and the Republican party were significant even to the casual observer. In sum, the lawmakers whose attitudes and voting habits this paper is investigating are definitely in Hofstadter's boss-machine-immigrant complex rather than the reformer-individualist-Anglo-Saxon complex.

But while the New Immigrant lawmaker in Illinois fit the qualifications mentioned above, his political behavior was not always what the Status Revolution historians have alleged. It has been the general view of middle-class reformers and many historians that the New Immigrant politician followed unthinkingly the dictates of the boss. In the case of Illinois this has been interpreted to mean allegiance to the will of Roger C. Sullivan. A second-generation Irish Catholic and self-made millionaire, Sullivan was universally regarded as the major force in Chicago and Illinois politics, although he held no elective office. The facts, however, suggest that while Sullivan was probably the most influential Democrat in the state, by no means was he the unquestioned ruler even of Chicago. There was a large anti-Sullivan force led by the Carter Harrisons, and some of the most purple prose regarding Sullivan comes not from Republican sources but from the younger Harrison's memoirs. With the ascendancy of Edward F. Dunne as mayor of Chicago and then governor of Illinois, New Immigrant loyalty was actually split three ways, and on many issues their representatives showed a proclivity toward independent voting which is disconcerting to the historian seeking patterns. Actually Sullivan suffered many serious reverses in the Progressive era, caused largely by New Immigrant defections. In 1913 both his candidate for Speaker of the House and his choice

Immigrants from southeastern Europe

Courtesy of the Illinois State Historical Library

for the United States Senate failed to be elected when the Dunne faction compromised with the Republicans. Sullivan's own candidacy for the Senate in 1914 also miscarried, at least partially because of the lack of enthusiastic support from the Dunne and Harrison forces. In the 1912 primary, Dunne was the candidate rated least acceptable to Sullivan; yet he carried Cook County by more than two to one over the combined total of the other two candidates. Inasmuch as the bulk of Dunne and Harrison support also came from the New Immigrants, it seems difficult to regard the group as monolithic.

Equally hard to justify is the reformer's claim that Sullivan's influence, all-pervasive or not, was universally unprogressive. Governor Dunne, for one, readily admitted Sullivan's influence, but insisted that it had been used often to effect the passage of progressive legislation, including the direct primary, women's suffrage, Chicago home rule charter, civil service, regulation of private banks, and the adoption of a state budgetary system. The official history of the Democratic party, while not an unimpeachable source, nonetheless made much more of Sullivan's role as a reformer than it could conceivably have done if there had been no justifiable evidence. Even the congenitally Republican *Chicago Tribune* noted in Sullivan's obituary that "it is not too much to say that the so-called 'reform laws' of the last ten or fifteen years bear more of Sullivan's thumbprint than of the professional reformers." And political scientist Harold Zink, in his critical study of political bosses, grants that Sullivan "occasionally supported progressive measures" and sometimes "threw his strength without reserve for strictly progressive measures."

. . . .

Thus it is possible . . . to question the implications of the Status Revolution theory as applied to Illinois' New Immigrant lawmakers. The most solid reasons for doubt come from an analysis of their attitudes toward the concrete economic, political, and cultural issues of the day. Such a study reveals that the New Immigrant legislator was not an unmitigated reactionary, but rather a pragmatist who gave very substantial support to several reforms, and who sometimes had legitimate reason to oppose others.

Of all the economic reforms of the Progressive era, Illinois' New Immigrant solons demonstrated the strongest support for welfare measures, largely because their constituents were the most tragic victims of the insecurity caused by industrialization, immigration, and urbanization. Even Richard Hofstadter is willing to grant them some contribution in this area, although he feels that this support of the welfare state did not really come to fruition until the New Deal years. Whether the motive of the New Immigrant lawmakers was sincere concern or, as some have suggested, an effort to shift the welfare burden of the machine to government, it nonetheless seems to indicate a somewhat earlier flowering of the welfare state impulse than historians have generally credited.

Old age pensions, for instance, were a major concern. The firemen's pension plan was the brainchild of Bob Wilson, a Sullivan lieutenant, and Senator Patrick Sullivan of Chicago; it passed with nearly unanimous support from the New Immigrant bloc. A Dunne lieutenant, Michael Igoe of Chicago, was the guiding force behind old age pensions for Chicago police, again with solid support from his fellows. Chicago house of correction employees were similarly benefited by a bill first introduced unsuccessfully by Anton Cermak in 1909, and later successfully by John Denvir, a Chicago labor leader. New Immigrants also supported pension programs for teachers and civil service employees, a petition to Congress requesting pensions for federal employees, and a resolution introduced by Medill McCormick, a Chicago Progressive of the famous *Tribune* family, to investigate the possibilities of a state system of old age pensions.

Minimum wage proposals also garnered much New Immigrant support. Proposals to investigate a possible minimum wage for women were introduced by Chicago Democrats J. J. O'Rourke and John Burns, and the votes of the Chicago Democrats were also instrumental in the success of a bill to create a commission to study a general minimum wage law, which was introduced by a Chicago Progressive. Even the highly sensational vice commission, chaired by Lieutenant Governor O'Hara, spent much of its time trying to establish a connection between prostitution and low wages for women, and the first bill which the committee introduced was a minimum wage for women. Concern for wages was also demonstrated by the considerable New Immigrant support for the semi-monthly payment of wages and the creation of wage loan companies, although there was some objection to the latter on the grounds of high interest.

Maximum hours laws were also a favorite cause. Bills to limit the hours of interurban railway employees were introduced by McLaughlin, Igoe, and Frank Ryan, all Chicago Democrats of Irish extraction. The fight for a minimum wage for women was a long and bitter one due to the opposition of the Illinois Manufacturers Association, but the urban immigrants were usually on the side of a strong law. Many of them opposed an early law because it only provided for a seventy-hour week and a maximum of twelve hours

per day, while Governor Dunne vetoed a fifty-four-hour law be-
cause it had too many exemptions and no limit per day. New
Immigrant support was also extended to stronger laws proposed by
Chicago Progressives McCormick and Walter Jones.

Unemployment, another serious concern for urban immigrant
workers who were always "the last to be hired and the first to be
fired," also merited much attention. A bill to create free employment offices in the state was introduced in the Senate in 1915 by
Edward Glackin, a confidant of Carter Harrison, and adopted by a
unanimous vote in which nine of the ten urban immigrant senators
participated. A similar measure was introduced in the House by
Patrick Sullivan and passed with the overwhelming support of his
fellow Chicago Democrats. Urban immigrants were also instrumental in the creation of a commission to investigate the causes of
unemployment in the state. Indeed the appropriation bill for the
commission was saved in the Senate when nine of the ten New
Immigrant senators voted against a motion by the Republicans to
refer it back to committee.

. . . .

Opposition to child labor was also a New Immigrant trait, although there was some disagreement as to whether it should be
abolished or just regulated. The middle-class reformers generally
favored abolition, but the New Immigrant was all too aware that
working children were often economically necessary. Therefore, he
frequently favored exemptions for newsboys and others, under
proper supervision. Joseph Weber, a Swiss immigrant, opposed
outright abolition since working children were sometimes the sole
support of their mothers. Business people who opposed child labor
laws often used the same argument, of course, but that does not
necessarily mean that all who reasoned similarly were insincere.
Many New Immigrants also clashed with reformers and organized
labor over the issue of children on stage, but it must be remembered
that a theatrical career was one of the few roads to success open to
a poor, uneducated immigrant boy. In general, though, Illinois' New
Immigrants favored strong regulation of child labor and voted for
the 1915 law.

Many other welfare measures also commanded the support of the
urban, immigrant legislator in Illinois, including aid to mothers with
dependent children, creation of schools for the handicapped, a
two-cent fare on urban railways, a bureau of labor statistics, public
washrooms for employees, and a commission to investigate working
conditions in factories. Most of these were designed to meet concrete problems which the urban representatives and their con-

stituents had experienced firsthand, and they do lead to the conclusion that the New Immigrants were more attuned to the development of the welfare state than most other groups in Illinois in this period.

Most welfare measures also had the support of organized labor in Illinois, and there were other areas of cooperation between the labor leaders and the New Immigrants. . . . In fact, nearly every significant measure which had labor support also had the backing of the New Immigrants in the legislature. The Illinois Federation of Labor's list of progressive reforms included a law to permit convicts to work at useful tasks, an improved child labor law, a health, safety, and comfort act, a miners qualification act, a ten-hour day for women, workmen's compensation, and an occupational diseases act. Every one of these had the support of the vast majority of New Immigrant lawmakers.

Some of Illinois' greatest accomplishments in labor and welfare legislation during the Progressive era concerned coal miners, and again the New Immigrant lawmakers were generally in support. This is all the more significant since there was little self-interest involved here for Chicago lawmakers. Their support has to be attributed to a general sympathy for other disadvantaged groups and a belief in the principle of safety and welfare legislation. In the 1909 session Morris proposed several bills relating to mine conditions and was generally backed up by most New Immigrant solons. Two of these, a safety bill and the creation of an investigation committee, eventually passed almost unanimously in the House. In 1913 a series of important mining laws were enacted, many of which were introduced by William McKinley of Chicago's thirty-first district, who had been elected Speaker of the House as a candidate agreeable to both Governor Dunne and Roger Sullivan. Included in this list were a mining investigation commission, a shot-firers act, a stronger health and safety law, the establishment of rescue stations, and mandatory fire-fighting equipment in the mines. These passed with the nearly unanimous vote of the New Immigrant lawmakers, although a dissenting vote was cast on occasion by John J. McLaughlin, one of Sullivan's chief cronies. The urban, immigrant legislators continued their backing of mining legislation in the next session by voting to strengthen the existing laws, and to create a board of examiners for potential miners.

Taken as a whole, then, the attitude of Illinois' New Immigrant legislators toward labor and welfare measures was generally a progressive one. Together with organized labor, social workers and middle-class progressives, the representatives of the urban, immigrant districts made a significant contribution in this area. This is certainly not to say that they made the only or even the most important one, but it is difficult to see how much of this legislation could have been enacted without their support.

. . . .

The attitude of the urban, immigrant legislators toward progressive taxation and regulation, while not as consistent as their devotion to labor and welfare measures, was usually progressive. In fact, the bulk of Illinois' New Immigrant legislators in the Progressive era were firmly committed to the idea of government responsibility in social and economic affairs to a degree which at least matched that of any middle-class, native reformer.

Nor can it be fairly said that Illinois' New Immigrant legislators were unalterably opposed to meaningful political reform. With some important qualifications, they often supported changes in the political system. To begin with, the New Immigrant evinced little sympathy for good government as an end in itself. With his aforementioned concern for welfare legislation, he was interested in equipping government with the tools necessary to promote economic and social well-being. Hence the New Immigrant was often unable to distinguish the reformer's cry for honesty, efficiency, and economy from the conservative's denunciation of the positive state. If the reformer's ideals could be realized without doing serious damage to the state's ability to provide for welfare matters, the New Immigrant lawmakers were often inclined to go along with them, as witnessed by the former's support of Governor Dunne's Efficiency and Economy Commission. On the whole, though, good government was not the burning issue for the New Immigrant as it often was for the middle class, and the ideal ran a distant second to the reality of the positive state.

. . . .

But if the New Immigrant lawmaker often agreed with the middle-class reformer on important political and economic questions, there were other issues which clearly divided him from the native solon; issues which reflected the ethnic and religious gap between the two. These might best be described as cultural, since they related to questions of morality and personal liberty.

The New Immigrant had brought with him a set of customs and religious practices which conflicted at various points with those of the old-stock American. Historically this had produced a struggle between the two value systems which manifested itself primarily in the attempts of the "native" to "Americanize" the immigrant. While the latter had no qualms about conforming in some things, he often was most adamant in clinging to his religious belief and to many of his customs, no matter how offensive these may have been to the "native" American. When the latter sought to change these by law, an often bitter struggle resulted over such issues as immigration restriction, parochial school attendance, and Sunday blue laws. Nowhere were the urban immigrants in the Illinois General Assembly more united, usually in opposition to the old-stock lawmakers, than on questions which touched this vital area of culture.

The school system was a constant source of argument. One controversial issue was free and uniform textbooks, a proposal backed by education groups, organized labor, and middle-class reformers. But while the urban immigrant might favor the free textbook, he had reservations about the uniform one, viewing it as part of a larger design to force conformity to the native ideal. Hence, as Charles Merriam later observed, the issue was complicated by a "Catholic-labor-foreign complex" and a "Protestant-capitalist-native American complex." In 1911 Catholic and Lutheran clergymen were among those who testified against the free and uniform textbook bill, as was Peter Collins, the Roman Catholic president of the International Brotherhood of Electrical Workers. Every time the issue was raised, opposition came mainly from urban immigrant lawmakers, although by no means all were against it. Urban immigrants likewise made up the entire opposition to a 1909 House bill to insure moral practices in public schools, an injunction which certainly meant something different to them than it did to the old-stock Protestant.

A similar split occurred over respective attitudes toward professional athletics. Many "natives" held professional athletes, especially boxers, in low repute, and succeeded in outlawing pugilism in several states. The urban immigrant, though, saw professional athletics as one of the few quick roads to success open to him in a strange world, as well as a cheap form of amusement. A mere glance at the sports pages during the Progressive era reveals the great predominance of New Immigrant names, and even several legislators had used professional athletics as a springboard to a political career. The main clash occurred over the attempt to legalize boxing and create a state athletic commission. Bills to this effect were introduced in several sessions, always by urban, immigrant legislators such as Al Gorman, Patrick Carroll, and Ed Santry, himself a former pug. None of these succeeded but they always provoked lively debate and a vote which split along ethnic lines; the New Immigrants provided a nearly solid bloc in favor.

But the issue which most divided along ethnic and religious lines was that relating to the consumption of alcoholic beverages. The matter was omnipresent, being regarded by many old-stock Protestants as the ultimate reform and by most New Immigrants as the ultimate horror. The assault on liquor took many forms in Illinois. Its advocates tried local option, county option, prohibiting its use on trains, near universities and old folks' homes, and finally throughout the state itself. The New Immigrants opposed all of these and managed to prevent nearly all of them from being enacted until 1919, when the fervor engendered by the national amendment led to statewide prohibition and ratification by Illinois. Even then the urban immigrant lawmakers refused to concur.

. . . .

On cultural matters, then, the New Immigrant lawmaker often found himself at odds with the middle-class, old-stock reformer. Whatever opinion at the time may have been, modern liberal thought, stressing pluralism and abhorring conformity, would be hard-pressed to hold the New Immigrant's cultural stand against him. Even on such controversial issues as the abolition of capital punishment, the rights of the accused, and compulsory sterilization of criminals, his stand was a progressive one, whatever the motivation. Lest we be too quick to laud the New Immigrant lawmaker and condemn the old-stock solon, it should be noted that the former could also be guilty of trying to force conformity to his standards. Hence he could vote for the censorship of movies, newspapers, and books when they violated his moral predilections. On balance, though, Illinois' New Immigrants, as a minority, were opposed to enforced conformity.

Thus the picture which emerges from an investigation of the voting records of Illinois' New Immigrant legislators during the Progressive era is a much more complex one than the Status Revolution theory seems to allow. Their influence was not a completely unprogressive one, but it did possess many gradations and conflicts. Basically the Chicago political machine was in a process of evolution, fast becoming the servant of the New Immigrant class, instead of its master. Part of this was due to the pressure from the machine's constituency for more effective relief from their ills than the boss's palliatives had formerly provided. Part of it was due to the predominance in high party circles of the New Immigrants themselves. Part of it may also have been the desire of the machine politicians to adjust their methods of control to new circumstances and a more educated electorate. This is a phenomenon which most historians, including Hofstadter, freely admit, but which they feel came to fruition in the late twenties or early thirties. It seems fairly clear from the evidence that, in Illinois at least, the process was well under way during the Progressive era.

Thus oriented, Illinois' New Immigrant lawmakers followed a highly pragmatic course in their attitude toward reform legislation, generally favoring labor and welfare laws, taxation of wealth, and the regulation of business. It would appear too that they were willing to accept many of the changes in the political structure proposed by other reformers, perhaps partly because these often did not really alter the power relationships involved. Here there was even a possible split between the old guard and the new, with the latter more willing to accept change. Lastly, they undertook to defend their customs, heritage, and religion against the attacks of the "native" reformers who sought to Americanize them.

None of this is meant to convey the impression that the New Immigrant lawmakers were the only real progressives in Illinois. Quite the contrary. There was no one group which could be objectively credited with that label. Progressivism was a series of movements; a cacophony of attempts by different groups to adjust to industrialization, immigration, and urbanization, which only accomplished something of value when a temporary and shifting coalition between organizations could be achieved. It is the sole contention of this paper that the New Immigrant and his representatives in Illinois contributed a great deal more to this process than has formerly been recognized.

Saint Jane and the Ward Boss

ANNE FIROR SCOTT

If Alderman John Powers of Chicago's teeming nineteenth ward had been prescient, he might have foreseen trouble when two young ladies not long out of the female seminary in Rockford, Illinois, moved into a dilapidated old house on Halsted Street in September, 1889, and announced themselves "at home" to the neighbors. The ladies, however, were not very noisy about it, and it is doubtful if Powers was aware of their existence. The nineteenth ward was well supplied with people already—growing numbers of Italians, Poles,

"Saint Jane and the Ward Boss": © 1960, American Heritage Publishing Co., Inc. Reprinted by permission from *American Heritage* (December 1960), pp. 12-17, 94-99.

Hull House

Russians, Irish, and other immigrants—and two more would hardly be noticed.

Johnny Powers was the prototype of the ward boss who was coming to be an increasingly decisive figure on the American political scene. In the first place, he was Irish. In the second, he was, in the parlance of the time, a "boodler": his vote and influence in the Chicago Common Council were far from being beyond price. As chairman of the council's finance committee and boss of the Cook County Democratic party he occupied a strategic position. Those who understood the inner workings of Chicago politics thought that Powers had some hand in nearly every corrupt ordinance passed by the council during his years in office. In a single year, 1895, he was to help to sell six important city franchises. When the mayor vetoed Powers' measures, a silent but significant two-thirds vote appeared to override the veto.

Ray Stannard Baker, who chanced to observe Powers in the late nineties, recorded that he was shrewd and silent, letting other men make the speeches and bring upon their heads the abuse of the public. Powers was a short, stocky man, Baker said, "with a flaring gray pompadour, a smooth-shaven face [*sic*], rather heavy features, and a restless eye." One observer remarked that "the shadow of sympathetic gloom is always about him. He never jokes; he has forgotten how to smile. . . ." Starting life as a grocery clerk, Powers had run for the city council in 1888 and joined the boodle ring headed by Alderman Billy Whalen. When Whalen died in an accident two years later, Powers moved swiftly to establish himself as successor. A few weeks before his death Whalen had collected some thirty thousand dollars—derived from the sale of a city franchise—to be divided among the party faithful. Powers alone knew that the money was in a safe in Whalen's saloon, so he promptly offered a high price for the furnishings of the saloon, retrieved the money, and divided it among the gang—at one stroke establishing himself as a shrewd operator and as one who would play the racket fairly.

From this point on he was the acknowledged head of the gang. Charles Yerkes, the Chicago traction tycoon, found in Powers an ideal tool for the purchase of city franchises. On his aldermanic salary of three dollars a week, Powers managed to acquire two large saloons of his own, a gambling establishment, a fine house, and a conspicuous collection of diamonds. When he was indicted along with two other corrupt aldermen for running a slot machine and keeping a "common gambling house," Powers was unperturbed. The three appeared before a police judge, paid each other's bonds, and that was the end of that. Proof of their guilt was positive, but convictions were never obtained.

On the same day the Municipal Voters League published a report for the voters on the records of the members of the city council. John Powers was described as "recognized leader of the worst element in the council . . . [who] has voted uniformly for bad ordinances." The League report went on to say that he had always opposed securing any return to the city for valuable franchises, and proceeded to document the charge in detail.

To his constituents in the nineteenth ward, most of whom were getting their first initiation into American politics, Powers turned a different face. To them, he was first and last a friend. When there were celebrations, he always showed up; if the celebration happened to be a bazaar, he bought freely, murmuring piously that it would all go to the poor. In times of tragedy he was literally Johnny on the spot. If the family was too poor to provide the necessary carriage for a respectable funeral, it appeared at the doorstep—courtesy of Johnny Powers and charged to his standing account with the local undertaker. If the need was not so drastic, Powers made his presence felt with an imposing bouquet or wreath. "He has," said the Chicago *Times-Herald*, "bowed with aldermanic grief at thousands of biers."

Christmas meant literally tons of turkeys, geese, and ducks—each one handed out personally by a member of the Powers family, with good wishes and no questions asked. Johnny provided more fundamental aid, too, when a breadwinner was out of work. At one time he is said to have boasted that 2,600 men from his ward (about one-third of the registered voters) were working in one way or another for the city of Chicago. This did not take into account those for whom the grateful holders of traction franchises had found a place. When election day rolled around, the returns reflected the appreciation of job-holders and their relatives.

The two young ladies on Halsted Street, Jane Addams and Ellen Starr, were prototypes too, but of a very different kind of figure: they were the pioneers of the social settlement, the original "social workers." They opposed everything Johnny Powers stood for.

Jane Addams' own background could hardly have been more different from that of John Powers. The treasured daughter of a well-to-do small-town businessman from Illinois, she had been raised in an atmosphere of sturdy Christian principles.

From an early age she had been an introspective child concerned with justifying her existence. Once in a childhood nightmare she had dreamed of being the only remaining person in a world desolated by some disaster, facing the responsibility for rediscovering the principle of the wheel! At Rockford she shared with some of her classmates a determination to live to "high purpose," and decided that she would become a doctor in order to "help the poor."

After graduation she went to the Woman's Medical College of Philadelphia, but her health failed and she embarked on the grand tour of Europe customary among the wealthy. During a subsequent trip to Europe in 1888, in the unlikely setting of a Spanish bull ring, an idea that had long been growing in her mind suddenly crystallized: she would rent a house "in a part of the city where many primitive and actual needs are found, in which young women who had been given over too exclusively to study, might restore a balance of activity along traditional lines and learn something of life from life itself. . . ." So the American settlement house idea was born. She and Ellen Starr, a former classmate at the Rockford seminary who had been with her in Europe, went back to Chicago to find a house among the victims of the nineteenth century's fast-growing industrial society.

The young women—Jane was twenty-nine and Ellen thirty in 1889—had no blueprint to guide them when they decided to take up residence in Mr. Hull's decayed mansion and begin helping "the neighbors" to help themselves. No school of social work had trained them for this enterprise: Latin and Greek, art, music, and "moral philosophy" at the seminary constituted their academic preparation. Toynbee Hall in England—the world's first settlement house, founded in 1884 by Samuel A. Barnett—had inspired them. Having found the Hull house at the corner of Polk and Halsted—in what was by common consent one of Chicago's worst wards—they leased it, moved in, and began doing what came naturally.

Miss Starr, who had taught in an exclusive girls' preparatory school, inaugurated a reading party for young Italian women with George Eliot's *Romola* as the first book. Miss Addams, becoming aware of the desperate problem of working mothers, began at once to organize a kindergarten. They tried Russian parties for the Russian neighbors, organized boys' clubs for the gangs on the street, and offered to bathe all babies. The neighbors were baffled, but impressed. Very soon children and grownups of all sorts and conditions were finding their way to Hull-House—to read Shakespeare or to ask for a volunteer midwife; to learn sewing or discuss socialism; to study art or to fill an empty stomach. There were few formalities and no red tape, and the young ladies found themselves every day called upon to deal with some of the multitude of personal tragedies against which the conditions of life in the nineteenth ward offered so thin a cushion.

Before long, other young people feeling twinges of social conscience and seeking a tangible way to make their convictions count in the world of the 1890's came to live at Hull-House. These "residents," as they were called, became increasingly interested in the personal histories of the endless stream of neighbors who came to the House each week. They began to find out about the little children sewing all day long in the "sweated" garment trade, and about others who worked long hours in a candy factory. They began to ask why there were three thousand more children in the ward than there were seats in its schoolrooms, and why the death rate was higher there than in almost any other part of Chicago. They worried about youngsters whose only playground was a garbage-spattered alley that threatened the whole population with disease. (Once they traced a typhoid epidemic to its source and found the sewer line merging with the water line.) In the early days Hull-House offered bathtubs and showers, which proved so popular a form of hospitality that the residents became relentless lobbyists for municipal baths.

Hull-House was not the only American settlement house—indeed, Jane Addams liked to emphasize the validity of the idea by pointing out that it had developed simultaneously in several different places. But Hull-House set the pace, and in an astonishingly short time its founder began to acquire a national reputation. As early as 1893 Jane Addams wrote to a friend: "I find I am considered the grandmother of social settlements." She was being asked to speak to gatherings of learned gentlemen, sociologists and philosophers, on such subjects as "The Subjective Necessity for Social Settlements." When the Columbian Exposition attracted thousands of visitors to Chicago in 1893 (*see* "The Great White City," in the October, 1960, *American Heritage*), Hull-House became—along with the lake front and the stockyards—one of the things a guest was advised not to miss. By the mid-nineties, distinguished Europeans were turning up regularly to visit the House and examine its workings. W. T. Stead, editor of the English *Review of Reviews,* spent much time there while he gathered material for his sensational book, *If Christ Came to Chicago.* By that time two thousand people a week were coming to Hull-House to participate in some of its multifarious activities, which ranged from philosophy classes to the Nineteenth Ward Improvement Association.

Neither her growing reputation nor the increasing demand for speeches and articles, however, distracted Jane Addams from what was to be for forty years the main focus of a many-sided life: Hull-House and the nineteenth ward. Much of her early writing was an attempt to portray the real inner lives of America's proliferating immigrants, and much of her early activity, an effort to give them a voice to speak out against injustice.

The Hull-House residents were becoming pioneers in many ways, not least in the techniques of social research. In the *Hull-House Maps and Papers,* published in 1895, they prepared some of the first careful studies of life in an urban slum, examining the details of the "homework" system of garment making and describing tumbledown houses, overtaxed schools, rising crime rates, and other sociological problems. The book remains today an indispensable source for the social historian of Chicago in the nineties.

Jane Addams' own interest in these matters was far from academic. Her concern for the uncollected garbage led her to apply for—and receive—an appointment as garbage inspector. She rose at six every morning and in a horse-drawn buggy followed the infuriated garbage contractor on his appointed rounds, making sure that every receptacle was emptied. Such badgering incensed Alderman Powers, in whose hierarchy of values cleanliness, though next to godliness, was a good bit below patronage—and he looked upon garbage inspection as a job for one of his henchmen. By now John Powers was becoming aware of his new neighbors; they were increasingly inquisitive about things close to Johnny Powers' source of power. By implication they were raising a troublesome question: Was Johnny Powers really "taking care of the poor"?

For a while, as one resident noted, the inhabitants of the House were "passive though interested observers of their representative, declining his offers of help and co-operation, refusing politely to distribute his Christmas turkeys, but feeling too keenly the smallness of their numbers to work against him." They were learning, though, and the time for passivity would end.

In company with many other American cities, Chicago after 1895 was taking a critical look at its political life and at the close connections that had grown up between politics and big business during the explosive era of industrial expansion following the Civil War. "The sovereign people may govern Chicago in theory," Stead wrote; "as a matter of fact King Boodle is monarch of all he surveys. His domination is practically undisputed."

The Municipal Voters League, a reform organization that included many of Jane Addams' close friends, was founded in 1896 in an effort to clean up the Common Council, of whose sixty-eight aldermen fifty-eight were estimated to be corrupt. The League aimed to replace as many of the fifty-eight as possible with honest men. But it was not easy: in 1896, as part of this campaign, a member of the Hull-House Men's Club ran for the second aldermanic position in the ward and against all expectations was elected. Too late, his idealistic backers found that their hero had his price: Johnny Powers promptly bought him out.

Jane Addams was chagrined but undiscouraged. By the time Powers came up for re-election in 1898, she had had time to observe him more closely and plan her attack. Her opening gun was a speech—delivered, improbably enough, to the Society for Ethical Culture—with the ponderous and apparently harmless title, "Some Ethical Survivals in Municipal Corruption." But appearances were deceptive: once under way, she took the hide off Powers and was scarcely easier on his opponents among the so-called "better elements."

She began by pointing out that for the immigrants, who were getting their first initiation in self-government, ethics was largely a matter of example: the office-holder was apt to set the standard and exercise a permanent influence upon their views. An engaging politician whose standards were low and "impressed by the cynical stamp of the corporations" could debauch the political ideals of ignorant men and women, with consequences that might, she felt, take years to erase.

Ethical issues were further complicated, she said, by habits of thought brought to the New World from the Old. Many Italians and Germans had left their respective fatherlands to escape military service; the Polish and Russian Jews, to escape government persecu-

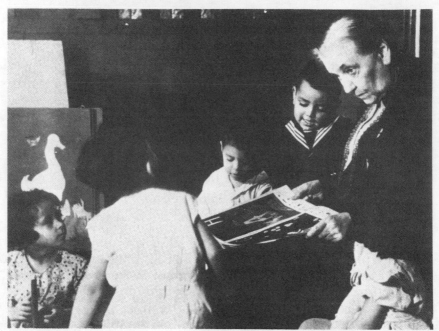

Courtesy of the Illinois State Historical Library

Jane Addams

tion. In all these cases, the government had been cast in the role of oppressor. The Irish, in particular, had been conditioned by years of resentment over English rule to regard any successful effort to feed at the public crib as entirely legitimate, because it represented getting the better of their bitterest enemies.

On the other hand, Miss Addams continued, there was nothing the immigrants admired more than simple goodness. They were accustomed to helping each other out in times of trouble, sharing from their own meager store with neighbors who were even more destitute. When Alderman Powers performed on a large scale the same good deeds which they themselves were able to do only on a small scale, was it any wonder that they admired him?

Given this admiration, and their Old World resentments toward government, the immigrants' developing standards of political morality suffered when Powers made it clear that he could "fix" courts or find jobs for his friends on the city payroll. It cheapened their image of American politics when they began to suspect that the source of their benefactor's largess might be a corrupt bargain with a traction tycoon, or with others who wanted something from the city of Chicago and were willing to pay for it.

Hull-House residents, Miss Addams said, very early found evidence of the influence of the boss's standards. When the news spread around the neighborhood that the House was a source of help in time of trouble, more and more neighbors came to appeal for aid when a boy was sent to jail or reform school, and it was impossible to explain to them why Hull-House, so ready to help in other ways, was not willing to get around the law as the Alderman did.

Removing Alderman Powers from office, Jane Addams told the sober gentlemen of the Society for Ethical Culture, would be no simple task. It would require a fundamental change in the ethical standards of the community, as well as the development of a deeper insight on the part of the reformers. These latter, she pointed out, with all their zeal for well-ordered, honest politics, were not eager to undertake the responsibilities of self-government 365 days a year. They were quite willing to come into the nineteenth ward at election time to exhort the citizenry, but were they willing to make a real effort to achieve personal relationships of the kind that stood Johnny Powers in such good stead?

On this last point, Hull-House itself had some experience. As Florence Kelley—a Hull-House resident who was to become a pioneer in the Illinois social reform movement—subsequently wrote:

> The question is often asked whether all that the House undertakes could not be accomplished without the wear and tear of living on the spot. The answer, that it could not, grows more assured as time goes on. You must suffer from the dirty streets, the universal ugliness, the lack of oxygen in the air you daily breathe, the endless struggle with soot and dust and insufficient water supply, the hanging from a strap of the overcrowded street car at the end of your day's work; you must send your children to the nearest wretchedly crowded school, and see them suffer the consequences, if you are to speak as one having authority and not as the scribes . . .

By 1898, after nine years of working with their neighbors, the Hull-House residents were ready to pit their influence against that of Powers. Jane Addams' philosophical address to the Ethical Culture society was followed by others in which she explained more concretely the relationships between Yerkes, Chicago's traction czar, and the city council, relationships in which Johnny Powers played a key role. With several important deals in the making, 1898 would be a bad year for Yerkes to lose his key man in the seats of power.

The election was scheduled for April. The reformers—led by Hull-House and supported by independent Democrats, the Cook County Republicans, and the Municipal Voters League—put up a candidate of their own, Simeon Armstrong, to oppose Powers, and undertook to organize and underwrite Armstrong's campaign. By the end of January, the usually imperturbable Powers suddenly began paying attention to his political fences. The newspapers noted with some surprise that it was the first time he had felt it necessary to lift a finger more than two weeks in advance of election day.

His first move was an attack on Amanda Johnson, a Hull-House resident who had succeeded Miss Addams as garbage inspector. A graduate of the University of Wisconsin and described by the papers as blond, blue-eyed, and beautiful, she had taken the civil service examination and duly qualified for the position. Alderman Powers announced to the world that Miss Johnson, shielded by her civil service status, was telling his constituents not to vote for him. The Chicago *Record* dropped a crocodile tear at the sad picture of the martyred alderman:

> General sympathy should go out to Mr. Powers in this, his latest afflic-
> tion. Heretofore he has been persecuted often by people opposed to bad
> franchise ordinances. He has been hounded by the upholders of civil
> service reform. He has suffered the shafts of criticism directed at his
> career by disinterested citizens. A grand jury has been cruel to him.
> Invidious comments have been made in his hearing as to the ethical
> impropriety of gambling institutions.... It is even believed that Miss
> Johnson in her relentless cruelty may go so far as to insinuate that Mr.
> Powers' electioneering methods are no better than those attributed to
> her—that, indeed, when he has votes to win, the distinctions of the civil
> service law do not deter him from going after those votes in many ways.

Powers' next move was to attempt a redistricting that would cut off the eastern, or Italian, end of his ward, which he took to be most seriously under Hull-House influence. It was reported that he also felt this area had been a "large source of expense to him through the necessity of assisting the poor that are crowded into that district." "These people," the Chicago *Record* reported, "formerly tied to him by his charities are said to be turning toward Hull-House and will vote solidly against him next spring."

Neither of Powers' first efforts was notably successful. A few days after his attack on Miss Johnson the *Tribune* reported:

> Trouble sizzled and boiled for Alderman John Powers in his own baili-
> wick last night. The Nineteenth Ward Independent club raked over the
> Alderman's sins ... and ... much indignation was occasioned by Alder-
> man Powers' opposition to Miss Amanda Johnson. One Irish speaker says
> Johnny is a disgrace to the Irish race now that he has descended to
> fighting "poor working girls."

Meantime, Powers' colleagues on the council redistricting committee had no intention of saving his skin at the expense of their
own, and stood solidly against his gerrymandering effort. Now the
shaken boss began to show signs of losing his temper. He told
reporters that if Miss Addams didn't like the nineteenth ward she
should move out. Later, still more infuriated, he announced that
Hull-House should be driven out. "A year from now there will be
no such institution," he said flatly, adding that the women at
Hull-House were obviously jealous of his charities. The *Record*
published a cartoon showing Powers pushing vainly against the wall
of a very substantial house.

The news of the campaign soon spread beyond the bounds of
Chicago. The New York *Tribune* commented that Powers

> wouldn't mind Miss Addams saying all those things about him if he
> didn't begin to fear that she may succeed in making some of his
> well-meaning but misled constituents believe them. She is a very practical
> person, and has behind her a large volunteer staff of other practical
> persons who do not confine their efforts to "gassin' in the parlors," but
> are going about to prove to the plain people of the nineteenth ward that
> a corrupt and dishonest man does not necessarily become a saint by
> giving a moiety of his ill-gotten gains to the poor.

By March the campaign was waxing warm, and Powers resorted
to an attempt to stir up the Catholic clergy against Miss Addams
and the reform candidate. One of the Hull-House residents, a
deputy factory inspector and a Catholic herself, went directly to
the priests to find out why they were supporting Powers. When she
reported, Jane Addams wrote to a friend:

> As nearly as I can make out, the opposition comes from the Jesuits,
> headed by Father Lambert, and the parish priests are not in it, and do
> not like it. Mary talked for a long time to Father Lambert and is sure it is
> jealousy of Hull-House and money obligations to Powers, that he does
> not believe the charges himself. She cried when she came back.

In another letter written about the same time, Miss Addams said
that Powers had given a thousand dollars to the Jesuit "temperance
cadets," who had returned the favor with a fine procession supporting Powers' candidacy. "There was a picture of your humble servant
on a transparency and others such as 'No petticoat government for
us . . .' We all went out on the corner to see it, Mr. Hinsdale
carefully shielding me from the public view."

By now the battle between Hull-House and Johnny Powers was
sharing headlines in Chicago newspapers with the blowing up of the
Maine in Havana's harbor and the approach of the war with Spain.

"Throughout the nineteenth ward," said the *Tribune,* "the one absorbing topic of conversation wherever men are gathered is the fight being made against Alderman Powers." It was rumored that Powers had offered a year's free rent to one of the opposition leaders if he would move out of the ward before election day, and the Hull-House group let it be known that the Alderman was spending money freely in the ward, giving his lieutenants far more cash to spread around than was his custom. "Where does the money come from?" Jane Addams asked, and answered her own question: "From Mr. Yerkes." Powers was stung, and challenged her to prove that he had ever received one dollar from any corporation.

"Driven to desperation," said the *Tribune,* "Ald. Powers has at last called to his aid the wives and daughters of his political allies." Determined to fight fire with fire, he dropped his opposition to "petticoat politicians" and gave his blessing to a Ladies Auxiliary which was instructed to counteract the work of the women of Hull-House. An enterprising reporter discovered that few of the ladies had ever seen Miss Addams or been to Hull-House, but all were obediently repeating the charge that she had "blackened and maligned the whole ward" by saying that its people were ignorant, criminal, and poor.

As the campaign became more intense, Jane Addams received numbers of violent letters, nearly all of them anonymous, from Powers' partisans, as well as various communications from lodging-house keepers quoting prices for votes they were ready to deliver! When the Hull-House residents discovered evidence of ties between banking, ecclesiastical, and journalistic interests, with Powers at the center, they proceeded to publicize all they knew. This brought upon their heads a violent attack by the Chicago *Chronicle,* the organ of the Democratic ring.

Suddenly a number of nineteenth-ward businessmen who had signed petitions for the reform candidate came out for Powers. They were poor and in debt; Powers gave the word to a landlord here, a coal dealer there, and they were beaten. The small peddlers and fruit dealers were subjected to similar pressure, for each needed a license to ply his trade, and the mere hint of a revocation was enough to create another Powers man.

When Alderman John M. Harlan, one of the stalwarts of the Municipal Voters League, came into the ward to speak, Powers supplied a few toughs to stir up a riot. Fortunately Harlan was a sturdy character, and offered so forcefully to take on all comers in fisticuffs that no volunteers appeared. Allowed to proceed, he posed some embarrassing questions: Why did nineteenth-ward residents have to pay ten-cent trolley fares when most of the city paid five? Why, when Powers was head of the city council's free-spending committee on street paving, were the streets in the ward in execrable condition? Why were the public schools so crowded, and why had Powers suppressed a petition, circulated by Hull-House, to build more of them?

Freely admitting Powers' reputation for charity, Harlan made the interesting suggestion that the councilman's motives be put to the test: Would he be so generous as a private citizen? "Let us retire him to private life and see."

Powers was pictured by the papers as being nearly apoplectic at this attack from Miss Addams' friend. He announced that he would not be responsible for Harlan's safety if he returned to the nineteenth ward. (Since no one had asked him to assume any such responsibility, this was presumed to be an open threat.) Harlan returned at once, telling a crowd well-laced with Powers supporters that he would "rather die in my tracks than acknowledge the right of John Powers to say who should and who should not talk in this ward." Summoning up the memory of Garibaldi, he urged the Italians to live up to their tradition of freedom and not allow their votes to be "delivered."

In a quieter vein, Miss Addams too spoke at a public meeting of Italians, where, it was reported, she received profound and respectful attention. "Show that you do not intend to be governed by a boss," she told them. "It is important not only for yourselves but for your children. These things must be made plain to them."

As the campaign progressed, the reformers began to feel they had a real chance of defeating Powers. Jane Addams was persuaded to go in search of funds with which to carry out the grand finale. "I sallied forth today and got $100," she wrote, and "will have to keep it up all week; charming prospect, isn't it?" But on about the twentieth of March she began to have serious hopes, too, and redoubled her efforts.

As election day, April 6, approached, the Chicago *Tribune* and the Chicago *Record* covered the campaign daily, freely predicting a victory for the reformers. Alas for all predictions. When election day came, Powers' assets, which Jane Addams had so cogently analyzed in that faraway speech to the Society for Ethical Culture, paid off handsomely. It was a rough day in the nineteenth ward, with ten saloons open, one man arrested for drawing a gun, and everything, as Miss Addams wrote despondently when the count began to come in, "as bad as bad can be." Too many election judges were under Powers' thumb. The reform candidate was roundly defeated. Hull-House went to court to challenge the conduct of the election, but in the halls of justice Powers also had friends. It was no use.

Even in victory, however, Powers was a bit shaken. Hull-House had forced him, for the first time, to put out a great effort for re-election. It was obviously *not* going to move out of the nineteenth ward; indeed, if the past was any portent, its influence with his constituents would increase.

Powers decided to follow an ancient maxim, "If you can't lick 'em, join 'em." Early in the 1900 aldermanic campaign, several Chicago papers carried a straight news story to the effect that Hull-House and Johnny Powers had signed a truce, and quoted various paternally benevolent statements on the Alderman's part. In the *Chronicle,* for example, he was reported to have said: "I am not an Indian when it comes to hate . . . let bygones be bygones." A day or two later another rash of stories detailed a number of favors the Alderman was supposed to have done for Hull-House.

Jane Addams was furious, and after considerable deliberation she decided to reply. It was one of the few times in her long public career when she bothered to answer anything the newspapers said about her. She knew that with his eye on the campaign, the master politician was trying to give the appearance of having taken his most vigorous enemy into camp. She had been observing him too long not to realize what he was up to, and she could not possibly let him get away with it.

On February 20, 1900, a vigorous letter from Miss Addams appeared in nearly all the Chicago papers, reaffirming the attitude of Hull-House toward Mr. Powers. "It is needless to state," she concluded, "that the protest of Hull-House against a man who continually disregards the most fundamental rights of his constituents must be permanent."

Permanent protest, yes, but as a practical matter there was no use waging another opposition campaign. Powers held too many of the cards. When all was said and done, he had proved too tough a nut to crack, though Hull-House could—and did—continue to harass him. An observer of the Municipal Voters League, celebrating its success in the *Outlook* in June, 1902, described the vast improvement in the Common Council, but was forced to admit that a few wards were "well-nigh hopeless." He cited three: those of "Blind Billy" Kent, "Bathhouse John" Coughlin, and Johnny Powers.

From a larger standpoint, however, the battle between "Saint Jane" (as the neighbors called Jane Addams when she was not around) and the Ward Boss was not without significance. It was one of numerous similar battles that would characterize the progressive era the country over, and many of them the reformers would win. Because of her firsthand experience, because she lived *with* the immigrants instead of coming into their neighborhood occasionally to tell them what to do, Jane Addams was perhaps the first of the urban reformers to grasp the real pattern of bossism, its logic, the functions it performed, and the reason it was so hard to dislodge. Years later political scientists, beginning to analyze the pattern, would add almost nothing to her speech of 1898. If copies of *The Last Hurrah* have reached the Elysian fields, Jane Addams has spent an amused evening seeing her ideas developed so well in fictional form.

The campaign of 1898 throws considerable light on Jane Addams' intensely practical approach to politics, and upon a little-known aspect of the settlement-house movement. If anyone had told her and Ellen Starr in 1889 that the logic of what they were trying to do would inevitably force them into politics, they would have hooted. But in due time politics, in many forms, became central to Hull-House activity. For Jane Addams herself, the campaign against Powers was the first in a long series of political forays, all essentially based on the same desire—to see that government met the needs of the "other half."

The regulation of child labor, for example, was one political issue in which Hull-House residents became involved because of their knowledge of the lives of the neighbors. The first juvenile court in Chicago was set up as a result of their efforts; it was a direct response to the anxious mothers who could not understand why Hull-House would not help get their boys out of jail. The first factory inspection law in Illinois was also credited to Hull-House, and Florence Kelley became the first inspector. Another Hull-House resident Dr. Alice Hamilton—pioneered in the field of industrial medicine. Because of their intimate acquaintance with the human cost of industrialization, settlement workers became vigorous advocates of promoting social justice through law.

It was a long jump but not an illogical one from the campaign against Powers to the stage of the Chicago Coliseum in August, 1912, when Jane Addams arose to second the nomination of Teddy Roosevelt by the Progressive party on a platform of social welfare. More remarkable than the ovation—larger than that given to any other seconder—was the fact that the huge audience seemed to listen carefully to what she had to say.

Some newspapers grandly estimated her value to T. R. at a million votes. "Like the report of Mark Twain's death," she commented, "the report is greatly exaggerated." But she campaigned vigorously, in the face of criticism that this was not a proper role for a woman, and when the Bull Moose cause failed, she did not believe it had been a waste of time. It had brought about, she wrote Roosevelt, more discussion of social reform than she had dared to hope for in her lifetime. Alderman Powers was still in office—as were many like him—but the sources of his power were being attacked at the roots.

When the 1916 campaign came around, Democrats and Republicans alike made bids for Jane Addams' support. The outbreak of war in Europe had turned her attention, however, in a different direction. As early as 1907, in a book called *Newer Ideals of Peace,* she had begun to elaborate William James's notion of a "moral equivalent of war," and had suggested that the experience of polyglot immigrant populations in learning to live together might be laying the foundations for a true international order. Like her ideals of social justice, those that she conceived on international peace had their beginning in the nineteenth ward.

To her, as to so many idealistic progressives, world war came as a profound shock. Her response was a vigorous effort to bring together American women and women from all the European countries to urge upon their governments a negotiated peace. In Europe, where she went in 1915 for a meeting of the Women's International Peace Conference, she visited prime ministers; at the end of that year she planned to sail on Henry Ford's peace ship (*American Heritage,* February, 1958), but illness forced her to withdraw at the last moment. At home she appealed to President Wilson. Unshaken in her pacifism, she stood firmly against the war, even after the United States entered it.

Her popularity seemed to melt overnight. Many women's clubs and social workers, who owed so much to her vision, deserted her. An Illinois judge who thought it dangerous for her to speak in wartime was widely supported in the press. For most of 1917 and 1918 she was isolated as never before or again. But she did not waver.

When the war ended she began at once to work for means to prevent another. Through the twenties she was constantly active in searching for ways in which women could cut across national lines in their work for peace. In 1931, in her seventy-first year, she received the Nobel Peace Prize—the second American to be so recognized. She died, full of honors, in 1935.

As for Johnny Powers, he had lived to a ripe old age and died in 1930, remaining alderman almost to the end, still fighting reform mayors, still protesting that he and Miss Addams were really friends, after all. From whichever department of the hereafter he ended up in, he must have looked down—or up—in amazement at the final achievements of his old enemy, who had been so little troubled by his insistence that there should be "no petticoats in politics."

. . . .

Original Narratives

The following are excerpts from the diary of Sydney and Beatrice Webb, both writers active in the socialist program in England. In 1898 they visited America and, among other things, investigated the government of Chicago. Municipal administration had a special attraction for Sydney because of his nineteen years of service on the London County Council. Beatrice describes former Governor Altgeld, Hull House, and Jane Addams. The account of the city council and the mayor was written by Sydney, whose less than favorable impression of Chicago may have been influenced by the fever and sore throat that hit him on his arrival in the city in early June and forced the Webbs to cancel much of their planned midwestern tour.

Chicago Diary

BEATRICE AND SYDNEY WEBB

Entry by Beatrice Webb

Lunched with Ex-Governor [John Peter] Altgeld, to whom Leonard Courtney gave us an introduction. Leonard had been sympathetic to the Bryan campaign and Altgeld was most anxious to be helpful.

The first impression of Altgeld when he called after dinner at the Zeublins was disappointing. A cross between a workman and a dissenting minister: I should have said if he had been English. In dress and general bearing a dissenting minister; in his slow literal speech a workingman unaccustomed to conversation. One expected

From *Beatrice Webb's American Diary, 1898*, ed. David A. Shannon (University of Wisconsin Press, 1963), pp. 100-109. Reprinted with the permission of the copyright owners, the Regents of the University of Wisconsin. Footnotes in the original have been omitted.

personal dignity and a certain "savoir faire" in a Governor who has made all America ring with his name.

When we lunched with him I listened to his account of his past life and of his political experiences, and watched his changing expression. A strong independent will and self-reticent manner; a man who is clearly not to be intimidated or put into the background by anyone. His mouth is firm, but his grey eyes have a curious visionary expression, a far off look as if he were always testing his opinions by some abstract reasoning. There is no American shrewdness, no quick perception of men; theory dominates his life and he is impatient of expediency. What makes him to my mind a dangerous ruler of men is the complete absence of tradition (inherited experience) and of science (present experience). He is a metaphysician and not a statesman.

We asked him about current American problems. All we could discover was a basis of Jeffersonian individualism and a superstructure of half accepted German Collectivism. He had no idea of an organic society, no vision of the need for the expert, or even for the representative. Any just man could administer justice; it was good for all citizens to take their turn at governing others; it was bad for any man to be too long in power, for power corrupted the heart of man. *Therefore* the cure for all American evils was the election of the judges of the Supreme Court by the whole people and for one term only. And they were to be ineligible for re-election! He believed every question could be settled by a guileless reference to some undisputed first principle to which all good men would agree. He was not the skilled brainworker: he was the skilled maker of things, brooding magnificently in his leisure about ultimate principles, speaking weighty words to his fellow workmen, exciting them to discontent.

. . . .

Entry by Sydney Webb

The government of Chicago, which as far as results are concerned, seems to reach the lowest depths of municipal inefficiency, is, in form, rather of an old type. The charter in force dates from 1870, though it has been much modified by special legislation. There is a single legislative council, of 68 "Aldermen" elected by 34 wards; and in this Council the Mayor presides (the only instance of this English practice that we have come across). But the Mayor seems to exercise no official influence in the Council. He does not, for instance, nominate the Committees, nor is he ex-officio or otherwise a member of them. (By exception, one special committee on the Elevation of Railroad Tracks, is always nominated by the Mayor, and he sits on it). The Mayor gets $10,000 a year ($7,000 down to 1897), and seems, for all his presiding over the Council, to fill the ordinary place of an American mayor, viz. the chief executive officer. He appoints all the heads of departments who are not directly elected (these latter are the Treasurer, City Clerk, City Attorney); and the principal officers so appointed (viz. the Commissioner of Public Works, the Corporation Counsel, Comptroller and Chief of Police) are said to form the Mayor's Cabinet.

. . . .

When we visited the Council we found the usual disorderly procedure—members smoking freely in spite of a Standing Rule expressly forbidding it; no agenda of any kind; everything read by a reading clerk; voting by call of ayes and nays and members rising to "explain their vote" after the vote had been taken: constant talking among the members, and between them and the visitors "on the floor;" and all the swinging of chairs, opening and shutting of desks, reading of newspapers and writing of letters that marks American public bodies from those at Washington downwards.

As we entered, "Bathhouse John" [John Coughlin], a saloon and private bathkeeper, and leading ward politician, was bawling at the top of his voice in Hyde Park style, reciting a flamboyant resolution denouncing any alliance between the U.S. and England on the ground that England had persistently oppressed all weaker nationalities from Ireland to the natives everywhere; that America had beaten her when America had but three millions of people, and had no need of her now that there were seventy millions; that they were not Anglo Saxons but Americans, and so forth. His claim of urgency for this resolution was lost on the vote, and it was, after another vote, referred to the Committee on the Judiciary! The whole thing was taken as a joke of Bathhouse John's.

It should be stated that the Council had got so far as to have distributed among the Aldermen a type-written list of the improvements they were to vote that evening (pavement, sewers etc. in various streets), and these were all voted en bloc without a word, each Alderman being allowed practically to put in the list whatever he pleased for his own ward.

These "improvements" (which with us would be the ordinary government) are charged, by way of special assessment, upon the owners of the property in the streets in question, and are not, in practice, even undertaken until a majority of the property owners along the street petition for them. Thus whether a Chicago street shall be paved or not, whether its sidewalks shall be of rotting planks or stone, whether its roadway shall be dirt, or wood, or brick or asphalt, is made to depend on a vote of the property owners, largely little property-owners, in the street affected, the vote being in all cases biassed by the feeling of the property-owners, not only that they will be mulcted in an indefinite sum for the "improvement," but also by the well-grounded suspicion that the Aldermen of the Ward and the Contractors will all get their picking out of the job. When a pavement wears out, as is constantly happening, the mere relaying of the pavement is deemed an "improvement" of this kind. Add to this the fact that it is usual to throw all the burden of keeping the pavement in repair on the Contractors for a long term, often five years; that the whole administration is so corrupt that no one sees that the Contractor lays the pavement decently in the first instance, still less dreams of enforcing his liability to keep in repair—and the reason why the Chicago pavements are bad becomes clear enough.

And the pavements are unspeakably bad! The sidewalks uneven and dilapidated even when of stone in the busy streets, are nothing but rotten planks in the slum streets, with great holes rendering it positively dangerous to walk in the dark. The roadways in the crowded business streets are, at best, of the roughest cobbles, most unevenly laid, with great holes and prominances. In the slum streets they are usually made of wood—not wood pavement as we know it, squared blocks on concrete—but merely round slices of tree-stems, placed on a dirt surface. This instantly wears uneven, and the unjoined circles of soft wood lie about loose on the mud. Imagine on sidewalks and roadways of this sort, the garbage and litter of some of the most crowded slums in the world, in an atmosphere as moist and as smoky as our Black Country towns, unswept, unwashed, untended from year's end to year's end. On the edge of the sidewalk are "garbage-boxes" large uncovered receptacles, loosely built of unjoined planks, for decaying vegetable matter, which is left to putrefy in the open air until the city's carts come round to empty it.

This utter inefficiency of municipal government so far as the streets are concerned is partly explained by the absurd state of the City's finances. The tax levied by the Council is limited by the Illinois State Constitution to 2 per cent of the assessed capital value of property. But the assessment is left to the tender mercy of one assessor, elected by the district which he assesses. As there are eight such districts in the city, and no check and no sort of machinery for keeping the districts level, each assessor does his best to keep his own district as low as possible, and usually reduces the total below what it was when he came in. The result of this competition of assessors as to which of them can bring his district down lowest, is that the valuation of Chicago to-day, with 1¾ million inhabitants, is less than it was in 1867, when the population was ¼ million. In the last six years, it has fallen by more than 10 per cent whilst the population has risen by over 25%. (This system is just being changed; a Board of Assessors to be elected by the whole city; with an appeal to a Board of Review, of three persons also elected by the whole city.)

The result is that the City Council and the Mayor can only levy about eight shillings per head in taxes for all their purposes. If it were not for the fact that they get nearly as much again from other sources,—mostly from saloon licenses—the City would be quite bankrupt. As it is, this City of 1¾ million inhabitants spends only £30,000 a year on street pavement repairs for all its 180 square miles, and only £120,000 a year on street cleaning.

The only decent municipal enterprise (beyond the Fire Department which is good in all American cities and may therefore be good even in Chicago), is the great system of parks and connecting boulevards. There are three Park Commissions, two appointed by the Governor of the State, and one by the Judges—the latter odd way of constructing a municipal body being said to produce the most efficient body. The parks are excellently laid out and kept, those on the South Side in particular, under the Judge-made Commission. This body carries to an extreme the principle of Direct Employment, even running successfully by its own servants, the park restaurants, where municipal ice-cream and other viands are sold. The boulevards between the parks are sometimes broad stretches of green with avenues sometimes merely an asphalted street through the heart of the city. Thus, Jackson Boulevard is only a street running from West Chicago to the Lake. It was handed over to the Park Commission, and accepted by them, merely as an expedient for getting it paved with asphalt, the necessary outburst of public opinion having been largely supplied by the bicyclists of Chicago. The expenses of the Park Commission are levied as an extra tax on the several districts graduated according to their assumed benefit.

. . . .

Entry by Beatrice Webb

On the Thursday, after our arrival at Chicago, we migrated from the attractive home of the Zeublins, surrounded by green lawns and avenues of trees, down to Hull House Settlement in the very heart of Chicago slums. Hull House itself is a spacious mansion, with all its rooms opening, American fashion, into each other. There are no doors, or, more exactly, no *shut* doors: the residents wander from room to room, visitors wander here, there and everywhere; the whole ground floor is, in fact, one continuous passage leading nowhere in particular. The courtyard, in front of the house, is always filled with slum children. At the back, opening out of the kitchen, is a rough and ready restaurant. There is the usual scanty service; the front door being answered by the resident who happens, at that time, to be nearest to it.

The residents consist, in the main, of strong-minded energetic women, bustling about their various enterprises and professions, interspersed with earnest-faced, self-subordinating and mild-mannered men who slide from room to room apologetically. One continuous intellectual and emotional ferment is the impression left on the visitor to Hull House.

Miss Jane Addams, the Principal, is without doubt a remarkable woman, an interesting combination of the organiser, the enthusiast and the subtle observer of human characteristics. Her article in the *International Journal of Ethics*—"Ethical Survivals in Municipal Corruption" is an exact analysis of the forces of Tammany organisation and its root in human nature. She has a charming personality, gentle and dignified, shrewdly observant: above all she excels in persistency of purpose and unflinching courage. She has made Hull House; and it is she who has created whatever spirit of reform exists in Chicago.

In the evening of our arrival we underwent a terrific ordeal. First an uncomfortable dinner, a large party served, higgledepiggledy. Then a stream of persons, labour, municipal, philanthropic, university, all those queer, well-intentioned or cranky individuals, who habitually centre round all settlements! Every individual among them must needs be introduced to us (a diabolical custom from which we have suffered greatly in America). Gradually the crowd pressed us into a large hall, with chairs for some hundreds and a small platform. From this place, Sidney and I were expected to orate to the assembly, on any topic we chose. We did our best and they were so far entertained, that they asked us innumerable questions.

For a right down exhausting business commend me to a dinner and a reception, preceding a lecture and a severe heckling. However, we seemed to give satisfaction.

The other days of our stay at Hull House are so associated in my memory with sore throat and fever, with the dull heat of the slum, the unappetising food of the restaurant, the restless movements of the residents from room to room, the rides over impossible streets littered with unspeakable garbage, that they seem like one long bad dream lightened now and again by Miss Addams' charming grey eyes and gentle voice and graphic power of expression. We were so completely done up that we settled "to cut" the other cities we had hoped to investigate, Omaha, St. Paul, Minneapolis and Madison; and come straight on here to the restful mountains.

. . . .

In contrast to the Webbs' disgruntled view of Chicago is the account written in 1896 by the English journalist George W. Steevens. That year he was sent to America by his newspaper, *The Daily Mail* of London, to report on the national political campaign between William McKinley and William Jennings Bryan. But Steevens was as much impressed with the vitality of American society, especially its urban life, as he was with its politics. Although he visited other cities, such as San Francisco and New York, Chicago was his favorite.

Land of the Dollar

GEORGE W. STEEVENS

Chicago! Chicago, queen and guttersnipe of cities, cynosure and cesspool of the world! Not if I had a hundred tongues, every one shouting a different language in a different key, could I do justice to her splendid chaos. The most beautiful and the most squalid, girdled with a twofold zone of parks and slums; where the keen air from lake and prairie is ever in the nostrils, and the stench of foul smoke is never out of the throat; the great port a thousand miles from the sea; the great mart which gathers up with one hand the corn and cattle of the West and deals out with the other the merchandise of the East; widely and generously planned with streets of twenty miles, where it is not safe to walk at night; where women ride straddlewise, and millionaires dine at mid-day on the Sabbath; the chosen seat of public spirit and municipal boodle, of cut-throat

From George W. Steevens, *The Land of the Dollar* (Edinburgh and London, 1897), pp. 144-52. Footnotes in the original have been omitted.

commerce and munificent patronage of art; the most American of
American cities, and yet the most mongrel; the second American
city of the globe, the fifth German city, the third Swedish, the
second Polish, the first and only veritable Babel of the age; all of
which twenty-five years ago next Friday was a heap of smoking
ashes. Where in all the world can words be found for this miracle of
paradox and incongruity?

Go first up on to the tower of the Auditorium. In front, near
three hundred feet below, lies Lake Michigan. There are lines of
breakwater and a lighthouse inshore, where the water is grey and
brown, but beyond and on either hand to the rim spreads the
brilliant azure of deep water—the bosom of a lake which is also a
sea shining in the transparent sunlight. White sails speckle its surface, and far out ocean-going steamers trail lazy streaks of smoke
behind them. From the Lake blow winds now soft and life-giving
like old wine, now so keen as to set every nerve and sinew on the
stretch. Then turn round and look at Chicago. You might be on a
central peak of the high Alps. All about you they rise, the mountains of building—not in the broken line of New York, but thick
together, side by side, one behind the other. From this height the
flat roofs of the ordinary buildings of four or five storeys are not
distinguishable from the ground; planting their feet on these rise the
serried ranks of the heaven-scaling peaks. You are almost surprised
to see no snow on them: the steam that gushes perpetually from
their chimneys, and floats and curls away on the lake breeze, might
well be clouds with the summits rising above them to the sun.
Height on height they stretch away on every side till they are lost in
a cloud of murky smoke inland. These buildings are all iron-cored,
and the masonry is only the shell that cases the rooms in them.
They can even be built downward. You may see one of them with
eight storeys of brick wall above, and then four of a vacant skeleton
of girders below; the superstructure seems to be hanging in air.
Broader and more massive than the tall buildings of New York,
older also and dingier, they do not appear, like them, simply boxes
of windows. Who would suppose that mere lumps of iron and bricks
and mortar could be sublime? Yet these are sublime and almost
awful. You have awakened, like Gulliver, in a land of giants—a land
where the very houses are instinct with almost ferocious energy and
force.

Then go out on the cable car or the electric car or the elevated
railroad—Chicago has them all, and is installing new ones with
feverish industry every day—to the parks and the boulevards. Along
Lake Shore Drive you will find the homes of the great merchants,

the makers of Chicago. Many of these are built in a style which is peculiarly Chicago's own, though the best examples of it are to be seen in the business centre of the city. It uses great blocks of rough-hewn granite, red or grey. Their massive weight is relieved by wide round arches for doors and windows, by porches and porticoes, loggias and galleries, over the whole face of the building from top to bottom. The effect is almost prehistoric in its massive simplicity, something like the cyclopean ruins of Mycenae or Tiryns. The great stones with the open arches and galleries make up a combination of solid strength and breeziness, admirably typical of the spirit of the place. On the other side of the Drive is the blue expanse of lake; in between, broad roads and ribbons of fresh grass. Yet here and there, among the castles of the magnates, you will come on a little one-storeyed wooden shanty, squatting many feet below the level of the road, paint and washed-out playbills peeling off it, and the broken windows hanging in shreds. Then again will come a patch of empty scrubby waste, choked with rank weeds and rubble. It is the same thing with the carriages in which the millionaires and their families drive up and down after church on Sunday. They are gorgeously built and magnificently horsed, only the coachman is humping his back or the footman is crossing his legs. These are trivialities, but not altogether insignificant. The desire to turn out in style is there, and the failure in a little thing betrays a carelessness of detail, an incapacity for order and proportion, which are of the essence of Chicago. . . .

It will be well worth your while again to go South to Washington Park and Jackson Park, where the World's Fair was held. Chicago, straggling over a hundred and eighty-six square miles, was rather a tract of houses than an organic city until somebody conceived the idea of coupling her up with a ring of parks connected by planted boulevards. The southern end of the system rests on the Lake at these two parks. Chicago believes that her parks are unsurpassed in the world, and certainly they will be prodigiously fine—when they are finished. Broad drives and winding alleys, ornamental trees, banks and beds of flowers and flowering shrubs, lakes and ornamental bridges, and turf that cools the eye under the fiercest noon—you bet your life Chicago's got 'em all. Also Chicago has the Art Building, which is the one remaining relic of the World's Fair, and surely as divinely proportioned an edifice as ever filled and satisfied the eye of man. And always beyond it is the Lake. Seeming in places almost to rise above the level of the land, it stretches along the whole western side, so that Chicago is perhaps the only one of the world's greatest cities that is really built along a sea-line.

Sparkling under the sun by day, or black beneath a fretwork of stars by night, it is a perpetual reminder that there is that in nature even greater and more immeasurable than the activities of Chicago.

. . . .

Chicago has a University hard by, which has come out westward, like Mahomet to the mountain, to spread the light among the twenty-five million souls that live within a morning's journey of Chicago. This University has not been in existence for quite five years; in that time it has received in benefactions from citizens of this place nearly twelve million dollars. Think of it, depressed Oxford and Cambridge—a University endowed at the rate of half a million sterling a-year! Two other prominent Chicago men found themselves in Paris a while ago, when a collection of pictures were being sold; promptly they bought up a hundred and eighty thousand dollars' worth for the gallery of their city. There is hardly a leading name in the business of the place but is to be found beneath a picture given or lent to this gallery. And mark that not only does the untutored millionaire buy pictures, but his untutored operative goes to look at them. It is the same impulse that leads school teachers of sixty to put in a course at the University during their summer vacation. Chicago is conscious that there is something in the world, some sense of form, of elegance, of refinement, that with all her corn and railways, her hogs and by-products and dollars, she lacks. She does not quite know what it is, but she is determined to have it, cost what it may. Mr. Phil D. Armour, the hog king, giving a picture to the gallery, and his slaughter-house man painfully spelling out the description of it on Sunday afternoon—there is something rather pathetic in this, and assuredly something very noble.

But there is another side to Chicago. There is the back side to her fifteen hundred million dollars of trade, her seventeen thousand vessels, and her network of ninety thousand miles of rail. Away from the towering offices, lying off from the smiling parks, is a vast wilderness of shabby houses—a larger and more desolate Whitechapel that can hardly have a parallel for sordid dreariness in the whole world. This is the home of labour, and of nothing else. The evening's vacancy brings relief from toil, the morning's toil relief from vacancy. Little shops compete frantically for what poor trade there is with tawdry advertisements. Street stretches beyond street of little houses, mostly wooden, begrimed with soot, rotting, falling to pieces. The pathways are of rickety and worm-eaten planks, such as we should not tolerate a day in London as a temporary gangway where a house is being built. Here the boarding is flush with the street; there it drops to it in a two-foot precipice, over which you might easily break your leg. The streets are quagmires of black mud, and no attempt is made to repair them. They are miserably lighted, and nobody thinks of illuminating them. The police force is so weak that men and women are held up and robbed almost nightly within the city limits; nobody thinks of strengthening it. Here and there is a pit or a dark cellar left wholly unguarded for the unwary foot-passenger to break his neck in. All these miles of unkempt slum and wilderness betray a disregard for human life which is more than half barbarous. If you come to your death by misadventure among these pitfalls, all the consolation your friends will get from Chicago is to be told that you ought to have taken better care of yourself. You were unfit; you did not survive. There is no more to be said about it.

The truth is that nobody in this rushing, struggling tumult has any time to look after what we have long ago come to think the bare decencies of civilisation. This man is in a hurry to work up his tallow, that man to ship his grain. Everybody is fighting to be rich, is then straining to be refined, and nobody can attend to making the city fit to live in. I have remarked several times before that America is everywhere still unfinished, and unless the character of the people modifies itself with time I do not believe it ever will be. They go half-way to build up civilisation in the desert, and then they are satisfied and rush forward to half-civilise some place further on. It is not that they are incapable of thoroughness, but that in certain things they do not feel the need of it. In Chicago there is added to this what looks like a fundamental incapacity for government. A little public interest and a small public rate would put everything right; both are wanting. Wealth every man will struggle for, and even elegance; good government is the business of nobody.

For if Chicago is the lodestone that attracts the enterprise and commercial talent of two hemispheres, it is also the sink into which drain their dregs. The hundred and twenty thousand Irish are not a wholesome element in municipal life. On the bleak west side there are streets of illiterate, turbulent Poles and Czechs, hardly able to speak a word of English. Out of this rude and undigested mass how could good government come? How could citizens combine to work out for themselves a common ideal of rational and ordered civic life? However, Chicago is now setting her house in order. It is thought a great step forward that there are now actually one-third of the members of the municipal body who can be relied upon to refuse a bribe. Some day Chicago will turn her savage energy to order and co-operation. Instead of a casual horde of jostling individuals she will become a city of citizens. She will learn that freedom does not consist solely in contempt for law. On the day she realises this she will become the greatest, as already she is the most amazing, community in the world.

. . . .

In the early 1900s, like today, the Chicago area received the greatest amount of attention from visitors to the Prairie State. Some travelers, however, have recognized that there was more to Illinois than Cook County. One such individual was the American journalist J. C. Burton, who in 1913 drove by car over the existing passable roads to the Rock River Valley. The following selection is his description of the towns and scenery in that part of the state at the end of the Progressive Era.

In Defense of Illinois

J. C. BURTON

Because the good roads enthusiast has sounded the slogan "Pull Illinois out of the mud," is the supposition correct that there are no highways winding through the fertile fields on which a speed of 20 miles an hour can be maintained without pounding a motor car to pieces and inviting Trouble to jump from Pandora's box to the bonnet of the machine? Are there no historic spots within the boundaries of this neglected state to warm the patriot's heart; no glens, no dells, no rippling streams to invite the admiration of the nature lover?

Crank up your car—if it is an early model and not equipped with a self-starter—and come with me on a journey of vindication. Leave Chicago, Phoenix city of energy consumed, behind and penetrate a region where the air is unpolluted by smoke, where the restful whir of mowers is heard instead of the wracking rattle of elevated trains, where ancient trails lead by fields of waving corn and bowed wheat.

It is late summer. The prairies are yellow with golden rod. The

From J. C. Burton, "In Defense of Illinois," *Motor/Age*, July 31, 1913. Footnotes in the original have been omitted.

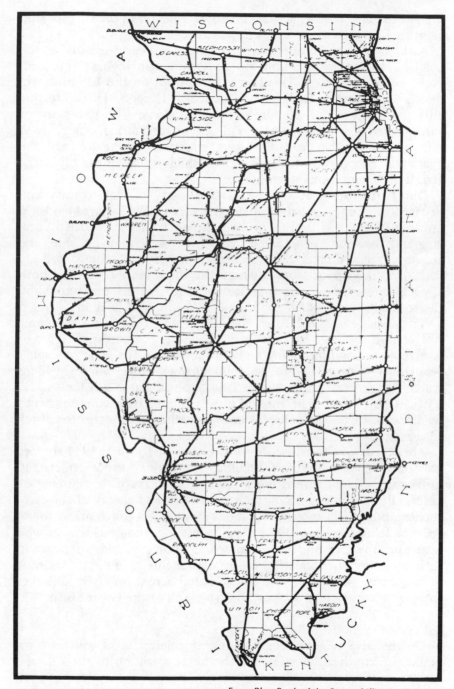

From *Blue Book of the State of Illinois, 1917-1918*

Illinois's proposed highway system, 1918

sky is blue and clear. There seems to be a nectar in the very air you breathe. Life is good on such a day as this.

With two exceptions—Louisiana and Delaware—Illinois is the most level state in the union, the government surveyors tell us, and they are truthful men. This fact is borne out on the 125-mile trip through aristocratic Rockford to peaceful Oregon. There are few hills to obstruct our 20-mile-an-hour progress. The roads are of hard-packed stone and gravel and excellent for touring, especially at this season of the year. For long stretches of the journey the overhanging branches of stately trees shield us from the blistering attack of an ambitious afternoon sun.

Our first stop is at Oregon, a small city of Ogle county and situated on the fertile banks of the Rock river. We have ridden for 6 hours—perhaps a trifle longer—and the air has been especially bracing and conducive to an appetite. We feel a vacuum amidships and are impetuous to enter the screened doors of a neat, quiet, orderly little inn, the Spoor House, where the unpretentious cuisine both appeals and satisfies. The appetite appeased, we are ready to enjoy the scenic beauties which abound in the vicinity of Oregon.

Two miles across the Rock river, in which a fiery sunset is being reflected, but visible for miles around stands an impressive figure of concrete—colossal, brooding and blanketed—on the crest of Eagle's Nest bluff, a mute but formidable sentinel which will keep silent watch for generations to come. This gigantic statue of Chief Blackhawk—it is 75 feet in height and was fashioned by the master hands of Lorado Taft—overlooks the most picturesque spot in the Rock river valley.

The statue of Chief Blackhawk was unveiled July 1, 1911, before an exclusive assembly of 500 sculptors, painters, authors, poets and millionaires. The figure is not a physical likeness of the famous Sac chief, ally of the English in the war of 1812 and enemy of the early settlers, but it is a most noble monument to an unrelentless foe, a redskin forced to don his war paint by unscrupulous whites who beat him, insulted him and encroached upon his fields of maize to ultimately conquer him after a year of slaughter and depredation. It is the statue of a stoic with arms folded across his chest and eyes looking into the great beyond, into the land of the Great Spirit.

. . . .

Oregon also is noted for its present celebrities as well as for a genius of another day, it being the nearest station to the Chicago artists' colony, where master and pupil, painter and sculptor, novelist and poet find inspiration, as did Margaret Fuller, in the winding river, green fields, rolling hills and forest of white pine. The colony, which is located on Eagle's Nest bluff, numbers among its members Lorado Taft, Charles Francis Brown, Ralph Clarkson and Hamlin Garland. Perched high on the thickly wooded bluff are the summer cottages where dwell the makers of masterpieces and the writers of best sellers. Pegasus now flaps his wings where the Indian pony once grazed. Easels are set up where the squaws of the Illini, Fox and Sacs pitched tepees for their painted braves.

Only a short distance from Eagle's Nest bluff is Congressman Frank O. Lowden's magnificent country estate of 5,000 acres, Sinnissippi farm. Here "Lowden's lawn mower"—the largest flock of Angora goats to be found in the middle west—moves over the prairie and trims the brush land. An inspiring view of the historic valley is to be obtained looking south from Castle rock, the winding river, dotted with islands and flanked by evergreen-covered bluffs, being visible for miles. Hemingway rocks form another one of the beauty spots in the vicinity of Sinnissippi farm.

Reluctantly leaving Oregon and the scenic beauties in the vicinity of Eagle's Nest bluff and driving down the river road for 11½ miles, we come to the little village of Grand Detour, an isolated hamlet 7 miles from a railroad station and very old as age is computed in Illinois. It was founded by the early French settlers and resembles a colonial town of New England with its towering elm trees, weathered stone houses and antique church where the great great-grandmothers of the present inhabitants, clad in rustling crinoline and wearing powdered wigs, went to worship.

It was in Grand Detour that the village blacksmith's assistant, John Deere, forged and welded the first steel plowshare ever made and freed the farmer from bondage to the clumsy wooden implement which Adam first fashioned to turn the sod.

The river bank, for a mile on either side of Grand Detour, is studded with cottages which are rented to motorists for week-end parties. Up and down the broad stream play the picturesque boats of the pearl fishers, for hunting for pearls is the leading industry of the quaint old town.

There are no hotels in Grand Detour. Hotels are too modern for a village of this kind. But there are two inns, the Sheffield and the Colonial, where the beaux and beauties of a century ago danced the Money Musk and minuet to the frantic bowing of the village fiddler. . . .

"There are many fine old houses in Dixon of a type built two generations ago when taste was classic and simple," writes a contemporary chronicler. "One is pointed out—a dilapidated, dejected-looking old structure with raw scars of a whilom verandah marring its front walls—as having been the once famous home of 'Governor'

Charters, 'Hazelwood.' These decaying walls once sheltered a hospitality so lavish, so all-embracing and ruinous that its owner died utterly poverty stricken, an object of charity. Many gay fetes champetres were given there with champagne flowing ad libitum and the 'governor' (I think the title was purely honorary) danced as lightly as air in spite of his 300 pounds. In his day, the saying was in Dixon, that after you cross the river to the north side, 'all roads lead to Hazelwood.' 'Governor' Charters may rest easy; Dixon is still celebrated for its hospitality as in romantic days of old."

Dixon's 300-acre public playground, Lowell park, is another link that binds the middle west to the east and the learned coterie of which Margaret Fuller was a member. When a brother of James Russell Lowell and his bride came west on a wedding trip they were so enchanted with the beauties of the Rock river valley that they purchased an estate on the shores of the winding stream with the intention of returning and building upon it. The Lowell mansion never was built, however, and at the death of the couple, their daughter gave the land to the city as a public park.

In connection with the popularity of the Rock river valley for touring, it is interesting to note that The Crusaders, a coterie of Chicago society people who have had an opportunity to tour America and Europe, and Friends of Our Native Landscape, a band of ardent nature lovers residing in the Illinois metropolis, have selected Oregon as the objective point in motor migrations this summer. The tourists were so charmed with the scenic beauties of Eagle's Nest bluff and Grand Detour that the services of Eames MacVeagh, the official guide of both organizations, are in constant demand for return visits.

Part II

MODERN ILLINOIS, 1920-1975

World War I veteran flyers selling airplane rides to fairgoers

Introduction

By the third decade of the twentieth century Illinois had clearly become one of the leading states in the Union. At the time of the centennial of its statehood in 1918, it numbered just under 6,500,000 inhabitants, more than a third of whom resided in Chicago. During World War I the state witnessed a spurt of industrial growth that produced a variety of manufacturers, especially in downstate cities. At the same time, Southern blacks migrated to growing metropolitan centers such as East St. Louis and Chicago, so that the latter's black population doubled in size from 1910 to 1920. Slums, already jammed with ethnic minorities, absorbed migrating blacks by the tens of thousands. Overcrowding became epidemic, unemployment commonplace, and vicious racial clashes more and more widespread.

Expansion and growth continued in the twenties. A revolution in transportation was taking place: electric railroads were added to the state's already bustling network of tracks and depots, and after them came the oil-powered diesel engine. To accommodate demands for modern roads for the new and increasingly popular automobile, the legislature passed a $60,000,000 bond issue to build 4,800 miles of hard-surfaced state highways. By 1930, with the steady support of three governors, Illinois's road system of 7,500 paved miles and its permanent constabulary of highway police had become one of the best in the nation. By that year the state was well into the automobile age, the first major step toward the modern era of suburbs, travel inns, distant vacations, traffic jams, expressways, and pollution. In addition, as Illinoisans became twentieth-century citizens, they saw their state develop into a crossroads of air transportation. Air travel had started just before World War I with the amateur pilots who participated in fairs, offered rides to the public at three dollars per person, and sometimes carried passengers from one city to another. Using planes produced for the war, Chicago became by 1920 the hub of an air mail service that ranged from New York to San Francisco and from

Minneapolis to New Orleans. By 1926 this service to and from the Windy City included four separate airlines. And the following year "Big Bill" Thompson dedicated the Chicago Municipal Airport, thereby officially beginning air service for both the mails and public passengers.

Everything flourished in Illinois during the 1920s—including crime and violence. Prohibition officially arrived on the seventeenth of January, 1920; and stepping in to fulfill the unquenchable and illegal demand for liquor was Alphonse Capone—"Scarface" Al as he was known—who applied the technique of syndicated crime inherited from "Big Jim" Colosimo and Johnny Torrio, all under the benevolent toleration of Chicago's Mayor Thompson. Gangland profits from supplying thirsty Chicagoans were enormous—tenfold in beer alone; the business peaked in 1927 at an estimated gross income of $110,000,000 going to the syndicate. Accompanying the illegal business were assassinations, torture, payoffs, and bribes, all used to accumulate and hold new gangland territories. Although Chicago mobsters did sell liquor to downstate bootleggers, that trade was carried on cautiously and at the exclusive risk of downstaters. This liquor traffic was sufficient to arouse the ire of the Ku Klux Klan, which used murder and threats of murder to suppress the booze trade and, in general, to harass Italians and other "foreigners."

Despite the ugliness of gangland violence and the illegal trade in alcohol, the 1920s was still the "prosperity decade" for Illinois. Then, in the autumn of 1929, progress halted and prosperity rapidly disappeared. For more than a decade Illinoisans were, to use an expression of the day, in for "hard times." The Great Depression, like the cold lake fog, crept in on the Prairie State. Within one year following the stock market crash, thirty per cent of the state's work force—about 700,000 individuals—was unemployed. The proportion was even higher in the Chicago area and in the downstate mining regions. And as the early efforts at relief by the state legislature proved inadequate, things went from bad to worse. Bank after bank folded and finally, on Inauguration Day, 1933, all of the banks in the state were closed by order of the governor. The Chicago Board of Trade shut its doors on the same day. By the winter of 1933 the Depression had bottomed out: a million-and-a-half people were unemployed, with one person out of seven in Chicago alone walking the streets looking for work.

Even though the federal government was by then pouring more relief money into Illinois than Pennsylvania and New York combined, it was not enough to meet the needs of families whose breadwinner was out of a job. This difficulty was further com-

Courtesy of the Illinois State Historical Library

The Saint Valentine's Day Massacre

pounded by the fact that over one-third of the unemployed were ineligible for federal relief because they could not demonstrate that the family's resources had been completely exhausted. Governor Horner accurately assessed the situation when he said that Illinois would have to augment the relief program with new state taxes. He pushed a special sales tax bill through the legislature and suspended the state property tax to aid farmers. Next he persuaded the legislature to pass a relief bond issue redeemable by a tax on gasoline. With the repeal of prohibition, a tax on the sale of liquor added another source of revenue for both the state and its municipalities. But even these efforts on the part of the state were insufficient to alleviate the Depression. Unemployment continued, and in some areas outbreaks of labor unrest occurred. A split in the ranks of Illinois miners over allegiance to John L. Lewis' United Mine Workers or to the Progressive Mineworkers of America resulted in pitched battles, which eventually required calling out the National Guard. In the Chicago area, the picketing of the Republic Steel plant by steelworkers precipitated a riot with the police. Sit-down strikers occupied the Fansteel Manufacturing Company for nine days, only to be forced out by tear gas and arrested.

Hope for ending the Depression in Illinois appeared only when the prospects for war in Europe increased. In 1938, with the demands for war materiel mounting, Illinoisans returned to work to build tanks and armaments. After Pearl Harbor the defense effort, in a flood of federal contracts, demanded rapid industrial expansion. Farm production, aided by scientific improvements in fertilizers and insecticides, also boomed. An indication of the extent to which the war pulled Illinois out of the Depression was the list of the unemployed: only 214,712 workers were on relief in 1945, compared to one million in 1939. Stimulated by the economic advance, prices inflated over thirty per cent, until they were placed under the control of the Office of Price Administration.

The postwar years saw continued growth in production. By mid-century Illinois was the third largest state in the nation in industrial output. The value of raw materials used in industry increased threefold—to $2,100,000,000 between 1939 and 1947. By then the state ranked fourth in the nation in population; and in 1970 it was still holding its own as the fifth most populous state. Although half of its citizens were living in Chicago and Cook County, recent demographic studies have shown a movement out of that region to downstate counties. Nevertheless, the urban problems of an earlier day continued: overcrowded slums, high taxes, and pollution. Then, with the widening American commitment in Southeast Asia during the 1960s, Illinoisans, like other Americans, became polarized in their feelings toward the war. The dissension exploded into violence in 1968 at the Chicago Democratic Convention, and under orders from Mayor Daley, parts of the city were, for the moment, turned into armed camps. However, Chicago, cocky as ever under Daley's leadership, confidently plunged forward with ambitious plans for urban development, symbolized in a building program that gave the city three of the tallest skyscrapers in the world. As Illinoisans moved into the last quarter of the twentieth century, they remained convinced that, with the Prairie State's abundant natural sources, crucial location in the center of the nation's transporation system, and steadily growing population, its future would be as successful as had been its past.

1: Prohibition Era

Despite a temporary recession, which resulted from the reconversion of the state's economy from war to peacetime, the decade of the twenties began with booming prosperity. George Soule, in selections from his 1947 study of Illinois between 1917 and 1929, believes that there were circumstances unique to the state which enabled it to adjust so quickly and easily to the ending of the war and to develop an economic plant of steadily increasing productivity. Soule, a graduate of Yale University, was the editor of the *New Republic* until 1946. He also was professor of economics at Bennington College, Colgate University, and the University of Tennessee. A prolific writer on economics and American history until his death in 1970, his most recent publications are *Economics: Measurements, Theories, Case Studies* (New York, 1967) and *Planning: U.S.A.* (New York, 1967). Illinois was not only unique in its economic situation in the twenties; it was also the location of a special cultural awakening known as the "Chicago Renaissance." Having its origins before World War I, it blossomed in the third-decade literary achievements of writers like Carl Sandburg, Vachel Lindsay, and Edgar Lee Masters. Bernard Duffey analyzes Sandburg in a selection from his *The Chicago Renaissance in American Letters: A Critical History* (East Lansing, 1954). The son of a Swedish blacksmith, Sandburg's career progressed from work as a teenage bootblack to that of a wartime newspaper correspondent, to editor of *Poetry Magazine of Verse* and biographer of Lincoln. Duffey picks up Sandburg's work at about 1907, when he moved to Chicago to become the associate editor of the magazine *The Lyceumite*. Bernard Duffey is a professor of English at Duke University. In addition to two monographs on twentieth-century poetry and literature, he has written "Humor Chicago Style" for *The Comic Imagination in America* (New Brunswick, N.J., 1973). But the twenties also had a seamy side: bootlegging, vice, gangland violence, and scandal pockmarked the decade. This tone was set for the prohibition era at the very beginning of the twenties, when it was learned that eight players of the Chicago White Sox had conspired with gamblers to fix the 1919 World Series with the Cincinnati Reds. Lewis Thompson and Charles Boswell tell the full story of the mysterious "Black Sox" Scandal in "Say It Ain't So, Joe!" published in the June 1960 issue of *American Heritage*. Thompson and Boswell, free-lance writers, collaborated on a number of books, mostly mystery novels, prior to Thompson's death in 1972. In 1955 they were awarded an "Edgar" by the Mystery Writers of America in recognition of "general excellence in the field of true crime writing."

Special Accounts

The Postwar Boom

GEORGE SOULE

When the armistice was signed on November 11, 1918, there were 4 million men in the armed services and 9 million persons, or about one fourth of the civilian labor force, engaged in war industries. Few in authority had given any serious thought to the problems of demobilization or to the reconversion of industry to civilian demands. The eyes of almost everybody were on Europe and the future peace terms. Dollar-a-year men in Washington rose from their desks, locked the doors of their offices, and went to Florida for a vacation before resuming their peacetime jobs. On November 12, the day after the German surrender, the telephone wires from Washington were overburdened with calls canceling contracts. The War Department had $6 billion worth of contracts outstanding, of which one third had already been completed. Considerably more than half of the remainder were canceled within four weeks. These orders for cessation of production usually included no more relief than allowance for a month's further operation at the current rate. Two days after the armistice the War Industries Board began to end price control. Within little more than a month no more priority orders were issued. Early in December, Congress instructed the United States Housing Corporation to stop work on all buildings not more than 70 per cent completed. Some Washington offices closed so suddenly that the executives had to lend money to the stenographers to get home.

Demobilization and Boom

Although somewhat more moderation was exercised by the Army in returning soldiers to civilian life, the demand to go home

From George Soule, *Prosperity Decade, from War to Depression, 1917-1929* (New York, 1947), pp. 81-85, 110-114, 121-125. Copyright © 1947 by George Soule. Footnotes in the original have been omitted.

was so strong that 600,000 men were released almost immediately, and by April of the following year nearly 2 million had been discharged. Monthly releases from the Army averaged over 300,000, and almost the entire force had been demobilized a year after the armistice.

In October, 1918, the War Department Committee on Classification of Personnel, in cooperation with the War Labor Policies Board, had begun to draw up plans for demobilization of the armed forces. In order to effectuate a smooth transition, it was the policy of these agencies, approved by Secretary of War Baker, to discharge first those men trained for jobs in which vacancies existed and to minimize unemployment by holding in the Army those who would be unlikely to find jobs when they came out. The Chief of Staff, however, ordered that the Army be demobilized by military units without regard to employment possibilities. The policy favored by Secretary Baker would in any case have encountered strong popular disapproval, since almost every soldier wished to doff his uniform as soon as possible and his family wanted to have him home.

The War Industries Board attempted to plan for the placement of returned soldiers, but failed to elicit the necessary information from employers. The task was then delegated to the United States Employment Service, which placed representatives in every army camp and set up special bureaus for veterans in towns and cities throughout the country, to coordinate local and voluntary bodies like the Red Cross and the Y.M.C.A. But Congress, in January, 1919, at a time when it was placing 150,000 men a week, curtailed the appropriation for the Employment Service by 80 per cent. Many of its staff then volunteered to work without pay, and it appealed for private funds to go on with the job. The agency managed to continue with 490 offices out of the 750 that had previously existed. On July 1, Congress appropriated enough more for it to continue until October on a still smaller scale. Eventually, the whole function was turned over to an unofficial Emergency Committee on Employment for Soldiers and Sailors, which sent boy scouts to employers to ask them to promise to rehire servicemen, and attempted to suppress peddling and panhandling by unemployed men in uniform.

A large federal program of public works had been advocated to stimulate employment after the war, but Congress made no appropriation for the purpose. A conference of governors and mayors, which President Wilson called to ask them to undertake more local building, met in Washington, March 3-5, 1919, but because of the lack of federal stimulation, the local governments did not respond to this appeal. The public works division of the Department of

Labor set in motion a "Build-Your-Own-Home" publicity campaign. The Emergency Committee on Employment inaugurated a
"spruce-up" drive to urge people to make necessary repairs to their
houses. The net result of all these activities was a construction
index that in 1919 was 11 per cent below the prewar level of
1910-1913. The only effectual governmental aid for returned soldiers was a plan sponsored by Secretary of the Interior Franklin K.
Lane to settle them on reclaimed farmland, but this opportunity
was necessarily narrowly limited.

Why, in these circumstances, did not the country at once experience a severe crisis of unemployment? It is true that production fell
sharply in the last quarter of 1918 and in the first few months of
1919. Unemployment was reported from numerous sections of the
country, but because no statistical measurement of it existed at the
time, nobody knows exactly how great it was. It is estimated that in
February, 1919, the total was 3 million. In spite of lack of any
advance provision for these eventualities, however, production and
employment turned upward in the second quarter of 1919 and a
boom followed that lasted well into 1920. Some would now call
this recovery sheer good luck, in so far as it was wholesome at all.
Others might allege that it gave testimony to the recuperative
powers of private enterprise when government controls were removed.

. . . .

A factor diminishing unemployment was that two or three million persons had been drawn into war industry who did not desperately need jobs and who retired from wage earning when the war
was over. Among these were many women, and persons from
agricultural regions who could go back and live on the farm.
Moreover, most industries did not have a difficult technical job in
turning back their plants and machinery to civilian production,
while there was still a considerable amount of civilian purchasing
power available to buy the goods that they could make. Automobile production, for instance, began to increase again. Output of
passenger cars, which in 1917 had been 1,750,000—the highest
volume in history—had during 1918 dropped to less than a million.
In 1919 it came back again to 1,650,000 and in 1920 was
1,900,000. Returned soldiers bought civilian clothing and so increased activity in the clothing and textile industries.

Consumers' demand for goods that had been scarce during the
war was probably not, however, an important factor in the boom.
Civilians had been deprived of relatively few goods and only for a
short period. Many of the shortages occurred in perishable com-

modities like food or coal for heating, and these cannot subsequently be made up. At that time, with the sole exception of automobiles, there had not developed a large market for consumers' durable goods such as electric refrigerators and other mechanical household equipment, while radios had not been offered for sale; hence the war economy had demanded little cessation in the output of such commodities. Furniture and house furnishings do not wear out in the space of less than two years, and the demand for them depends to a great extent on the construction of new houses, which was still at a low level.

. . . .

Why Production Expanded

What, then, was the reason why production began to expand again in 1922? Clearly it was not because prices as a whole had fallen to any mathematically "correct" level. It is true that, partly because of their fall, the gold reserve had now become more than sufficient, and the reserve ratio had risen to a point where credit could be freely extended. But this was a passive rather than an active factor. Money is not always borrowed just because it is available. The borrower must expect that he can make profitable use of money before he will pay the interest on a loan. What was it that gave businessmen this assurance? In part, the drastic fall of prices may have provided what is called by economists a "psychological motive," since businessmen shared the general belief that when prices had fallen sufficiently recovery was certain to come. Nevertheless, no one of them could be sure the bottom had been reached until after an upturn of prices had actually occurred. Some more specific influence must have been at work.

The stimulus, whatever it was, must be sought in the private sector of the economy. The excess of governmental expenditures over receipts had been replaced by an excess of receipts over expenditures. No more public loans were being made to foreign governments; indeed, by this time these governments had begun to pay back interest and principal. Since the Treasury had ceased flotation of bonds on a large scale, there was no longer any impulse from this source leading to the expansion of bank loans to private borrowers. Nor had the new administration introduced positive measures of any kind to aid recovery or relieve unemployment, if one excepts removal of the excess-profits tax. Its avowed purpose was to withdraw as far as possible from exerting any influence on the economic life of the country except the encouragement that might be derived from a balanced budget and nonintervention with private enterprise. Although the standard Republican prescription for prosperity, the protective tariff, had been administered, it was incapable of producing recovery because there had been little competition from imports.

In the area of private enterprise itself, no important stimulus came from outside the country. While some effects of European reconstruction and relief expenditures was still being felt, and while a trickle of private credits flowed to foreign purchasers, the value of exports continued at about the same low level they had reached in 1921. In sum, an economic order that for about six years had largely been nourished by orders from abroad and huge governmental spending by the United States was now left to its own devices.

There is good ground for believing that the turning point was marked by nothing more substantial than changes that had taken place in figures on the books of business concerns. At the beginning of the deflation, many a manufacturing or distributing company had found itself in the following position: It had a large stock of goods on hand bought at high prices. While prices fell and this inventory was either being sold at a loss or revalued at the lower current prices, the mere change in value turned up on the books as an operating deficit. It therefore looked as if production and trade were unprofitable. Nevertheless, all through the period of deflation, there was a sufficient margin between the prices of materials and the prices of finished products so that the company in question could have made a profit on the purchase and sale of new goods at any given moment. When the inventory losses had been absorbed and the loans on the inventories had been liquidated, the possibilities of profit-making in current production and trade became clear. They had existed all the time, but had been obscured by the fog of accounting and credit symbolism.

The size of the incubus that was rolled off the back of the business order may be judged by the estimate that during 1919 the value of business inventories had been increased by $6 billion, or nearly four times as much as that of any other single year in the ensuing decade except 1923. Of this increase about $4 billion was due to a growth in the actual quantity of goods on hand and $2 billion to the mere rise in prices. These figures were enhanced in the early months of 1920 and then underwent a rapid reduction after the speculative boom cracked. Observation of this phenomenon has led many economists to describe the period as one of inventory boom and depression.

The question may be asked how businessmen could be sure, even though there was a sufficient margin of profit on each unit of production, that the goods could be sold. Doubtless they had little assurance except the perennial hope that rises in the breast of the seeker after profit. Nevertheless, at this time a number of substantial factors made certain the fulfillment of the hope. Study of economic statistics over a long period of years shows that consumers' demands, especially for perishable goods, are remarkably stable, varying less than any other element in the economy, even between full prosperity and extreme depression. Because of unemployment, wage reductions, and the difficulties of the farmers, the dollar volume of consumers' spending, of course, dropped somewhat during the depression. It did not, however, drop so rapidly as the prices of the goods that consumers bought. Actual expenditures by consumers fell, it is estimated, from $62.9 billion in 1920 to $56.1 billion in 1921, or about 11 per cent. They remained about at this level in 1922. When, however, the effect of price changes is taken into consideration, and these spendings are expressed in terms of dollars of constant value (1929 = 100), there was an increase of $3.7 billion from 1920 to 1921 and a further increase of $3.2 billion from 1921 to 1922. In the latter year, consumers were buying a volume of goods and services more than 12 per cent larger than at the peak of the postwar boom. The purchasing power flowing into the retail markets from consumers thus constituted a steadily increasing reinforcement to the profit possibilities noted by businessmen.

One important element in this increase of purchasing power has previously been noted. During the deflation, wage rates had fallen less than the cost of living. For every hour's work, therefore, the average wage earner could now buy more than he had been able to purchase at any time during the war or the postwar boom. As production was resumed and the total hours of employment increased, a sharply augmented total of purchasing power in the hands of the wage earners sustained the advance. Thus the business community now profited from the resistance labor had offered to wage reductions when employers had been arguing that drastic reductions were necessary in order to stimulate recovery.

The average annual earnings of employed wage earners in terms of constant purchasing power (1914 = 100), according to Paul Douglas, was 8 percent above the base year in 1921, 13 per cent above in 1922, and 19 per cent above in 1923. During the next two years, the figure remained about at this level and then increased again, reaching 32 per cent above in 1928.

Aside from this increased consumer buying, the major factor adding to the stream of purchasing power was the revival of residential construction. A good estimate of the amount spent in this way indicates an increase of slightly more than $1 billion between 1921 and 1922. Every factor was favorable: the price of materials had fallen, rents still remained relatively high, plenty of money was available for mortgages, the labor supply was abundant, and a severe housing shortage was still to be made up. At the time, construction was the only outlet for savings, in which a considerable expansion occurred. Business construction increased between 1921 and 1922 only about $500 million. There was an actual reduction between these years in the investment in other producers' durable goods, as well as in inventories and the foreign balance. The government, of course, was paying off loans instead of borrowing. In subsequent years, savings found an outlet not only in residential building but in capital investments of business as well, and the building boom remained a powerful factor of expansion for five years.

The federal reserve index of value of construction contracts awarded (1923-1925 = 100) rose steadily from 56 in 1921 to 135 in 1928. A similar index of residential construction increased from 44 to a temporary peak of 124 in 1925, dropped slightly in the next two years, and finally attained its high point for the period at 126 in 1928.

. . . .

Rapid Advance in Productivity

A development of critical importance in this period was a great gain in efficiency of production. For the decade between 1919 and 1929 the output per person employed, as well as the output per man-hour, increased with unusual rapidity. In manufacturing, the index of number of wage earners per unit of output was reduced from 84 in 1919 to 51 in 1929. The man-hours per unit fell in the same period from an index number of 74 to 42, or by 43 per cent (1899 = 100). There was little or no increase in productivity during the war. Immediately after it, however, immense gains were made, the index of man-hours per unit falling from 74 in 1919 to 55 in 1922, or by 26 per cent. Gains continued in the following years at a more moderate rate (see table below).

Increases in productivity were also registered in mining, in transportation, and even in agriculture. On steam railroads employment per unit of product decreased from 124 in 1919 to 100 in 1929. The index of the number of gainfully occupied per unit of product in agriculture fell from 84 in 1919 to 67 in 1929 (1900 = 100). The number of hours worked weekly did not fall as in manufacturing, and therefore the output per man-hour did not show such striking gains as in factories.

INDEXES OF EMPLOYMENT PER UNIT OF OUTPUT

Year	Manufacturing (1899 = 100)		Agriculture (1900 = 100) Gainfully Occupied	Railroads (1929 = 100) Man-Days	Mining (1929 = 100) Man-Days
	Wage Earners	Man-Hours			
1919	84	74	84	124	135
1920	78	67	83	120	128
1921	74	61	82	130	130
1922	64	55	81	119	119
1923	65	56	79	114	116
1924	64	53	76	114	118
1925	59	50	74	108	112
1926	57	48	71	105	112
1927	55	47	70	106	108
1928	53	44	68	102	103
1929	51	42	67	100	100

Source: Solomon Fabricant, *Labor Savings in American Industry, 1899-1939* (New York: National Bureau of Economic Research, 1945), pp. 43, 44, 45, 46, 50.

The first effect of an increase in efficiency is to reduce unit labor costs. The gain may be retained by the employer as a larger margin of profit. It may also be utilized either to pay higher wages or to reduce selling prices, or to do both at once. Increase of wages serves to enlarge the purchasing power of the wage earners, while reduction of prices naturally augments the purchasing power of all consumers. Thus the manufacturer may, through larger volume of sales, gain more in aggregate profits than he loses by cutting his widened profit margin.

If output and sales do not increase or do not increase rapidly enough, gains in productivity are likely to result in reduced employment. If the technical gains, however, are rapidly translated into increased production and sales, employment may not suffer or may even increase.

The nature and effects of the productive advances of this period will be considered in greater detail in subsequent chapters. Here it is sufficient to point out what actually happened to wages, consumers' purchasing power, employment, and the reward of capital in the aggregate.

In the accompanying table the figures for employee compensation include the effect of both the changes in wages and salaries and the changes in volume of employment, for all occupations in the country. They reveal a considerable advance during the recovery

DISTRIBUTION OF INCREASED PRODUCT, 1923-1929

Year	Employee Compensation (Million dollars)	Cost-of-Living Index	Consumers' Outlay (Billion dollars)	No. of Employees (Thousands)	Property Income (Million dollars)	Dividends (Million dollars)
1922	37,003	97.7	56.1	28,585	11,925	2,962
1923	43,339	99.5	63.0	31,351	13,211	3,745
1924	43,323	99.8	66.2	31,068	13,818	3,683
1925	45,019	102.4	66.8	31,680	14,469	4,270
1926	48,017	103.2	72.3	33,121	14,565	4,615
1927	48,433	101.2	71.9	33,201	15,065	4,918
1928	49,361	100.1	74.3	33,394	15,707	5,344
1929	52,214	100.0	77.2	35,059	16,822	6,117

Source: Kuznets, *National Income and Its Composition*, pp. 314, 145, 137, 318, 316.

from 1922 to 1923 and then a slower growth to the peak of 1929, the gain for the entire period being about 40 per cent. The dollars received changed little in their purchasing value throughout the period, as is shown by the cost-of-living index, which rose slightly, with a bulge in the middle of the decade. The figures for consumers' outlay include what was spent not only by employees, but also by all other members of the population. They exclude, however, that part of their incomes which people saved, as the figures for employee compensation do not. They indicate a rise in consumers' purchases for the period of slightly more than 37 per cent. The totals for numbers of employees offer a rough guide as to how much of the growth in employee compensation was due to expansion of the number employed. This gain was about 23 per cent, as compared with the 40 per cent increase in total compensation. The gain in earnings per capita was, thus, approximately 15 per cent.

Property income includes dividends, interest, and rent, as well as that part of the income of individual enterprisers which is not attributed to payment for their labor. Farmers, of course, bulked largely in this latter category. It shows a gain of something over 41 per cent, or slightly more than the gain in employee compensation. It should be remembered, however, that this total income was divided among a number of people which probably did not increase markedly during the period, as did the number of employees. While the number of stockholders grew, the number of farmers declined. The number of individual enterprisers grew about 5 per cent.

The column for dividends, which shows the gains in current income registered by the owners of corporations, takes no account of that part of the profits retained by corporations in surplus accounts. The total of dividends paid grew in the period by slightly over 100 per cent. Obviously, the corporation owners were the greatest winners from the increase in productivity. It is unlikely that their numbers increased more rapidly than those employed.

Wholesale prices reached their high point for the period in 1925 and then declined for the next two years. Though the decline was relatively moderate, the experience of an expansion of production while prices were falling was so unfamiliar that business spokesmen complained that this was a time of "profitless prosperity." Apparently investors and speculators did not regard it as profitless, however, because the stock market enjoyed a heavy increase in transactions during most of the period and the averages of stock prices had a rising trend.

In addition, the growth of profits led to a change in the methods of financing business. Many companies, especially the larger ones, accumulated enough working capital so that they financed themselves instead of resorting to borrowing, and the commercial loans extended by the banks declined. This development was, of course, accompanied by a corresponding retardation in the expansion of demand deposits. Business kept its surplus cash in time deposits,

A view of Chicago's Michigan Avenue in 1920

Courtesy of the Illinois State Historical Library

which grew almost three times as much as demand deposits between 1924 and 1927. Thus bank resources were released for collateral loans on securities, and these grew 40 per cent during the three years. This development facilitated activity in the stock market.

Agricultural Distress

The prosperity of the industrial sectors of the community was not shared by the agricultural regions. It is true that the city populations increased their purchases of food, particularly of the higher grades, such as milk and other dairy products, fresh vegetables, fruit, and the better cuts of meat. This did not bring much relief to the growers of the great staples like grain and cotton. When standards of living rise above a certain point, individuals eat less bread rather than more. There was no permanent revival of the foreign markets for these crops. The average of farm prices, which had been more than double the 1913 level at the peak of the postwar boom, fell to only 16 per cent above it in 1921; although it rose slightly thereafter, it did not register a net gain of more than 10 per cent during the years of economic expansion. The prices received by farmers for their crops remained low in relation to the prices they had to pay for what they bought. In 1921, the relation of these prices was such that a farmer selling the same amount of produce that he had sold in 1913 could buy only three fourths as much with the proceeds. In 1922, he was still at a disadvantage of about 19 per cent. Although the disparity narrowed in subsequent years, it did not disappear during the whole period of industrial prosperity.

Meanwhile, mortgage debts incurred during the years of high prices were slowly and painfully being liquidated. The more fortunate farmers succeeded in retaining their property while paying the necessary charges, but a large acreage passed under the control of banks, insurance companies, and other mortgage holders.

The plight of the farmers was not, however, one of unrelieved gloom. The purchasing power of the money received for a single bushel of wheat or a bale of cotton does not tell the whole story of agricultural welfare. Output of the farms steadily increased, while the number of those engaged in agriculture slowly declined, so that there was more income to be divided among a smaller number of persons. The index of agricultural output (1900 = 100) rose from 126 in 1920-1921 to 144 in 1929, while the index of those gainfully occupied fell from 104 to 97. Farmers did, therefore, benefit from the general increase in productivity.

Sandburg and the Chicago Renaissance

BERNARD DUFFEY

In 1907 [Carl Sandburg] settled in Chicago as an associate editor of *The Lyceumite,* the magazine of the International Lyceum and Chautauqua Association. The organization which he had joined descended in a straight line from the New England Lyceum of the early century and so continued in its way that optimistic and liberal effort toward moral uplift and the establishment of vision as an essential. He addressed the convention of the association in 1908 on Whitman and made Lyceum dates speaking on the same subject. How far his poetry had progressed by this time is not known, but with these explicit references to Whitman one can guess that its final ingredient, a commitment to the free verse as well as the free thought and sympathy of the older poet, was completed.

During 1907 or 1908 Sandburg met Winfield R. Gaylord, a state organizer for the Social Democratic party, and in the latter year he became a professional party worker. This connection, which he maintained until his second move to Chicago in 1912, represented a sudden but thorough focusing of all his earlier interests. The hitherto diffused lines of his life were drawn together in what was far more a vocation than a job. He had his living, in part, from the Socialists, he took his wife, Lillian Steichen, from their ranks in 1908, and he performed the work they gave him to do. As he had become part of a dedicated and idealistic group, these qualities could not help but affect his own life at its roots.

The Socialism he espoused was, among members of the left generally, regarded as a conservative variety. It had been born in 1897 out of a union between the remnants of Eugene Debs' American Railway Union and the Cooperative Commonwealth and was headed by Debs and the Milwaukee Socialist leader, Victor Berger—the only man ever to be elected to Congress by any Socialist group. Much of its strength lay in the Chicago and Milwaukee areas.

. . . .

Concurrently with Sandburg's Socialist activities began also his regular work as a newspaper writer which was to continue without major interruption until 1932. Its general tone echoed his political interests. Indeed, two of the papers for which he worked were avowedly Socialist, and his writing for the others was apt to be on

From Bernard Duffey, *The Chicago Renaissance in American Letters* (East Lansing, Michigan: Michigan State University Press, 1956), pp. 212-222. Reprinted by permission.

Courtesy of the Illinois State Historical Library

Carl Sandburg

subjects connected with labor and industry. After moving to Chicago in 1912 he had an odd lot of alliances including E. W. Scripps'
Day Book, an early experiment in tabloid journalism without advertising, a business efficiency paper called *System*, and the *National
Hardware Journal*. But in 1918 he made a connection with the
Daily News which lasted until 1932 and which confirmed his place
in the Chicago renaissance.

His first introduction to that force had come in 1914 with
Poetry's publication of his "Chicago Poems," which was also his first

appearance in a major literary magazine. He had mailed a group of his verses headed by the famous "Chicago," to the *Poetry* office where they were opened by Harriet Monroe's assistant, Alice Henderson, and thence passed on to the editor herself. For Harriet the poem's first impression was that of shock, but she recovered in time to give the group the lead position in her March issue projecting Sandburg thus into the midst of the Chicago renaissance. He was from his first appearance a cynosure of admiration and, thanks to his deliberate and inward personal manner, of some awe. Edgar Lee Masters wrote excitedly to Dreiser in April, "Next Monday I am going for a tramp to the sand dunes with a Swede bard. He is a new find and I think has the right fire." And Sandburg's importance to the Liberation, if it needed confirming, was sealed by an attack from the *Dial* upon him and upon *Poetry* in its subsequent issue. "We have always sympathized with Ruskin," wrote its critic, "for the splenetic words about Whistler that were the occasion of the famous suit for libel, and we think that such an effusion as the one now under consideration is nothing less than an impudent affront to the poetry-loving public." By this last phrase the *Dial* perhaps had in mind such a public as that constituted by The Little Room. If so, its conclusions were correct. "Chicago" was an act of war.

By 1916 Sandburg had accumulated enough verse to make a volume, *Chicago Poems,* and again it was Alice Corbin Henderson who served as mediatrix. She interested Alfred Harcourt, then representing Henry Holt and Co., in Sandburg, and Harcourt in turn persuaded his firm to take on publication of the book. What *Chicago Poems* achieved was of a double kind, success and failure, but the two poles were not absolute in particular poems. These latter ranged over every possible level of the romantic spectrum, from the concreteness of imagism to avowedly cosmic affirmations without vestige of concreteness. Such a range was to be characteristic of Sandburg's whole poetic output, and an analysis of *Chicago Poems,* consequently, would serve to point out some of the differing kinds and levels in his seemingly undifferentiated achievement. Despite this range, however, *Chicago Poems* held firmly to two elements and strove continually to make a harmony of them.

He was later to fashion a series of definitions for poetry, most famous among which was his image of the art as a fusion of hyacinths and biscuits. Here indeed lay figures for two extremes, the two elements out of which Sandburg's verse was compounded. On the one hand, ineffable beauty, and on the other, mundane reality. It was the tension between these romantic and realistic elements, the pattern of their relationship like those of Whitman's before him, out of which Sandburg created his verse.

In all of his poetry a single effort was represented—that of refounding his derived romanticism, its vision and imaginative ecstasy upon the common realities of a labor and populist experience. This latter remained for him a fixed element, one he would not place in perspective and seemingly could not alter. It was a datum which the poet by his own temperament and experience was fastened to. Consequently, the only mobile or adaptable part of his work lay in its other half—the essentially rhetorical and willful exercise of fancy to embellish and stage impressively his obdurate poetic matter. Like the other midwesterners, Sandburg was a poet of subject. Where his subject was in itself arresting, moving, and satisfying, his poem likewise could achieve these qualities. "Chicago," thus, was a striking and shocking poem because its subject, highlighted by Sandburg's rhetoric, was striking and shocking. "Who Am I?" on the other hand, remained as diffuse and pointless as the generality itself of truth unrealized.

. . . .

A subject sufficiently commanding to hold the poet's imagination, and sufficiently friable to allow working and cultivation, seemed clearly to be needed. This came only when Sandburg began serious work on his biography of Lincoln. Here, beginning in 1919, he struck what was for him the natural subject. Lincoln, the native midwesterner, epitome of the people, who in his own life had begun as a raw frontier boy, had known hard labor, kept store, studied to raise himself, wrestled and played, piloted river boats, suffered racking sorrow, practiced law in an intimate and homely community, immersed himself in its politics, and taken on character ultimately by a native streak of high poetry compounded of wit and tragedy in often intense ironies of experience, such a man was in concrete fact the poetry Sandburg had for years been trying to write. He was popular substance, and myth at once. The hitherto discrete elements of Sandburg's verse came together in a subject who, by careful and sympathetic reporting, could speak for himself the word which the poet had never been able to pronounce finally—that word which was the accumulated poetry of midwestern American life.

If Sandburg's knowledge of smoke and steel had seemingly little part in Lincoln's life, all the forces which were to produce them were present, for Lincoln was a Whig and a Republican who began his political career opposing Jackson and the Democrats, supporting a national bank and internal improvements in accord with the dictates of his party leader, Henry Clay. He was the embodiment, as President, of the current in American life which found its impetus in the northern cities and directed itself cruelly and destructively against both the agrarian West and the corrupt, aristocratic South. His administrators, however divided their loyalties, were Seward, Chase, and Stanton, and his battle was won by that behemoth of unenlightened force, Ulysses Grant. Lincoln was the President who fought the Civil War to preserve the Union—and to deliver it into the hands of the pillaging and gutting capitalism of the seventies, eighties, and nineties against which Sandburg himself stood in angry opposition. But Lincoln was also the scrupulous and committed democrat, the man of the people whose origins were wholly himself, or he them, raised to a poignant degree of compassion, perspicuity, and reality. His task lay always with the next step ahead; his wisdom was most often that shrewdness about doing what had to be done which was also the common wisdom of his people. "If I could save the Union without freeing any slaves, I would do it; and if I could save it by freeing some and leaving others alone, I would also do that." But to his task and to his wisdom he gave himself in utmost measure and so achieved for the people from whom he sprang and for himself a dignity which could never have been theirs or his in mere success. Lincoln's life was the mixed stuff of Sandburg's verse, but his compassion, wit, eloquence, devotion, and suffering gave a heightening and point to that life which turned it into poetry and so brought its uncritical but comprehending biographer into high literary distinction.

Sandburg's *Lincoln* was the fulfillment of a singularly homogeneous intellectual and emotional development which cast meaning upon the poems by revealing at last what they had been driving at, by completing the task they had begun. And the completion, furthermore, was made by the same talents which had created the poetry—those of an articulate devotion to the common but commanding and moving elements in midwestern life and of a romantic imagination which stood ready to transmute those elements into high significance. In the case of Lincoln that significance could become one of true and tragic insight rather than willful rhetoric which it had been too often and too centrally in the poems; the poetry of the *Lincoln*, consequently, could have both substance and stature. Lincoln was a man for anecdote and vision both; he was at once hyacinth and biscuit. They were of his nature inextricably, and they made of him Carl Sandburg's greatest poem.

Sandburg's work on the six volume biography formed the greatest part of his creative life from 1919 until the publication of *The War Years* in 1939. Like Masters' *Spoon River* and Anderson's *Winesburg, Ohio,* the work stood as the cumulated result of its author's long training in the school of native dissent and liberated affirmation. He was not to pass this point. During his Chicago years, from his joining of the *Daily News* in 1918 until his move to Harbert, Michigan, in 1932, Sandburg was to be in the midst of Chicago's literary life. His colleagues in the *News* office included Vincent Starrett and Ben Hecht, Henry B. Sell and Harry Hansen among others. But he showed little if any effect from these more exotic blooms of the Liberation. His nearest affinity was Lloyd Lewis, whose interest in midwestern history may well have been a contributing factor in the formation of the *Lincoln,* and with whom he held himself at something of a distance from the more esoterically literary members of the *News* group. His Imagist period lay behind him and his growing absorption with Lincoln ahead. The Liberation had done its work for him by recognizing him as a poet and so helping him to recognize himself as a poet. This had been the office of *Poetry's* acclaim and continued to be the office of the *Daily News'* liberal attitude toward his staff duties. To the extent that he had become a free and personal agent, the Liberation had made him its greatest gift, that of the free and creative personality itself.

After 1932 he retired from regular journalistic work, and his time since then has been spent first on his Michigan farm and later in North Carolina with frequent and long visits to Chicago. His *Lincoln,* by 1941, had sold nearly half a million copies. His reputation as an American folk-singer and folk-song collector spread, and his career issued into a fulfilled maturity. Sandburg's novel, *Remembrance Rock,* published in 1948, added little to his reputation and detracted little. It was essentially a return from the triumph of the *Lincoln* to the mixed achievement of the poetry. If its great length can be accepted, its fault again lay in the author's failure to harmonize fact and vision. Where it was history, *Remembrance Rock* spoke with some authenticity and power, but where it was fiction the failure was the familiar one of vaporousness, of good visionary intentions doing duty for imagined reality. But the author had sufficiently established the validity of his method, imagination, and attitude in his twenty-year labor on the *Lincoln.* It, taken alone, affirmed his life and literary way.

. . . .

"Say It Ain't So, Joe"

LEWIS THOMPSON AND CHARLES BOSWELL

On November 6, 1920, a grand jury in Cook County, Illinois, issued to an aroused public a statement of reassurance on a question that seemed to eclipse in significance even the landslide presidential victory of Warren Gamaliel Harding just four days earlier. In spite of the jury's recent disclosures, the game of baseball was "clean."

Only five weeks before, this same jury had disclosed that the 1919 World Series had been fixed; eight players of the Chicago White Sox team of the American League had been indicted for accepting bribes. The grand jury had exposed what soon came to be celebrated as the "Black Sox" scandal—in the public mind, the most brazen conspiracy in the annals of American sports.

The outcry at this revelation was universal. Newspaper editorials thundered imprecations. In the Philadelphia *Bulletin,* for example, the disgraced players were compared with "the soldier or sailor who would sell out his country and its flag in time of war." More poignant was the plea of one or more small boys to their idol, "Shoeless Joe" Jackson, as he left the building where the grand jury met. It has come down to us, one of the most pitiful fragments of the American idiom: "Say it ain't so, Joe!"

The proprietors of baseball have watchfully guarded the integrity of the game ever since the Black Sox scandal; that a similar conspiracy could take place today seems quite improbable. It is unlikely that the public reaction would be so emotionally charged as in 1920. Though baseball is still our national pastime, it is regarded with a diminished sense of reverence. The notion that it is a big business, run for profit, is now widely embraced.

In contrast to the enormous publicity of the scandal, exact documentation of it is slight, and based almost entirely on circumstantial evidence. Those involved in the conspiracy were understandably reticent at the time, and have remained so ever since. After the case was closed, Shoeless Joe Jackson and his teammate, George "Buck" Weaver, spoke openly about their roles—to insist that they were innocent as the lilies of the field. In 1956, a third player, Chick Gandil, told his version of the inside story in a sports magazine, admitting a guilty part but only further confusing an already confused picture.

There is no doubt, however, that once a fix had been arranged

From Lewis Thompson and Charles Boswell, "Say It Ain't So, Joe": © American Heritage Publishing Co., Inc. Reprinted by permission from *American Heritage* (June 1960), pp. 24-27, 88-93.

between eight of the White Sox players and a group of gamblers, it was one of the worst-kept secrets of all time. The first game of the Series was played on October 1, 1919, at Redland Park, the home grounds of the Cincinnati Reds, winners of the National League pennant. Among the sports writers who covered it were Hugh Fullerton and the baseball great, Christy Mathewson, who had been commissioned by a syndicate to write interpretative articles on the fine points of the Series play. Before the first game, the two compared notes. What was this talk about the Series being in the bag? Both had heard rumors. Both agreed that the possibility was too monstrous to believe. But others in the reporting fraternity, as well as an indeterminate number of ordinary citizens, had heard the same rumors.

One significant fact did give credence to the reports: the betting odds. These had started out overwhelmingly in favor of the White Sox, but by October 1 they were virtually even. It was curious that a heavy influx of Cincinnati cash into betting channels had brought about the change, for almost everyone agreed that the Sox were vastly superior to the Reds.

The 1919 White Sox were one of the notable teams in the history of baseball. Owned by Charles A. Comiskey—nicknamed the Old Roman—the team had Eddie Collins at second base and Ray Schalk as catcher. It would be risky to say they were the greatest ever at their positions; but there have been none better.

No less outstanding was the left fielder, Shoeless Joe Jackson. This back-country boy from South Carolina who could neither read nor write was one of the most colorful and idolized players the game has ever known. Described by some as the "greatest natural batsman that ever played," Jackson compiled a batting average of .356 during ten years in the majors.

There were other fine players on the team: "Shineball" Eddie Cicotte, an accomplished spitball pitcher; Claude "Lefty" Williams, a marvel of control on the mound; Oscar "Happy" Felsch in center field; and a great infield that, in addition to Collins, included Gandil at first, Charles "Swede" Risberg at shortstop, and Weaver at third. Under the management of William "Kid" Gleason, the Sox had romped through the American League that season: with the pennant clinched, the only question seemed to be how quickly they would win the required five-out-of-nine games of which the Series then consisted. By contrast the Reds, who had beaten seven listless, ineffectual teams to win their first National League pennant, were at best a competent outfit.

The result of the first game amazed everyone—except, as it later developed, eight of the Sox and certain other shadowy figures. As *The New York Times* said in its page one story: "Never before in the history of America's biggest baseball spectacle has a pennant-winning club received such a disastrous drubbing in an opening game as the far-famed White Sox got this afternoon. . . . The heralded White Sox looked like bush leaguers."

These were not irresponsible words. In the bottom of the first inning, Eddie Cicotte took the mound to pitch against the Reds. He hit the first batter, lobbed up an easy single to the second, and twice sent Heinie Groh, the third Cincinnati hitter, into the dirt with beanballs. Cicotte's control seemed to have deserted him, and when the inning was over, the Reds were ahead, one to nothing.

In the bottom of the fourth, Cicotte blew up completely. The first batter flied out. The second singled, but then was thrown out on a fielder's choice. There were two out and one on. Two singles followed, which brought in a run and put men on second and third. Up to the plate stepped Dutch Ruether, the Reds' pitcher and one of the weakest hitters of a traditionally weak-hitting position. But Ruether leaned into a slow, easy pitch and whacked it for a triple. A double and a single followed, and when the third man was finally out, the Reds had enjoyed a five-run inning. The final score was nine to one.

As soon as the game was over, talk of a fix grew louder. Much of it was bruited about the lobby of the Hotel Sinton, quarters for the visiting Sox and hence a natural gathering place for Series-minded sportsmen and gamblers. Presently, the gist of the rumor reached Kid Gleason; he in turn told Comiskey what he had heard—namely, that gamblers had bribed some members of the team.

Gleason was of two minds about the truth of the rumor. On the one hand, he knew that it would take a large number of players to throw a game, a possibility which seemed as unlikely as it was painful. On the other, Gleason was impressed by the peculiar gyrations of the betting odds, and he had heard that well-known gamblers had made a killing on the opening game. Then, Cicotte *had* pitched an extraordinarily bad game, and many of the Sox' big bats had been remarkably ineffectual.

Comiskey was not so vacillating. Having seen his players' performance on the field, he felt there was something wrong.

Yet, what could he and Gleason do? The Series had to go on. They had no actual proof of wrongdoing, and without it, they could not very well suspend any of the players. Comiskey worried through the night, and the next morning approached an old friend, John A. Heydler, president of the rival National League. The natural person for Comiskey to have consulted was Byron Bancroft "Ban" Johnson, the president of Comiskey's own league; but the two were not on speaking terms.

In Heydler's view, Comiskey's concern was unwarranted. He

believed that the White Sox had simply been taken "unawares" in the first game, and that they would quickly revert to form. Some-time during that day, however, Heydler sought out Ban Johnson and repeated what he had heard. Heydler later quoted Johnson as saying that the bribery explanation for the loss of the first game was like the "crying of a whipped cur." There Heydler let the matter rest.

The course of the second game, played on October 2, did nothing to reassure Gleason and Comiskey. Lefty Williams pitched for the Sox and performed well for three innings. But in the fourth, he walked three men and allowed two hits, for a total of three runs. The final score was four to two. Even the Sox's two runs were tainted, for they had scored on a wild pitch.

The teams moved to Chicago for the third, fourth, and fifth games at the home stadium of the Sox, Comiskey Park. For Gleason and Comiskey, it was a gloomy trip. By now, the manager was certain that some of his men were throwing the Series, but like Comiskey he realized there was no practical move he could make at the moment.

Then, on October 3, "Wee Dickie" Kerr shut out the Reds, three to nothing. Gleason and Comiskey felt better. Perhaps the bribery talk was so much nonsense, and the Sox were at last finding themselves. Yet, in Chicago hotel lobbies there was talk of a double cross between the gamblers and the players involved, of a double-double cross; and talk that all was well between the conspiring parties, that the third game had been won in order to bring the betting odds into a more reasonable alignment.

It was Cicotte's turn to pitch the fourth game, and if Gleason hesitated to start him, the manager's doubts were allayed when Shineball made an earnest appeal for the starting assignment. Per-haps this reflected a change of heart—if indeed there had been dirty work. Perhaps the men involved were now determined to play to win.

The Sox were shut out in the fourth game, two to nothing. The Cincinnati runs were largely made possible by two glaring fielding errors committed by Cicotte in the fifth inning. Regarded in the best light, these errors were singular examples of maladroitness by an experienced pitcher; at worst, they were highly suspicious. In any case, the Reds were now ahead in the Series, three games to one.

The fifth game, scheduled for Sunday, October 5, was postponed until the next day because of rain; when it was over the Reds had won again and the world championship seemed virtually clinched. The Sox had been shut out again, in a contest marked by the ragged fielding of Felsch and Risberg, and a disastrous four-run sixth inning. Lefty Williams, Chicago's starting pitcher, had lost again.

Back in Cincinnati for the next two games, the White Sox electrified the sports world by taking both. In the first, Wee Dickie Kerr pitched skillfully for ten innings for a five to four victory; in the second, Cicotte was at his best, while Felsch and Joe Jackson led a batting attack which placed the Sox on the long end of a four to one score.

The Series now stood at four games to three, and the teams returned to Chicago for what the White Sox adherents hoped would be the final *two* games. The American League team needed both to win the Series. But in the eighth game, played on October 9, the Reds jumped on Lefty Williams for four runs in the first inning, and went on to a ten to five victory—and the world championship.

Although Charles Comiskey was deeply suspicious of his team's integrity, he could not make any invidious public admission without proof. Pressed for comment on the still-persisting fix rumors, he was quoted as being "sure of the fidelity of the players. I believe my boys fought the battle of the recent World Series on the level as they have always done, and I would be the first to want information to the contrary." In the same breath, he offered $20,000 for evidence of any thrown games, and soon after, he visited Maclay Hoyne, state's attorney for Cook County. He told Hoyne he believed he had been "jobbed" in the Series, asked for help, and expressed willingness to foot the investigative bill.

Two months later, on December 10, Comiskey admitted to reporters that an inquiry was in progress. No evidence had been found, but he vowed that "if we land the goods on any of my players, I will see that there is no place in organized baseball for them."

By this time, Comiskey had heard a great deal more than he admitted publicly. Yet what he knew was still based largely on tip and rumor. He believed the Series had been thrown, and thought he knew the players involved. There were eight suspects: Cicotte, Williams, Gandil, Risberg, Felsch, Jackson, Weaver, and Fred McMullin, a utility infielder. Detectives had reported to Comiskey a remark Cicotte allegedly had made to a relative who commiserated with him after the Series. "Don't worry," Cicotte had said, "I got mine." And, too, there was the wire Gandil reportedly sent to his wife before the Series began. "I have bet my shoes," it read. After the Series was over, Gandil seemed to be spending freely, and it was argued that if he had bet his shoes on his own team, he would have been in no position to throw his money around. Sketchy as this evidence appeared, Comiskey felt justified in holding up the World

Series checks of the suspected players, each of whom had more than $3,000 coming to him. But on the advice of his lawyers, and after much pressure from the players, he finally released the payments.

The identity of the gamblers involved was even more uncertain; and in a sense it still is. No one able to speak with complete authority has ever publicly named all the persons, aside from the players, who manipulated the fix, or has explained the complexities of their interrelationships. Perhaps this authoritative voice does not exist, and never did, for there is reason to believe that some of the dozen or so gamblers whose names hover over the scandal were not even aware of the involvement of others. The higher echelons of the fraternity kept quiet; what we do know of the elaborate maneuvers and brisk footwork that went on (and the information, so far as it goes, is probably accurate enough) has come from the lesser ranks of those concerned.

In the early stages of Comiskey's investigation, specific emphasis fell on certain personalities. The most notorious was Arnold Rothstein, the gambler and manipulator whose name is synonymous with the shady aspects of the twenties. Equally as suspect was Abe Attell, the onetime featherweight boxing champion of the world. Then there was a former big-league pitcher, William "Sleepy" Burns, who had played for the White Sox and the Cincinnati Reds before going on to more lucrative endeavors in the Texas oil fields. Allied with Burns was one William Maharg, a Philadelphian who, like Attell, was an ex-prizefighter. Supposedly, these were the principal gamblers in the World Series fix; but others—in Boston, Des Moines, St. Louis, and elsewhere—were mentioned as accomplices.

Early in the new year, 1920, Comiskey sent out season contracts to his players, including—in spite of his doubts—the eight suspects. In the bargaining that ensued, Gandil's demands were too high for Comiskey, and the first baseman retired from big-league baseball; but after some maneuvering, the others signed.

The White Sox of 1920 were virtually the same team that had won the pennant the year before; and as the season drew to a close in September, they were in a hot race for the flag with the Cleveland Indians. Quite suddenly the scandal was exposed—in a curiously indirect manner.

All that summer, there had been disquieting speculation about the integrity of baseball; early in September, it centered on a game played on August 31 between the Chicago Cubs and the Philadelphia Phillies of the National League. Before the game there had been rumors that it would be thrown by the Cubs, and in a countermove, the Cub management decided not to start the pitcher previously announced. Instead, the great Grover Cleveland Alexander was named to pitch, and he was offered a bonus of $500 if he won. Nevertheless, the Cubs lost.

The fix rumors eventually came to the attention of Charles A. McDonald, Chief Justice of the Criminal Court of Cook County. McDonald wondered what action, if any, should be taken, and conferred with Ban Johnson. Johnson advised that a grand jury look into the matter, and McDonald followed his suggestion.

The jury opened its hearings on September 7; for two weeks a parade of witnesses marched through its chambers. These included ballplayers, owners, managers, officials of both leagues, and sports writers. Speculation about their testimony grew intense, especially when it became known that the 1919 Series had replaced the Cub-Phillies game as the focal point of the inquiry.

On September 22, Assistant State's Attorney Hartley Replogle asserted bluntly that the 1919 World Series had been fixed and that the grand jury had heard the testimony implicating eight of the White Sox. The eight, whom he named, were those on Comiskey's list.

Comiskey acknowledged that he had been suspicious of the Series, that he had spent $20,000 in investigating it, and had been unable to prove a thing. For that matter, he declared, he was *still* without proof. But if he received any, he swore to "ruin the evil-doers."

Meanwhile, in Philadelphia, Billy Maharg, the friend of Sleepy Bill Burns, had decided to talk. He told his story to Jimmy Isaminger, a sports writer for the Philadelphia *North American,* and what Isaminger wrote became a national sensation.

Maharg declared that in September, 1919, he had received a wire from Burns, inviting him to go hunting at the latter's New Mexico ranch. To make further arrangements, Maharg met Burns at the Hotel Ansonia in New York. There it developed that Burns had gambling, not hunting, on his mind. He introduced Maharg to Eddie Cicotte and Chick Gandil, who were in town with the White Sox to play the Yankees. The two players indicated that they would "deliver" the Series—for a price. The price was $100,000, to be paid in installments of $20,000 before each game and split among the eight players involved.

After this meeting, Burns asked Maharg if he knew of any gamblers who would underwrite the proposition. Maharg said he would go to Philadelphia and try to interest some men he knew there. His Philadelphia contacts refused the proposal, but suggested that Rothstein was the man to see. Back in New York, Maharg and

Burns met with Rothstein, who declined the deal. According to Maharg, "Rothstein said he did not think such a frame-up could be possible."

Maharg returned to Philadelphia, just before the World Series was scheduled to start, and there he received a wire from Burns that "Arnold R. has gone through with everything. Got eight [players] in, leaving for Cinn." The next day, Maharg went to Cincinnati, where he met Burns, who told him he had run into Abe Attell in New York and that Attell had persuaded Rothstein to finance the deal.

On the morning of the first Series game, Maharg and Burns visited Attell at the Hotel Sinton, and asked him for the $100,000 to parcel out among the eight players. Attell told them he needed all the cash he could muster for betting; he proposed instead that the players be given $20,000 *after* each losing game. Burns talked to the players, who agreed to it.

The following morning, Maharg and Burns again called on Attell in his room; they were impressed by the great stacks of currency in evidence. Once again Attell demurred at paying off the players. Maharg and Burns were now suspicious, and pointedly questioned Attell as to whether Rothstein was actually backing him. As proof, Attell flashed a telegram which read: "Abe Attell, Sinton Hotel, Cinn. Have wired you twenty grand and waived identification. A. R." Later, said Maharg, he became convinced the wire was spurious, and that Rothstein had not been involved.

At the moment, however, Burns was angry because there was no money for the players. He told Maharg that he would turn over to them $110,000 worth of oil leases. Maharg dissuaded Burns "and thereby saved him that money."

After the second game—and the second Sox loss—Maharg and Burns saw Attell and demanded the players' payoff. Attell stalled, but finally handed over $10,000. Burns gave this to one of the players (whom Maharg did not name), and afterward told Maharg that the eight White Sox were restless and might not go through with their agreement. On the other hand, Burns did not believe they would try to win for Dickie Kerr, the third-game pitcher, who was not in on the plot, and who had been referred to by those who were as a "busher." Consequently, Maharg and Burns bet their roll, including their winnings from the first two games, on the third—and lost everything when Kerr shut out the Reds.

For all its sensationalism and aura of authenticity, Maharg's story must be regarded as the account of one who was only a peripheral participant in what *The New York Times* characterized as "one of the most amazing and tangled tales of graft and bribery and interlocking 'double-crossing.'" Bill Burns and certain of the eight players were to affirm that Maharg's story was, in general, accurate; but others in the plot offered emendations and additions which suggested that his knowledge was limited.

A somewhat different story, for instance, was told by Chick Gandil in the magazine *Sports Illustrated* almost forty years later. Although it conflicts with Maharg's account, Gandil's version is probably just as accurate—and just as limited in its perspective.

According to Gandil, the 1919 White Sox were ripe for trouble. The players quarreled among themselves, and the one common bond among them seemed to be their dislike for Comiskey, who paid his pennant-winning team the lowest salaries in the league. "I would like to blame the trouble we got into on Comiskey's cheapness," Gandil commented, "but my conscience won't let me."

Gandil claimed that the plot originated in Boston, in September, 1919, when he and Cicotte were approached by a gambler named "Sport" Sullivan, who suggested that they get together seven or eight players to throw the Series. The pair consulted with the others, and the group decided to accept the offer—cash in advance. Sullivan, however, explained that it was difficult to raise so much money quickly, and made arrangements to meet the players again in Chicago.

Not long after, Cicotte introduced Gandil to Sleepy Bill Burns. Burns had heard of Sullivan's offer, and asked for a chance to interest a gambler in Montreal, who might make a better one. At a meeting, the players decided to consider Burns's terms.

A few days later, Sullivan and a friend from New York joined the players at the Hotel Warner in Chicago. The friend was introduced as "Mr. Ryan," but, said Gandil, "having met this man two years before in New York, I recognized him as Arnold Rothstein."

Rothstein's plan was to *win* the first game, in order to raise the odds on the White Sox; then the players could lose the Series as they wished. When it came to paying the players the promised $80,000, Rothstein demurred; he finally handed over ten $1,000 bills, with a promise to pay the rest in installments. "When the gamblers left," Gandil recalled, "we entrusted the money to Cicotte until it could be changed inconspicuously. He put the bills under his pillow." Gandil claimed that he never received a cent of the money.

By the time of the first game, talk of a fix was so prevalent that the players were reluctant to go through with it. According to Gandil their intention was to double-cross Rothstein by keeping his money and playing to win; in effect, this is what they did. But it was a demoralized White Sox team which took the field against their National League opponents—and the Reds played much better than anyone expected.

After the third game, which the White Sox won, Gandil received a visit from Burns, who was panicky. "He and some other gamblers, going on the assumption that the Series was fixed, had bet heavily on the Reds. Now they had their doubts." Burns offered Gandil $20,000 personally if he could guarantee that the Sox would lose the Series; but Gandil turned him down.

At any rate, it was Maharg's story that broke the Black Sox scandal. In Chicago, its publication set off a limited chain reaction. On the morning of September 28, 1920, the pressure became too much for Eddie Cicotte. Troubled by his conscience, he went to Comiskey's house to say that he wished to get something off his chest. The Old Roman told him that the proper place for any confession was the grand jury room, and that morning Cicotte appeared there, to testify that Maharg's story was substantially correct and that he was one of the ring. Later in the day, Shoeless Joe Jackson and Lefty Williams visited the grand jury chambers to add their *mea culpas.* Before the day was over, the grand jury had indicted the seven players still on the team, together with the now-retired Gandil, for "conspiracy to commit an illegal act." The crime carried with it a penalty of from one to five years in jail and/or a maximum fine of $10,000.

Comiskey at once suspended the tainted players, and in so doing ruined any chance of wresting the pennant from the Indians, who at the moment were leading the league by only one game, with three left to play. Yet outwardly he maintained his composure. "Thank God it did happen," he declared. "Forty-four years of baseball endeavor have convinced me more than ever that it is a wonderful game and a game worth keeping clean."

The stories told by Cicotte, Jackson, and Williams to the grand jury, as reported in the press, were the first embellishments of Maharg's account. Cicotte, for example, said:

> The eight of us got together in my room three or four days before the [first] game started. Gandil was the master of ceremonies. We talked about "throwing" the Series. Decided we could get away with it. We agreed to do it.
>
> I was thinking of the wife and kids and how I needed the money. I told them I had to have the cash in advance. I didn't want any checks. I didn't want any promise, as I wanted the money in bills. I wanted it before I pitched a ball.
>
> The day before I went to Cincinnati, I put it up to them squarely for the last time, that there would be nothing doing unless I had the money.
>
> That night, I found the money under my pillow. There was ten thousand dollars. I counted it. I don't know who put it there, but it was there. It was my price. I had sold out "Commy"; I had sold out the other boys; sold them for ten thousand dollars to pay off a mortgage on a farm. . . .

After receiving the money, according to a statement later made by Burns, Cicotte vowed to lose the first game if he had "to throw the baseball clean out of the Cincinnati park."

Williams asserted that he and Jackson had been promised $20,000 each, but received only $5,000. According to Williams, Gandil had approached him at the Hotel Ansonia in New York with the fix proposition. Later, in Chicago, he met with Cicotte, Gandil, Weaver, Felsch, and two gamblers, Joseph Sullivan of Boston and Rachael Brown of New York. Williams said the group bargained over price. At the end of the *fourth* game, Gandil handed him $10,000 and said: "Five for you, five for Jackson. The rest has been called off." After that, nothing further was said.

One other player made momentary public acknowledgment of complicity. This was Happy Felsch, who told reporters the day after the indictments were handed down that he had received $5,000 for his part in the plot.

On September 29, *The New York Times* reported that when Shoeless Joe Jackson left the grand jury room the previous day, "a crowd of small boys gathered round their idol and asked: 'It isn't true, is it, Joe?' Shoeless Joe replied: 'Yes, boys, I'm afraid it is.' " Other newspapers and two wire services reported the same basic story, and the only question that remains is one of grammar. The version that has passed into popular mythology cannot be documented, but perhaps it is reasonable to assume that small boys are not overly sensitive to niceties of phraseology; perhaps the words actually were: "Say it ain't so, Joe!"

At this point Arnold Rothstein was subpoenaed by the Chicago grand jury. Protesting that he had long ago renounced gambling for an honest career in the real-estate business, Rothstein nevertheless took the precaution of hiring one of the slickest trial lawyers of the day, William J. Fallon. Rothstein emerged "exonerated completely from complicity in the conspiracy." In fact, the jury even acknowledged that his testimony had strengthened the case against some of those already indicted.

Although Rothstein was cleared, other gamblers were not. Before the case ultimately came to trial, in the summer of 1921, Attell, Burns, Sullivan, Brown, Hal Chase (a former Giant player who had been fired by John McGraw in 1918 for "shady playing"), and others had been indicted.

Meanwhile, organized baseball had taken a step that was greatly to affect the destinies of the indicted players. At the time the Black Sox scandal broke, baseball's top authority was vested in a three-man committee; but the club owners felt that a single executive with wide powers would better serve the game. On November 12,

1920, they appointed Federal Judge Kenesaw Mountain Landis as baseball's first commissioner. His first important act occurred on March 12, 1921, when he banned the eight guilty players from organized baseball by placing them on the ineligible list.

On June 27, 1921, the long-delayed trial finally got under way, with seven of the eight Black Sox present. Fred McMullin, who was not there, was said to be hurrying to Chicago from the West. Other notable absentees were Abe Attell (whose lawyer had wangled his freedom on a *habeas corpus* writ), Hal Chase, Joseph Sullivan, and Rachael Brown.

The proceedings attracted feverish interest on the part of the public. The courtroom was jammed daily to its capacity of five hundred, including many small boys, and special guards were needed to hold back those who could not be accommodated. Most of the spectators sweltered in their shirtsleeves, and collars were conspicuously absent.

A hard fight was expected, since it was no secret that Jackson, Cicotte, and Williams had repudiated their confessions; the admissibility of these statements as evidence would be briskly debated. At the same time, there was an air of near-joviality. The "clean" White Sox players, who were called into court by the defense, talked easily and with humor to their former teammates. And Joe Jackson, much impressed by the zealous infighting of the battery of defense attorneys, brought a laugh when he remarked: "Those are certainly smart men, and that lawyer of mine is one lawyerin' bird. They better not get him riled up." But always, the vocabulary of baseball prevailed. One exchange, involving the confessions, went as follows:

Michael Ahern, a defense attorney: "You won't get to first base with those confessions."

George E. Gorman, assistant state's attorney: "We'll make a home run with them."

Ahern: "You may make a long hit, but you'll be thrown out at the plate."

After the selection of a jury, which took over two weeks, the prosecution presented its case—which rested mainly on the testimony of Sleepy Bill Burns. The presence of Burns as a witness was due, it was said, to the persistence of Ban Johnson, who had tracked him to Mexico and persuaded him to testify. A representative of the state's attorney had met Burns at the border town of Del Rio, Texas, and there, "in the middle of the night," had discussed the implications of his giving evidence. One implication, of course, was that Burns would be spared prosecution.

His testimony was quite consistent with Maharg's earlier story; he insisted that the only money the players received was the $10,000 which he had conveyed to them from Attell before the third game. And on one point Burns was emphatic: the players, and not the gamblers, had conceived the idea of throwing the Series.

A sensational loss was revealed on July 22, following Burns's testimony, when it became known that the waivers of immunity signed by Cicotte, Jackson, and Williams, as well as the original transcripts of their statements, had disappeared. Ban Johnson immediately came forward to charge that Arnold Rothstein had paid $10,000 to have the confessions stolen soon after they had been obtained and, after satisfying himself that he was not implicated, had turned them over to a newspaperman. What ultimately happened to the confessions and the waivers remains one of the unsolved mysteries of the case.

The trial ended on August 2, after the prosecutor, asking for conviction, had asserted that "the crime strikes at the heart of every red-blooded citizen and every kid who plays on a sand lot." The defense, of course, called for acquittal.

The jury deliberated for two hours and forty-seven minutes, and then came in with a verdict of "Not Guilty." The outcome was not surprising, in view of the judge's charge that for conviction "the law required proof of intent of the players not merely to throw baseball games, but to defraud the public and others."

The verdict was greeted in the courtroom with a wild demonstration of approval. The spectators cheered, and the judge congratulated the jury, whose members responded by carrying the vindicated players from the courtroom on their shoulders.

To Buck Weaver and Happy Felsch, the acquittal may have seemed unnecessary, for before the case went to the jury, the judge had announced that, on the basis of the evidence, he would not let a verdict against them stand. Chick Gandil seasoned *his* joy with a dash of gloating. He said: "I guess that will learn Ban Johnson that he can't frame an honest bunch of players."

The press and organized baseball were hardly as jubilant. The Associated Press reported that the news was received with "surprise, disappointment and chagrin" by sports editors and writers. The outcome of the trial was a "travesty" as "stunning and disturbing as the original disclosures." The New York *World* asserted that "if the crooks who were acquitted try to show their faces in decent sporting circles, they should be boycotted and blackballed."

As a matter of fact, Commissioner Landis had precisely that in mind. On the day after the verdict, the eight were suspended for life. Landis stated:

> Regardless of the verdict of juries, no player that undertakes or promises to throw a ball game; no player that sits in a conference with a bunch of

crooked players and gamblers where the ways and means of throwing games are planned and discussed and does not promptly tell his club about it, will ever play professional baseball.

From that day on, organized baseball never retreated from this position.

It is no exaggeration to say that every one of the Black Sox bitterly regretted his role in the scandal. Although they had been held legally guiltless, they were nevertheless cut off from their livelihood—a livelihood that, at best, could offer relatively few working years. For a while, some of the Black Sox played exhibition baseball, but they found the public indifferent and their existence harassed by the hostility of the game's rulers. Ball parks were closed to them, and other obstacles appeared in their path. Gradually, most of them turned to other fields.

In the years immediately following the scandal, several of them tried to obtain through the courts what they considered equitable redress. None succeeded. Perhaps the most persistent protester of his own innocence was Buck Weaver, who, while admitting that he knew of the plot, was adamant in asserting that he had had no part in it. From time to time he addressed appeals to Landis. They were never answered. From time to time, too, baseball fans signed petitions for the reinstatement of various of the players— particularly Jackson—but none was ever effective.

It is doubtful if the ultimate truth will ever be known. Some of those concerned—like Rothstein, Jackson, McMullin, Weaver, and Williams—are dead, and those who survive are at the mercy of their memories and their pride. Chick Gandil's comment on his banishment may perhaps serve as a last word. "I felt it was unjust," he said, "but I truthfully never resented it because, even though the series wasn't thrown, we were guilty of a serious offense, and we knew it."

Original Narratives

The documents reprinted below portray in grim detail the race riot of July 2, 1917, at East St. Louis. The editor, Robert Asher, holds a Ph.D. from the University of Minnesota and teaches at the University of Connecticut, Storrs, where he specializes in labor history. For a contemporaneous report of the grisly event, consult the Illinois Attorney General's *Biennial Report, 1917-1918* (Springfield, 1918), p. 16.

Documents of the Race Riot at East St. Louis

ROBERT ASHER (ED.)

The savagery of the East St. Louis race riot of July 2, 1917, shocked the nation. At least 50 persons were killed and 240 buildings destroyed; estimates of property damage ran as high as $1,400,000. Reaction across the country was immediate. William Yates Sherman, United States senator from Illinois during the years 1913-1921, was one of the first to protest the violence and demand a congressional investigation after President Woodrow Wilson refused to intervene.

A scholarly study of the riot and its aftermath—by Elliott M. Rudwick, professor of sociology at Southern Illinois University, Edwardsville—was published in 1964. Many new documents relating to the riot have become available since the return to Illinois of the papers of Senator Sherman. Two accounts received by Sherman are printed below.

The first letter was written on July 19, 1917, by Senia W. Madella, a black woman from Washington, D.C. The purpose of her letter was to ask Sherman's help in finding jobs for two public school teachers from East St. Louis, Cora and Daisy Westbrook, who were afraid that the city's schools would not be reopened in the fall of 1917. Mrs. Madella also sent the Senator a letter that had been written to her daughter Louise by Daisy Westbrook, director of music and drawing at Lincoln High School. In the letter Miss

From Robert Asher, "Documents of the Race Riot at East St. Louis," *Journal of the Illinois State Historical Society*, LXV (1972), pp. 327-336. Reprinted by permission of the author and the Illinois State Historical Society. Some footnotes in the original have been omitted.

Westbrook poignantly describes the physical violence and destruction she witnessed on July 2, 1917.

3946 W. Belle
St. Louis, Mo.

Dearest Louise:

Was *very* glad to hear from you. Your letter was forwarded from what used to be my house.

Louise, it was *awful.* I hardly know where to begin telling you about it. First I will say we lost everything but what we had on and that was very little—bungalow aprons, no hats, and sister did not have on any shoes.

It started early in the afternoon. We kept receiving calls over the 'phone to pack our trunks & leave, because it was going to be *awful* that night. We did not heed the calls, but sent grandma & the baby on to St. Louis, & said we would "stick" no matter what happened. At first, when the fire started, we stood on Broadway & watched it. As they neared our house we went in & went to the basement. It was too late to run then. They shot & yelled some thing awful, finally they reached our house. At first, they did not bother us (we watched from the basement window), they remarked that "white people live in that house, that is not a nigger house". Later, someone must have tipped them that it was a "nigger" house, because, after leaving us for about 20 min. they returned & started shooting in the house[,] throwing bricks & yelling like mad "kill the "niggers," burn that house.["]

It seemed the whole house was falling in on us. Then some one said, they must not be there; if they are they are certainly dead. Then some one shouted "they are in the basement. Surround them and burn it down. Then they ran down our steps. Only prayer saved us, we were under tubs & any thing we could find praying & keeping as quiet as possible, because if they had seen one face, we would have been shot or burned to death. When they were about to surround the house & burn it, we heard an awful noise & thought probably they were dynamiting the house. (The Broadway Theatre fell in, we learned later). Sister tipped to the door to see if the house was on fire. She saw the reflection of a soldier on the front door—pulled it open quickly, & called for help. All of us ran out then, & was taken to the city hall for the night—(just as we were). The next morning, we learned our house was not burned, so we tried to get protection to go out & get our clothes, & have the rest of the things put in storage. We could not, but were sent on to St. Louis. Had to walk across the bridge with a line of soldiers on each side—in the hot sun, no hats, & scarcely no clothing. When we reached St. Louis; we tried to get someone to go to our house, & get the things out, but were not successful.

On Tuesday evening at 6 o'clock our house was burned with two soldiers on guard. So the papers stated. We were told that they looted the house before burning it. We are in St. Louis now trying to start all over again. Louise it is so hard to think we had just gotten to the place where we could take care of our mother & grandmother well, & to think, all was destroyed in one night. We had just bought some new furniture & I was preparing to go away, & had bought some beautiful dresses. Most of my jewelry was lost also. I had on three rings, my watch bracelet and LaValliere—Everything else was lost. 9 rings, a watch, bracelet, brooch, locket, and some more things. I miss my piano more than anything else.

The people here are very nice to us. Several of our friends have brought us clothing, bed clothes etc.

Tell me how you got in the Gov. Printing Office. Do you take an examination, if so what does it consist of. I might take it. I have had a *good* position in E. St. L., but don't know whether there will be enough children to teach there this fall or not. People are moving out so fast. The papers did not describe all the horrors. It was awful. People we[re] being shot down & thrown back into fire if they tried to escape. Some were shot & then burned; others were dragged around with ropes about their necks, one man was hung to a telegraph post. We saw two men shot down. One was almost in front of our house. One man & his wife, a storekeeper, were burned alive, a cross in front of our house.

I must close now it makes me blue to talk about it Write again.

Tell Miss Black I received her card. Will you tell Florene & Mrs. Bowie, I haven't their address. Will expect to hear from you *real* soon. All send love.

Lovingly,
Daisy

The second document was sent to Sherman by Hallie E. Queen, a member of the staff of Howard University. Miss Queen's report is a compilation of interviews with survivors of the July violence. It is noteworthy not only for its sensitive description of the emotional reactions of blacks in East St. Louis but also for its keen social observations. Many of the developments Miss Queen outlines corroborate the conclusions drawn by Professor Rudwick. Her account was typewritten and is printed here as she wrote it, except for the correction of obvious typographical errors.

East St. Louis as I saw it.
Hallie E. Queen

Like a tired human being the great train gasped and groaned and moved more slowly after its journey of twenty seven hours from Washington. The porter, who had been almost too affable, stared at us strangely and, giving a look of resentment out of the car window, stalked out of the coach. Passengers who knew the road better than we, began to get restless and move toward the windows. Strange, disagreeable odors met our nostrils and everywhere there was a peculiar tensity which we could not understand until the white conductor, taking the place of the colored porter called out "EAST ST. LOUIS." So we understood. The strange look which the porter gave us was the look which dark men and women must always give when EAST ST. LOUIS is mentioned. And he had gone away because he hated to call out the name of the accursed town. Twenty some railroads run into EAST ST. LOUIS and our train stayed at the Junction for some time. Box cars have been parked and sidetracked all along the way as if purposely to prevent the window observer from seeing the wreckage of the city. But high above it all, above windows and trains and even houses, stand piles of burnt timber that once formed the homes of human beings, but are marked with careless indifference, "Kindling for sale." So our train sped on to St. Louis Mo. On the following morning we crossed the "Bridge of Mercy["] back into EAST St. Louis.[1]

Had you been with us you could never forget, as we can never forget, the sight of that city. When, in wild fury, a southern mob lynches a man or two men or even five, as it did one time in Georgia, the tree is burned and the grass around the tree is seared. But the city stands as it did before. Not so with EAST ST. LOUIS. The city is a living monument to its own shame. A riot of half burned houses, masses of broken beds, stoves, baby carriages and other furnishings piled here and there, solitary chimneys standing out amid whole blocks of debris, an endless procession of heavily laden moving vans, groups of soldiers sitting on doorsteps laughing, talking and playing games with idle young white men, four or five saloons in every block, dark narrow blind alleys, between the streets . . .[2] and everywhere that same disagreeable stench we had noted from the train . . . and that is EAST ST. LOUIS today.

In some places a whole row of houses has been burned or destroyed with the pickaxe—in others the mob has been careful to

---

[1] The Municipal Free Bridge, which crossed the Mississippi River into St. Louis, Missouri.
[2] There has been no deletion of text here or where other ellipses appear. They are copied from Miss Queen's original report.

pick out only the colored home between the houses of white residents. In such cases no burning has been done but the house has been literally smashed to pieces. We learned a little later that there was no racially segregated district in EAST ST. LOUIS but that white and colored lived side by side. And so, saddened in heart by what we had seen, we set about our task.

As I see it, there were three main causes of the riot: economic competition, racial antipathy and southern intervention. You know the story of the increased demand for labor because of war orders. There had been continued trouble in EAST ST. LOUIS between Capital and Labor and strike after strike had occurred. In nearly every case the employers had refused the demands of the strikers and had put Negroes in their places. The owner of a certain Aluminum Plant testified that in order to prevent strikes he had maintained his business on a principle of hate. He employs one third white Americans, one third Negroes and one third foreigners, knowing that each group hates the other so heartily that they will never combine against the shop. The Negroes who took the places of the strikers became interested in their work and were promoted so rapidly that they began to acquire better homes, furniture and clothing than the whites. At this point the economic competition developed into racial hatred. White men who delivered furniture to colored homes sneered the purchasers and noted the purchase. Neatly dressed colored children were hooted in the streets. Finally on May 28 the memorable meeting was held and the mob marched out to murder and riot.[3] You know the story of how the mob went wild on Third Street, how armed colored men drove it back, how a secret investigation was held, how no results were ever known and how the Negroes were continually harassed until the final riot broke out on July second. As to the third cause of the riot, it seems that about five days before the riot began, three Mississippi planters, Messrs. Leroy W. Valiant, James Mann (nephew of Rep. Mann), and Henry Crittenden, appeared at the office of the city councilman and asked permission to solicit Negro labor in EAST ST. LOUIS to return to the South. This Committee was very much in evidence after the riot. Mr. Mann stated that his city with a population of 1200 had lost 700 Negroes and that Mr. Litch of the Department of Immigration had told him to go ahead and solicit labor if he wished to. They were told (both before and after the riot) that this could not be done in EAST ST. LOUIS as there was still a shortage of

---

[3] On that day delegates from the East St. Louis Central Trades and Labor Union had appeared before the city council to protest Negro migration into the city. Following the meeting, a mob of about three thousand attacked black pedestrians and merchants in the area near City Hall.

labor even with the influx of Negroes. The Committee persisted for a while, even offering to charter a flatboat or train to take as many Negroes as wished to go back South. They left when they were finally told that their project was unfeasible. One may draw his own conclusions from their visit, but at least it does not absolve the South from blame. Of one thing I felt certain after much questioning and investigation, the German agents had no more to do with the riot than American agents had to do with the German atrocities in Belgium or the Belgian atrocities in the African Congo.

During the last days of June, frequent labor meetings were held in EAST ST. LOUIS. On Saturday the 30th. the policemen were especially invited to a meeting and a notice was posted in police Headquarters. The next morning policemen and soldiers appeared at the homes of colored men and demanded their weapons.[4] Most of the men were at work, and the women, respecting the uniform, surrendered their arms without question. Some, however, evidently did not. Several colored men became suspicious of this move and warned others. All during the early part of Monday morning colored residents of EAST ST. LOUIS were receiving telephone calls warning them to get their women and children away as it was going to be bad in the city that night. On the testimony of a white woman, the actual riot started about noon, when a colored man came to her house to deliver gasoline. White men attacked him on the porch and beat him up. The woman held the mob at bay with a revolver and got the man into her house. When she let the man out of the back door, the mob pursued him, gathering strength all the time and finally killing him and leaving his body in the street. Then it turned toward the home of Scott Clarke [Clark], a teamster. Clarke was in his house at the time. The mob caught him, tied a rope around his neck and was about to lynch him, when some one said "Let's drag him around a little." So Clarke was dragged through the streets of EAST ST. LOUIS with the sun shining down on him while women members of the mob showed the ancient spirit of intolerance by stoning him to death. Some persistent spark of life or some reflex action was left in him when they reached the corner of Fourth Street and Broadway. The mob, now tired out, attempted a second time to hang Clarke but he was rescued? by Col. Tripp. He died soon in St. Mary's Hospital.[5] His blood inflamed the mob. "Get a Nigger" became the slogan, and the mob rushed on to out-do St. Bartholemew's Night and the terrors of

---

[4] The East St. Louis police had similarly concentrated their efforts after the May 28-30 riot on disarming the city's blacks; *ibid.*, pp. 31, 246.
[5] Two of Clark's murderers were later arrested and brought to trial; they were found guilty and sentenced to fifteen years in prison.

Armenia. I have often thought that as they rushed along the echo of their cry was carried on to Springfield and he, the man of many sorrows, turned uneasily in his grave because he was unable to "Hit that thing and hit it hard".

There is a section of EAST ST. LOUIS known as the Denver Side. It is a thick colored settlement and has for many years been known as a retreat for "Bad Men." On Sunday night, just after a labor meeting, an automobile of white rioters rushed through this section, firing shot in every direction. A little later another automobile filled with white men rushed through the same street. Both cars were Fords and both were filled with white men dressed in citizen's clothes. The colored men, who by this time had got together, fired on them, killing one mortally, wounding another and inflicting minor wounds on several of the others. It happened that these plain clothes men were detectives; the man instantly killed was Detective Sgt. [Samuel] Coppedge and the mortally wounded one was Detective [Frank] Wodley [Wadley]. It has been said that the killing of these two policemen explains the fact that the police later took the side of the rioters rather than that of the Negroes.

Judge Lynch[6] was not long in making his appearance. Chasing a Negro until he fell, his head laid open by a piece of curbstone, the mob attempted to lynch him in a blind alley on Fourth Street. They used a clothesline, which of course broke. An old white man came out of his house and ordered the rioters away, crying, "Don't you dare to hang that man on this street" but he was pushed away by the angry mob. A stronger rope was brought and Mr. Carlos Hurd of the St. Louis (Mo.) Post Dispatch, saw a man stick his fingers into the wound and bathe his hands in blood in order to adjust the rope. Then the crowd called out "Get hold of the rope and pull for EAST ST. LOUIS." The man's body was elevated and left hanging as was done with several others.

As the mob turned away from this Negro, it encountered a colored man running from an alley in hope of being protected on the street. He was met with a rain of missiles and blows and fell prone on the ground. The crowd did not leave him then but kicked his skull to pulp.

As the day wore on, the men grew tired of rioting alone so they invented another means of torture. Going to the "Red light District" of the town they let out the denizens and stationed them at the corners of the street. As soon as they (the men) would catch a colored woman they would take her to these underworld dwellers who would strip her entirely and make her run back forth between

[6] This was a common way of referring to justice administered by lynching.

them firing at her feet until she fell dead. More than one half
stripped woman escaped and ran across the Bridge of Mercy to St.
Louis Mo. Even this was not enough. Every one admits that the
women were far more vile in this riot than were the men and far
more inventive of cruelty. How they killed infant after infant
before the face of the mothers, shooting them, burning them and
cutting their throats, is a story too horrible to tell and the mothers
are too sorrowful to look upon. One mother, half crazed, wrapped
her infant in a crash towel and fled. She was overtaken by a group
of female demons but fought like a thing wild and escaped. Crossing
the Bridge of Mercy she rushed to the Municipal Building, crying
"Thank God, I saved my baby". When she opened the towel it was
empty. In the fight they had taken the baby and the mother lost
her reason.

Fearing that some of those who fled to St. Louis Mo. would get
hospital treatment, the rioters cut the wires, thus plunging the
operating room into darkness and causing the surgeons to have to
work by the light of small electric flashes.

Turning to Broadway and Eighth Street, the mob surrounded a
colored barber shop and two of the rioters went in to search for
Negroes. Two bullets were fired by the Negro barbers who were in
hiding and both white men fell. The mob then set fire to the shop
and guarded the entrance knowing that the Negro would be cre-
mated alive. After the building had been burning a few minutes the
mob was fired upon by the Negroes from within and a white man
and boy fell. Then the Negroes made a dash through the flames into
the street only to fall under a fusillade of shots.

There is [a] bridge between EAST ST. LOUIS and ST. LOUIS
Mo. Out there they call it the MUNICIPAL FREE BRIDGE but to
me it will always be the BRIDGE OF MERCY. When the city was
given over to flame and carnage and the disarmed Negroes saw that
it was a choice between escape and sacrifice, they rushed to the
street cars on the Ead's Bridge only to find that all cars had been
stopped at the order of the mayor. Those who tried to go over on
foot had their bodies thrown into the Mississippi. So by the Free
Bridge they passed over the Red Sea into SAINAI. May some poet
of my race write a paean of thanks at the wonderful way in which
that city took care of the wretched and may all our children and
our children's children rise up and call it blessed!

There follow here a few of the personal stories of refugees—just
the top from that cup of gall that is running over with bitterness.
What the riot engendered was hatred, anger, resentment and a desire
for revenge. These are strange children of a country that is striving
to democratize the world and bring lasting peace to the entire

world. But if out of this chaos of riot and fire and lynching and drowning there arises a respect for the power of the LAW; and if on the ruined homes of these martyrs there are builded homes where black men may live in peace and work in happiness; if it really needed the sacrifice of this innocent blood to purge the guilt of the rioters and this trial by fire to cleanse the stain of LYNCH LAW from our civilization . . . then the dying has not been in vain.

Mayhap, from those ashes shall rise the dismembered bodies of my people, and, joining hands with those who come from graves hidden deep in the waters of the Mississippi, they may look upon a true democratic civilization in EAST ST. LOUIS and say "ALL IS WELL."

. . . .

The second document in this section of original narratives outlines the state's plan to give Illinois a modern system of highway transportation in an ambitious $60,000,000 bond issue—a rather impressive figure for 1918. The author of the report, S. E. Bradt, was then Superintendent of Highways. The sequel to this commitment is told well by David R. Wrone in "Illinois Pulls Out of the Mud," *Journal of the Illinois State Historical Society*, LVIII (Spring 1965), 54-78.

Sixty Million Dollar Bond Issue

S. E. BRADT

It was not until about 1911 that the people of the State of Illinois began to realize the condition of our highways as compared to other states and the handicap under which we were working in the marketing of products and the carrying on of that part of our ordinary business which required the use of our highways. Most of you will remember the oft repeated statement that the State of Illinois, standing first in agriculture, second in wealth and third in population, occupied twenty-third place among the states of the union in the matter of highways which were improved.

From *Blue Book of the State of Illinois, 1917-1918*, ed. Louis L. Emmerson (Danville, Illinois, 1918), pp. 67-73.

This awakening resulted in the passage of the Tice Road Law by the Forty-eighth General Assembly in 1913. Under the working of this law and its influence on all the road work of the state, Illinois stands today in the sixteenth place among the states in road improvement instead of twenty-third. This change from twenty-third to sixteenth place in so few years would appear to be a very satisfactory increase; but it falls far short of the increased demand for road improvement as evidenced by the public sentiment of the State. This public sentiment indicates that the people of the great agricultural State of Illinois with all its teeming thousands and its unbounded wealth will not be content until it has attained its proper rank in road improvement; until its farming population can carry the products of its farms to market as cheaply as the farmers of any other state, and until it has reached the same place in road improvement that it occupies in agriculture, wealth and population. This insistent demand is continually broadening our view of the subject and hence calls for a continually broadening treatment.

The Tice Law

Under the Tice law there has been laid out a 16,000 mile system of State Aid Roads out of a total of 95,000 miles of country highways in the state; this system to be improved at the joint expense of the state and the respective counties. We have been working upon this 16,000 mile system since July 1, 1914, the day when the first contract was awarded; and during this time over 500 miles have been improved. The location of the improvement in each county has been determined by the county boards. In some instances the county boards have pursued the wise course of placing the improvement in each consecutive year upon the most important and most heavily traveled road in the county. In other instances they have started with the improvement in three or four directions from the center of the county population. In a majority of cases, however, the money has been scattered and the improvement placed upon several widely separated stretches of road with mud at each end and where they can be of little benefit to anybody until they are connected with main centers of population and with each other. The day when these scattered sections will be connected is so far distant in the minds of the people that they are becoming dissatisfied with the working of the law.

It should be said that while the work carried on under the State Aid system has been widely scattered, yet it has given to each county its proportion of money expended and has been of great educational value to the people of the entire state, because of the fact that in nearly every county has been constructed one or more sections of durable hard surfaced road, or the improvement of one or more sections through proper draining and grading.

To improve this 16,000 miles of roads in a durable manner will require not less than $160,000,000. Therefore to complete this work within a period of 20 years will require not less than $8,000,000 per year of which $4,000,000 would be the proportion furnished by the State and $4,000,000 by the respective counties. For the great State of Illinois to appropriate $4,000,000 for each year is not beyond the possibilities, but for the counties to raise $4,000,000 per year in addition to the revenue required for the regular county expenses would in many cases be an impossibility. During the past three years the counties have been called upon to raise $1,000,000 per year to meet a like appropriation of the General Assembly. A number of counties have been unable to meet their proportion of the million dollars required and their state allotment has gone to other counties. It is very evident that if this amount were increased to $4,000,000 many other counties would be unable to meet their proportion, and thus unable to carry on their improvement on a scale required to improve this 16,000 mile system within the 20 year period. But even if the people could be guaranteed $4,000,000 annually from the state and $4,000,000 annually from the counties, they would still be dissatisfied and unwilling to wait that length of time for the improvement of our roads. The evidence of this is seen in the rapidly growing sentiment in favor of County Bond Issues.

County Bond Issues

Two counties, Vermilion and Cook, have already voted the bonds and the roads are in process of construction. Not less than eight other counties have voted upon the proposition, but because of the failure to take the necessary length of time to reach the people with the required information the proposition has failed to receive the necessary votes except in one county, St. Clair, where the vote for the bond issue was carried, but the vote for an additional tax, beyond the constitutional limit to meet the bond and interest payments, was defeated. The counties in which bond issues were defeated are already making preparations to present the question again to the people, and in no less than twenty-five other counties the bond issue is being agitated.

In practically every county there are one or two main arteries of travel through the county which rise to the level of interstate or

Courtesy of the Illinois State Historical Library

Illinois Route 13 in the early 1920s

state highways, and that these main arteries of travel require different treatment from the other State Aid Roads of the county. They should be wider and of a more durable type.

In issuing county bonds, however, the desire to reach all parts of a county, that is, to cover as many miles of the State Aid System as possible, will in many cases prevent the proper improvement of these main arteries. Therefore, when constructed, they may not be of proper width or proper type to give an adequate system of main state highways, hence may require reconstruction at some considerable loss in order to accommodate the traffic on these main roads.

Again, the County Bond System will give us patchwork results. In a county where public sentiment is favorable the bonds will be approved by the voters; in adjoining counties if the question is put up at all the voters will fail to give this method of financing their approval and will insist that the piecemeal method be followed. Thus we shall have excellent roads through one county with mud roads through the adjoining counties; and this hit or miss plan will exist over the entire state. Assuming that twenty-five or thirty counties of the state should vote in favor of the county bond issues, the result would be that in those counties the voters would disapprove a state bond issue that would give a system of state roads to every county in the state and thus prevent the construction of a State Road System for the use of all the people.

Classification of Highways

From another standpoint it is a well-known fact that our roads naturally divide themselves into four classes:

First, the Interstate or National Highways, consisting of the roads of national importance because they are the roads used for practically all of the interstate and transcontinental traffic. These comprise practically 1 per cent of the total mileage of the state. Second, the State Highways, being the main state thoroughfares crossing the state in different directions. These comprise practically 4 per cent of the total mileage of the state.

A state-paved road in the mid-twenties

Courtesy of the Illinois State Historical Library

Third, the County Highways, consisting of the roads carrying the through county traffic. These comprise 10 per cent of the total mileage of the state.

Fourth, the Township Roads, being those purely local in character, which comprise 85 per cent of the total mileage of the state.

These various classes should be at least partially constructed at the expense of the different taxing units; namely, the federal government, the state, the county and the township. The amount of traffic per mile on the roads of the first class is greatest and decreases in the order named. These roads should, therefore, be constructed in the same order if we are to accommodate the greatest number of people.

Necessity for State Bond Issue

To those familiar with the necessity for road improvement in the State of Illinois and the public sentiment back of it, together with the method of construction and financing, it became a firm conviction that the next great step for us to take was the laying out of a system that would include the first and second classes above referred to; namely, the National and State Highways, comprising about 5 per cent of the total mileage of the state, to be constructed with such funds as are to be provided by the federal government combined with a State Bond Issue.

Provisions of the Law

In order that such a plan should be made effective it was first necessary that a bill be passed by the Legislature and then ratified by a vote of the people at the next succeeding general election. Accordingly there was presented to the Fiftieth General Assembly and passed by it a bill providing for a system of roads comprising about 4,600 miles of the main thoroughfares of the state. This system reaches into every county and connects practically all of the cities and villages in excess of 2,000 population, as well as hundreds of smaller ones. Sixty-six per cent of the people of the state reside in the cities and villages which it connects or in the country beside the system. Eighty-six per cent of the people of the state either reside upon the road itself or within five miles of it. These figures are given in order to convey the idea of the service which this system, when improved, will give to the people of this great state.

The law as passed fixes the routes only in a general way; naming the county seat and the larger centers of population as points which must be reached by the system. It leaves the determining of the exact road between the points named to be made by the Department of Public Works and Buildings. Before this is determined a survey will be made covering the different roads connecting the points named in order to determine the most feasible road from the standpoint of cost of construction. Investigations and estimates will also be made as to the traffic which the different roads are carrying and various other points which will assist in determining the best road to take.

The bill further provides for the issuing of $60,000,000 in bonds to cover the cost of construction, said bonds to be issued in annual amounts as required to meet the cost of each year's work and each annual issue to mature in series over a period of 20 years.

. . . .

Bonds Paid from Motor Fees

The most interesting feature of the bill and the one which differs from any other similar bill ever drawn is that the bonds including interest are to be retired from the proceeds of the motor license fees of the state. The bill as written first provides that a tax shall be levied annually to pay the interest on outstanding bonds and the principal of those maturing during the succeeding year.

It says further that income from any other source may be appropriated to pay said bonds and interest; the amount thus appropriated from such source is to be deducted from the amount to be levied.

Still further, if motor fees, which are to be used for the purpose of paying said bond and interest, shall be sufficient in any year to pay the amount due for principal and interest, then no tax shall be levied for such purpose.

The motor fees law passed by the Fiftieth General Assembly provides that after bonds have been issued by the state for the improvement of its highways, the amounts collected for motor and kindred license fees shall *first* be used for each year for the payment of principal and interest due on the said bonds. The amount collected in 1917 on the basis of the old rates will not be less than $1,650,000. Under the new schedule for 1920 this would mean $3,300,000. This sum collected for twenty-five years would total $82,500,000, which is sufficient to retire the bonds, principal and interest, even though there be no further increase in the number of motor cars in this state. . . .

The justice of this proposition is sometimes questioned. People generally recognize that road improvement benefits all classes of people and all lines of business, hence should be paid at least in part by general taxation. If this bond issue system of roads were to be the only roads improved, then it would, beyond a doubt, be an unjust proposition, but when you consider that this system constitutes only 5 per cent of the roads, that the county roads and the township roads will be paid for generally by local taxation; further that the largest part of the benefit through saving in the cost of operation goes to the motor car owners, and that the motor driven cars are so rapidly supplanting all other modes of transportation, it is not considered a matter of injustice that the cost of this improvement should be placed on their shoulders.

It would also be well to look at the matter from another standpoint; namely, the rapidly increasing cost of our State government. It is a well known fact that because of the constant increase in the number of people dependent upon the state; the constant demand for better surroundings for these people; the new activities into which the state is obliged to enter in order to keep pace with our civilization, has caused appropriations to increase by leaps and bounds. This situation caused the state officials and many of the influential members of the Legislature to take the position that they would not favor this plan for road improvement, unless it could be financed outside of the general revenues of the state. Again, from this viewpoint, it appeared to be entirely proper that the motorists should stand sponsor for this improvement.

Questions Submitted to the People

The people of this state should all understand that the bill passed by the Legislature does not authorize the issuing of bonds or the improvement of this system of roads, but is only an enabling act which will permit the people to express themselves, either for or against the proposition, at the general election to be held November, 1918. Unless the majority of the people voting at said election for members of the General Assembly shall vote in favor of the said proposition the bonds cannot be issued and the work cannot go on.

As was said in the beginning this state is now far below its proper place in the matter of road improvement. Our farmers are handicapped in delivering their products to market. In many sections of the state business is practically stopped for many months of the year because of the mud. The improvement of this main system of highways will stimulate the improvement of connecting roads and be the means of redeeming the entire State of Illinois from its present bondage. Only through an extraordinary effort on a big project such as is placed before the people at this time can this be accomplished.

We call upon every man to inform himself thoroughly upon the question so that he will have all the facts before him, be able to judge clearly for himself and impart the necessary information to his neighbor in order that all may vote intelligently upon the proposition in November, 1918.

The English journalist E. Harold Spender, who visited America after World War I as part of an official effort to improve relations between his country and America, toured Illinois in a series of lecture appearances between Chicago and Springfield. His description of the two downstate cities of Springfield and Bloomington appeared in *A Briton in America* (London, 1921).

Springfield and Bloomington, 1920

E. HAROLD SPENDER

Springfield, Nov. 17

We started from Chicago early this morning, and travelling in a pleasant Pullman car we have traversed throughout the day the great plains of the Mid-West. We journeyed south-west across the great State of Illinois, one of the most famous States of the earlier American Union. It is the country of Abraham Lincoln, and there seems always a touch of that great man's spirit in the little western towns through which we have passed. From the train we get glimpses of the little two-storied houses with large porches and verandahs, standing in their own grounds, rather shabby and badly painted, a little ramshackle like "Uncle Abe" himself, but always with the same sense of space and freedom that marked his character. Though the houses are small, the roads are wide and bordered with trees. The houses stand well back from the thoroughfares, with no railings or fences, and always with a certain genial openness

From E. Harold Spender, *A Briton in America* (London, 1921), pp. 56-67, 82-89. Reprinted by permission of William Heinemann, Ltd., Publishers. Footnotes in the original have been omitted.

about the appearance of even the smallest homestead—a hospitable accessibility, like that of Abraham himself.

. . . .

We arrived at Springfield in the dark. The railway station was full of friendly faces and welcoming hands. Committees pounced upon us from the gloom and carried us, bag and baggage, to waiting motor-cars. We rolled smoothly through broad thoroughfares to the Leland Hotel. The lounge of the hotel was full of eager crowds, for many things are happening in this city. A Convention—another Convention!—is sitting here in the capital of Illinois to revise the Constitution of the State, and the town is full of important delegates and lawyers. The revising of the State Constitution is a rare and vital event in an American State, and all these men are full of a high exhilaration and excitement. I noticed again in the lobby of this hotel that few of them sat down, but persisted in standing quite as remorselessly as members of the British Stock Exchange.

I have talked to many of the members of this Convention Committee, including several Ministers of the State. I am deeply interested to find that this Convention recognises as the basis of its new Constitution all the great documents of English freedom— Magna Charta, The Petition of Right, The Bill of Rights. Nothing is admitted to their Constitution which is inconsistent with any of these great British standards. The walls of America are built on British foundations, and it is really useless for people to say that British traditions count no more than any other foreign traditions in the making of America.

For in discussing their new Constitution with these men, I realise instantly that they are bound by the laws of British freedom almost as closely as we are ourselves. They inherit the achievement of British ancestors: they build on the deeds of British heroes. All the time they hark back to British origin and think in terms of British faith. Certainly the best Americans can never forget this aspect of their lives.

But while talking to these distinguished men we have been witnesses of a pretty spectacle which presented the lighter and gayer aspect of American life. A fashionable wedding took place in the hotel this evening—for American weddings always take place in the evening. A great party assembled, including all the rank and fashion of the town and all the beauty of Springfield womanhood. Two things have impressed us. One is the grace and charm of the women; and the other is the elegance of their dress. The women in this Mid-West capital are as finely dressed as any women in Europe. Thanks to their great wealth, they can indulge in this taste freely, and certainly there is no sign of excessive thrift in this matter of dressing. American women are fond of wearing their jewels, and it appears to be a pleasanter habit than that of keeping them in boxes at home. It is surely an amiable thing to share the glitter and delight of your possessions with the world at large!

November 18

Springfield is indeed the city of Abraham Lincoln. He dominates the place, even in memory. For this is where he lived during that important period of his life between the early Mid-West backwoods experiences and the later grandeur of his Presidency. At Springfield he was something "betwixt and between"—not yet the great man of America, but already emerged from the obscurity of his early days. He had become a lawyer and given up the vague, shiftless life of the Mid-West pioneer store-keeper which he had led for so many years.

. . . .

During the morning we have been taken in a motor-car loaned to us, with the usual American hospitality, to visit all these great memorials of Abraham Lincoln's life and death. We have journeyed in this way round this beautiful spacious town, now beflagged in our honour with French and British bunting.

. . . .

The Lincoln home is in Eighth Street, four blocks from the Courthouse. It is open to the public at certain times, and we were most graciously received by the charming lady who now owns it. She is the grand-daughter of the sister of Mrs. Lincoln, and she showed us through the rooms with a loving enthusiasm for the man who had lived there. Like the chamber at the tomb, those rooms are full of mementoes. But the simple furniture best bespeaks the life. One gains the impression of a smooth, middle-class existence, intensely domestic: the life of a man who had passed right beyond his pioneering state, and had settled down to tranquil ways. One wonders how that gawky, long, lank man was contained in those little rooms. I caught a fancy that he was probably more often to be found on the open verandah outside the house, perhaps sitting there in a long chair on the summer evenings with his feet on the railings, pouring out his unending stream of stories to the mixed crowd which probably surrounded him there, as all through his life.

The neighbourhood of the house is full of tales about Abraham Lincoln, many of them bizarre and grotesque. But the one I like best is that which tells how Abraham Lincoln, going down the street outside to an important engagement at the Capitol, passed a little girl who was carrying a very heavy basket. He stopped and insisted on taking the basket from the little girl and carrying it himself all through Springfield. That was characteristic of the man, his indifference to external dignity, his unbounded compassion for the weak, his readiness to bear the burdens of others, his essential and fundamental goodness of heart.

From the house we passed to the Capitol, and there we paused to look at Lincoln's second statue. It is a representation of a younger Abraham, probably during the period of his State political life, and alongside of it stands the statue of his great friend and rival Stephen Douglas—a stout, thick-set little man, rather recalling Charles Fox. The interesting fact about this second statue of Lincoln is that it represents him without the goatee beard conspicuous in the statue presented to London by the United States, and now generally associated with his features. Shorn of that ugly appendage, the face is far more interesting. The close-lipped mouth and the square jaw reveal the secret of his strength and determination, hidden from the world afterwards by the straggling beard.

. . . .

We now hastened back to the hotel, where we were to be entertained at lunch by the Springfield Luncheon Club. It was a great and enthusiastic gathering, and certainly Springfield did her best to show both England and France what she could do in the way of welcome and hospitality. When I ventured to ask that gathering whether they would, in the end, after they had finished with their politics, come back to the assistance of afflicted Europe, they replied with one unanimous shout—"Yes! We will!" Whether that shout was merely the exhilaration of the moment, or whether it represented the deeper mind of America time alone will show.

We have spent the afternoon motoring round the suburbs, and paying a series of visits to the homes of hospitable Americans, who have overwhelmed us with invitations. I will not trespass upon their privacy except to note the beauty of their houses. We visited ex-Senator Hays, who possesses one of the finest private libraries that I have yet seen in an American home. Then we visited the villa of a rich business man which seemed the last word in artistic luxury. Every bedroom, including also the servants', has a bath room with a shower bath. The guest's room is the best of all, a happy touch in home-making. It has a marble bath worthy of a Roman Emperor. There are sleeping porches and verandahs all round the house for use in the hot weather. The study of the master of the house is in the basement, and is surrounded with pictures of the American Revolution, showing that no luxury abates the patriotism of the true American. We ended by glimpsing into a house where the hostess was entertaining a bevy of American girls. For in Springfield, as in most other American towns, the women are quite happy with their own company. A prettier set of girls one could not wish to see: their tea frocks exquisite, with short sleeves, but otherwise covering the body in a way that puts the present nudity of Europe to some shame. One more point—they were really drinking tea, and not smoking cigarettes!

. . . .

. . . Bloomington, Nov. 19.

We rose this morning at 5 a.m. in the Leland House Hotel at Springfield. In the dim dark we finished that precarious process of packing which "vexes public men" on travel intent.

We had been promised a five o'clock breakfast. But one of the weak spots in these admirable American hotels is the supply of early food. The instructions seem to get handed on from one head of department to another—and it is marvellous how many heads of departments there are in the smallest of these Mid-West hotels. The only real "servants" appear to be the negroes. Every white man or woman becomes a "manager"—of sorts: and managers don't like early rising. Division of labour leads to efficiency up to a point, but beyond that point it becomes a form of industrial stagnation.

This morning at Springfield, Illinois, for instance, it shocked up against the earliness of the hour and sank in deep water.

Compelled at last to make a bolt for our train we had the hungry experience of passing our breakfast on our descent to the hall—we in the lift and the breakfast on the stairs. We climaxed in a game of hide and seek. The breakfast and the negro dodged us. At last, despairing of our quest, we took refuge in the hospitable car of our friend and were whisked breakfastless to the station.

Then came a glorious relief. For lo! there stood to hand in the station restaurant a gracious breakfast of fresh fruit—apples rosy-red and grape fruit bulging—steaming coffee and hot rolls—such as one could not dream of in war-worn Europe. Thus refreshed, we quickly forgave and forgot.

So we started back eastward to this little town of Bloomington in mid-Illinois, where I was booked to address the students of the Wesleyan University at ten o'clock. We travelled in an "Observation Car"—a car attached to the rear of the train, and provided with "big windows"—which gave us an admirable vision of the Mid-West prairies and vast corn fields which used to supply Europe with maize at a time when the exchange permitted it. To-day the county is in its winter dress. The golden maize has been plucked and the fields are a dirty yellow, dotted with bare stalks. But it is all new to us, and we loved every little village that we passed—the freedom of the little wooden houses and the pretty thoroughfares.

At the station we expected the usual committee. But instead we were greeted by an old Oxford friend—a contemporary from the eighties—who, seeing our arrival notified in the Press, had walked down to the station to welcome us. My friend is typical of the American human kaleidoscope. He came to America twenty years ago as a railway manager and remained to become an Episcopalian minister. He is now in charge of the principal church in this little town of Bloomington. Although now a fully equipped American, he remains British in heart and memory. How often throughout this tour we have met this type of British American! Prosperous and patriotic, true to "The Star Spangled Banner" but still always, with a touch of the exile, eager to see an English face and to hear an English voice!

"I just thought I'd come and meet someone from the old country," is the way they put it. Or if he is a Yorkshireman then rather wistfully, "And how may they be doing up Bradford way." Or if he be a Lancashire man—"Do you happen to have been down Manchester of late?" Or if he be from Somerset, he grips me with both hands and smiles all over his face when he hears that my native town is Bath.

It is wonderful how long these memories of the old country survive. It is not only the Irish-Americans who love their old country.

We have been lucky to-day. For these good British-Americans—this old Balliol man and his American family—have looked after my travel-weary wife, letting her rest in their house, while I have been lecturing and speaking.

The sight of the morning was the crowd of eager young faces of the boys and girls at the Wesleyan University—a vast hall packed with young men and women allowed to sit as they liked and with whom they liked—just left to their own sense of discipline and order. When I looked at these glad and happy faces, and received their joyous welcome, I thought of how differently we order these things at Oxford—of the young men and women separated into their flocks and eyeing one another furtively over their books—and I wondered which was the better way, the English or the American!

They are good listeners, these young Americans. But I think we all enjoyed ourselves best when the lecture was over. Then they told me all about their University, and their happy life there, and they brought out their Kodaks and took photographs of me, and made me sign autograph books and do a number of other trivial things, just expressive of their general pleasure at meeting a visitor from England. At the gates we parted, and I suppose I shall never see again any of that great crowd. May they live happy lives!

But America leaves one no pause for regret. My guide and guardian immediately switched me off to eat with the inevitable Town Luncheon Club. What I said at that luncheon does not matter, for most of the time was occupied by a formidable American orator—"spell-binder" is, I believe, the word—who was billed to lecture on Abraham Lincoln. It was a gathering of lawyers, well-dressed, prosperous men, and I think I told them that Europe was not quite so prosperous as they were. But my chief recollection of that luncheon is that our speeches were preceded and followed by a band which played jazz music with amazing violence, and comfortably drowned most of our conversation. Listening to this music I was not surprised to hear from my neighbour that many of the melodies were of African origin. A fearful thought then possessed me—that possibly the musical tradition of America is destined to be submerged by the aboriginal music of the negro!

For it is a curious fact that although America shines in many of the arts—especially in painting and sculpture—she has, as yet, struck no original line in music except along these semi-barbaric paths.

Finding it impossible to talk, I spent most of my time watching the keen, mobile, clean-shaven faces of the men sitting around me, and I became conscious of a certain boredom and weariness reflected on their countenances, as if the endurance of these jazz noises were merely accepted as one of the sacrifices of life offered on the altar of convention.

Luncheon over and its turmoil abated, we enjoyed a few hours of afternoon rest in the British-American home of our hosts. We obtained here a vision of that large American class which has procured no increase of wealth during the war, and feel only the incidence of high prices. It is a class that must never be forgotten if we are estimating the comparative well-being of the English-speaking peoples. For it is through the common experiences of that class on both sides of the water that America and Britain have the best chance of being drawn together.

Here was a household built on an income corresponding to £400 English sterling—with three children ranging from ten to fifteen—a small house but no servants. It is a hard life.

The difference indeed between such a house in America and England is the far ampler supply in America of facilities for cooking, warming and cleaning. Central heating alone saves much work on fires. Shopping is easier and quicker in the wonderful American stores. Holidays are simple and cheap. For such a family in America is freed from the British tribute to the seaside lodging-house keeper. They enjoy an almost free holiday in the vast spaces of this continent. For three months every summer they go camping out on the shores of Lake Michigan, living in tents, fishing, bathing, and renewing their energies in a glorious experience of the simple life. That is one signal advantage to set against the drudgery of the domestic life.

For an hour or so we have wandered about this town, visiting the fine bookshops and other stores, all bespeaking the wonderful wealth and well-being of this Middle-West city. All round you is a sense of national well-being, but perhaps most of all in the multitude of motor-cars which crowd the streets. It is a low estimate to say that one out of three adults in any of these Mid-Western towns possesses a motor car. At mid-day you see all of the side streets blocked with them. There are practically no chauffeurs: nearly everyone drives his own car.

Our host has been telling us of some glorious examples of the motor-mania which now possesses America. The workmen spend much of their spare cash in purchasing motors, usually on the hire system. A strike crisis recently arose because the workmen engaged on a new building did not consider that sufficient facilities were provided for "parking" their motor cars. Walking around, I expressed a surprise at seeing a number of cars "parked" behind one of the great stores. "You have a rich shopping class here," I ventured to say. My friend laughed.

"It is not the shopping class," he said. "It's the girls in the stores. That's where they put their cars while they are at work."

Perhaps not a bad investment; because, after all, it enables the girls to live out in the fresh air at lower rents instead of being crowded up in expensive lodgings in the centre of the town. But it all speaks of high wages and a great national reserve of wealth and energy.

A lady engaging a charwoman recently in one of these American towns, was faced by the charwoman with the following interesting dilemma.

"Have you room for my car in your garage, or will you fetch me in yours?"

Surely a very perplexing question, and likely to add very much to the problems of the modern mistress.

. . . .

Len Small, a farmer by trade, was born in Kankakee in 1862. Prior to being elected governor in 1921, he was state treasurer and state senator, among other offices. The following selection shows that, like Dr. Pangloss in Voltaire's *Candide*, Governor Small—along with most Illinoisans—believed that he was living in the best of all possible worlds in late 1928, even while America was on the brink of economic disaster—the Great Depression.

Governor Small's Annual Message

LEN SMALL

Mr. President, Mr. Speaker, and Members of the Fifty-Sixth General Assembly Representing the People of the State of Illinois.

Ladies and Gentlemen:

The constitution of our State requires that the Governor shall at the close of his term of office give to the General Assembly information by message of the condition of the State and shall recommend such measures as he shall deem expedient.

In obedience to this duty, as well as for the purpose of recording in organized form the progress of our State and the activities of our state government from the beginning of my first term, January 10, 1921, to the end of my second term in January, 1929, I am transmitting in some detail a resume of various activities and accomplishments that have marked that period.

The fullest cooperation of the various Departments of State government has attained the purpose and aim of government which is to assist in promoting and preserving the health, comfort, safety, convenience and morals of the people. It has to a degree relieved the burdens of the poor and oppressed, has brought comfort to the diseased, distressed and helpless, has assisted in education and enlightenment, has aided the worthy and ambitious to become established in life, and has to a measurable extent maintained the equality of opportunity that furnishes to talent and ambition a chance to rise to success and prosperity.

The past eight years have been marked by growing prosperity and wealth throughout Illinois as well as throughout the United States. The comforts and conveniences of modern life have been enjoyed by a constantly increasing number of people. Many conveniences, which as recently as ten or fifteen years ago were looked upon as luxuries, have become common to a vast majority of the people.

From Len Small, *Illinois Progress, 1921-28* (Springfield, 1929), pp. 5-9.

Courtesy of the Illinois State Historical Library

Governor Len Small

We have witnessed in an amazingly brief period of time a tremendous and unprecedented spread of higher education. Enlightenment and learning have become the rule rather than the exception. Not only has formal education through organized institutions of learning been given to a larger number of people, but other means of education and enlightenment have developed apace, so that today there is probably no nation in the world where intelligence and knowledge is as general as in our land.

Modern invention has broken down the isolation that formerly limited the horizon of those who live on farms, and even of those who live in villages and cities. The automobile and the hard roads enable all to travel considerable distances, and the radio enables almost every family daily to keep in touch with the events and progress of the world.

Government has created the conditions under which the inventions of science and the arts could be enjoyed by an ever increasing number of people, and has relieved its citizens of those burdens which business and commerce cannot or will not carry.

Our State during the past eight years has kept pace in all respects with the most prosperous and progressive states in the Union and in many outstanding instances has assumed unquestioned leadership.

Economy and Finances

The finances of our State are in splendid condition. The treasury balance as of January 1st, 1929 was over $40,000,000, as compared with a treasury balance of $15,132,658.03 on January 1st, 1921. This balance includes the general revenue fund as well as such special funds as roads, waterways, conservation, and education. In all of those branches, the activities of the State have greatly increased in recent years.

When I became Governor in 1921, the Legislature was called upon to appropriate nearly $2,500,000.00 to take care of deficiencies which had occurred in the operation of the State institutions and in the Departments of Health, Education, and Agriculture, and that were necessary to cover the operation of those departments to the end of the biennium which had begun in 1919.

Since that time, during the past eight years there have been practically no deficiency appropriations necessary, excepting for cyclone and flood relief, and small amounts, totaling about $43,000.00, for newly created departments where the expenses could not be accurately anticipated. On the other hand, during the six years from 1921 to 1927, out of appropriations made by the General Assembly for State purposes, we have saved $16,737,720.00 which, although appropriated, has not been spent and was not drawn out of the State treasury. In addition, a sum of more than $2,000,000.00 has been saved to the State in the past eight years in discounts earned by the prompt auditing and payment of bills through the Finance Department. This reflects great credit on those officials whose duty it is to pass upon the requisitions and vouchers presented for payment.

A detailed report of the building program and construction at the various institutions and educational plants of the State will be made when speaking of the activities of those departments. The total amount spent for buildings and permanent improvements during the past 8 years has been very large and has proven an enormous task. Permanent improvements at the State institutions during the past 8 years have cost in excess of $22,000,000.00, and in addition $8,000,000.00 has been spent for buildings at the University of Illinois.

Budget

In accordance with the provisions of the Civil Administrative Code, the Department of Finance has, at the beginning of each session of the General Assembly during my term of office, prepared a budget of the needs of the Code Departments for the following biennium and the requests of the elective State Officers and the

University of Illinois, which has been transmitted by me to the General Assembly.

The law requires that "The Governor shall, as soon as possible and not later than four weeks after the organization of the General Assembly, submit a State Budget, embracing therein the amounts recommended by him to be appropriated to the respective departments, offices and institutions, and for all other public purposes, the estimated revenues from taxation, the estimated revenues from sources other than taxation, and an estimate of the amount required to be raised by taxation." In accordance with the law, the Director of Finance is, at present, engaged in compiling the requests from the several State Officers and the suggestions of the Directors under the Civil Administrative Code on their requirements for the ensuing two years, which may be of assistance to the incoming Governor.

. . . .

2: The Great Depression

Beginning the special accounts on the Depression, Thomas B. Littlewood, in a selection from *Horner of Illinois* (Evanston, 1969), concentrates on the years 1933 to 1935 and on the heroic efforts of Governor Henry Horner to provide adequate relief to victims of an ever-worsening economic crisis. Goaded by the stubborn insistence of Harry Hopkins that Illinois develop its own relief program, Horner forced a reluctant legislature first to approve a bond issue referendum, and then to pass a sales tax in order to finance state relief. Littlewood was the *Chicago Sun-Times'* Springfield correspondent from 1953 to 1965. For the past decade he has been a member of the Washington bureau. Such measures were indeed necessary, according to David J. Maurer's study of unemployment in the state during the Depression. Maurer believes that Illinois was a microcosm of the nation's economy and, as such, reveals much of the American experience during the 1930s. His article was published in *Essays in Illinois History in Honor of Glenn Huron Seymour* (Carbondale, 1968), edited by Donald Tingley. Maurer, who specializes in recent American history, is a member of the history department at Eastern Illinois University. For other insights into the Great Depression in Illinois, see Alex Gottfried, *Boss Cermak of Chicago: A Study of Political Leadership* (Seattle, 1962) and Cabell Phillips, *From Crash to the Blitz, 1929-1939* (New York, 1969).

The Battle for the Dole

THOMAS B. LITTLEWOOD

In the context of today's social dialogue, Henry Horner's Standard Club orientation would probably warrant the label of social "moderate" or "conservative with a heart" or something of that

From Thomas B. Littlewood, *Horner of Illinois* (Evanston, 1969), pp. 108-119, 240-242. Reprinted by permission of Northwestern University Press. Footnotes in the original have been omitted.

sort—his political posture fell short of social liberalism as we know it in the modern welfare state. He combined an intense feeling for people with an emotional reverence, typical of his well-to-do cronies, for the platitudes that are said to have made the nation great—private initiative, business enterprise, etc.

Oftentimes Horner spoke of the "constant danger of the establishment of a permanent dole and a pauper class" in America. To one friend he wrote that "a dole . . . is bound to be enervating to what we have been proud to call American vitality and courage." Another time he wrote, "I realize how difficult it is to get out of the dole once we are in it. However, all of us must realize that the dole is one of the dangers of American life, and the sooner we get out of it, the better it will be for the normal process of both government and community life." Horner coupled fundamental economic conservatism with a feeling for people in trouble. In 1933, though, theoretical pronouncements about the danger of the dole were to be proven academic.

Three hundred policemen donned steel helmets and took up axe handles to deal with hungry demonstrators at city relief stations in Chicago. "It has been brought to our attention," reported the National Guard military intelligence officer, "that the possibility or desirability of revolution is being openly discussed . . . in Chicago, the Tri-Cities area, Springfield, and Granite City. . . . Certain leaders of farm organizations prophesied that unless the economic condition of the farmer improved in the near future there would be revolution within twelve months. . . . Talk of revolution is common through Illinois among the small businessmen's group."

Looking back, it now seems incredible that Horner's hardest legislative struggle involved a proposed tax for the feeding of starving families. The tax structure bore heavily upon land, buildings, and farm equipment. An income tax already had been held unconstitutional. And Horner had promised to relieve the disproportionate load on property owners. But in 1933 no tax—including his only practical alternative, the sales tax—would have been greeted with anything like pleasure in Illinois. Although Democrats had majorities in both houses of the legislature, a rare privilege, the minority Republicans made political capital by being against taxes—period. The sales tax did not set well with either the ideological liberals, who were disturbed by its regressive impact upon the poor, or with the retail merchants. Horner's old friendships in the commercial community proved helpful though. D. F. Kelly of The Fair store wrote the governor in February that although he could not publicly advocate the tax, "my private opinion is that there is no other way to take care of the poor during these trying times." Kelly became Horner's ambassador on State Street, trying to persuade other leading merchants to see his point of view.

For more than a year now local governments and private charities had been unable to hold back the waves of destitution and suffering. The Illinois Emergency Relief Commission administered bond issues and other appropriations, with county relief commissions being formed to set local standards for assistance. Later this aid was supplemented by the first of the special federal programs, the Civil Works Administration. Governor Horner and Pat Nash traveled to Washington pleading for still greater federal assistance. As it turned out, in the year ending August 1, 1933, the federal government contributed 99 per cent of the $68,000,000 spent for relief in Illinois.

. . . .

Those who expected the benevolent New Deal to continue its prolonged bankrolling of virtually all the relief burden in the industrial states failed to reckon with Harry L. Hopkins. The son of a harness shop proprietor in Sioux City, Iowa, this former social worker on the lower East Side of New York City was brusque, cocky, and ambitious. As much as Governor Horner admired Harold Ickes, he despised Harry Hopkins. And Hopkins functioned not only as federal relief administrator but also as administrator of the New Deal's work-relief program, the Civil Works Administration. In both capacities he cultivated Mayor Kelly and the other big-city leaders with an eye on the presidency in 1940. This farsightedness was shared, though, by two of his enemies within the administration, Postmaster General Farley and Ickes.

In the fall of 1933 Hopkins advanced federal funds to Illinois on condition that the state take immediate steps to raise money on its own for the winter needs. Governor Horner recalled the legislature in special session and proposed a $30,000,000 bond issue for the November referendum ballot.

. . . .

Although the bond issue did succeed, the petty, politically inspired bickering in the Statehouse chambers over this relief project and others that followed is one of the sorry chapters in the history of Lincoln's state. The Decatur *Herald* commented, sympathetically, that "politics [in the relief situation] will not be adjourned until the specter of anarchy is in sight." Bishop Griffin, whose casual friendship with his neighbor in the Executive Mansion had now been bound firmly through personal fellowship, told the governor in a letter:

"I fear that the United States is becoming one big insane asylum. . . . Our elected representatives are watching the passing show and leaving you to take full responsibility before the public. When there is any honor and credit, they like to take it. When there is any grief, the Governor is expected to go it alone."

Whenever the sniping opposition lacked for ammunition, they were helped by the barely disguised animosity between Horner and Harry Hopkins. The federal official recognized no Illinois authority other than Mayor Kelly, and the governor finally had to complain to the president that he could not even get through to Hopkins by telephone. Hopkins dispatched two investigators to check into alleged irregularities in the Illinois CWA program and later made an army district engineer the state administrator of CWA instead of placing this responsibility with the relief commission. A tapering off of the CWA in Illinois at the end of the year also proved damaging. In November, two hundred thousand heads of families were working on CWA projects. But the National Guard reports informed the governor that in Rock Island "much of the money paid CWA workers has gone to pay old bills in neighborhood stores." In the same community "some mass meetings have been held by the so-called CWA Protective Association and another to raise funds for the Daily Worker. Efforts are being made [by the Communists] to organize the steelworkers' union. Curtailment of only 11 per cent in CWA work brought people back to the relief agency." "Pessimistic utterances" were also reported in Kankakee and Bloomington "about what will happen when CWA funds are depleted." In Springfield "the mental attitude of the public has taken a distinct turn to the pessimistic, caused mostly by the cut in CWA workers. . . . The Communist Party has been holding a series of meetings. Mining conditions are very unsettled. Loaning agencies, both farm and city, report their borrowers depressed and pessimistic."

Nature did little to soften the hardship on the farms. In 1933, hail, wind, and rain devastated fifteen hundred farms in the northeastern part of the state. Half the farmers were without resources to buy seeds for replanting, until the relief commission and the state agriculture department came to their rescue. Then in the following summer, severe drought, cinch bugs, and ear worms cut the corn crop to about twenty bushels per acre, the lowest yield in sixty-eight years.

Another part of the National Guard report stated that "stevedores on the barge lines at Cairo are being organized by the Marine Workers Industrial Union, a purely Communistic organization of the most direct actionist type." In Rockford, said the guard, "the Unemployed Councils (slightly red) hold regular meetings and make demands upon relief agencies—nothing serious."

In Illinois the legislature meets in regular session every other year from January to the end of June. Because of the recurring problems Governor Horner kept the legislators in special session much of the rest of the time too. After the regular session of 1933, there were four special sessions. Except for a two-week break, the two houses were in session from October of that year until May of 1934.

. . . .

The members of the Illinois Legislature, like those of other states in which the business of legislating is an underpaid, part-time job, have generally not been of superior quality. Independent of mind, hungry for patronage and other favors, they are usually convinced that they could govern the state better than the man elected to try to do it. An impetuous, quick-tempered orator from Chicago, twenty-eight-year-old Benjamin Adamowski, became Democratic House leader in 1935 after Horner had rejected him as being too young in 1933. The governor had barnstormed the state in 1934 asking for the election of legislators who sympathized with FDR's recovery program. His campaigning evidently helped, for twenty-two additional Democrats won.

. . . .

Despite his yeoman's service implementing the New Deal in Illinois, the governor's federal patronage rewards proved disappointing. Hopkins, furthermore, made it plain that federal relief money would be cut off if the state did not raise its ante and implied that there had been wasteful political administration of the Illinois program. Auditor Barrett, a member of the state relief commission, clashed repeatedly with the professional social workers, alleging "looseness" in the issuance of relief checks. A legislative investigating committee was formed to look into these charges. Howard O. Hunter, Chicago field representative for the Federal Emergency Relief Administration, wrote Horner that he considered the investigation "an obscene farce." He said the committee members had no idea what they were supposed to be investigating and studiously avoided the assistance of anybody who knew anything about the subject.

Even before the new legislature could organize in January of 1935, the governor was compelled to bring back the old legislature for a fourth special session. If the property tax were to be suspended again, forfeiting $30,000,000 a year in potential revenue, Horner had to be certain that the sales tax, due to expire in mid-1935, would be continued. "After fifteen months of experience," he informed the legislators, "the sales tax has been found practical and efficient. . . . No tax is of itself popular. It can only be said to be popular in the sense that it is preferred over other taxes. To my mind it is unthinkable that we shall take the backward step of discarding our present constructive and beneficial method of obtaining state revenues."

The Monmouth *Daily Review Atlas,* a downstate newspaper, disagreed. "Who is best able to pay for expenses of state government?" asked the paper. "The rich, the big corporations, or the poor to whom Jewish Horner's 2 per cent toll is a real hardship? The sales tax is a blessing to the rich. It is a damn outrage on the poor and those unable to pay it."

Such talk pained Horner because he knew it to be essentially true. . . .

Within a few weeks it was necessary not only to continue the sales tax but to raise it. Governor Horner advised the new legislature that President Roosevelt was now pursuing a policy of finding work for the employables but was turning back to local communities the responsibility of caring for the unemployables, other than the aged and blind. Cash relief replaced disbursing order relief. Illinois also began making its first old-age "pension" grants (under the 1935

The inauguration of Governor Henry Horner

Courtesy of the Illinois State Historical Library

federal Social Security Act), widely supplemented by general assistance for medical care. Horner emphasized that he remained strongly opposed to restoring the property tax. Still there were about one million unemployed in Illinois who "through no fault of their own are denied the opportunity to labor for their daily bread. They cannot wait while we seek to perfect or adjust an economic system which will assure a job to every employable person and livelihood to each wage-earner."

With Mayor Kelly's backing, the administration sponsored legislation raising the tax rate to 3 per cent. The governor used his personal persuasion on legislators who cringed under anti-tax pressure from home. Paul Powell, a young Democrat from Vienna in southern Illinois, where the folks were "thinning out the soup a little more," showed a stack of telegrams to Horner. The governor thumbed through the telegrams, and anger flashed in his beady eyes. "That one cost a buck! That one cost 75 cents! I'm interested in the people who don't have a buck, who don't have a nickel!"

But, ever the dignified judge, he could not bring himself to the sordid practicality of swapping jobs for votes. Ben Adamowski, his House leader, reported that he could dredge up three Republican votes in exchange for twelve patronage jobs. Horner's mustache twitched with indignation. "How can they . . . when human misery is involved . . . put this on that level?" Leaving the governor's office, Adamowski mentioned his problem to Mayor Kelly, who was waiting to see Horner. "Will they take city jobs?" the mayor inquired. The leader checked and, finding city jobs acceptable, was able to chalk up three more Republican votes.

Despite the governor's persuasiveness and the mayor's patronage generosity, the bills failed miserably in both houses. They fell again and again, along with companion measures extending the sales tax rate to public utilities. . . .

On April 18, Hopkins cut off federal funds until Illinois raised taxes. But the Republicans maintained their opposition, on the contention that waste and extravagance dominated relief administration. Representative Lyons called Horner's statement a "silly symphony." He said he had received no mail response to the speech, "proving that Horner is dead. Deader than Cermak. He is a political corpse." The legislative stalemate dragged on. Compromises were tried and failed. . . . By May 2nd the last food orders were exhausted. Transient relief stations in Chicago for fifteen thousand residents of other states closed. Horner took to the radio again, warning that every twenty-four hours without legislation would bring an additional twenty thousand families face to face with starvation. He called the Republicans "obstructionists." In conclusion, he said "the hearts that had remained indifferent to the pleas of the hungry beat in ready response to the call of the officials of the power companies of the state."

Hopkins explained in Washington that "I've got to see $3,000,000 a month on the line before Illinois will get any further federal allotments." Horner arranged an emergency conference with Hopkins in Cleveland, and on May 24, $5,000,000 in federal funds were released to end the crisis at a time when the Illinois Emergency Relief Commission had virtually ceased operations and shut down its relief stations.

With the pressure finally off, the legislature passed the sales tax increase on the sixth roll-call vote. The crisis had been averted, and, stewing silently at the lack of help from Washington, the governor was confined to bed with what was described as a bad cold. Actually, Dr. Nathan Rosen, Horner's Springfield physician, had been alarmed by his rising blood pressure, racing heart beat, and the appearance of a metallic sound in his aortic region. A nineteen-year-old graduate nurse was brought in to enforce the doctor's rules, which included another try at a low-protein, reduced-salt diet. The patient balked, of course, at being bedridden. "You tell me what I should do and then I'll do as I damn please," he instructed the nurse. "No slip of a girl is going to give me a bed pan." The arrival, at long last, of the federal relief check in the amount of several million dollars was deemed by the governor an occasion worthy of celebration. He popped the cork on a bottle of imported champagne and shared it with the young nurse. She recalled many years later that, inspired by the champagne, the governor forgot his blood pressure and chased her about the mansion later in the evening, a clear violation of all the doctor's orders and a startling experience for a damsel fresh out of nurses' training. The governor lost the foot race and soon recovered.

. . . .

For many reasons, the years through which Horner served as governor marked the start of a turning point in Illinois political history. Early in this century, progressivism penetrated the power structure of Chicago and Illinois in only a very limited way. Power in the old Chicago was monopolized by self-made men—industrialists, grain merchants, department store owners, editors, and politicians—unburdened by any notable tradition of public responsibility. It will be recalled that Horner himself was reluctant about taking Finnegan's advice to strike hard at the Insull scandal. But the conscience of Illinois was disturbed by what happened to Horner. Although the Democratic organization would continue to be a boss-led party through the 1960's, its leader would never again be able to act in as arbitrary and blatantly disdainful a way as had Tony Cermak and Ed Kelly. Although the leader of the Democrats in the 1950's and 1960's, Mayor Richard J. Daley, does not enjoy a glittering national reputation, politics *is* several shades cleaner now in Illinois than it was then. Of course, it would be foolish to suggest that the Cash-Value School of Politics has disbanded altogether in the state. As Horner once put it, there are few saints on this earth, and politics is certainly the last place to look for them. But the machine is not monolithic, Daley *does* reflect a substantial segment of the community, and—by Chicago standards—he is, in some respects, almost semi-saintly. Moreover, in time of dire need the party has turned, albeit reluctantly and only occasionally, to distinguished Democrats like Adlai Stevenson and Paul Douglas. Almost certainly, the processes of change that began with the Horner-Kelly experiences and are being exacerbated by today's almost unmanageable urban social problems will produce the end of party bossism when Daley retires, and maybe sooner.

Many of the most enduring monuments to Horner's administration involved his role as middleman for the New Deal in Illinois. Kelly and Nash were not ideological New Dealers, and neither was John Stelle. Nor can it be said that Chicago, the capital of the conservative heartland of the nation, appeared initially receptive to the economic reforms. Horner stood out as an articulate spokesman for NRA, social security, unemployment insurance, and emergency relief, even though Roosevelt persisted in working with the big-city bosses and simply ignored whatever indiscretions they perpetrated. Horner's changing attitudes only reflected the shift in public opinion that has led to today's general acceptance of our version of the welfare state. Despite his Standard Club background, he had as instinctive a feeling for the victims of the depression as any radical. On his deathbed, Horner's last words to Arch Bowen were, "I am glad to know we have been able to do so much—you and I—for those who need help."

Crisis and federal assistance combined to strengthen the office of governor in the 1930's. In Illinois a historical parallel can be drawn between Horner's experience and that of the Civil War governor Richard Yates. The war resulted in a significant enlargement of the scope of the office, just as the depression did later. Governors were called upon by the president to fulfill many direct obligations. In 1863 the Democratic-controlled legislature refused to appropriate funds, and the governor had to negotiate loans from private financial institutions to run the state. In the 1930's the Republican-controlled legislature came close to doing the same by refusing to appropriate funds for relief. Both Yates and Horner exploited the crisis situation and the demands of the federal government to enlarge the powers of the office. Although Horner clashed continuously with Harry Hopkins on one hand and Mayor Kelly's Chicago administration on the other, he used the twin levers of federalism and crisis to enhance the powers of the governor.

Always the skilled politician, Roosevelt mobilized his natural allies, labor leaders for instance, in his battles with his natural enemies in the business community. Horner could never untangle the coal mine union mess in Illinois. Although public opinion probably favored the Progressives, UMW leader John Lewis had access to the national administration, canceling out the governor's effectiveness. . . .

Through it all, Horner emerges as a superb politician. He projected simplicity, sincerity, and goodness. He would most likely have been a master at modern television campaigning because of those qualities and the force of his personality—attributes it is now fashionable to call *charisma.* Henry Horner—a Jew—bridged the cultural and emotional gap between metropolitan Chicago and rural downstate as no one else has done before or since.

If the message of this story is the effect of stress in high office upon a man with "thoroughgoing integrity," perhaps we should also devote a moment of reflection to the wonder of a system which could give Illinois at its moment of greatest civil peril a one-time precinct worker for Hinky Dink Kenna who a few eventful years later would be universally regarded as "the Real Goods."

. . . .

Unemployment in Illinois During the Great Depression

DAVID J. MAURER

For a great many Americans the phrase, the Great Depression, means mass unemployment. An older generation of Americans

From *Essays in Illinois History in Honor of Glenn Huron Seymour*, pp. 120-132, edited by Donald F. Tingley. Copyright © 1968 by Southern Illinois University Press. Reprinted by permission of Southern Illinois University Press. Footnotes in the original have been omitted.

realizes the implications of high unemployment figures (breadlines, mortgage foreclosures, evictions, lost opportunities, and despair), but the younger generation can only note the devastation of the Depression by examining the written record. From the bleak pages of government documents between 1930 and 1941 inclusive, come the unemployment and relief figures, but only through interpretation in a narrative form are they intelligible. Because the state of Illinois contained within its boundaries the elements of the American economy in microcosm, it reflected with a high degree of accuracy the condition of the nation. Therefore, by spotlighting the unemployment relief story of Illinois in the decade, we can learn something of the circumstances of the United States during the Great Depression.

After the stock market crash in 1929 the American public began to realize that its economy was in trouble, but difficulties appeared to be local. Illinois' agricultural and manufacturing diversity delayed the full effect of the Depression on its citizens until the fall of 1930. Until then unemployment seemed no worse than in the winter of 1921-1922. But by the winter of 1930-1931 the number of unemployed increased alarmingly. In December 1930 payrolls in manufacturing were over 30 per cent lower than they were twelve months earlier and in January 1931 unemployment in Illinois was estimated in excess of 700,000. Hardest hit were Cook County and southern mining counties like Franklin and Williamson. In Chicago the factories were laying off thousands and hardly anyone was hiring. Few of the mines were open even part time. Frank Bane, director of the American Association of Public Welfare Officials, reported many families in the mining communities lived in actual destitution and there wasn't any possibility of county relief.

By the fall of 1931 almost every county in the state reeled under the impact of staggering unemployment. According to the census of 1930, there were 3,184,875 gainfully employed workers in the state. The best estimate for October 1931 reported 1,100,0000 men and women unemployed. In succeeding months the unemployment rate continued to rise until the figure peaked at 1,500,000 unemployed in January 1933.

The above facts are valuable but they cannot relate how parents suffered because their children lacked shoes to go to school or how men despaired over their condition. A checkup of the Chicago public schools in June 1931 revealed that sympathetic and generous teachers already hit by payless paydays were providing lunch for over 11,000 hungry children. On September 19, 1931, Mrs. Elizabeth Conkey, commissioner of public welfare in Chicago, related that several hundred homeless unemployed women slept nightly in

Maxwell Street during the Depression

Chicago's parks. The one free women's lodging house accommodated only one hundred persons. A social worker related the following story to her co-workers. "A woman in Chicago, when her husband was idle, worked all summer on farms outside the city. She left at four in the morning and returned at seven o'clock at night." Multiply these stories a million times and the magnitude of the Depression in Illinois will be seen.

Neither individuals, charitable organizations, nor government ignored the mountain of misery created by the Depression. From the beginning families, friends, relatives, and strangers helped those less fortunate than themselves. And many who helped, in time, needed help too. Charitable organizations increased the scope of their activities. Throughout the state of Illinois the government strove to provide assistance. In the end, all were overwhelmed. Treasuries, public and private, were exhausted. The records indicate a rout by 1933 in the battle to provide relief for the unemployed in Illinois.

In 1929 most private, public, and church charities in Illinois expended their income on their traditional concerns. Only a small share of their monies and energies were devoted to relief work of all

1. Relief expenditures from private
funds for all types of relief,
1929-1935[1]

Fiscal year ending June 30	Expenditures
1929	$1,045,748
1930	1,411,180
1931	7,925,388
1932	8,431,823
1933	3,501,525
1934	1,403,489
1935	942,480

1. Source: *Biennial Report of the Illinois Emergency Relief Commission,* Covering the Period July 1, 1934, through June 30, 1936 (Chicago, 1936), p. 136. Among the leading charitable organizations engaged in relief work were: Red Cross, Catholic Charities, Jewish Social Service Bureau, Joint Emergency Relief Stations, Salvation Army, and United Charities.

types, but by 1930 a significant increase in relief expenditures was noted. By the following year a fantastic growth in their relief efforts indicated the seriousness of the unemployment problem. In 1932 charitable organizations which had redoubled their fund-raising campaigns were unable to raise significantly their relief expenditures. In the first year of the New Deal, relief activities on the part of these organizations declined dramatically. Partly because the New Deal shouldered the burden, but more because the sources of funds were drying up and the organizations had to maintain their support of their traditional interests. Thereafter their solicitude waned until in 1935 their expenditures for relief of all types dwindled below the 1929 figure.

The state government did not remain oblivious to the plight of the unemployed. In October 1930 Governor Emmerson appointed a Governor's Commission on Unemployment and Relief to explore ways of creating work and distributing relief. The governor did not believe that state involvement was necessary, so the commission did not disburse money for relief purposes. In the following year the governor still believed that local government and private charity could carry the relief burden; therefore, he did not request an appropriation for relief purposes from the General Assembly. By December 1931 state aid became imperative. For several months the Governor's Commission had urged state support to the counties. On Feburary 6, 1932, the Third Special Session of the 57th General Assembly passed legislation providing $20,000,000 for relief of the unemployed. It also created the Illinois Emergency Relief Commission to administer the funds. The IERC, as it was commonly referred to, was empowered to establish rules and regulations relating to the expenditure of its funds in every county. Moreover, in Cook County the IERC would administer directly the state's aid. The General Assembly had hoped the appropriation would suffice for the year, but on July 30, 1932, only $34,127.29 of the original sum was unencumbered. Beginning in August 1932 Illinois began "to rely on the Federal Government for practically all relief funds through August, 1933."

Illinois desperately needed outside help; charitable organizations and government, state and local, had exhausted their financial resources. In Washington, President Hoover recognized the acuteness of the relief situation in Illinois and many other states. He supported the Congress which passed the Emergency Relief Act (ERA) of 1932 which allocated $300,000,000 to be loaned to needy states for direct- and work-relief purposes by the Reconstruction Finance Corporation (RFC). Illinois received more funds from this Act up to April 1933 than any other large state (Table 4).

. . . .

4. *Emergency Relief Act funds to the four largest states to April 1933*

States	Amount
Illinois	$48,463,621
Pennsylvania	29,929,875
New York	19,800,000
Ohio	15,283,937

With the advent of the New Deal, the IERC would be the state's administrative arm for the federal relief program. Prior to the Works Progress Administration (WPA) in 1935, the commission organized and administered the federal government's relief projects in the state. It established the Illinois Emergency Relief Administration which was funded by the Federal Emergency Relief Administration (FERA), and was designated formally the Federal Civil Works Administration for Illinois to handle the Civil Works Administration (CWA) program during the latter's brief existence. The substantial aid provided for needy citizens through the commission can best be illustrated by a brief résumé of the projects undertaken, the number of people served, and the expenditures for relief activities before WPA.

Beginning in the spring of 1933, hundreds of thousands of Illinois citizens benefited from direct- and work-relief projects. The majority received direct relief: food and clothes (in-kind), medical services, and payment of rent. Also the recipient in many areas availed himself of services developed on work-relief projects: literacy, sewing, nursing, nutrition classes. A minority, approximately 20 per cent, found jobs on work-relief projects. Most of the jobs involved construction or maintenance work, but other projects provided clerical workers with jobs in organizing and distributing relief supplies. Teachers found relief employment on the educational projects. A transient program extended relief to nonresidents in the state.

It should be noted that, although an average of over a million persons received some kind of relief every month between March 1933 and July 1934, there were still over six hundred thousand persons classed as unemployed employables in the state not receiving relief. The simple fact of the situation was that thousands had not been reduced yet to circumstances where relief was the only alternative. With the introduction of the Civil Works Administration program many unemployed persons not on the relief roles acquired jobs for the few months the project existed.

The CWA project proved a godsend to Illinois. Not only were people paid living wages for their labor during an exceptionally severe winter, but the state benefited from the construction of parks, airports, and stadiums, and the improvement of public buildings, streets, etc. Although minor scandals, administrative lapses and ill-conceived projects marred the success of the effort, nothing detracted from the observation that the unemployed wanted work.

After CWA was phased out in February 1934 the IERC continued many of the unfinished CWA projects and initiated others under its own auspices and with FERA funds appropriated under the Civil Works Emergency Relief Act of 1934. Between April 1934 and June 1936 the number of work-relief projects totaled 9,116 (Table 5).

Other New Deal agencies contributed to the welfare of those hit hard by the Depression even though the functions were not administratively a part of the relief system. The Civilian Conservation Corps (CCC) would employ tens of thousands of Illinois' young male population during the 1930's. Although the Public Works Administration (PWA) did not become effective in promoting in-

5. *Work relief projects, April 1934-June 1936*

Location	Number	Cost
Cook County	1,026	$22,507,613
All other counties	8,073	23,740,022
Statewide	17	582,867
Total	9,116	46,830,502

creased employment through the funding of large projects in the state until late 1934, many men and women would eventually find jobs in private industry because of PWA-sponsored projects. Before the end of 1935 many on relief were able to supplement relief allowances with surplus foods distributed by the Federal Surplus Relief Corporation (FSRC). New Deal legislation like the Agricultural Adjustment Act, the Emergency Farm Mortgage Act, the Farm Credit Act, the Home Owners' Loan Act, and the National Industrial Recovery Act all helped to stimulate the state's economy and provide jobs—the best kind of relief.

In taking stock of the effort made to provide relief through the IERC prior to the second New Deal (February 1, 1932-June 30, 1935), we find that the state of Illinois, and the federal government, spent $291,028,458.28 for unemployment relief purposes in Illinois. In spite of this enormous expenditure, a little long division indicates that only a bare minimum of aid was extended as a glance at the figures of the number receiving relief between April 1933 and June 1935 shows (Table 6).

6. *Number of persons (transient and resident) receiving relief in Illinois in selected months, April 1933-June 1935*

Month	Year	Number	Per cent of total population
April	1933	1,278,752	16.8
Aug.	1933	929,385	12.2
Dec.	1933	871,291	11.4
April	1934	1,033,837	13.5
June	1934	1,080,865	14.2
Dec.	1934	1,141,518	15.0
June	1935	1,022,161	13.4

The records of IERC indicate that relief support hardly put enough food on the table for the average family. In December 1934 the number of resident families on relief totaled 326,533. Around two-thirds of this number received direct-relief payments, averaging $22.54 per month throughout the state. Approximately one-third were on work relief, and the average relief pay in the state was $32.67 per month. The records suggest that it was better to be on relief in Cook County than elsewhere in the state (Table 7).

7. *Average direct-relief payments for June 1934 and June 1935*

Location	June 1934	June 1935
Entire state	$24.57	$30.66
Cook County	33.11	38.65
10 urban manufacturing counties	18.55	25.95
7 coal mining counties	13.24	23.53
33 agricultural counties	10.91	17.77
51 other counties	14.12	22.66

With the advent of the second New Deal in 1935 the method of providing relief and jobs for the unemployed was altered. When the Congress of the United States passed the Emergency Relief Appropriation Act which set up the Works Progress Administration in April, those needing relief were divided into two classes: the unemployables and the unemployed employables. The former would receive aid from the state and the federal government. The latter were expected to find work on WPA projects.

The establishment of WPA and the passage of the Social Security Act in 1935 drastically altered the business of providing relief. In Illinois all FERA work-relief projects were discontinued in forty-three rural counties in July 1935 and in the remaining counties projects were terminated by September 30, 1935. On July 1, 1935, local government took over direction of relief to unemployables and those employables not on WPA projects or whose WPA wages failed to provide enough income (the latter became eligible for a supplementary relief grant). The IERC certified the allocation of federal and state funds which together with local funds provided aid to unemployables and the other classes noted previously. Table 8 shows the number of people on relief in the state between 1936 and 1941; but the figures do not include workers on WPA projects, or persons dependent on Old Age Assistance, mother or blind pensions.

Relief support per person for those dependent on general relief averaged $4.30 per month for all Illinois counties outside of Cook in July 1936. In subsequent years the figure began to rise slightly. In spite of the low relief payments, Illinois spent large sums on general relief. When one considers that in the fiscal year July 1, 1934-June 30, 1935, the state of Illinois supported relief activities with only $18,231,579.82 and the support of local governments was considerably less, the assistance in the latter half of the decade is a measure of the state's commitment to those suffering as a result

8. *Number of persons in Illinois dependent on general relief in selected months between 1936 and 1941*

Month	Year	Number
July	1936	400,847
June	1937	427,427
June	1938	530,459
June	1939	536,866
Dec.	1939	471,735
June	1940	420,109
Dec.	1940	441,444
June	1941	315,096
Nov.	1941	268,989

of the Depression. Table 9 illustrates the contributions by state and local governments from July 1, 1936, to June 30, 1940.

9. *Obligations for general relief and administration in Illinois, July 1936-June 1940*

Fiscal year ending June 30	State government	Local government
1937	$35,126,284	$19,690,345
1938	36,763,951	24,767,432
1939	46,497,783	20,654,602
1940	46,410,943	16,717,642

Although there were a greater number of persons dependent on general relief (including Old Age Assistance, mother's pension, and aid to the handicapped) than on projects of the Work Progress Administration, National Youth Administration, and Civilian Conservation Corps, the latter activities received greater public acclaim and criticism. The visibility of WPA, NYA, and CCC projects accounts for the public's acquaintance and comment: hundreds of recreational areas were built or restored, sidewalks were laid, trees planted, drainage ditches were dug, students were kept in school, murals were painted on post-office walls, and, most importantly, hundreds of thousands worked on projects that preserved or improved their skills. WPA's security wage was less than the prevailing local wage but it was a wage for the performance of dignified labor. A great deal of criticism was leveled at the WPA nationally for boondoggling and political involvement but in Illinois these charges hardly mar the record of achievement. The CCC and NYA were universally praised.

The employment figures for WPA, CCC, and NYA indicate that Illinois citizens were dependent on the projects until the late summer of 1941. In Illinois the economy reacted sluggishly to increased defense spending and higher draft calls. Not until mid-1941 did the enrollment in WPA, CCC, and NYA fall below one hundred thousand. Table 10 provides an interesting comment on the growth and decline of these projects in Illinois.

10. *Selected enrollment figures for WPA, CCC, and NYA between 1936 and 1942*

Month	Year	WPA	CCC	NYA
July	1936	150,286	18,334	8,285
June	1937	120,998	10,890	26,137
June	1938	226,342	16,500	27,737
June	1939	193,981	11,518	29,356
June	1940	135,700	11,545	38,673
Mar.	1941	116,256	10,566	50,984
Aug.	1941	64,659	5,579	21,321

In the preparation of this article the author could not help but notice the contrasts and similarities of the relief problem in the Depression decade and in the mid-1960's. If a study of the past is to have any merit other than for its own sake, it must analyze what is significant in order to understand the present situation.

One striking similarity is high Negro unemployment. Then as now the problem goes beyond just providing jobs. If current programs would be recognized as an investment in human resources, perhaps some real success might be achieved.

In the 1930's mass unemployment was dealt with by establishing work programs, but in the 1960's mass unemployment of the Depression variety hardly exists. Underemployment in the form of low wages and poor job security still affects millions of Americans. Unfortunately the underemployed of today are not as visible as were the unemployed of the Great Depression. Perhaps if the same spirit of the 1930's could be reborn today solutions could be found. We must recognize that millions of Americans are underemployed through no fault of their own, and they need society's help.

. . . .

Original Narratives

Louis "Studs" Terkel received his J.D. degree from the University of Chicago in 1934 and, after holding a number of jobs in Washington, D.C. during the Depression, joined the radio station WFMT in Chicago. Among his many writings are *Division Street: America* (New York, 1967) and *Working: People Talk About What They Do All Day and How They Feel About What They Do* (New York, 1974). The experience of the Depression left a deep psychological scar on many Americans—a lingering feeling that those individuals who did not feel the middle-class financial insecurity were somehow unappreciative of the post-Depression economic accomplishments. This is brought out subtly in Terkel's interview with the Chicago school principal, the first of the oral history interviews printed below.

Hard Times

STUDS TERKEL

ELSA PONSELLE

She is the principal of one of the largest elementary schools in Chicago.

I was the youngest one in the family, so I got the college education. My brothers and sisters wanted me to go. They couldn't. It was a step up for us to have one daughter go to college.

I began to teach in December, 1930, and I was paid until June, 1931. When we came back, the city had gone broke. We kept on teaching, of course. I didn't go hungry and had a place to live. My father provided me with enough money to get by. But it was another thing for the men who were married and had children.

They began to pay us with warrants, which carried six percent interest. A marvelous investment. But not for the teachers who had to take them for pay. They had to peddle those warrants for what they could get. It was a promise to pay when the city got some money. We didn't think we'd ever get paid, but the businessmen knew better.

There were some stores downtown we will always remember with gratitude. They took those warrants at a hundred percent. Remember the Hub, Lytton's? They were wonderful. Old-timers like us still go there. There are some stores that will not be remembered with any love. They took it with a sixty, seventy-five percent discount. Many teachers were credited with only fifty percent. As time went along, they got it up to ninety. One of my friends bought a grand piano because she got a hundred percent on the warrant. (Laughs.) That was—if I may be forgiven for saying so—a hell of a note.

Finally, with F.D.R. in the White House, somebody went to Washington and we got a federal loan. And that didn't happen without a shove. At the time, the chairman of the Board of Education said we should be happy with what we were getting. We asked him if his wife could live on what we were making. A group got together and organized us. Everybody was heart and soul in the unions those days. Somebody said, "Why not a teachers' union?" And why not?

There were objections, of course: We're not tradespeople, we're not laboring class. We're professionals. As professionals, we're entitled to starve to death quietly and with refinement. Some of us weren't that much interested in being refined and professional. We were much more interested in improving our conditions.

We didn't have sit-ins, of course. That would hurt the children. We determined on one thing: We were not going to hurt the children. We went on teaching, whether we were being paid or not. We kept them apart from it.

We marched down LaSalle Street, we marched down Dearborn, we marched down Michigan Avenue. We marched everywhere. People were appalled. Teachers were supposed to be meek and mild. We were supposed to be the bulwark of the status quo and here we were, joining the revolution. (Laughs.) We were on the side of the great unwashed. How could we do that? I'm really surprised at how many teachers joined the movement, especially the older ones. They marched. It gave the establishment a turn. One of them went to Washington and got the money for us.

The Depression hit other members of my family. My brother, a tailor, like my father, was working one day every three months. He had a wife and two children. We were able to help him out. My sister-in-law came to me one day and said: "You want to hear something really funny? Johnny came home and said he had to bring some canned goods to school for the poor children. Where the hell is he gonna find kids poorer than we are?" We protected the kids from any idea that they were deprived.

Today the kids blithely make $50 and off they go and spend it.

As they very properly should. One time, somebody said to me, "What these kids need is to experience a Depression." Two of us, remembering the hard times, screamed at him, "Never! Not in a thousand years!" I don't care how blithe they are in spending money. Nobody should experience a Depression. No young person should.

Do you realize how many people in my generation are not married? Young teachers today, they just naturally get married. All the young men are around. There were young men around when we were young. But they were supporting mothers.

It wasn't that we didn't have a chance. I was going with someone when the Depression hit. We probably would have gotten married. He was a commercial artist and had been doing very well. I remember the night he said, "They just laid off quite a few of the boys. It never occurred to him that he would be next. He was older than most of the others and very sure of himself. This was not the sort of thing that was going to happen to him. Suddenly he was laid off. It hit him like a ton of bricks. And he just disappeared.

At our school, we had many Mexican children. When I get violent against big business, I think of those poor little kids. The Mexicans were imported to come up and work on the railroads, and when the work gave out, well, brother, can you spare a dime? They were thrust out, just like that. And they accepted it. I mean, this was the way the world was.

At a time, when it was raining and snowing and the middle-class children were all bundled up, or else kept at home, these kids came to school every single day, whether they had anything to wear or not. 'Cause it was warm, the classroom was warm.

The Mexican and Negro children were more used to being poor and hungry. The Italian and Greek children and their parents were stunned by it. You hear the saying today: if you really want work, you can get it. My nephew, not so long ago, said to me, referring to the Negroes: Ah, if they want a job, they can get it. I said, "If you ever say that again—I don't care if you're damn near forty years old—I'll slap you! Your father couldn't get a job in the Depression, and he wanted one." Of course, he's forgotten. But, ohhh, I felt all that old rage coming back.

The parents of the children I have today are working, but some of them are very, very poor. During the Depression, when you were poor, you weren't looking around and seeing . . . here's a society in which everybody has something except me. What's wrong with me? What's wrong with my parents, that we don't have these things? By God, I'm gonna get some. I can't blame them. They watch television, and everybody has everything. Why not me?

In the Depression, it wasn't only "not me," it was "not you," too. The rich, then, had an instinct for self-preservation. They didn't flaunt their money, if you remember. They didn't have fancy debutante parties, because it was not the thing to do. They were so God-damned scared they'd have a revolution. They damn near did, too, didn't they? Oooohhh, were they scared! What's more scared than a million dollars?

The Depression was a way of life for me, from the time I was twenty to the time I was thirty. I thought it was going to be forever and ever and ever. That people would always live in fear of losing their jobs. You know, *fear.* And, yet, we had, in a way, a wonderful time. We were young.

Remember? The one great thing was the end of Prohibition. The liquor we drank before was awful. Whoever thought about enjoying a drink? I'm talking about the bootleg. To this day, I can't drink gin, because every time I get a very fine Beefeater martini, all I can remember is that white stuff I drank during Prohibition.

How can you talk about the Depression without talking about F.D.R.? I remember when he was at the Chicago Stadium and all of us ran from school to get there. He came in on his son's arm. We didn't realize that he was really and truly crippled until we saw the braces. He got up there and the place just absolutely went up in smoke. What was tremendous about him was—with all the adoration—his sense of humor. He acted as though he didn't take himself seriously.

And Eleanor, Eleanor. I think she's the greatest thing that ever happened to anybody. I think of the way they talked about her, about her looks, about her voice. I used to get so rabid. Why I didn't have high blood pressure, I don't know.

Not so long ago, one of the parents said to me, "You know, you kind of talk like Eleanor Roosevelt." I said, "You mean her voice?" She said, "Oh, no, your voice isn't like hers." I said, "What do you mean?" She said, "I don't know. You just talk like Eleanor Roosevelt." Wasn't that something?

. . . .

BEN ISAACS

It is a house, with garden and patio, in a middle-class suburb on the outskirts of Chicago.

I was in business for myself, selling clothing on credit, house to house. And collecting by the week. Up to that time, people were buying very good and paying very good. But they start to speculate, and I felt it. My business was dropping from the beginning of 1928.

Depression victims advertising themselves

They were mostly middle-class people. They weren't too rich, and they weren't too poor.

All of a sudden, in the afternoon, October, 1929 . . . I was going on my business and I heard the newspaper boys calling, running all around the streets and giving news and news: stock market crashed, stock market crashed. It came out just like lightning.

I remember vividly. I was on my route, going to see my customer. It didn't affect me much at the time. I wasn't speculating in the market. Of course, I had invested some money in some property and some gold bonds, they used to call it. Because I have more confidence in the gold bonds than the stock market. Because I know the stock market goes up and down. But the gold bond, I was told from the banks, is just like gold. Never lose its value. Later we found to our sorrow that was fake.

They turned out to be nothing. Those banks, they'd take the people's money that they were saving, they would loan it out a mortgage on the property. The property was worth $100,000, they would sell $200,000 gold bonds on that property. The banks.

I have suspicions the bankers knew. They were doing it for their own personal gain. If it wasn't for the Crash, this fake would probably keep going on. Lotta these banks closed down overnight.

We lost everything. It was the time I would collect four, five hundred dollars a week. After that, I couldn't collect fifteen, ten dollars a week. I was going around trying to collect enough money to keep my family going. It was impossible. Very few people could pay you. Maybe a dollar if they would feel sorry for you or what.

We tried to struggle along living day by day. Then I couldn't pay the rent. I had a little car, but I couldn't pay no license for it. I left it parked against the court. I sold it for $15 in order to buy some food for the family. I had three little children. It was a time when I didn't even have money to buy a pack of cigarettes, and I was a smoker. I didn't have a nickel in my pocket.

Finally people started to talk me into going into the relief. They had open soup kitchens. Al Capone, he had open soup kitchens somewhere downtown, where people were standing in line. And you had to go two blocks, stand there, around the corner, to get a bowl of soup.

Lotta people committed suicide, pushed themselves out of buildings and killed themselves, 'cause they couldn't face the disgrace. Finally, the same thing with me.

I was so downcasted that I couldn't think of anything. Where can I go? What to face? Age that I can't get no job. I have no trade, except selling is my trade, that's all. I went around trying to find a job as a salesman. They wouldn't hire me on account of my age. I was just like dried up. Every door was closed on me, every avenue. Even when I was putting my hand on gold, it would turn into dust. It looked like bad luck had set its hand on my shoulder. Whatever I tried, I would fail. Even my money.

I had two hundred dollars in my pocket. I was going to buy a taxi. You had to have your own car to drive a taxi, those days. The man said: You have to buy your car from us. Checker Cab Company. So I took the two hundred dollars to the office, to make a down payment on the taxi. I took the money out—he said the kind of car we haven't got, maybe next week. So I left the office, I don't know what happened. The two hundred dollars went away, just like that. I called back: Did you find any money on the table? He said no, no money.

Things were going so bad with me, I couldn't think straight. Ordinarily, I won't lose any money. But that time, I was worrying about my family, about this and that. I was walking the street just like the easy person, but I didn't know whether I was coming or going.

I didn't want to go on relief. Believe me, when I was forced to go to the office of the relief, the tears were running out of my eyes. I couldn't bear myself to take money from anybody for nothing. If it wasn't for those kids—I tell you the truth—many a time it came to my mind to go commit suicide. Than go ask for relief. But somebody has to take care of those kids. . . .

I went to the relief and they, after a lotta red tape and investigation, they gave me $45 a month. Out of that $45 we had to pay rent, we had to buy food and clothing for the children. So how long can that $45 go? I was paying $30 on the rent. I went and find another a cheaper flat, stove heat, for $15 a month. I'm telling you, today a dog wouldn't live in that type of a place. Such a dirty, filthy, dark place.

I couldn't buy maybe once a week a couple of pounds of meat that was for Saturday. The rest of the days, we had to live on a half a pound of baloney. I would spend a quarter for half a pound of baloney. It was too cold for the kids, too unhealthy. I found a six-room apartment for $25 a month. It was supposed to be steam heat and hot water. Right after we move in there, they couldn't find no hot water. It wasn't warm enough for anybody to take a bath. We had to heat water on the stove. Maybe the landlord was having trouble with the boiler. But it was nothing like that. The landlord had abandoned the building. About two months later, all of a sudden—no water. The city closed it for the non-payment of the water bill.

My wife used to carry two pails of water from the next-door

neighbors and bring it up for us to wash the kids and to flush the toilet with it, and then wash our hands and face with it, or make tea or something, with that two pails of water. We lived without water for almost two months.

Wherever I went to get a job, I couldn't get no job. I went around selling razor blades and shoe laces. There was a day I would go over all the streets and come home with fifty cents, making a sale. That kept going until 1940, practically. 1939 the war started. Things start to get a little better. My wife found a job in a restaurant for $20 a week. Right away, I sent a letter to the relief people: I don't think I would need their help any more. I was disgusted with relief, so ashamed. I couldn't face it any more.

My next-door neighbor found me a job in the factory where he was working. That time I was around fifty. The man said, "We can't use you." They wouldn't hire nobody over forty-five. Two weeks later, this same man said, "Go tell Bill (the name of the foreman) I sent you. He'll hire you." They hire me. They give me sixty cents an hour. Twenty-year-old boys, they were paying seventy, seventy-five cents an hour. They were shortage of hand, that's why they hire me.

I read in the paper that some place they're paying a good salary, dollar an hour. I took the street car to go look for that job. On the way . . . I don't know what happened . . . something, like kicked me in the head. I said: I'm going back to my old business. People are now doing good, people's working in the war factory. So I got off the street car and I came into the store I was dealing with before.

I told them I was gonna go back to my old business. They laughed at me: What are you gonna sell? You can't find no merchandise. I said: Whatever you people are selling, I'll do the same thing. All this time that I was working, skimping, and my wife was working, I had saved $400. So I invested that $400 and start to go back into business.

Thank goodness, things changed. I came back. I came back. It was the end of 1944. If I had stayed in the factory I would probably still be on relief. Lotta people, even my wife, they told me don't go. We have only a few hundred dollar saved, you're gonna throw it out into the street. I said I'm not going back in the factory.

So for you the hard times were—

1928 to 1944. I was realizing that many and many other people are in the same boat. That gave me a little encouragement. I was looking at these people, waiting in line to get their relief, and I said,

My God, I am not the only one. And those were wealthy people . . . they had failed. But still my heart won't tick. Because I always prayed in my heart that I should never depend on anybody for support. When that time came, it hurted me. I couldn't take it.

Shame? You tellin' me? I would go stand on that relief line, I would look this way and that way and see if there's nobody around that knows me. I would bend my head low so nobody would recognize me. The only scar it left on me is my pride, my pride.

How about your friends and neighbors?

They were the same thing, the same thing. A lot of them are well-to-do now and have much more money than I have. But in those days, we were all on relief and they were going around selling razor blades and shoe laces.

We were going to each other's. That was the only way we could drown our sorrow. We were all living within a block of each other. We'd come to each other's house and sit and talk and josh around and try to make a little cheerfulness.

Today we live far away from the rest of our friends. Depression days, that time, we were all poor. After things got better and people became richer and everyone had their own property at different neighborhoods, we fell apart from each other.

. . . .

The Depression unemployed selling apples

Courtesy of the Illinois State Historical Library

TOM SUTTON

A lawyer, with offices in a suburb, west of Chicago, His wife, a physician, shares the quarters.

He heads Operation Crescent, an organization of white property owners:

"The wealthy have a place to run. My people are caught in a trap. They're lower middle class, the forgotten ones. Every member on our board is a former liberal. Our best ideas come from the skilled laborers. They have the pulse of the people. They feel abandoned by their priests and their schools. They are hurting, hurting, hurting. . . . They have no place to go but themselves. They don't hate negroes. They may prefer whites, but that doesn't mean they hate Negroes. And nobody really wants to admit hate. . . ."

The reason a man works is not because he enjoys work. The only reason any of us work is because if we don't work, we don't eat. To think that any man may sit in society and say: I don't wanna. O.K., if you want to starve, starve. He'll work. Believe me, he'll work.

Those who went through the Depression have a little more pride in their possessions, have a little more pride in the *amount* of possessions they have. They know that it was a fortunate person in the Thirties who have as much as they have today. They're much more money conscious.

Money is important to people, especially children of the Depression. You can see when they come into the office here, they're trying to see: Am I a wealthy or am I a poor lawyer? If I'm poor, they don't have that much confidence. They're sort of happy that they're shaking hands with some of the wealthy.

I hate people to know how much money I have. I would never want to admit it if I was broke. I would never want to admit I was a millionaire. One thing the Depression did was to make us secretive. It was ours. During the Depression, nobody would admit that they were broke. My friends who went through the Depression with me, I'll never know how much money they have, because they won't talk about it. Whether they're broke or wealthy.

In the Depression, you didn't want to admit you had problems, that you were suffering. This is mine. If I don't have the money, that's my problem, not your problem. If I did have money, that's not your affair. I don't know if our family was particularly secretive. . . .

The last Depression was blamed on the lack of regulation. This Depression which is coming will be blamed on too much regulation. The way we'll try to get out of it is to truly go back to a free system of exchange. Whether that'll work, I don't know.

People blamed Hoover for the Depression. He had no control over it. If the Depression hits now, they'll blame the Government. You always have one danger when you blame Government: disturbances tend to create chaos. Chaos will create a demand for a strong man. A strong man will be most repressive. The greater the Depression, the greater the chaos.

I don't think we're basically a revolutionary country. We have too large a middle class. The middle class tends to be apathetic. An apathetic middle class gives stability to a system. They never get carried away strongly, one way or the other. Maybe we'll have riots, maybe we'll have shootings. Maybe we'll have uprisings as the farmers did in Iowa. But you won't have revolution.

I remember standing in my father's office in the Reaper Block,* watching a march on City Hall. I was seven or eight. I remember his comment about red flags and revolution. He said, "The poor devils are just looking for bread." They weren't out to harm anyone. All they were marching for was food. I thought: Why were they looking for food? There were plenty of stores.

There was always talk in the house about the financial crisis. I remember listening to Father Coughlin about money changers in the temple. I lived in a Protestant neighborhood. It seemed there were more Protestants listening to Father Coughlin than there were Catholics. My father listened to him. He was like everybody else: anybody that had a solution, they'd grab onto it.

But he was a liberal and a Democrat and a strong supporter of Roosevelt. One of my favorite pastimes, during the campaign, was sitting across the front room, watching him repeat after Roosevelt as Roosevelt talked. You know, telling off the other side. Since most of his brothers-in-law were conservative Republicans, he enjoyed that particularly.

I went along with him. I can remember writing a term paper in high school: "The Need for a Planned Economy." I take it out and read it once in a while, just to see how foolish youth can be. How could anyone take that seriously?

The income tax changed me. I was making some money. It burned me up thinking now I had to file it with the Government. It was the fact that I had to sit down and report to somebody what I made. I had to keep records. And I'm so tired of keeping records.

I'm a happy-go-lucky Irish type. As long as I've got enough money to pay rent next month, I'm happy. I don't like to sit down: Did I make a big fortune or did I lose a deal? How much did I pay the secretary? How much did I pay for the cabs? Half the time when I had arguments with Internal Revenue, I don't keep

*An office building in the Loop, since torn down. Many lawyers had their quarters there.

track of those things. We have to be bookkeepers: ten cents for the cab tip, twenty-five cents for a meal, what have you. We're building the bookkeeper type. The New Deal and all those agencies contributed to this. . . .

Of course, we had social problems thrown in with the Depression. We had the beginning of the liberal movement in which Communists were in the forefront. They made use of labor with strikes, sit-ins, the many problems we had at that time. A free economy would have straightened out these problems.

Looking back, many individuals would have been hurt, etc. But as a result of the programs, many more are now hurt than would have been hurt at the time. In an attempt to alleviate a temporary situation, they've created a monstrosity.

Many of the people I knew in law school, children of the Depression, talked about how they had to quit school for help. The father who had been a doctor took a janitor's job. They would do anything rather than take public money. Then it was just the thought that you couldn't take someone else's money. It was a matter of pride. Now I have some of that left over. . . .

Postscript: "And there's the added feature: I am somewhat of a snob. My children are going to know some of the best of society. Not the best, necessarily. Though money is an indication. They're going to know the best who are working a little harder, applying themselves with greater effort, and will be going further. We work a great deal for our children. It's nice to think there are wonderful ditchdiggers in the world, but that it's for somebody else's daughter."

. . . .

HARRY HARTMAN

It is somewhere in the County Building. He overflows the swivel chair. Heavy, slightly asthmatic, he's a year or two away from retirement. He's been with the bailiff's office for "thirty-three and a half years"—elsewhere, a few years. He had begun in 1931.

During the Depression, "I was the only guy working in the house at the time. So the windup is they become big shots and I'm still working." But he has had compensations: "It boils down to having a front seat in the theater of life." As court bailiff, he had had in his custody a sixteen-year-old, who had killed four people on a weekend. During the trial, "he bet me a package of cigarettes, understand, he'd get the chair. And I bet him a package of cigarettes he wouldn't. When the jury come up and found him guilty, he reached back in a nonchalant way to me and said, 'O.K., give me the cigarettes.' I gave it to him in open court and pictures were taken:

KILLER BETS PACKAGE OF CIGARETTES. *You know what I mean, and made a big thing about it." The boy got the chair—"it was quite a shock to him."*

During the Thirties, "I was a personal custodian to the levy bailiff." Writs of replevin and levies were his world, though he occasionally took part in evictions. "Replevins is when somebody buys on a conditional sales contract and doesn't fulfill their contract. Then we come out and take the things back. 'Cause it ain't theirs till the last dollar is paid for. Levy, understand, is to go against the thing—the store, the business—collect your judgment."

We had 'em every single day. We used to come there with trucks and take the food off the table. The husband would come runnin' out of the house. We'd have to put the food on the floor, take the tables and chairs out. If they were real bad, we'd make arrangements, you understand, to leave a few things there or something. So they could get by. But it was pretty rough there for a lot of people.

Once we went to a house and there were three children. The table seemed to be part of the furniture company's inventory. That and the beds and some other things. The thing that struck us funny was that these people had almost the whole thing paid for, when they went to the furniture company and bought something else. So instead of paying this and making a separate bill, the salesman said, "You take whatever you want and we'll put it on the original bill." They paid for that stuff, and then when they weren't able—when the Depression struck—to pay for the new articles they bought, everything was repossessed.

You know, like radios. You remember at that time, they used to take the radio and put it in a cabinet that would cost $200 or so. The cabinet was the big thing. These people paid off the bedroom set and the dining room set. Next thing they'd want is a nice radio. The radio was put on the bill and boom! everything, the whole inventory, went.

It was a pretty rough deal. But we arranged that we left a lot of things there. On the inventory, we overlooked the beds and some of the other stuff. When we got enough, we said that the mattresses were unsanitary and we weren't gonna take it. If we had our way, we'd see that these people—if the original bill was $500 and they paid $350—we'd figure, well, you could leave a bed for $350 and you could leave a table. Or we'd say the mattress was full of cockroaches. We'd never touch the stuff. I'd just put down: bed missing. I'd ask the guy, "Can you identify that bed as the one sold?" And I'd say to the guy, "Hey, that ain't your bed. Say your brother-in-law's got it, and he gave you this one instead." Or something like that.

I mean, we always had an out. It was a real human aspect. If you really wanted to help somebody, you could. By making it easier for them, you made it easier for yourself. In most cases, people had plenty of warning that if they couldn't pay it, something would have to be done. They were broke and they were holding out as long as they could. But when it came around, a lot of cases they just gave up.

Some of the most pitiful things were when you went into a fine home, where if they were able to sell an oil painting on the wall, it could more than pay their judgment. When you went into factories, where the guy pleaded with you, so he could have his tools, understand, and do his work at home. When you took inventory, if you let him take his stuff, you know, if there was a beef, it'd be bad. But if you let him take what he needed, he didn't care about the rest. 'Cause he'd have bread and butter to go. So you'd use your head in a lot of cases.

It was a question of going in like a *mensch*. There was a rewarding part of it. If you treated that guy good, he appreciated it. And in the long run, we did better than any of the guys that went out on the muscle stuff. When we took inventory, it was our inventory that stood up. I could open a brand new box, say in haberdashery, for shirts. What's to stop me from marking one box "partly full?" All I had to do is take out a shirt and throw it out and I can call it "partly full."

We'd even go out at night to repossess cars in a different way. The attorney would want this or that car, and he'd give you an order to take it. But if we thought the guy was a nice guy and he could get some money up, understand, and he needed the car for his business, we'd tell him to park it half a block away and be sure to get hold of a lawyer, or otherwise we'd tow it in the next time. You see? We did some good.

At that time, they tried all their pullers, the companies, they tried to recover on their own. So they wouldn't have to file in the municipal court. They tried to save that. They had their own pullers. We put a check on them and we took all kinds of phony stars away from them. Chicken Inspector 23, you know. They tried everything. It got so, people were so mad at me—or, you know, anybody to come out. These guys would come out with their fake stars and say they were deputies. Then when we come out, they were ready to shoot us.

One of your greatest guys in town, a fella that's a big banker today, when we went to his home, he met us at the head of the stairs with a rifle. And my boss at the time said, "Yeah, you'll get one of us, but we'll get you, too. Why don't you cool off, and maybe we can discuss this. We don't want this place. We knew you had the money, we knew that. Why don't you get together with the lawyer and work something out? What good would it do if you shot us? We didn't ask to come here." People would get emotionally disturbed.

One time I went to take out a radio and a young girl undressed herself. And she says, "You'll have to leave. I'm in the nude." I said, "You can stay," and we took it out anyhow. All we did was throw her in the bedroom and take the thing out. But we had to have a police squad before the old lady'd let it out. Screamed and hollered and everything else. It was on the second floor and she wanted to throw it downstairs. There were many times we had sofas and divans cut up by a person in a rage.

The only way to gain entrance is if people would open the door for us. Whoever wouldn't let us in, we'd try to get it another way. There are ways, if you want to get it bad enough, you can do it.

I used to work quite a bit at night. We'd go around for the cars and we'd go around for places we couldn't get in in the daytime. We did whatever the job called for.

Remember your feelings when you had to go out on those jobs?

In the beginning, we were worried about it. But after you found out that you could do more good and maybe ease somebody's burden—and at the same time, it was very lucrative as far as you were concerned—why then you just took it in your stride. It was just another job. It wasn't bad.

But we had places where we had to take a guy's truck and take his business away, and he's gone to the drawer and reached for a gun. We'd grab him by the throat, you know what I mean, and muscle and something like that. I don't know if he reached for the gun to kill himself or to scare us or what. Anyway, he went for the drawer and boom! I slammed the door on his hand and my partner got him around the neck. I opened the drawer, and there's a gun there. I said, "Whataya goin' for the gun for?" He said, "I'm going for my keys." (Laughs.) The keys were in his pocket.

We've had guys break down. We've had others that we thought would, and they were the finest of the lot. No problem at all. No matter how much they were burning on the inside.

There were some miserable companies that wanted to salvage *everything.* When we got a writ from them, we didn't want it. But we had to take it. Some of 'em really turned your guts. And there were others, it was a pleasure to know. All in all, we used to look at it and laugh. Take it for whatever it was. If you got so, you knew how to allay hard feelings there, and you knew how to soft soap 'em, you did all right.

Aside from the bed, the table—I suppose the humiliation . . .

We tried to keep it down. That they were sending the stuff back or that they were gonna get new stuff. Frankly, their neighbors were in the same classification as they were. It was things that people knew. It was part of the hardship.

When you say guys around the house, they'd just stand by . . . ?

Depressed . . . if you came in there and they thought they were failures to their wife and children. But like everything else, they always got over it. Look, people were trying to get by as best they could, and this was our way of getting by. We might as well make it as pleasant as we possibly can. And that's what our boss wanted: less trouble. Because after all, he held a political office and he wanted good will.

The poor people took it easier and were able to much better understand than the people who were in the middle or better classes.

If I walked in a house, say, where they had furniture from Smyth* and you come into them . . . first of all on account of being ashamed of never having had things of this type . . . they were the ones who hit hardest of all. They never knew anything like this in their whole career. They'd have maybe a Spanish cabinet, with all the wormwood and that. And realize that if they could have sold that, they could have paid their bill what they owed, what the guys were closin' in on 'em for. We had men walk out of the house with tears in their eyes. And it was the woman who took over. The guys couldn't take it. Especially with cars, you know what I mean?

The poor mostly would make the best of it. They knew it was gonna be taken. They knew what they were up against and they knew it was only a matter of time, you know, until somebody took it away. We had less trouble with the poor. Not, I mean, that we enjoyed going against them, 'cause if they were poor, you had to help 'em more than anybody else.

It was a real rough time, but we tried to make it along with a smile. Instead of being a vulture, we tried to be helpful. But they were interesting times.

Did you encounter much resistance in your work?

No. I'd say one in a hundred.

If you'd walk in another room and somebody all of a sudden gets

*John M. Smyth Co., one of the better furniture stores in Chicago.

hot and grabs a knife and goes for one . . . I mean this can happen. But you usually get 'em when they start crying, understand. When they start crying, they're already spent. Most of all, it was surprising how they accepted their fate.

What we did then, I don't think we could do today. With the way the people look at the law. And with their action and their feeling, you know what I mean. They wouldn't accept today as they did then. What we did then was different. People still respected the courts and respected the law. They didn't want to revise our laws to satisfy them. (Weary, resigned.) What am I gonna tell you?

Today you get a guy in court, you don't like what the judge says, he calls him a *mf,* you know what I mean? So how can you go in a house, understand, where we had law-abiding citizens like we had in the Thirties? Today we'd possibly run into a lot of trouble. If we started these evictions, we'd move 'em out on the street, they'd move 'em right back in. Whataya gonna do then? Today I think it's different, a different type people.

Before if you wore a badge, it meant something. Today you wear a badge, you better watch out, 'cause somebody'll try to take you to see if they're as good a man as you are. And we're getting older, not younger. (Laughs.)

Today it's tougher for evictions than it was in our day. Today if you evict anybody, you not only have to evict the people, you have to evict about seven or eight organizations that want the people in there. And each can come up with some legal point, why they should remain without giving the landlord any rent. Now I'm not for the landlord. They bled 'em in some of these buildings, I understand. They may be perfectly right. But as far as following the law is concerned, that's something else.

John F. Cernocky, a Chicago native, completed undergraduate studies at Western Illinois University in 1970 and began graduate work in history at the same institution. His master's thesis, completed in 1973, examined the effects of the depression in McDonough County through interviews with local residents. He currently teaches at the Edna Keith School in Joliet, Illinois.

Oral History of the Depression in McDonough County

JOHN CERNOCKY

The Most Useful New Deal Agency

Of all of the New Deal agencies, which do you believe was the most beneficial? Some of them would be the CCC, WPA [and] PWA. . . .

> Electrician, No. 5. Well, I think the PWA was. Them men, a lot of their men, went out and done a full day's work. They dug the sewer right over here on Orchard Street. And that sewer over there I think is seventeen or eighteen foot deep. And them men dug that. You couldn't get a man to go down that deep today. (He laughs) . . . Right there at the corner of Western Avenue, years ago, that was nothing but an old chuck pile. Chuck was in there twenty foot deep. And the sewer pipe factory over here had hauled old chuck into that place for years to fill that up. All right, during the depression they got a machine down there that would mash up that chuck. All right, that's the WPA part of it, and they'd haul that around and put it on our roads, alleys and one thing and another. . . . And this alley right through here [on Carroll Street] has got a lot of it in it.

Of all the New Deal agencies, such as CCC, PWA . . . which do you think was the most beneficial? Do you think there was one that you really remember?

> High School Teacher, No. 9. Of course, I remember NYA [National Youth Administration] because I was involved in it. But I have an idea that CCC may have been one of the highlights. Again, it was working with young people and these were young men; this could have been the revolutionary group. And you were taking this group out and giving them a place. In fact, this land right across the road [near the intersection of Adams Street and Wigwam Hollow Road] was the old CC Camp here in this county. And I can remember the CCC boys coming in here and these, of course, were from families that didn't have any money at all. And it did give them something to do.

The Civilian Conservation Corps recruited nationwide a quarter of a million unemployed young men and put them to work in the country's national forests and parks. In addition to room and board, they received thirty dollars a month. The CCC was the most

From John Cernocky, "An Oral History Approach to the Effects of the Depression, 1929-1941, in McDonough County, Illinois" (Master's Thesis in History, directed by Victor Hicken, Western Illinois University, 1973), pp. 6-11, 17-18, 20-22, 34-36, 47-50, 64, 76-77, 83-86, 90-93, 136-137.

widely accepted of the New Deal agencies, for much productive labor, such as tree planting, road construction and land reclamation, was accomplished. In addition, CCC provided its men with leadership training that later proved valuable in other fields.

. . . .

President Roosevelt and Politics

What did you think of President Roosevelt?

High School Teacher, No. 9. Well, I'm naturally a Democrat. To me, because I went through the Depression, I still think that Roosevelt was a far cry over Hoover. Although I do realize that—I happen to be a social science major—and I realize that probably Hoover was only doing what he could do at the time. But I think Roosevelt certainly was a man of the times. That probably we were saved from a revolution in our country by the strong action that he took. And by sweeping in a [Democrat] Congress he was able to get through the program that a Republican could not have gotten through.

F.D.R. was loved by the "little man," who regarded him as their champion. What did you think of President Roosevelt?

Newspaper Owner and Editor, No. 11. Well, President Roosevelt was the greatest man that ever lived as far as I'm concerned. I've worked with my hands all my life. Prior to his being there, there was one constructive piece of labor legislation enacted by the Republicans. And he took the laboring man and almost made a white-collar man out of him. Another thing, as far as I'm concerned, he'll be great 'cause I can take a dollar bill and put it in a bank and go back twenty years later and the dollar bill is still there. . . .

We lost several prominent citizens of this county due to suicide, heart conditions [or] just pining away, because they lost all their money in the bank. It's hard to realize that you had a substantial savings of—back in those days, ten to fifteen thousand dollars was a lot of money—and suddenly you didn't have any money; you were a poor man. This is terribly hard to realize, as I realize, having lived all through the Roosevelt administrations, that there are several things that he did that probably history will condemn him for. But as far as the little person was concerned, he was a great man.

. . . .

Transients on the Road

During the 1930s, thousands "took to the road," hitchhiking by car or rail to escape poverty at home. Some were landless farmers while others were unemployed factory hands. Whatever their background, most searched either in city or country for some kind of work. The number of transients who roamed across America in the 1930s will probably never be known for certain, but the figure certainly ran into the hundreds of thousands.

The court records of Macomb reveal that only three people were actually arrested for loitering. But certainly there were more transients in McDonough County than would be indicated by the number of arrests. The interviews show that transients who passed through the county were in most cases provided food and humanitarian treatment. In most instances, unless a job was provided—which was unlikely—transients were only permitted to remain in the county for a short time. The data concerning transients is very incomplete. Figures for Macomb are the only county records available. Both the county and city law enforcement officials of that era have either died or are retired and living in other parts of the United States.

How was the problem of many jobless transients coming in the area [handled]?

> *Bank Clerk, No. 18.* Now [when] we were married in 1935, there was no social security for the aged. We're just a block from the railroad. And we moved in here July 1, 1935, and I don't think there was a day passed but what my wife didn't feed some transient. We always heard, "Well, they've got your house marked." Well, we had a big white picket fence around here. But we fed 'em all. And like I say, there was old men and there were young.
>
> And one rainy night a young fellow came to the door, said he was hungry, could we give him something to eat. Well, always before we had never let 'em in the house. So this rainy night [on] a little table right over here my wife brought him in. And we happened to have hash that night. And he ate and enjoyed himself. And when he left, he left a tape measure on the table, see. I suppose he just wanted to try and pay for something. So a transient problem, they were just on the road. They were just not tramps, not bums, but just men out of work and no place to go. Those that didn't have any brothers or sisters to stay with or just didn't have anybody and was just on the road. And every night they would go to the jail, and the city marshal would let 'em sleep in the jail and the next morning, out they go.

An official of the Missouri Pacific Railroad stated before a Senate Subcommittee of the Committee on Manufactures that in 1931, the peak year of transient-related accidents, 372 people were killed or injured on the Missouri Pacific line alone.

During the Depression, what was the railroad's response to the number of people that used to hitch rides on trains or would congregate in the rail yard . . .? Did you see much of this and how did the company handle it?

> Railroad Freight Claims Clerk, No. 3. Well, as you mentioned, there . . . was an awful lot of what were called hobos in those days I guess. They were really hitch-hiking; they'd get in the empty cars and ride for long distances—things like that. And get off, maybe in towns like this, and maybe want to stay a while. And then they would mooch their food from residents and go down the streets. We had a lot of that in those days. . . . But I do recall, too, that the railroad did try to discourage all of that they could. Because [the] thing that I'm thinking about mainly is the responsibility of them getting hurt or killed. We had at different times people that were killed riding a train, getting off or on and then would be run over. . . .

. . . .

Jobs in the '30s

Would you please describe your job situation in the 1930s, the type of work that you did and how long you were in this line of work?

> Banker, No. 17. Well in 1930, I mean the beginning of the 1930s, I had been here five years as the managing officer of the association which at that time was quite small. Of course, you realize today that it's considerably larger. We have about thirty one and a half million [in deposits]. At that time I was the only employee at a salary of $175.00 a month. And out of that I paid a girl for a half [day's] work. It gave me an opportunity to go to the bank and the courthouse and do whatever else I had to do on the outside.
>
> And I was also the janitor. I shucked down the ashes in the coal furnace and shoveled the coal in, and washed the windows, swept the office and the sidewalk. And as a consequence of all this I was also working a lot at night, something I don't do now, by the way, only very, very rarely. As far as the Depression is concerned, me and my family never felt it in the 1930s. Because things were reasonably cheap and I did have a job which a lot of people didn't have. And as a consequence we got along very well in spite of the fact that I was paying forty-seven dollars and twenty-five cents a month on my loan covering my house. And my first son was born in 1925 and the other one five and one half years later. But even with that added expense we didn't seem to be cramped.

This couple farmed for nearly forty years. Her husband died a couple of years ago, but she likes the country too well to move into town. She enjoys reminiscing about farm life in the 1930s.

Describe your job situation in the 1930s, the type of work, and length of time you did this.

Farm Housewife, No. 13. We were farmers and we were [just] a young married couple and we moved to this place. He and his father owned the place north [of us]. He had inherited it. And then this land that connected with them on the south was put up for sale. And they thought that they would like to have that to add to what they did have, so, you know, to buy this one. And it meant a lot of hard work. In those days, money was so tight. So there were three sons in the family and Kenneth, my husband, was the middle one—one older and one younger. And the older boy and Kenneth pledged to their dad that they'd stick with him till they got the additional land paid off so he wouldn't lose his home that he inherited.

. . . so the other boy stuck with it about eight months or so and he grew tired of it. He wanted to go to the city to work. So he took off. So they paid him out in cash which was the way he wanted it. And the younger boy, well, he was never very strong and he didn't care for the farm work. He really wasn't able to do it. He wanted an education, so he went to town to live with his grandmother. . . . [So my husband and his father were left to do the whole thing.] And that was the reason things were so tight for us in those days. They had this ground to pay for and just the two of 'em to do it.

Do you recall how many acres this was?

Farm Housewife, No. 13. [This section of land was about one hundred acres] . . . that they were paying for. And, boy, I tell you, we didn't have a penny for anything. When the kids were little I told 'em many a time to go to town and get groceries, just to get the staples, what we had to have. And there wouldn't be enough left to buy 'em a candy bar or package of chewing gum. Things were that tight for us all of those years, and that was the 1930s, I'll tell you. (She laughs.)

. . . .

As of this writing, this teacher of more than thirty-five years will be retired. Her new home emphasizes the style of the seventies, which expresses her own progressive attitudes. While this woman enjoys talking about the past, she is not one to glorify a vanished age.

Could you describe your job situation in the 1930s. . . ? And, if you so desire, how much you were paid? It must have been a king's ransom.

High School Teacher, No. 9. Well, in the early part of the '30s I was still a student going to Western. [At that time it was known as Western Illinois State Teachers' College.] And in order to get enough money to pay tuition, I worked on an NYA job [National Youth Administration] and got paid thirty cents an hour.

I had a question about the NYA. Go ahead.

> High School Teacher, No. 9. I was grading papers for an English teacher and being paid this thirty cents an hour during that time. Later on in the '30s, I received my degree and went out to teach in a rural school. My first salary was $35.00 a month. The total for the year was less than $400.00. It was an eight-month school.

I imagine it was pretty difficult finding a teaching job?

> High School Teacher, No. 9. I remember that we wandered all over the state of Illinois trying to locate some kind of job at that time. We went as far as Woodhull from here and as far south as down around Quincy trying to locate a job of any kind.

Where was your first teaching job?

> High School Teacher, No. 9. My first teaching job was about twelve miles from here down southwest of Colchester called Eagle's School. The school house is still there.

There was, I imagine, what—one through eight?

> High School Teacher, No. 9. Yes, this was one through eight. I had thirty-two children in all grades and we didn't even skip grades. And at the same time we cooked their hot lunch at noon.

. . . .

Starting in 1918, [this man] spent nearly fifty years working for the Chicago, Burlington and Quincy Railroad. He gave an excellent account both of railroading and the industrial establishments of Macomb in that Depression decade.

Describe conditions of your work for the railway in the 1930s and for railroading in this area. . . .

> Railroad Freight Claims Clerk, No. 3. Now Macomb has always been known in the past as a manufacturing center more or less and that's where a lot of the rail business came from, that is the freight. By the late 1920s a good deal of freight entered and left Macomb. From the Chicago, Burlington and Quincy Railroad, the main artery that linked the town with the outside world, this freight included 3,800 carload shipments outbound and 5,000 carloads inbound. In addition there were 2,800 carloads of L.C.L. freight.

For what industries?

> Railroad Freight Claims Clerk, No. 3. Well, now at that particular time when it was at its height, we had two sewer pipe and tile manufacturing

plants here, one down where Sandy's Restaurant is now and the other one up here where King-Seeley are now located. In fact, that building— part of that building—is the old building that was operated by the W. S. Dickie Clay Manufacturing Company. And they at that time were operating those two plants and employed a lot of people.

But as business went down why they began to shut down a plant and lay off. And then at one time we had down where King-Seeley plant number two—that's down here, oh, back of the YWCA grounds—they own that and use it for a warehouse now. And that has been a thriving business ever since they took over. It started out as Hemp and Company and then it was sold to King-Seeley. Then we had another thriving plant called the Buckeye Pottery Company—that's where Haegers are now. And then at the [place] where their lamp works are located, down there at the west end of town, that was Western Stoneware Company. They made flower pots mainly and things.

So [by the] time you got them all to working that was the nucleus of business in Macomb. And it was really something, because the clay manufacturing companies shipped in all their coal for steam and kiln purposes burning. And I recollect there were times when we had as high as fifty carloads of coal in one month for that clay manufacturing company for the both plants. And then another one that we mustn't forget, too, started out as the Illinois Electric Porcelain Company which is now McGraw-Edison and Company. And put them all together and when the slump, as we might say, came on, that began to close down some of it. You know their business began to fall off and then following that they would have to lay off help.

. . . .

Could you describe the condition of the railroad brotherhoods in McDonough County in the 1930s?

Railroad Freight Claims Clerk, No. 3. Well, of course, the brotherhood I belonged to, it was voluntary at that time, belonging to them, it was the Brotherhood of Railway Clerks. Since that time it has been taken to include the airlines and steamships and so forth. . . . Well, the union we belonged to, we had no local lodge at all, we just belonged in general and the lodge was located in Kansas City. And they were supposed to handle any grievances that came up, but they were very few so far as that's concerned. But they were beneficial due to the fact that when it came to employment or unemployment, too, in securing another job.

They established what was called the seniority rules or rights that made it helpful in getting another job. If your job was taken off, or if it was changed to a particular place, you had the opportunity then of what we call "bumping," going into your same line of work, which was your Brotherhood of Railway Clerks, in other places and "bumping" or taking the job of someone with lower seniority than you had. And it had its benefits quite a lot in that respect, which we didn't have before.

Did any of the railway workers, either the clerks, the engineers, or the brakeman, go on strike in the 1930s?

> *Railroad Freight Claims Clerk, No. 3.* Well now let's see. I don't know whether if I can hardly tell you. There was during the time that I worked in that—over forty-eight years—there was a strike or so for just a day or two that they were out of work, but not of any extent at all during my time of tenure there. Of course, there were strikes, but you see the government steps in with the railroads. If a strike was coming up, they would enact legislation to stop it right away. That's one thing that I felt wasn't exactly fair, to work with one union like that, like the railroad organization [while allowing the dock workers to remain on strike for one hundred sixty-five days]. Still they went back of their own accord with the government getting ready to enact legislation to put them back. It never seemed fair to me, it never did, that they wouldn't let the railroads strike.

. . . .

Prices in the '30s

Could you go into the prices for some of the different meats in the '30s?

> *Butcher, No. 7.* I've sold lard for two pounds for five cents. I've sold beefsteak for ten cents a pound. I've sold beef roast for eight cents a pound. And everything else in conjunction, coffee [from] about eighteen to twenty cents a pound [and] bread [from] a nickel to a dime a loaf.

What did you do? I imagine a lot of people couldn't pay their bills. . . ?

> *Butcher, No. 7.* Many people would, who were friends—I suppose you'd have to call 'em friends, acquaintances at least—would give you a check for a dollar and a quarter on up to two dollars for a few groceries. Maybe they were having company, might be a death in the family or something. It wasn't any good, you'd send [the check] to the bank and bring it back. We'd usually throw them in the stove. There was nothing else to do. You couldn't collect it because this we had tried. And they would ask you to sit down and have a meal with them, which wasn't much when you [went over there]. And the friendliness that they offered you, it was almost impossible to ask them for the little debt which neither made you very much richer or them very much poorer, as Shakespeare would say. (He chuckles)

. . . .

How would you compare that business, the shoe business, to other places in Macomb, other stores [and] other shops?

> *Shoe Salesman and Store Owner, No. 2.* They all run about the same way. It wasn't felt here in general like it was in a great many other

[places]. You get forty miles away from Macomb and it was different than it was here. Over in Carthage, Illinois [in Hancock County], they had bank failures. They had a man who used to be from Carthage in the bond business in Chicago. And all the sour bonds he had to sell, it seemed like that Carthage had got 'em. And we had none of that. . . .

Would you describe the prices that shoes were selling at in those days. . . ?

Shoe Salesman and Store Owner, No. 2. Of course, shoes had gone up some by that time, but I know [that] when we opened [Walker Baymiller and I] the store in 1937 for ourselves, we had Nunn-Bush shoes and Edgerton, which is another line, [for] five or six dollars [and] Nunn-Bush shoes [selling for] seven and eight. That was the price of those shoes then. Now today, those shoes will run from twenty-two dollars and ninety-five cents, there in that bracket, up to forty-five or fifty dollars. In those days, you could buy shoes and other merchandise and what you didn't sell out this season that would carry over and be good next season. Today, in all kinds of merchandise, styles change so fast that merchandise carried from one season to the next is not worth very much, except in just basic staple-type shoes. . . .

Being in business for yourself and knowing that times were bad, what were some of the things you used to try to get people to want your services. . . ?

Electrician, No. 5. Well, I'll tell you. Things were just so bad they didn't want your services. (He laughs) They didn't want your services, things were just that bad.

But you were able to get by, your business didn't fold. . . .

Electrician, No. 5. I can remember one time there were these people who lived over here on Pierce Street. That it wasn't one year, it was every Christmas, they would have some little thing for me to do. I suppose that was their Christmas and it was mine, too. Putting in a doorbell, chimes or something like that, and I often thought about them, never did forget about 'em.

. . . .

Farming in the Depression

In McDonough County, where farming plays such an important role in the economy, it is impossible to include agriculture under one heading, for farming overlaps into so many different areas. In

this section the discussion centers on agricultural prices, farm policy, and methods of reducing farm costs.

McDonough County's greatest resource is its fertile soil. This is
evident by the advanced development in the field of agriculture.
But in the prosperous 1920s the farmer did not share propor-
tionately in the national income. Both farm mortgages and tenancy
increased as farmers found it more difficult to balance their production costs against their profit margin. The staggering blow of the
Great Depression brought a further decline in an already depressed
farm economy. In the Midwest, including McDonough County,
farmers were forced to burn corn for fuel because it was cheaper
than coal.

In 1933, McDonough County corn farmers received only about
one-third of the 1868 price. For oats, the price comparison with the
sixty-year price index varied from one-fourth to one-fifth in value.
The price for wheat was around one-fourth the post-Civil War level.
In the '30s, farm mortgage foreclosures, already high, increased still
further both in McDonough County and nationwide. Under the
New Deal, relief measures were applied to aid the farmer. For the
first time, under the Agricultural Adjustment Act, the attempt was
made on a national scale to limit farm production with the incen-
tive being the farm subsidy. While the farm policies of the federal
government have done much since the New Deal to relieve the
farmer, the problem of low agricultural prices versus the high fixed
costs of production still persists.

This man is now in his sixties. Both he and his wife responded to
questions asked during the interview.

*What devices as a farmer did you try to do for your land or
equipment to cut your expenses [and] save money so you would
make it through those difficult years?*

Farm Housewife, No. 14. Well, I can recall one thing: that our daughter
started high school in '32 and we were limited on the gasoline you could
get for the car. Well then the next year the boy started high school and
they drove the car. . . . When she started driving the car, we were allowed
so much gasoline for the kids to drive to school. And we weren't limited
on gas now, we didn't put the car in the shed and try to save gas. We used
what little they allowed us to have. And then on account of the children
we did get—I didn't remember how many gallons—but we did get a little
extra gas. But that car only went when it needed to.
. . . .

This man is the father of a large family. He has a friendly manner which reflects his attitude about living.

What did you do [as a farmer] to try to make it during the Depression? Could you describe some of the ways you . . . cut corners to keep body and soul together during those times?

> *Farmer, No. 1.* I know one of the main things that dad did [was that] we cut the electricity off for about two years. And as I say we put the car in cold storage and used a horse as much as possible. And pretty near all my running around was done either afoot or with [a] horse. . . .

What would you consider in those days a good price for your grain crops and your pigs?

> *Farmer, No. 1.* Well, probably five cents, five dollars a hundred on hogs, two cents on old sows. Corn at one time was ten to fifteen cents a bushel. And wheat, I just can't recall. Beef, I can't recall just what it was selling for at that time.

When would you say was the worst time for farmers losing their land in the '30s?

> *Farmer, No. 1.* Well, possibly right in here I would say before the '30s, actually in the late '20s was when most of 'em here really lost. I know the place right across the road from us went in—probably about 1929 they lost it. And the big farm down on the corner here, probably in about . . . '27 [or] '28, along in there. And the eighty [acres] right north of us here was lost probably in about '26 there. . . .

When do you think was the worst [part of the Depression] for you, the hardest to make a living?

> *Farm Housewife, No. 14.* I think about '31 and '32. We had two kids in school and a little fellow, and you didn't have money to buy anything. . . . That was better than a year that we went to town—[and] it was shoes or sugar. And with three kids you know what we bought, we bought shoes. That's one of the worst things that I remember, was not being able to have the average amount of food, the kind of food we wanted. We had to buy corn meal and such stuff as that in an effort to get good flour and sugar. We were limited on that. And we had to buy other kinds. What hurt me the worst was not being able to have the variety of food we wanted. . . .

. . . .

Social Leisure in the 1930s

What means of social leisure did you employ in the 1930s?

> *Bank Clerk, No. 18.* I remember because that was my accordion days. Thirty [miles] from the river, my wife lived in a little town called Denver, thirty miles from here. And every Sunday, all summer long, my friend and I, and my wife now and her sister would go to the river. . . . We'd have a fish-fry or ride up and down the river. We got eight gallon of gas for a dollar. That's right. Of course, you get back to this sixty-five dollar a month [salary]. Eight gallon of gas for a dollar.
>
> We had no money to go to the picture show very much. Occasionally, the girls would have a supper; well, they'd have us for supper. Now that's just the way we lived. And when we did go to the show, Thursday night was dime night. Thursday night was the night that the picture shows were full. And the rest of the nights, the twenty-five cent nights, there just weren't anybody there. 'Course, we didn't have a radio till the middle of [the] 1930s. 'Course, a radio then probably cost you a hundred and fifty dollars. Getting back to sixty-five dollars a month salary, now there's two months' salary.

What were some of the things you used to do to try and relax?

> *High School Teacher, No. 9.* Oh, we once in awhile got a dime to go to the old Royal Theater on the South Side of the Square. . . . But you were lucky if you had the dime; it only took a dime or fifteen cents to get in at this time.

. . . .

The Effects of the Depression—A Comparison: McDonough County Versus the Nation

How did the Depression affect McDonough County compared with the rest of the nation during the 1930s? Was McDonough County better or worse off? From the interviews it was determined that McDonough County came through the Depression in better shape than many other localities, and the reasons given by the respondents make a good deal of sense. For one thing, the county is located in a rural agricultural section of the state. Even if a farmer could not realize a profit on his crops, he could at least provide food for his family.

The conservative bank management in the county prevented a good deal of the poor financial practices which were found in other places. So when the Depression struck and mortgage payments became due, the impact on McDonough County residents was not as severe. Furthermore, every attempt was made by the banking community to arrive at a just settlement with the mortgagee. The absence of large urban centers generally removed problems which would have existed if thousands of factory workers had been idled. The people of this small, stable county knew each other, so if a family down the road was having problems with food or shelter, they would probably receive assistance either from the county or a neighbor. With these favorable conditions existing in McDonough County, the impact of the Depression, in terms of unemployment and overall suffering, was considerably reduced. The economic picture of the county would have been far worse if the population had been predominantly urban and industrial in character.

How do you think the county fared compared with the rest of the state or the nation?

> *Farmer and Farm Auctioneer, No. 12.* Well, this county was always just a little better county, not because I lived here . . . but McDonough County in central-western Illinois is perhaps the best garden spot of the world. Now the banks have always been good in Macomb. We weren't hit as bad as they were in other counties. In Hancock County, there was only one bank left. When the banks closed in the moratorium, the Hill-Dodge Banking Company in Warsaw was the only bank that opened. Even the supervisors of Hancock County had to move their accounts and everything to Warsaw because that was the only one [that remained sound] . . . .
>
> There must have been six or seven banks that stayed open in McDonough County, whereas the other counties around didn't have so many. I think Monmouth was pretty fortunate. I think they maybe had two banks or three banks, I think, that opened up. . . . Now Schuyler County only had one bank—that's the little town of Camden—all the banks closed in Schuyler County but one. But McDonough County has been very fortunate. We've had some pretty good factories here. . . .

How do you think the county fared compared with the rest of the state or the nation? Do you think it was better off? Do you think it was worse off in the Depression?

> *Newspaper Owner and Editor, No. 11.* Well, very similar. We didn't have the marvelous ·positions under the federal administration that other counties had because of the political makeup of our county. So consequently, we didn't fare quite as well. The laborers or the common people, or actually the people down at the bottom scale, fared just as well. But we didn't have the high-paying positions that a lot of the counties had.

In other words, this county, being heavily Republican, didn't get some of the high administrative positions?

> *Newspaper Owner and Editor, No. 11.* You couldn't get the high administrative jobs that other counties had.

. . . .

3: War and Recovery

In an analysis of changing modern transportation needs in Illinois, Cary Clive Burford examines the demise of a "community institution," the local passenger train. The first of this section's special accounts, this article first appeared in the 1958 *Journal of the Illinois State Historical Society*. Burford is the author of *The History and Romance of Danville Junction; or When Rails Were Only Trails* (Danville, Ill., 1942) and *We're Loyal to You, Illinois* (Danville, 1952). Two Chicago writers discuss an essential element of modern Chicago—Mayor Richard J. Daley. In selections from *Daley of Chicago: The Man, the Mayor, and the Limits of Conventional Politics* (New York, 1970) Bill Gleason gives a sympathetic portrait of the accomplishments Daley has recorded in his long and colorful tenure. Other books by Gleason are *Footsteps of a Giant* (New York, 1966), with Emlen Tunnell, and *The Liquid Cross of Skid Row* (New York, 1966). Quite another perspective of the mayor and his city is provided by Mike Royko, the witty columnist for the *Chicago Daily News*, in *Boss: Richard J. Daley of Chicago* (New York, 1971). Royko began his career as a reporter in 1956, after serving for four years with the United States Air Force. For yet another view of Daley, see Len O'Conner, *Clout: Mayor Daley And His City* (Chicago, 1975).

The Twilight of the Local Passenger Train in Illinois

CARY CLIVE BURFORD

Just as it formerly clattered down the track to become a speck on the horizon, so has the local passenger train faded from the Illinois scene. And with it has passed a way of life. For most of our small towns and many larger ones it was as much a community institution as the public square, or Main Street, or the old bank corner.

The day's events were tuned to "train time." Those were glamorous moments for the community. Most of the citizens made a habit of going down to the depot to see the train come in—it was pronounced "dee-po," and was seldom referred to as the station. On these occasions the more sedate residents used the thin excuse of having letters to mail "on the train." In my own home town of Farmer City, Illinois, I remember the arrival of the 4:38 on Sunday afternoons as a particularly gala event—the area in front of the depot was filled with buggies, surreys and carriages, and there would be well over a hundred greeters in attendance.

It would be difficult to set definite years for the "Golden Age" of the local passenger train in Illinois, but I would estimate that it extended from about 1880 to the end of World War I—or, approximately, 1920. Beginning at that time, there was a gradual "annulment" of local trains until the few that are now left are mostly in the Chicago area where they still make their daily commuter runs.

For instance, the *Official Guide of the Railways* shows that in 1918 the Chicago, Burlington & Quincy operated a vast network of branch lines in northern Illinois and Iowa. It ran local passenger trains between Quincy and Keokuk; Buda and Rushville; Concord, Jacksonville and Herrin; Davenport, Rock Island and Sterling; Streator and Walnut; Galesburg and West Havana; Galesburg, Galva, Keithsburg and Burlington; Quincy and Burlington; Shabbona and Sterling; Aurora and Streator; Oregon and Forreston; and Rochelle and Rockford. Business was so brisk on the Aurora-Streator branch that two deports were maintained at Ottawa—one in the city proper

From Cary Clive Burford, "The Twilight of the Local Passenger Train in Illinois," *Journal of the Illinois State Historical Society,* LI (1958), 161-163, 167-180. Reprinted by permission of the Illinois State Historical Society. Footnotes in the original have been omitted.

and one across the Illinois River in South Ottawa. These were only a few of the Burlington's branches. Passenger service has now been discontinued on all of them.

Similarly, the Illinois Central operated its network of branches connecting with "main lines" at such towns as Clinton, Champaign, Mattoon, Decatur, Freeport, Bloomington, Kankakee, Carbondale and DuQuoin. There were lines between Effingham and Indianapolis; Havana and West Lebanon, Indiana; Bloomington, Pontiac and Kankakee; and Freeport and Madison, Wisconsin. The Peoria-Decatur branch was the former Peoria, Decatur & Evansville road (the P.D. & F.) and served Peoria, Decatur, Mattoon and Evansville.

Passenger service has been discontinued on all of these branches as well as on what was the I.C.'s original main line—one of its "Charter Lines." This runs through Vandalia, Decatur, Bloomington, LaSalle, Mendota and Dixon to Freeport, and in 1958 carries freight only. At Dixon there were two depots, one north and one south of the Rock River.

Another road with an extensive local passenger service was the Chicago & Alton—now a part of the Gulf, Mobile & Ohio. Two of its important branches entered the Peoria Union Station. One was the Springfield-Peoria line and the other extended northeast to meet the main line at Dwight. From Bloomington another branch ran southwest to serve Delavan, Mason City, Petersburg, Jacksonville, Roodhouse, Alton and St. Louis. Roodhouse was a terminal where still another branch operated west through Missouri to Kansas City.

In Alton the downtown depot overlooked the Mississippi River and the old city hall where the seventh Lincoln-Douglas debate took place. Trains operating north from this old station had to climb one of the steepest grades in Illinois. This station has long since been abandoned for a newer one in Upper Alton and the older tracks are now used only for freight.

Other roads with their fleets of local passenger trains in Illinois were the Wabash; Chicago, Rock Island & Pacific; Chicago & North Western; Chicago, Milwaukee & St. Paul; and the former Big Four, now operated as a part of the New York Central.

. . . .

The old-time local passenger train—which so many towns no longer have—usually consisted of a steam locomotive and its tender, a mail car, a baggage and express car, a "smoker" and a "ladies car." Sometimes the mail compartment was compressed into the end of the baggage car and frequently the train baggageman doubled as the express messenger. Incidentally, railroad men, or "railroaders," as they call themselves, still use the word "consist" as a noun when describing the composition of their trains.

The "crew" of this local train was composed for years of the engineer, fireman, mail clerk, baggage master, expressman, conductor and brakeman. The engineer was, of course, in charge of the enginer—he was the boss of the "front end." His assistant, the fireman, stoked the coal from the tender into the engine and also climbed, squirrel-like, over the pile of coal in the tender to operate the pipe from the water tank at the frequent water stops.

The mail clerk worked in the mail car or compartment but his assignment was far lighter than it would be today. Newspapers and magazines did not have the tremendous circulation they now enjoy, direct-mail advertising had not yet been developed, and parcel post did not enter his picture until 1912. The myriad of packages now moving through the mails was handled by the express messenger, or the baggageman-express messenger if, as they frequentiy were, these two busy tasks were given to one man. The train baggageman needed to be a strong and durable individual, for it was his duty to handle the many ponderous trunks and sample cases "checked" by the traveling salesmen or "drummers" using the trains. Some "carried" from six to ten trunks, and one representative of a Baltimore clothing "house" checked twenty-five trunks and sample cases.

Wholesale dry-goods houses, such as John V. Farwell & Co. of Chicago, "traveled" their salesmen with heavy trunks. Shoe and jewelry wholesalers also employed their drummers. Passengers, during this local-train period, "checked" their valises and telescopes and frequently they had trunks as well. Then, too, all college and university students used the local trains and each of them "checked" a trunk heavy with books. Still other additions to the baggageman's burdens were the heavy trunks and awkward scenery of the medley of theatrical companies or "show troupes" that were constantly "on the road."

The express messenger was another busy member of the local train crew—even if he was not doing double duty as baggageman. In the 1890's and early 1900's he was responsible for the thousands of small packages which now are moved through the mails—then they were handled by the individual express companies. Adams, American, United States, Wells-Fargo, Pacific, National and others, which were consolidated into the Railway Express Agency during World War I. The messenger also handled a dizzying array of bread baskets, ice-cream freezers, crates of live chickens, beer kegs, laundry baskets, milk cans, egg crates and other bulky items. Then, too, he had charge of money shipments—usually bags of silver dollars shipped from big city banks to those in small towns. Also, he received the remittances of all agents along the line and gave receipts therefor. These valuable packages were placed in the safe in the express car for delivery to the "top office" of the road—usually in Chicago, St. Louis or Cincinnati.

The one "dressed up" man on the train was the conductor, who was in charge of this little empire on wheels. Some were even elegantly attired with a white vest in summer and a boutonniere. They were usually "lodge men" and wore their fraternal insignia on heavy gold watch chains extended across frequently bulging "tummies."

The conductor was the one contact between the company and the passenger—to whom he was the company, just as he is on the sleek transcontinental trains of today. He collected the tickets and, if there was "trouble" regarding a fare or some disturbance on the train, he was the one who "straightened things out"—or attempted to do so. Conductors varied tremendously in their attitudes toward passengers. Many were kindly and treated women and children with every consideration. Others were stern or even haughty in their dealings. Some were known to be "easy" when inquiring about the

The Illinois Central Railroad depot at LaSalle, Illinois

Courtesy of the Illinois State Historical Library

age of children who were then, as now, supposed to pay half-fare after the age of six and full fare when they were twelve and above. Many pious Presbyterian and godly Methodist parents would insist their offspring was only five years old when he or she was really nine, or only eleven when the child was evidently fifteen. Parents often pushed their darling into a corner between them and the window sill so that they could not be observed too closely by the conductor, especially when he was considered the "hard-boiled" type who would insist upon the last farthing for the company.

The "easy" conductors were known to the men who wanted to ride without paying their full fares. They would stroll to the last seat in the "ladies' car" where they would slip the conductor fifty cents when the fare was three dollars or more. It was alleged that many conductors "made good money on the side" in this way. Rumor said that one man, after he retired, purchased three farms with what he had "knocked down." Actually, though, most conductors were scrupulously honest with the company.

Many of the conductors were picturesque characters and were known personally to their regular passengers by their first names or nicknames. One of these was Frank Green who commanded a local Wabash train on the Effingham-Bement branch, which turned onto the main line at Bement and made a local passenger run to Danville and return, then back "home" to Effingham. He was mayor of Effingham (1901-1903) and a master politician. Everyone knew Frank and Frank knew everyone. He was a hand-shaker and numbered as his close friends the scores of passengers he carried every day. His train was always called "Green's Train."

Another well-remembered conductor was a wiry little chap who wore a beard that reached to his waist. He braided it and tucked it beneath his vest so it would not get caught when the car door slammed—car doors were always slamming, it seemed. Another wore boots, hand-made to his order, of exquisite soft leather. Shoes hurt his feet, he insisted. Since there was no retirement rule at that time some conductors continued in active service until they were more than eighty years of age.

The train's all-around handy man was the brakeman, who was usually only slightly less "dressed up" than the conductor—after all he was an apprentice conductor. He would call the names of the station—although ninety-five per cent of the passengers knew the towns as well as he did—and would alight from the train in all sorts of weather to throw the switch if the train had to "run into the hole," as the side track was called, when meeting another train. The brakeman assisted the ladies up the steps and usually was alert to note the exposure of a bit of feminine stocking above a high button shoe. When a lady inadvertently turned at the top of the steps toward the smoke the brakeman would call up, "Smoking car, lady." Whereupon, she fled in terror to the shelter and protection of the "ladies' car." Ladies, of course, never thought of smoking, hence had no need for "the smoker."

Another, but ex-officio, member of the crew was the "train boy," "train butcher," or "Butch," who sold a variety of goods— newspapers, magazines, fruit, candy, chewing gum and novelties— from a large basket swung over his arm. Although there was a train boy—sometimes as young as fifteen years old—on every local train he was not employed by the railroad but by the Union or Western News Company. His stock of goods, supplied by his company, was called his "slam." His surplus was piled in the front corner seat of the smoker where it was safe from pilfering. In fact, snitching from the slam of a train boy was considered worse than high treason.

Butch sold apples, pears and bananas at three for a dime. Apples at this price seemed outrageously high to country folks who could go out in their own or their neighbors' orchards and pick up all they wanted—for free. And a dime was an immense sum to many passengers. In the smoker Butch found his steady and "quick" money. There he sold cigars and, on the sly, cigarettes which, of course, were utterly "taboo" in the ladies' car. It was the period of "roll your own" when "the makings" were sold by the pack with "the papers" free. Cigarettes were denounced by the older generation as "coffin nails"—young men were admonished that every time they smoked a cigarette they were driving one more nail into the lid of their coffins

Butch also found an attractive quick profit in articles he bought and sold "on the side" from his slam. One of these was eyeglasses or spectacles, which he peddled through the ladies' car. He purchased them at two or three dollars a dozen and sold them at three dollars each to dear old ladies who were certain they could see much better after buying their new "specs" from the train boy.

Another big profit-maker for Butch was his "hot stuff" department—pictures and "sex books." The pictures were of beautiful girls in scanty attire which he purchased at perhaps a dollar a dozen. Then, when he cornered a country lad in the smoker enjoying, or trying to enjoy, his first "see-gar"—he unloaded them at fifty or seventy-five cents each. The country boy would hide them in the haymow at home to bring out for special showings to visiting neighbor lads.

Butch's "sex books" were merely the physiology texts of today. He bought them in paper backs or cheap hard covers at thirty-five or forty cents each and sold them to the "hired hands" or "corn shuckers" in the smoking car at two dollars and a half, or three dollars. In that period when patient station agents and telegraph operators worked for $40 or $50 a month some train boys on preferred runs were clearing as high as $50 or $75 a week.

If Butch had few bargains in his "slam," the railroads of the period did offer something that was a bargain then and would be at any time—that was the special excursion train. Sunday excursions were featured for years by many roads with "special rates" sometimes as low as a dollar for a round trip of a hundred miles or more. Those were the years when the silver dollar was king. A veteran ticket agent told this writer that one Sunday morning he sold so many excursion fares to Indianapolis at one dollar each and received so many silver dollars that he could not possibly put them in the conventional cash drawer. So he threw them into a bucket and when the train of sixteen cars pulled out he had a bucket full of silver dollars.

Not all excursions were relatively short-distance affairs, for a number of railroads ran special trains to Niagara Falls with fares as low as seven dollars for the round trip. "Cheaper than staying at home" was the comment frequently heard. All of these Niagara Falls excursions with their fifteen to twenty wooden coaches, jammed with humanity, made the round trip safely with the exception of one Toledo, Peoria & Western train which was involved in the historic Chatsworth wreck. And it more than made up for all of the safe trips. This train of approximately twenty coaches, on the night of August 10-11, 1887, plunged from a burning trestle near Chatsworth, Illinois, with a loss of 85 killed and perhaps 300 injured. The property damage and claims against the road were so heavy that it was thrown into receivership.

Naturally, when people depended so greatly upon passenger trains, especially local passenger trains, a familiarity grew up whereby they affectionately nicknamed the roads and the trains. Thus the Toledo, Peoria & Western came to be known as "The Tip-Up." The Lake Erie & Western, which ran from Peoria to Sandusky, Ohio, handled a heavy local passenger business for many years and its trains, stopping at every station, were necessarily slow. Hence, the road was dubbed the "Leave Early and Walk,"—a good walker, it was alleged, could outdistance a Lake Erie train. An interesting little road operated for many years between Sidell and Olney, Illinois, parallel to the Indiana state line. Its official name was the "Chicago & Ohio River Railroad" and the wiseacres declared it was correctly named since it reached neither Chicago nor the Ohio River. Its train was nicknamed "The Doty." For years the butt of jokesmiths was the Hooppole, Yorktown & Tampico Railroad, east of Rock Island. Without a turntable on the line, the locomotive, known as "The Dummy," had to back up in one direction. There were a number of these one-way operations throughout the state. One was on the Sidney Champaign branch of the Wabash, which for years carried many passengers to and from the University of Illinois.

One local passenger train that deserves a book rather than just a few lines was "The Dolly," which traveled her route for more than eighty years as a part of the Burlington system. Her full name, of course, was "The Dolly Varden" but this was shortened by her friends to simply "The Dolly." Often called "the old girl," she was named—along with a style of women's dresses and hats, and a trout—for a coquettish lass in Dickens' *Barnaby Rudge* and the popular American entertainer, Dolly Varden O'Dell.

Originally, the Dolly had been a four-unit train, with locomotive and tender, combination mail, baggage and express car, a smoker and a ladies' car. But by the time of her last run she was reduced to a "doodlebug" in size—a diesel car with mail and baggage compartments and an area for passengers. The Dolly operated between Burlington, Iowa, and Galesburg, Illinois, via Oquawka, Aledo and Galva. She left Burlington at 6:45 A.M., arrived at Galesburg at 10:45, and "laid over" until 2:30 P.M., when she began her return trip, arriving at 6:40 P.M. Her schedule changed, of course, across the years.

The last run of the Dolly was made February 16, 1952, a date long to be remembered. It was a real "Old Home Week," a Roman holiday, indeed. Kind housewives along the route brought cakes, cookies, pies and other tidbits for the crew. Usual business was neglected while everyone went to the depot in Viola, Alpha, New Windsor, Keithsburg, New Boston (where the Dolly backed in or out of town), Joy, Oquawka and other towns on the route.

The conductor on this last run was Louis Astle, then seventy-nine, and almost as much a Burlington institution as the Dolly herself. The mail clerk contrived a special stamp reading, "Death of the Dolly. Last Trip," which he affixed to all mail handled that day. Newspapers in nearby cities—Rock Island, Moline, Davenport, Burlington, Muscatine, Galesburg and others—sent photographers and reporters to record the last trip of this old veteran of the rails. Incidentally, Robert T. Glenn, a mail clerk, wrote a column headed "The Dolly, By Golly," which ran for about five years in the *Aledo Times-Record.*

I have taken rides on several "last trains" in the half-dozen years since the Dolly waved farewell to her friends and passengers and have noticed a waning enthusiasm for such events. Probably there have been too many "last runs." The most recent of these was on October 14, 1957, when the Peoria & Eastern, an old-time Big Four route now leased to the New York Central, made its final trip from Indianapolis to Pekin and return. There was a coach filled with passengers, sure enough, but there was little interest shown at the various stations along the route. When we arrived in Farmer City I found businessmen who did not realize that the P.&E., as it was called, was making its last run on a line that had been serving the people since 1870. "Oh, was this the day for the last train?" several inquired.

. . . .

Daley of Chicago

BILL GLEASON

The Place

Chicago is the name—Chicago, a calculating city that conceals the truth about itself because it prefers to be misunderstood. Chicago strives to conceal its realities from those who see the city infrequently. Chicago doesn't want to know the stranger on his first day in town, and Chicago doesn't want the stranger to know the city on his fifth day in town. Chicago has a need to awe a visitor, and Chicago is convinced that familiarity breeds contempt. This is why those who profess to know Chicago best know Chicago least. Chicago is not a woman, not a "she" as so many cities are. Chicago is the "he" among cities. Chicago is always the seducer, never the seduced. Chicago does not lie there at the western turn of Lake Michigan waiting for things to happen. Chicago moves, moves, making things happen.

Chicago is, has been and will be violent. When Chicago heard that Abraham Lincoln had been shot and gravely wounded, a man who was standing in the crowded lobby of the Matteson House said that Lincoln had got what was coming to him. Almost immediately the Lincoln critic was shot to death. The reaction of the witnesses to the Matteson House murder? Most in the huge crowd applauded. The killer stepped over the body of his victim, strolled from the lobby and walked into the street. Free? More than free. A hero. The police neither pursued him nor looked for him later. He merely had done what others would have done.

Almost a century later, after John Fitzgerald Kennedy was destroyed by an assassin, another Chicagoan put his gun into his pocket and went to the jail in Dallas. Jack Ruby, well remembered by refugees from Chicago's West Side as a hustler, a slugger, a tough guy with a marshmallow heart, is part of the legend now—a folk hero.

Chicago is violent. Five phases of its history have brought to it conditions that inspire violence and individuals who incite to violence. Chicago was a frontier fortress-outpost. Chicago was a river village. Chicago was a canal town. Chicago was a railhead city. Chicago was a Prohibition metropolis. In each of those phases violence was a way of life or of death. Citizens killed and citizens were killed.

Chicago is conservative. Rooted in history, as is the violence, the conservatism has been the reaction to the violence. The violent and the conservative are the contradictions that analysts from other places rarely comprehend. Chicago has had a reputation as a wide-open town, but this renown is based on misconceptions from the past. The illegalities of Chicago exist, and have existed, for the visitors from out of town and for those who promote the illegalities and profit by them. Chicago now may be one of the few large cities in the world that do not have a whorehouse that operates with the sanction of elected officials, and it is a city in which a person cannot make a wager on the outcome of a horse race in surroundings conducive to dignity and serenity.

. . . .

Chicago is conservative, but Chicago is not cheap. If you need money for any purpose Chicago will lend it to you, but Chicago will not pay for a lay. Chicago stays out in the neighborhoods on Friday and Saturday nights and leaves Old Town, Rush Street and State Street to those visitors from other places. Chicago may covet its neighbor's wife in the corner tavern just after closing on Sunday morning, but Chicago will not go downtown to pay for what it can get free.

. . . .

The city says, "If you can't make it in Chicago, you can't make it anywhere." What the calculating city means to say is, "If you can make it in Chicago, you can make it anywhere." Natives of other places may see themselves with similar confidence, but Chicago's men and Chicago's women, children of the man-city, reject the premise that any other city and the residents of any other city are comparable to Chicago and Chicagoans. The citizens of Chicago know, beyond any doubt, that they could slow their speed to three quarters of the pace they move at when at home and lead the field in other places.

The Tribune Tower overlooks the place where Chicago's first non-Indian inhabitant made his home. This first settler was a black man in the eyes and in the minds of those who accept Chicago's premise that a person who is half Negro, or any fraction thereof, is all Negro. Chicago's conscience prefers to skip over this black man who lived on the riverbank and think instead of the man who bought the Negro's property. The purchaser was "the first white settler," and those few words explain all that is wrong with Chicago.

Chicago's slogan of a generation ago—"I will"—is laughed at by older citizens and is unknown to the younger. Chicago's authentic, unwritten slogan is "I'm with you," which is pronounced "I'm witchoo."

An easy air of conspiracy permeates day-to-day life outside the home. Chicago is a city of alliances. Those who stand apart from one another by tradition and background become allies when they are thrown together. The Pole and the Negro who work side by side in a machine shop confide in one another with the motto of a brotherhood that does not run as deep as blood. "I'm witchoo."

They work together, conspire together, laugh together and drink together. When the working day is done each returns to the sanctuary of the tavern in his neighborhood and tells ethnic jokes about the other.

The Pole and the Negro in the machine shop. The Irishman and the Lithuanian on the police force. The Jewish merchant and the Bohemian janitor. The Wasp stockbroker and the hillbilly waitress.

They understand one another and the understanding is complete. Each knows that the other will be "witchoo" until a more profitable alliance can be worked out. Today's ally may be tomorrow's enemy. The ritual is a big-city square dance in which the original partners "go on to the next" but rarely "come on home." Chicago is the caller.

The most skillful dancers are Chicago's politicians. Alliances, like campaign promises, are made to be broken. *I'm with you.* The unsaid part of this affirmation of loyalty is "We're against everybody else."

The Man

Daley is the name—Richard J. Daley, a secretive man who has managed to keep himself from being known to the millions who have watched him and listened to him and been governed by him for more than fourteen years. Richard J. Daley is like a king of olden times who daily came down from his castle into the town to walk among his subjects, to touch them and to be touched by them; but when the king returned to the castle at dusk his subjects realized that he had learned much about them and they had learned nothing about him.

Richard J. Daley is a private man in a public job. He is at least as calculating and as complicated as Chicago, his city. He also makes a deliberate effort to be misunderstood. Nobody asks him, "How do you feel about this?" Instead the question invariably is, "What do you think about this?" His feelings are kept under lock in the strongbox of his soul except on rare occasion when he turns the lock with the key that is temper. Then he says, "Shoot to kill," and the millions who admire him realize that he does feel.

According to one who studies the derivation of surnames, *Daley* means "He who goes to meetings." If this name did not have that meaning, Richard Daley would have brought the meaning to it. He goes to meetings and to wakes. It has been said of him that he has attended more wakes than any politician in Chicago history. To this chore, which even a few among Irish-Americans find to be onerous, he brings genuine respect for the dead and practical compassion for the mourners. In his quiet, diffident way he is saying, "I'm with you."

He is elderly now, but he remains charged with the energy of youth. He is a born walker, a parader, a marcher. Even when he is standing, he looks as though he is in motion. When he enters the Council chambers at City Hall to preside at a meeting of aldermen, he moves so quickly it seems as though he will stride through the large room and exit at a far door before he can stop.

When he arrives at a funeral home, he whirls through the entrance door, members of the retinue taking large steps to keep pace, and if it is not a Catholic wake and there is no kneeler upon which a man can say a prayer beside the casket, he looks to be in motion even when he is talking earnestly and comfortingly to the widow. He moves, moves, moves, making things happen.

His carriage and his posture, carefully cultivated, are magnificent.

Chins in, abdomen tucked up. Because he looks so much like the politicians of the editorial-page cartoons, he does everything possible to avoid the stereotype. He is not a tall man. He is not a slim man. But he walks tall and slim. This is a trick he learned well from others. He has disciplined his body, but his face got away from him. It is a good face, but instead of having been stretched it was folded and piled. Just as he has an extra chin, he has a profusion of jowls. There are, within the jowls, great dimples and small crevasses. At times students of his face see Mr. Pickwick there; at other times they see Santa Claus; and at still other times the character portrayed so often by Sidney Greenstreet, the late movie villain. In 1955 critics made fun of the clothes worn by Daley. Now he makes "best-dressed men" lists, an accomplishment that amuses him.

His malapropisms, tautologies and syntactical errors are collector's items. But he is not the "dese, dem and dose" mispronouncer that some among the literati have made him out to be. His basic speech impediment is one shared by most Irish-Americans, even to the third and fourth generation. There is something in the Gaelic language that makes the sounding of *th* all but impossible. For Richard J. Daley and millions like him *thanks* becomes *tanks* and *think* becomes *tink*. Even *the* is difficult—it usually emerges sounding like *tuh*—and *these, them* and *those* are more so.

For a very long time he infuriated his constituents by speaking as though he were sure that Chicago's major airport, O'Hare Field, actually was O'Hara Field. The explanation offered and accepted was that Daley knew many O'Haras and hardly any O'Hares. The true explanation may very well have been buried in the subconscious of this man who has an aversion for anything that reflects upon the fair name of Chicago. Daley knew that the airport had been named to honor the deed and the memory of a young man who had been one of the great heroes of the dismal days early in World War II. Daley also knew that the hero's father had been a powerful associate of Al Capone, the boss of Chicago's crime syndicate, and that the elder O'Hare had been shot to death in a Chicago street, another victim of the contract killers of the Syndicate that contributed so largely to giving Chicago a notorious name.

It has been said that his approach to press relations is abominable, that he does not know how to handle the questions volleyed at him by the men from newspapers, television and radio. The fact is that he uses a press conference or an interview for his purposes and that he loses control only on those rare occasions when his short temper routs his good judgment. One of his first major interviews was a question-and-answer session with a reporter from a news weekly. That was Daley's first opportunity for a national demonstration of a skill he had learned from masters—the knack of pretending to answer a question by talking away from the question. These are examples from that interview:

> Q. Is there any organized crime remaining [in Chicago]?
> A. Well, you have crime always, whether it's the large city or the village or the neighborhood.
> Q. But what about the Syndicates, like the Capone gang—do they exist?
> A. Well, whether it's organized or unorganized, it's still crime and it has to be met on all the various levels by very rigid law enforcement.

Those answers were accepted by the reporter in 1955, and the editors printed them. Reporters and editors have been taking and publishing similar answers from Daley ever since.

In 1955 Richard J. Daley became the fortieth mayor of Chicago. His opponents were certain that he would be a very bad mayor. His supporters hoped that he would be a mediocre mayor who would not disgrace his city, himself or his party. He was reelected in 1959, in 1963 and in 1967. He has been mayor of Chicago longer than any other man, and many contend that he is the best mayor the city has had. When he came to City Hall in 1955 his task, as he saw it, was to "restore, revitalize and rebuild the spirit of Chicago." His successes are unparalleled. His failure is singular. His failure is the failure of all of us, of the nation. Race. He is good with buildings, but he is poor with people—and deplorably poor with people who are black.

He is The Mayor.

. . . .

For more than fourteen years, going on sixteen, The Mayor had been Chicago. Almost everything accomplished within the city, for good or for ill, had his name or his imprint upon it. Almost nothing had been done in Chicago that he had not wanted done. When Richard J. Daley took office in 1955, he saw himself as the city. In 1970 those who had studied him through his years in City Hall realized that he had understood Chicago, in 1955, far better than his critics had.

The Mayor's vision had not been dramatic or poetic. It was realistic. Chicago had been his "subject" for a lifetime, and he had pursued his research assiduously. The once and future mayor had been twelve years old on November 1, 1914, when Chicagoans who cared about such things read that *Poetry Magazine*'s first prize of $200 had been won by a citizen named Sandburg, who lived at 4646 North Hermitage Avenue. The poem written by Sandburg was titled "Chicago," which wasn't a bad start, and the city seen by the Chicago newspaperman was the one that natives expected a country boy to see. Sandburg came from Galesburg, Illinois, and as Eleventh Warders of that day put it in their patronizing Big City manner, "Once a rube, always a rube."

Sandburg wrote of Chicago as "Hog Butcher for the World . . . City of the Big Shoulders." During his boyhood and young manhood Dickie Daley's neighbors had been the broad-shouldered men who stuck the hogs in the nearby Union Stock Yards. The man who became mayor was certain that the Chicago of 1955 no longer was the Chicago that had been brought alive by the imagery of the man from Galesburg. And The Mayor had been right.

As the city waited for The Mayor to decide whether he would run for a fifth term in 1971, the question that many citizens were asking was whether The Mayor comprehended that the Chicago of the Seventies no longer was the Chicago of 1955. Nobody could be certain of the answer.

So many have said so often that he is "the best mayor" or "the greatest mayor" in Chicago's history, the accolade has come to be taken for granted, although it does not necessarily withstand examination. . . .

Has Richard Daley truly been a better mayor than Edward Kelly, who brought Chicago through the Depression and built the subway under the Loop and accommodated the bookmakers and the vice bosses and had such magnetic appeal to the black residents of the city? Has Dick Daley truly done a better job than William Hale Thompson, who was the first of the great builders and who also won the hearts and the minds of the black voters?

John Dienhart, the venerable newspaper editor, who has seen them all come and go, says of Daley, "I like him as a man and as a public official. He's a clean man. The politicians didn't trust Dick, in the beginning because he never has been reachable, even by inference. I can't conceive of him doing anything wrong."

. . . .

Nick Bohling, the Republican alderman who remained in his neighborhood until his was one of only two white families in a city block of high population density, says thoughtfully, "I don't think there's any doubt that he'll go into history as the greatest mayor Chicago has had."

As to the Chicago of tomorrow, Bohling says, "Much is dependent upon how long Daley will be around. He has the ability, and thankfully so, to run a tight ship. What will happen when he's gone [long pause] I just don't know. In another generation this hatred and resentment we have on the basis of color will be gone. Chicagoans of the future will look back and laugh at us just as we now laugh at some of the things that our predecessors did because they thought they were right."

Will Chicago or any other major city be able to afford the luxury of waiting a generation before the hatred and resentment blow away upon the winds of progress? One year after the release of the Kerner Report, which was a best seller in Chicago, the National Advisory Commission on Civil Disorders concluded its anniversary report with these words: "A year later, we are a year closer to being two societies, black and white, increasingly separate and scarcely less equal."

The overpowering question, the question being asked in every metropolis of the world, was one that frightened men. "Can the city of the 1970's be made to work?" John V. Lindsay, the mayor of New York, had the gift that Daley was denied—the instinct that enabled him to get into the hearts of the citizens—but New York was falling apart before Lindsay's eyes. Richard Daley, the mayor of Chicago, had the talent that Lindsay lacked—the ability to get things done—but Chicago was being sundered while Daley worked so energetically. Daley and, to a lesser extent, Lindsay knew how to play the political game by the rules of the Sixties and the Fifties, but by now the game itself had changed. The strategies of conventional politics were falling everywhere.

To paraphrase the words written more than fifteen years earlier by Meyerson and Banfield for their book on the Chicago Housing Authority, ". . . whether one liked it or not and whether one ignored it or not, The Mayor's problem and the race problem are inseparably one."

If the man who vowed to be "the mayor of all the people" should decide to run again, he will have an opportunity to do something now about bringing together all the people. The motto of the Daley Clan is "Faithful to God and King," a rather contradictory battle cry for a family which sprang from a land whose patriots never hesitated to shout "to hell with the King" for the honor and glory of God.

During recent years this common man from a common background has so often revealed that he does not have the common touch. He has been much more at home with the kings. It is time for this king to learn more about his people, and the most dramatic way for him to communicate his willingness for contact would be to leave behind forever the castle at 3536 South Lowe Avenue. He has done enough for Bridgeport. His children are old enough now to permit him to do what Ed Kelly did, to move away from the old neighborhood and dwell on neutral ground in a high-rise luxury apartment east or north of the Loop. From that distance he may more clearly see that the good people of Bridgeport are much better than he thought them to be.

It is time for him to listen to those who say no. It is time for him to understand that Dan Mallette, Warner Saunders, Jesse Jackson and even Dick Gregory are on his side, as he has come to comprehend that Martin Luther King Jr. and he were on the same side.

"In modernizing the political system, Daley surrounded himself with bright young men who submerged their talents in order to exercise their talents telling him what a great gift he is to the people of Chicago," Father Mallette says with typical bitterness. "Daley's office is either modeled on, or is a model for, Archdiocesan chancery offices, where bishops surround themselves with handsome young monsignors whose main talents are their Irish names, handsome faces and ability to remain unfrustrated rubber stamps and soothsayers."

If he chooses to give of himself for four more years, The Mayor must leave the buildings to those who will come after him and concentrate on the people. Should he do this he will be remembered not as Chicago's most efficient mayor, not as the mayor who made State Street and LaSalle Street work with City Hall, but as the mayor of all the people, the greatest mayor Chicago ever had.

If he cannot do this he will be memorialized by the epitaph that this man would detest more than any other. He will be remembered as just another political boss.

. . . .

Boss

MIKE ROYKO

> *WILLIAM KUNSTLER: What is your name?*
> *WITNESS: Richard Joseph Daley.*
> *WILLIAM KUNSTLER: What is your occupation?*
> *WITNESS: I am the mayor of the city of Chicago.*

The workday begins early. Sometime after seven o'clock a black limousine glides out of the garage of the police station on the corner, moves less than a block, and stops in front of a weathered pink bungalow at 3536 South Lowe Avenue. Policeman Alphonsus Gilhooly, walking in front of the house, nods to the detective at the wheel of the limousine.

It's an unlikely house for such a car. A passing stranger might think that a rich man had come back to visit his people in the old neighborhood. It's the kind of sturdy brick house, common to Chicago, that a fireman or printer would buy. Thousands like it were put up by contractors in the 1920s and 1930s from standard blueprints in an architectural style fondly dubbed "carpenter's delight."

The outside of that pink house is deceiving. The inside is furnished in expensive, Colonial-style furniture, the basement paneled in fine wood, and two days a week a woman comes in to help with the cleaning. The shelves hold religious figurines and bric-a-brac. There are only a few volumes—the Baltimore Catechism, the Bible, a leather-bound *Profiles in Courage,* and several self-improvement books. All of the art is religious, most of it bloody with crucifixion and crosses of thorns.

Outside, another car has arrived. It moves slowly, the two detectives peering down the walkways between the houses, glancing at the drivers of the cars that travel the street, then parks somewhere behind the limousine.

At the other end of the block, a blue squad car has stopped near the corner tavern, and the policeman sits in a car. Like Gilhooly, he has been there all night, protecting the back entrance, behind the high wooden fence that encloses the small yard.

Down the street, in another brick bungalow, Matt Danaher is getting ready for work. He runs the two thousand clerical employees in the Cook County court system, and he knows the morning routine of his neighbor. As a young protégé he once drove the car, opened the door, held the coat, got the papers. Now he is part of the ruling circle, and one of the few people in the world who can walk past the policeman and into the house, one of the people who are invited to spend an evening, sit in the basement, eat, sing, dance the Irish jig. The blue-blooded bankers from downtown aren't invited, although they would like to be, and neither are men who have been governors, senators, and ambassadors. The people who come in the evening or on Sunday are old friends from the neighborhood, the relatives, people who take their coats off when they walk in the door, and loosen their ties.

Danaher is one of them, and his relationship to the owner of the house is so close that he has served as an emotional whipping boy, so close that he can yell back and slam the door when he leaves.

They're getting up for work in the little houses and flats all across the old neighborhood known as Bridgeport, and thanks to the man for whom the limousine waits, about two thousand of the forty thousand Bridgeport people are going to jobs in City Hall, the County Building, the courts, ward offices, police and fire stations. It's a political neighborhood, with political jobs, and the people can use them. It ranks very low among the city and suburban communities in education. Those who don't have government jobs work hard for their money, and it isn't much. Bridgeport ranks low in income, too.

It's a suspicious neighborhood, a blend of Irish, Lithuanian, Italian, Polish, German, and all white. In the bars, heads turn when a stranger comes in. Blacks pass through in cars, but are unwise to travel by on foot. When a black college student moved into a flat on Lowe Avenue in 1964, only a block north of the pink bungalow, there was a riot and he had to leave.

Well before eight o'clock, the door of the bungalow opens and a short, stout man steps out. His walk is brisk and bouncy. A nod and smile to Patrolman Gilhooly and he's in the limousine. It pulls out from the curb and the "tail car" with the two detectives trails it, hanging back to prevent the limousine from being followed.

It's a short drive to work. The house is about four miles southwest of the Loop, the downtown business district, within the problem area known as the "inner city." If the limousine went east, to Lake Shore Drive, it would go through part of the black ghetto. If it went straight north, it would enter a decaying neighborhood in transition from white to Latin and black. It turns toward an expressway entrance only a few blocks away.

The two cars take the Dan Ryan Expressway, twelve lanes at its widest point, with a rapid-transit train track down the center. It stretches from the Loop, past the old South Side ghetto, past the giant beehive public housing with its swarming children, furious street gangs, and weary welfare mothers.

He built that expressway, and he named it after Dan Ryan, another big South Side politician, who was named after his father, a big South Side politician.

The limousine crosses another expressway, this one cutting through the big, smokey, industrial belt, southwest toward white backlash country, where five years ago Dr. Martin Luther King was hit in the head with a brick when he led marchers into the neighborhood for the cause of open housing—which exists only on a few pages of the city's ordinance.

He built that expressway, too, and named it after Adlai Stevenson, whom he helped build into a presidential candidate, and whom he dropped when it was time.

The limousine passes an exit that leads to the Circle Campus, the city's branch of the University of Illinois, acres of modern concrete buildings that comprise one of the biggest city campuses in the country. It wasn't easy to build because thousands of families in the city's oldest Italian neighborhood had to be uprooted and their homes and churches torn down. They cried that they were betrayed because they had been promised they would stay. But he built it.

Another mile or so and the limousine crosses another expressway that goes straight west, through the worst of the ghetto slums, where the biggest riots and fires were ignited, for which the outraged and outrageous "shoot to kill" order was issued. Straight west, past the house where the Black Panthers were killed, some in their beds, by the predawn police raiders.

He opened that expressway and named it after Dwight D. Eisenhower, making it the city's only Republican expressway.

As the limousine nears the Loop, the Dan Ryan blends into still another expressway. This one goes through the Puerto Rican ghetto and the remnants of the old Polish neighborhood, where the old people remain while their children move away, then into the middle class far Northwest Side, where Dr. King's marchers walked through a shower of bottles, bricks and spit. It ends at O'Hare Airport, the nation's busiest jet handler.

He built that expressway, too, and he named it after John F. Kennedy, whom he helped elect president, and he built most of the airport and opened it, although he still calls it "O'Hara."

During the ride he reads the two morning papers, the *Chicago Sun-Times* and the *Chicago Tribune,* always waiting on the back seat. He's a fast but thorough reader and he concentrates on news about the city. He is in the papers somewhere every day, if not by name—and the omission is rare—at least by deed. The papers like him. If something has gone well, he'll be praised in an editorial. If something has gone badly, one of his subordinates will be criticized in an editorial. During the 1968 Democratic Convention, when their reporters were being bloodied, one of the more scathing newspaper editorials was directed at a lowly Police Department public relations man.

He, too, was criticized, but a week after the convention ended, his official version of what had happened on Chicago's streets was printed, its distortions and flat lies unchallenged. He dislikes reporters and writers, but gets on well with editors and publishers, a trait usually found in Republicans rather than Democrats. If he feels that he has been criticized unfairly, and he considers most criticism unfair, he doesn't hesitate to pick up a phone and complain to an editor. All four papers endorsed him for his fourth term—even the *Tribune*, the voice of Middle West Republicanism—but in general, he views the papers as his enemy. The reporters, specifically. They want to know things that are none of their business, because they are little men. Editors, at least, have power, but he doesn't understand why they let reporters exercise it.

The limousine leaves the expressway and enters the Loop, stopping in front of St. Peter's, a downtown church. When the bodyguards have parked and walked to his car, he gets out and enters the church. This is an important part of his day. Since childhood he has attended daily mass, as his mother did before him. On Sundays and some work days, he'll go to his own church, the Church of the Nativity, just around the corner from his home. That's where he was baptized, married, and the place from which his parents were buried. Before Easter, his wife will join the other neighborhood ladies for the traditional scrubbing of the church floors. Regardless of what he may do in the afternoon, and to whom, he will always pray in the morning.

After mass, it's a few steps to the side door of Maxim's, a glass and plastic coffee shop, where, in the event he comes in, a table is set up in the privacy of the rear. It is not to be confused with Chicago's other Maxim's, which serves haute cuisine, has a discotheque, and enjoys a social-register clientele. He won't go to those kinds of places. He doesn't like them and people might think he was putting on airs. He eats at home most of the time, and for dinner out there are sedate private clubs with a table in a quiet corner.

He leaves a dollar for his coffee and roll and marches with his bodyguards toward City Hall—"the Hall" as it is called locally, as in "I got a job in the Hall," or "See my brother in the Hall and he'll fix it for you," or "Do you know anybody in the Hall who can take care of this?"

He glances at the new Civic Center, a tower of russet steel and glass, fronted by a gracious plaza with a fountain and a genuine Picasso-designed metalwork sculpture almost fifty feet high.

He put it all there, the Civic Center, the plaza, the Picasso. And the judges and county officials who work in the Civic Center, he put most of them there, too.

Wherever he looks as he marches, there are new skyscrapers up or going up. The city has become an architect's delight, except when the architects see the great Louis Sullivan's landmark buildings being ripped down for parking garages or allowed to degenerate into slums.

None of the new buildings was there before. His leadership put them there, his confidence, his energy. Everybody says so. If he kept walking north a couple more blocks, he'd see the twin towers of Marina City, the striking tubular downtown apartment buildings, a self-contained city with bars and restaurants, ice rinks, shops and clubs, and balconies on every apartment for sitting out in the smog.

His good friend Charlie Swibel built it, with financing from the Janitors' Union, run by his good friend William McFetridge. For Charlie Swibel, building the apartment towers was coming a long way from being a flophouse and slum operator. Now some of his friend Charlie's flophouses are going to be torn down, and the area west of the Loop redeveloped for office buildings and such. And his friend Charlie will do that, too. Let people wonder why out-of-town investors let Charlie in for a big piece of the new project, without Charlie having to put up any money or take any risk. Let people ask why the city, after acquiring the land under urban renewal powers, rushed through approval of Charlie's bid. Let them ask if there's a conflict of interest because Charlie is also the head of the city's public housing agency, which makes him a city official. Let them ask. What trees do they plant? What buildings do they put up?

Head high, shoulders back, he strides with his bodyguards at the pace of an infantry forced march. The morning walk used to be much longer than two blocks. In the quiet of the 1950s, the limousine dropped him near the Art Institute on Michigan Avenue, and he'd walk a mile and a half on Michigan Avenue, the city's jeweled thoroughfare, grinning at the morning crowds that bustled past the shops and hotels, along the edge of Grant Park. That ritual ended in the sixties, when people began walking and marching for something more than pleasure, and a man couldn't be sure who he'd meet on the street.

He rounds the corner and a bodyguard moves ahead to hold open the door. An elderly man is walking slowly and painfully close to the wall, using it as support. His name is Al, and he is a lawyer. Years ago he was just a ward boss's nod away from becoming a judge. He had worked hard for the party and had earned the black robe, and he was even a pretty good lawyer. But the ward boss died on him, and judgeships can't be left in wills. Now his health was bad and Al had an undemanding job in county government.

He spots Al, calls out his name, and rushes over and gives him a two-handed handshake, the maximum in City Hall affection. He has seen Al twice in ten years, but he quickly recalls all of his problems, his work, and a memory they shared. He likes old people and keeps them in key jobs and reslates them for office when they can barely walk, or even when they can't. Like the marriage vows, the pact between jobholder and party ends only in either's death, so long as the jobholder loves, honors, and obeys the party. Later that day, Al will write an eloquent letter in praise of his old friend to a paper, which will print it.

The bodyguard is still holding the door and he goes in at full stride. He never enters a room tentatively—always explosively and with a sense of purpose and direction, especially when the building is City Hall.

Actually, there are two identical buildings—City Hall and the Cook County Building. At the turn of the century, the County Building was erected on half a city block, and shortly thereafter City Hall was put up. Although identical, City Hall cost substantially more. Chicago history is full of such oddities. Flip open any page and somebody is making a buck.

Although the main lobby and upstairs corridors extend through both buildings, he never goes through the County Building. That's a political courtesy, because the County Building is the domain of another politician, the president of the Cook County Board, known as "the mayor of Cook County," and, in theory, second only to him in power. But later in the day, the president of Cook County will call and ask how his domain should be run.

The elevator operators know his habits and are holding back the door of a car. The elevators are automated, but many operators remain on the job, standing in the lobby pointing at open cars and saying, "Next." Automation is fine, but how many votes can an automatic elevator deliver?

He gets off at the fifth floor, where his offices are. That's why he's known as "the Man on Five." He is also known as "duh mare" and "hizzoner" and "duh leader."

He marches past the main entrance to his outer offices, where people are already waiting, hoping to see him. They must be cleared first by policemen, then by three secretaries. He doesn't use the main entrance because the people would jump up, clutch at his hands, and overexcite themselves. He was striding through the building one day when a little man sprung past the bodyguards and kissed his hand.

Down the corridor, a bodyguard has opened a private door, leading directly to his three-room office complex. He almost always uses the side door.

The bodyguards quickly check his office then file into a smaller adjoining room, filled with keepsakes from presidents and his trip to Ireland. They use the room as a lounge, while studying his schedule, planning the routes and waiting. Another room is where he takes important phone calls when he has someone with him. Calls from President Kennedy and President Johnson were put through to that room.

Somewhere in the building, phone experts have checked his line for taps. The limousine has been parked on LaSalle Street, outside the Hall's main entrance, and the tail car has moved into place. His key people are already in their offices, always on time or early, because he may call as soon as he arrives. And at 9 A.M. he, Richard Joseph Daley, is in his office and behind the big gleaming mahogany desk, in a high-backed dark green leather chair, ready to start another day of doing what the experts say is no longer possible—running a big American city. But as he, Daley, has often said to confidantes, "What in hell do the experts know?" He's been running a big American city for fifteen of the toughest years American cities have ever seen. He, Daley, has been running it as long or longer than any of the other famous mayors—Curley of Boston, LaGuardia of New York, Kelly of Chicago—ran theirs, and unless his health goes, or his wife says no, he, Daley, will be running it for another four years. Twenty is a nice, round figure. They give soldiers pensions after twenty years, and some companies give wristwatches. He'll settle for something simple, like maybe another jet airport built on a man-made island in the lake, and named after him, and maybe a statue outside the Civic Center, with a simple inscription, "The greatest mayor in the history of the world." And they might seal off his office as a shrine.

. . . .

Daley has no . . . luncheon circle, and he eats only with old and close friends or one of his sons. Most afternoons, he darts across the street to the Sherman House hotel and his office in the Democratic headquarters, where as party chairman he will work on purely political business: somebody pleading to be slated for an office or advanced to a judgeship, a dispute between ward bosses over patronage jobs. He tries to separate political work from his duties as mayor, but nobody has ever been able to see where one ends and the other begins.

Lunch will be sent up and he might be joined by someone like Raymond Simon, the Bridgeport-born son of an old friend. Daley put him in the city legal department when he was fresh out of law school, and in a few years he was placed in charge, one of the highest legal jobs in the country. Now Simon has taken on an even bigger job: he resigned and went into private practice with Daley's oldest son, Richard Michael, not long out of law school. The name Daley and Simon on the office door possesses magic that has the big clients almost waiting in line. Daley's next oldest son, Michael, has gone into practice with a former law partner of the mayor, and has a surprisingly prosperous practice for so young and inexperienced an attorney. Daley filled Simon's place in his cabinet with another bright young lawyer, the mayor's first cousin.

When there is time, Daley is driven to the private Lake Shore Club for lunch, a swim, or a steam bath. Like most of the better private clubs in the fine buildings along the lake front, the Lake Shore Club accepts Jews and blacks. But you have to sit there all day to be sure of seeing one.

It's a pleasant drive to the club. Going north on Michigan Avenue, he passes the John Hancock Building, second in size only to the Empire State, and twice as high as anything near it. It was built during Daley's fourth term, despite cries of those who said it would bring intolerable traffic congestion to the gracious streets that can't handle it and lead to other oversized buildings that would destroy the unique flavor of the North Michigan Avenue district. It's happening, too, but the Hancock is another tall monument to his leadership.

From Michigan Avenue, he goes onto Lake Shore Drive, with the lake and beaches on the right, which were there when he started, and ahead the great wall of high-rise buildings beginning on the left, which wasn't. Dozens of them, hundreds, stretching mile after mile, all the way to the city limits, and almost all constructed during his administration, providing city living for the upper middle class, and billions in profits for the real estate developers. They are his administration's solution to keeping people in the city.

Behind the high-rises are the crumbling, crowded buildings where the lower-income people live. No answer has been found to their housing problems because the real estate people say there's not enough profit in building homes for them. And beyond them are the middle-income people, who can't make it to the high-rises and can't stay where they are because the schools are inadequate, the poor are pushing toward them, and nothing is being done about their problems, so they move to the suburbs. When their children grow up and they retire, maybe then they can move to a lake front high-rise.

By two o'clock he's back behind his desk and working. One of his visitors will be a city official unique to Chicago city government: the director of patronage. He brings a list of all new city employees for the day. The list isn't limited to the key employees, the professional people. All new employees are there—down to the window washer, the ditch digger, the garbage collector. After each person's name will be an extract of his background, the job, and most important, his political sponsor. Nobody goes to work for the city, and that includes governmental bodies that are not directly under the mayor, without Daley's knowing about it. He must see every name because the person becomes more than an employee: he joins the political Machine, part of the army numbering in the thousands who will help win elections. They damn well better, or they won't keep their jobs.

He scans the list for anything unusual. A new employee might be related to somebody special, an important businessman, an old political family. That will be noted. He might have been fired by another city office in a scandal. That won't keep him from being put to work somewhere else. Some bad ones have worked for half the governmental offices in the city. There might be a police record, which prompts a call to the political sponsor for an explanation. "He's clean now." "Are you sure?" "Of course, it was just a youthful mistake." "Three times?" "Give him a break, his uncle is my best precinct captain." "Okay, a break, but keep your eye on him." As he has said so often, when the subject of ex-cons on the city payroll comes up, "Are we to deny these men honest employment in a free society . . . are we to deprive them of the right to work . . . to become rehabilitated . . ." He will forgive anything short of Republicanism.

The afternoon work moves with never a minute wasted. The engineers and planners come with their reports on public works projects. Something is always being built, concrete being poured, steel being riveted, contractors being enriched.

. . . .

Regardless of where he goes, the speech will be heavy in booster-ism, full of optimism for the future, pride in the city, a reminder of what he has done. Even in the most important of gatherings, people

Courtesy of the Illinois State Historical Library

Mayor Richard J. Daley

will seek out his handshake, his recognition. A long time ago, when they opposed him, he put out the hand and moved the few steps to them. Now they come to him. He arrives after dinner, in time to be introduced, speak, and get back to the car.

The afternoon papers are on the back seat and he reads them until the limousine stops in front of a funeral home. Wakes are still part of political courtesy and his culture. Since he started in politics, he's been to a thousand of them. On the way up, the slightest connection with the deceased or his family was enough reason to attend a wake. Now he goes to fewer, and only to those involving friends, neighbors. His sons fill in for him at others. Most likely, he'll go to a wake on the South Side, because that's where most of his old friends are from. The funeral home might be McInerney's, which has matchbooks that bear a poem beginning, "Bring out the lace curtains and call McInerney, I'm nearing the end of life's pleasant journey." Or John Egan's, one of the biggest, owned by his high school pal and one of the last of the successful undertaker-politicians. The undertaken-politicians and the saloon keeper-politicians have given way to lawyer-politicians, who are no better, and they don't even buy you a drink or offer a prayer.

He knows how to act at a wake, greeting the immediate family, saying the proper things, offering his regrets, somberly and with dignity. His arrival is as big an event as the other fellow's departure. Before leaving, he will kneel at the casket, an honor afforded few of the living, and sign the visitor's book. A flurry of handshakes and he is back in the car.

It's late when the limousine turns toward Bridgeport. His neighbors are already home watching TV or at the Pump Tavern having a beer, talking baseball, race or politics. His wife Eleanor, "Sis" as he calls her, knows his schedule and will be making supper. Something boiled, meat and potatoes, home-baked bread. She makes six loaves a week. His mother always made bread. And maybe ice cream for dessert. He likes ice cream. There's an old ice cream parlor in the neighborhood, and sometimes he goes there for a sundae, as he did when he was a boy.

The limousine passes Comiskey Park, where his beloved Sox play ball. He goes to Wrigley Field, too, but only to be seen. The Sox are his team. He can walk to the ball park from the house. At least he used to be able to walk there. Today it's not the same. A person can't walk anywhere. Maybe someday he'll build a big superstadium for all the teams, better than any other city's. Maybe on the Lake Front. Let the conservationists moan. It will be good for business, drawing conventioneers from hotels, and near an expressway so people in the suburbs can drive in. With lots of parking space for them, and bright lights so they can walk. Some day, if there's time, he might just build it.

Across Halsted Street, then a turn down Lowe Avenue, into the glow of the brightest street lights of any city in the country. The streets were so dark before, a person couldn't see who was there. Now all the streets have lights so bright that some people have to lower their shades at night. He turned on all those lights, he built them. Now he can see a block ahead from his car, to where the policeman is guarding the front of his home.

He tells the driver that tomorrow will require an even earlier start. He must catch a flight to Washington to tell a committee that the cities need more money. There are so many things that must be built, so many more people to be hired. But he'll be back the same day, in the afternoon, with enough time to maybe stop at the Hall. There's always something to do there. Things have to be done. If he doesn't do them, who will?

. . . .

Original Narratives

The modern age began for Illinoisans, as for all Americans, with the Cold War. In the years following World War II the threat of advancing Communism increasingly haunted the imaginations of concerned citizens. With the impending fall of China to the Communists in 1948, cries of alarm against the "red threat" intensified. An example of the Cold War mentality is the following paper, which was read before the Illinois State Historical Society on November 1, 1947, by Herbert O. Brayer. After noting the weakened condition of America's allies in the wake of Hitler's defeat, he points to the sudden ascendency of Russian Communism in Europe and to the astonishing internal progress of one Russian "totalitarian" state in the industrial revolution. In 1952, along with Garnet M. Brayer, he published *American Cattle Trails, 1540-1900* (Denver, Colo.).

The Duty—or Dilemma—of Every Illinoisan

HERBERT O. BRAYER

On every hand today—in the press, on the air, in our clubs, in our schools, and in our churches—we are faced with the startling and tragic picture of a starving and disorganized Europe torn between two conflicting philosophies of life—the one our own and the other that professed by the Union of Soviet Socialist Republics. Since my recent return from Europe, I have listened patiently and faithfully for someone, preferably some career member of our State Department, to give to the American people a concise, straightforward, and fearless account of what that struggle is about, and how it is manifest throughout the so-called "civilized world." I have waited in vain. The conflicting accounts of even present conditions in Europe are disheartening and sometimes even ludicrous. Representative John Taber, for example, reports he found no starvation in Europe while his own colleagues on the very same congressional visit report food conditions to be critical and even chaotic. A Scripps-Howard reporter with a liberal expense account and twenty-four hours in Paris reported several weeks ago that he could get excellent food in the French capital and saw no starvation. What that gentleman forgot to report to his readers was that he purchased his breakfast, lunch, and supper on the black market, and that only

From *Journal of the Illinois State Historical Society*, XLI (1948), 28-33, 37-42. Reprinted by permission of the Illinois State Historical Society.

ten or twelve per cent of the French people could afford the meals
he had bought! Paris is not France. I remember all too well last
June witnessing an incident in northeastern France in which a mob
attempted to seize a shipment of sugar en route to the American
Army in Germany.

There is no question that much of Europe is badly in need of
good food. Unfortunately, food is but one of Europe's critical
needs—there is an equally serious need for clothing, housing, medical
facilities, education, public welfare work, and re-establishment and
expansion of public utilities and social services. Europe is now short
of electricity, water and gas, of coal and wood, of cement, iron,
glass, and of wire, and pipe. . . . The problem is complicated by the
breakdown in government resulting from prolonged enemy occupa-
tion in certain areas. Years of subjection and terror and living under
rigid controls have altered both the moral code and the sense of
values of millions of people. Larceny, black marketing, smuggling,
sexual promiscuity, juvenile delinquency, and outright murder are
part of the daily European picture which Americans must not only
recognize but understand. Understanding is essential; thoughtless
condemnation is not only foolish but fails to recognize that under
similar circumstances Americans would likely be no better. This,
then, is the social and economic situation in Europe today.

. . . .

You will note that up to this point nothing has been said about
Russia or Russian communism—not that communistic elements
were not present and aggravating, but up to 1939—with the exception of Spain—Russian communism was not a dominant factor in
Western Europe. What the American press so frequently termed
"communistic" during that hectic pre-World-War-II era was in fact
"socialistic"—and the difference between the two was not academic, but one of basic fundamentals. Another popular fallacy
must also be exploded at this point. Many Americans still believe
that previous to the war the Western European democracies were
also believers in the free enterprise form of capitalism—some even
think that except for Great Britain "free enterprise" is the economic philosophy among most of the European democracies today.
Both impressions were and are erroneous. The democracies—
England, France, Belgium, Holland, Norway, Sweden, Denmark,
and formerly Finland—are firm believers in monopolies, cartels,
subsidies, and other internal and external commercial trade controls. Before labeling such actions undemocratic let the American
critic remember that our own tariff wall is but one of the methods
utilized internally and externally by these United States to prevent

"free" enterprise or perfect competition. Democracy and "free enterprise" are not synonymous, in fact, the latter can be, and historically has been, a potent weapon of every form of government from democracy to absolute monarchy. Thus it was that, in 1939, on the eve of World War II, the European world—economically ill and therefore politically chaotic—had found capitalism unsuited to economies with limited national resources, "captive" or closed markets, and most of all they had discovered somewhat bitterly that they could not compete with America's mass production methods, Japan's heavily subsidized, highly concentrated consumers' goods factories, or the restrictive colonial systems of Great Britain, France, Holland, and Belgium.

It seems hard to believe that only eight years ago, when Hitler marched into Poland, Communist Russia had not one real friend or ally among all the countries of Europe. Not one; yet today, eight years later, Russia counts as "friends and allies" Poland, Finland, Bulgaria, Rumania, Hungary, Yugoslavia, Czechoslovakia, parts of Germany and Austria, an apparent majority of the voters in Italy, a large part of the French population, and tens of thousands of others in Spain, Denmark, Norway, and Sweden. It is a relatively simple matter to account for Russian influence in those countries and areas which were occupied by troops of the Soviet, but what about the astounding success of the "Reds" in Italy, France and elsewhere in Western Europe?

First, nothing succeeds like success, and Russia's heroic battle against the Fascist hordes justly earned the plaudits of all men. But along with that military victory went a propaganda victory of which Herr Doktor Goebbels would have marveled. From 1917 to 1939, Russian publicists in every part of the world strove mightily to sell the working classes on the "people's revolution" and the Utopia to be found in the communistic Soviet. Not since the conversion of pagan Europe to Christianity had so widespread and militant a propaganda campaign been planned and executed. The comparison with religion is intentional. Communism has its theology, its dogma, an elaborate hierarchy and priesthood, its hero martyrs and damned persecutors, its ritual and exacting discipline. It utilizes the "revival" technique and thrives on "persecution." It would be foolish to minimize the success of this campaign. "Cells" were founded throughout Europe, America, and Asia. To the jobless and dispossessed, the bankrupt and downtrodden, the "people's revolution" held great appeal—gone would be "the scheming banker," the "slave-driving boss," the "grasping politician," the "warmongering international capitalists." Colonies would be freed; there would be no domination of one people by another. Clericalism would no longer oppress the ignorant. There would be no imperialism—cultural or political. The necessities of life would be publicly owned. Such was to be the good life. No wonder it appealed to the "exploited" laborers of threescore nations. Of course, not a few such "exploited workers" turned out to be professional agitators, pseudo intellectuals, and not a few misguided individuals who believed the way to clean a house—admittedly in need of a thorough overhauling—was to burn it down.

Such was the propaganda line. Many people, even in this country, took not only the bait, but the hook, line, and sinker. Thus it was that, when the guns fell silent two years ago, Europe was more than prostrate—she was economically bankrupt, socially disintegrated, politically chaotic, and spiritually confused.

. . . .

This, then, is the story of Europe as of November 1, 1947. Communism is still on the ascendancy, despite our avowed intention to meet and contain it on all fronts.

What is this "monster," this "horror" which fills our radio, our newspapers, and our daily life with grim forebodings of a new war? Actually it is half propaganda and half fact. Russian communism is in fact just another form of totalitarianism. It amounts to the control of some two hundred million people in Russia by not over two per cent of the population. Through its hierarchy, it controls all forms of enterprise within the country. It operates all factories, stores, shops, foundries, and even the farms through the appointment of managers and superintendents. It establishes production goals for each enterprise, allocates material, drafts labor, and distributes and markets all products of this state business. It owns and operates all the means of communication and transportation— radio, telephone and telegraph, newspapers, magazines, wire press services, trams, busses, airlines, railroads, and intercoastal ship lines as well as overseas transport. The Soviet administration organizes labor unions in each industry—one union to a plant and all employees must belong to it. Labor leaders are responsible to the government and production goals are as much their responsibility as they are those of the plant management. Strikes and labor disputes, such as we know them, are unknown, but "grievances committees," representing the workers, do confer with the management and can appeal over the head of the plant operators.

. . . .

It should be realized, however, that despite all wishful thinking, the government apparently is popular within Russia and supported vigorously by the people. This is understandable. In the thirty years since the revolution, Russia's millions have seen the complete redesigning of their country. The peasants are no longer serfs in the feudal sense, lands are no longer in the hands of an intrenched land-exploiting nobility, and the national income is not used for the aggrandizement of a corrupt and vicious government. The Russian today can say in all honesty that he is one hundred per cent better off than were his parents. Never having experienced our form of personal freedom, however, he can not conceive of its being better than his own. The *internal* propaganda of his government tells him daily of labor strikes in America, anti-labor legislation, the Negro and other minority problems in the United States and has convinced him that American labor is ruthlessly exploited by "bloated Wall Street capitalists," "Washington imperialists," and "industrial warmongers." When I described for a Russian my own home with a refrigerator, electric toaster, and bathtub, his reply was, "You could only have such luxuries by exploiting the workers who make such things." I described for a "Red" soldier who had been a farmer the equipment and methods used by a friend of mine on his farm in Colorado. My interested listener's visage clouded up with incredulity when I described the new Buick owned by my beet-sugar-growing agriculturist in America. This was impossible, he commented, unless my friend was taking the fruit of the labors of his hired hands and paying them little or nothing in return. In that answer, I saw the result of years of constant repetition of that same theme by the controlled press and radio.

The truth is that Russia, in thirty years, has risen from the semi-feudalistic state of the tzars to a modern nation striving to overcome centuries of backwardness in the shortest possible time. That she has succeeded so well is nothing less than astounding. She is producing jet airplanes, automobiles, trucks, busses, street cars, locomotives, tractors, tanks, guided missiles, automatic rifles, ammunition, and tires. She is building huge power dams, railroads, highways, and by her own admission, atomic energy plants. She has accomplished all of this in three decades by the simple process of subordinating everything, especially men, to the program of the state. Americans must realize that despite certain notable failures in specific fields, the internal program of Russia has been highly successful from the point of view of the Soviet government.

At the same time the rulers of Russia have carried on an external program designed first to prevent aggression against the Soviet; secondly, to prevent the permeation into Russia, and now its satellites, of ideas and principles contrary to the established propaganda line; thirdly, to foment and encourage political chaos in neighboring countries so as, ultimately, to be in a position, through its "fifth-column cells," to take over and establish "friendly" states on its borders; and lastly, to establish and support Communist parties throughout the world as the basis for the "coming world-wide revolution of all workers." The Communist slogan, "Workers of the World Unite," and the words of the "International" are clear warning of the long-range intentions of the Soviet. To the long-established external "party line," Stalin, Molotov, and company have now added other intentions, some of which date back to the reign of Catherine the Great: a warm-water port on the Baltic, full access and at least joint control over the Dardanelles, and latterly an ice-free port on the Pacific. To these, add the obvious desire for a share or control of the rich Iranian oil fields, and a "friendly administration" in Greece and Turkey. Quite an ambitious program, and, as of this date, only one obstacle stands in the way of its complete realization—the United States of America.

That these United States now face a serious decision is obvious even to the Russians. We have a choice: either to bolster Europe's western democracies so that they can stand off the "Red" menace within their own borders until their own economies can be rehabilitated to carry their own weight, or to withdraw from the so-called "cold war," permitting the Communists to take over and integrate their vast holdings. Reducing it to practical terms in the first instance, it means the underwriting of some twenty billion dollars worth of European purchases—purchase of American food, clothing, machinery, and supplies. In all probability most of this aid will never be repaid. At least we should be prepared for that eventuality.

Our adoption of the second choice is more complicated. We must face the fact that the Communists, whatever their national origin, will readily unite with Russia. Our European markets would, of course, be lost. The united Communist front would compete with us in Latin America, and efforts to communize that portion of the new world would be augmented. In Asia and Africa the Russian influence would be redoubled. For our own protection we would have to be prepared to build and maintain the best army, navy, and air force in the world. In order to protect ourselves against unforeseeable pressures and surprise attacks, we should also have to be prepared to surrender, for a time at least, a part of our personal rights and privileges to the federal government in order that it could be instantly prepared to meet any eventuality. That is the trouble with allowing the spread of totalitarianism—in order to meet its threat, we should be forced to adopt some of its methods.

The first alternative—that now termed the "Marshall Plan"— seems preferable and has promise of success, the other choice is strategically nothing more than a holding or delaying action—you don't win even "cold wars" that way! The expense of the latter choice would within five years be at least tenfold the cost of the first alternative. In concluding this analysis, there remains one additional factor to be considered. How serious is the threat of internal infiltration by American Communists? At the present moment this danger is relatively small, but it must be remembered that communism thrives on internal strife. If American labor and management are foolish enough to permit their rivalries to degenerate into an internecine struggle thereby sapping the strength from the very vitals of the American economy and contributing to political chaos within the nation, then both must be prepared for the inevitable result.

Some one hundred years ago, Governor Thomas Ford, having experienced a situation in Illinois in which the people of this state had been victimized by propaganda, rumor and unreasoning prejudice to the point that they were irreconcilably divided, wrote a terse description of the result which all Americans should read. With deep insight he recorded:

> . . . Both parties were thoroughly disgusted with constitutional provisions, restraining them from the summary attainment of their wishes for vengeance; each was ready to submit to arbitrary power, to the fiat of a dictator, to make me a king for the time being, or at least that I might exercise the power of a king, to abolish both the forms and spirit of free government, if the despotism to be erected upon its ruins could only be wielded for its benefit, and to take vengeance on its enemies. It seems that, notwithstanding all our strong professions of attachment to liberty, there is all the time an unconquerable leaning to the principles of monarchy and despotism, whenever the forms, the delays and the restraints of republican government fail to correct great evils. . . .
>
> If the people will have anarchy, there is no power short of despotism capable of forcing them to submission; and the despotism which naturally grows out of anarchy, can never be established by those who are elected to administer regular government. . . . But it is a fundamental law of man's nature from which he cannot escape, that despotism is obliged to grow out of general anarchy, as surely as a stone is obliged to fall to the earth when left unsupported in the air. Without any revealed special providence, but in accordance with this great law of man's nature, Cromwell rose out of the disorders of the English revolution; Charles the Second was restored to despotism by the anarchy which succeeded Cromwell and Bonaparte came forth from the misrule of republican France. The people in all these cases attempted to govern, but in fact, did not. They were incapable of self-government; and by returning to despotism admitted that they needed a master. Where the people are unfit for liberty, where they will not be free without violence, license, and

injustice to others; where they do not deserve to be free, nature itself will give them a master. No form of constitution can make them free and keep them so. On the contrary, a people who are fit for and deserve liberty cannot be enslaved.*

The question now facing the American people is relatively simple: Are we fit for liberty or is our despotism to be that which we now call "communism"?

British writer Graham Hutton describes the hustle and bustle of postwar Chicago in this selection from *Midwest at Noon* (Chicago, 1946). "The tempo of life in Chicago," he observed, "has to be experienced to be believed." He goes on to sketch the unique character of Illinois state politics in the 1940s and the real appeal of the Machine.

The Cities Rise

GRAHAM HUTTON

All over the world, cities and city life arose in the wake of communications, trade, and industry; but nowhere and at no time did they arise as quickly as in the Midwest. One of the most striking Midwest extremes or paradoxes today is between its cities and its country. There are two distinct Midwests: one, the older agricultural Midwest with separate, scattered farms and small village towns, each with anything from a few hundred to twenty-five hundred inhabitants; the other, the larger, newer Midwest with a network of towns and cities above that limit, forming wide industrial areas. The Old Midwest was broadly settled, in its present familiar outlines and way of life, by the end of the Civil War. The industrial, urban Midwest dates from after the Civil War. Both Midwests have interacted and changed, but the change has been vastly more striking in the New Midwest.

In the Civil War, survivors of which are still alive, the center of

Reprinted from *Midwest at Noon* (pp. 96-97, 140-149, 301-304) by Graham Hutton by permission of The University of Chicago Press. Copyright © 1946 by Graham Hutton.

*Thomas Ford, *A History of Illinois* (Chicago, 1854), 361-62, 435-36.

population and of industry of the United States was inside Pennsylvania, though it was over the mountains and in the west of that state. The center of industry and population by 1890 had passed westward into Ohio. Today it is in eastern Illinois. This westward movement of industrialism was naturally linked with the transcontinental development of America and the spread of cities and towns, for since the industrial revolution, manufacture has been an urban process. Consequently, the way Americans live, "the American way of life," has rapidly changed from an overwhelmingly rural to an overwhelmingly urban way. You can tell a people by its songs. Today the majority of midwesterners are city dwellers or townsmen. But at the Rotary or other service clubs their songs are of Dobbin and the shay, of the old mill stream, or of working on the first railroads, or the songs of Stephen Foster and of other regions of America. Since those songs were written, the only new and popular songs are the radio ditties of all-American cities. There is Midwest history in a nutshell: from cornfield to neon signs without a pause.

In this rapid change within half a century—roughly from 1840 to 1890—the older East of the country underwent almost as striking a change as the newer Midwest and West. The only outstanding difference was that in the East the older commercial towns were magnified into industrial cities as the country towns were drained of their population, while in the Midwest entirely new towns sprang up and soon became big industrial cities. In both regions the rural country towns were drastically reduced in their total number and in their size. They have never regained their former importance, either in the East or in the newer Midwest. While the total population of America between 1790 and 1890 was multiplied only 16 times—and that is a fantastic growth compared with any other people's—the population living in towns was multiplied 139 times. Rural towns, townships, villages, and even counties lost population after 1880, while towns and cities picked it up and added waves of immigrants to it. This was the beginning of the great cleavage between town and country which so strikingly divides the Midwest, its people, and their ways of life to this day.

In 1860 there were only three cities in the Midwest with 100,000 inhabitants or more—St. Louis, Chicago, and Cincinnati. They were engaged in handling the agricultural products of the region and serving its farmers and settlers. In the most thickly populated Midwest states not more than one-seventh of the people then lived in towns of 2,500 inhabitants or more. Yet by the end of the century, within only half a lifetime, the region had fourteen cities each with more than 100,000 souls; in the entire region one-half of the people lived in towns of 2,500 inhabitants or more; and more than half the people of some Midwest states had become urban dwellers. Chicago had a population of more than 1,500,000 in 1900, whereas half a century earlier it had well below 100,000.

· ·

Chicago is the metropolis of the West. To describe this great city, now the fourth largest in the world, defies one's powers. Abler pens than mine have done it, and yet Chicago changes so fast that their written descriptions are largely out of date or out of truth in a few years. Here is a city of nearly four million souls, with another two millions in satellite communities round it; composed of almost all Caucasian nationalities, Negroes, and Orientals; and dependent on agriculture, mining, oil, electricity, the seaborne traffic of the Great Lakes or the canals and rivers, and the most intricate texture of railroads and highways on earth.

The most impressive first sight of the New World is when you sail into New York harbor—if it is on a clear day. But the most impressive first sight of the Midwest is when you fly into Chicago at night from the East, descending over the blackness of the prairie to the great, ruddy blast furnaces and steel mills, catching the first winkings of the Lindbergh beacon from the Palmolive Building away on the starboard bow, and watching the brilliant rectangles formed by a thousand square miles of straight streets and buildings. Huge, sprawling city of swamp and prairie; one community of many communities, *communitas communitatum;* it is both a Pittsburgh and a Detroit; a financial and commercial center; a warehouse, department store, mail-order house, granary, slaughter-house, and inland seaport; a repository of great wealth and great poverty; a center of learning; metropolis of that million square miles which is the heart of America. It is something of a national metropolis, too, because of its position. It is the national headquarters of the medical, surgical, and hospital associations; of Rotary and other service clubs; of America's library associations; of the mail-order business; of the musical and juke-box industry, which plays so large a part in American life; of the *Encyclopaedia Britannica;* and of the cinematograph equipment trades. It is a part of all American life.

Driving into the city from the airport up Archer Avenue, you could be on the outskirts of Warsaw, Budapest, Prague, Bucharest, or almost any other big central or eastern European city except Berlin or Vienna, which have too many apartment blocks. And in a sense you are, for the names above the stores and on the windows of offices speak all European tongues. Little clapboard houses with unfenced patches of garden remind you of a dozen European nations and their cities. Miles and miles of streets go by, with

railyards and warehouses, corner stalls and markets, before you see
the strange billowing vastness of the inland sea; the great cluster of
skyscrapers and the biggest hotels in the world that sprout inside
the central "Loop" of the elevated lines, like precocious overgrown
plants in a wired-in forcing-bed; and perhaps the noblest front that
any city in the world ever deliberately put on: Michigan Avenue.

. . . .

In Chicago all the extremes and extremisms of the region reach a
grand climax. Within a minute or two's walk of the splendid stores
and hotels and offices in the Loop you pass the flophouses of West
Madison, Canal, and North Clark streets; the hiring offices for
casual railroad laborers ("Good Eats Provided" painted white on
the windows); the terrible slums and Negro district near the stockyards; the waste lands near the railyards; the hangouts of the bums
and especially of the old, wrinkled, slow-moving, pathetic bums. I
think "bums" and "bumming around" are still used more frequently in the Midwest than anywhere else because of the size of
the region, the importance of its vast railroad network, the building
of that network and its maintenance. It is natural, in the region of
the greatest mobility in America, that the Germans' *bummeln*
should have thus passed into the general slang.

. . . .

Who are the Chicagoans? More than New Yorkers, Jersey Citizens, Philadelphians, Pittsburghers, Clevelanders, Detroiters, St.
Louisans, New Orleannais, or San Franciscans, they come from
almost every race and people. There are Americans from all regions.
Germans form solid districts all over, but chiefly in the north and
northwest, like the working-class quarters of Hamburg. Poles with
their pseudo-baroque Catholic churches with green cupolas make
whole areas look like Cracow or Lodz. Czechs and Slovaks keep
their homes and little gardens more neatly and reproduce Brünn or
Pilsen, Brno or Plzen, in the Midwest. Lithuanians, Latvians, and
Estonians have their homes out in the southwest, looking severe and
North European in winter. There are Scandinavians of all kinds;
Italians of all kinds, too, who keep their feast days and market days
as if in the old country and live in solid blocks of the city; Greeks,
Yugoslavs, and Syrians mainly on the West Side; Mexicans, Chinese,
and Japanese, in their characteristic quarters; Hungarians down in
the South and also on the North Side, mixed in with the Czechs and
Germans and Yugoslavs, whom in Europe they dislike; British,
Dutch, Belgians, Spaniards, Portuguese, Russians, Ukrainians, and
Armenians; and of course, the Negroes.

It was estimated in 1940 that two-fifths—nearly one-half—of adult Chicagoans did not generally speak English (or, as Illinois puts it, American) in their own homes. Nearly all of them can speak it and do, outside, or with their American children. But there are many Chicagoans over the age of fifty who cannot speak it at all; they live in one or other of these compact groupings and do not need to. No wonder there are so many confusing accents in Chicago. New Yorkers and other Americans can make fun at the Brooklyn or Italian accent because in New York these stand out, firm and clear. No one in Chicago makes fun of any particular accent, because there is no single Chicago accent as a standard from which to deviate; there are so many. Chicagoans of German, Italian, Polish, and Czech national origin of the first or second generation, with their children, accounted in 1940 for more than one-third of the people. The others of non-English-speaking origin and the Negroes brought that proportion to more than one-half; a clear majority. Here is a potent source of variety and difference as well as of vigor and restlessness. The same pattern can be traced, with less degree of clarity and intensity, in almost every Midwest city and large town.

Americans from outside the Midwest tend to think of Chicago as Sandburg's "hog-butcher to the world," as being composed of vast stockyards and slaughter houses ("everything used but the squeal"), surrounded by some fairly decent apartment blocks and some necessary hotels and offices in a downtown section called the Loop or the North Side, and peopled by a scared race who go to and from work under a periodic hail of gangsters' lead. Nothing could be more grotesquely inaccurate. The stockyards are vast, surprisingly trim and clean, and localized in a compact area away from the main thoroughfares and traffic (except, of course, the huge railyards which serve them). You can live in Chicago for years and not know that meat-packing goes on there.

. . . .

The visitor generally sees only the Loop, the Outer Drive, the Near North Side, the offices and hotels, and perhaps one or two institutions on the outskirts: factories, mail-order houses, universities, hospitals. He seldom sees the Chicagoans at home. Their homes are their pride, and rightly so. From over thirty miles north of the Loop to thirty miles west and southwest, or fifteen miles south, and from as near as only three miles, the commuters come into the Loop by steam and electric trains, trolley cars, busses and automobiles. They are very early risers. Chicago starts work at the same hour as New York, where time is an hour later, and often before it.

All factories and most Loop offices are working by eight or eight-thirty. From six-thirty in the morning until eight-thirty the commuters go into town; and from four-thirty in the afternoon until six-thirty they go out again. They have little time for lunch; half an hour is quite common. They are a hardworking community.

Their homes are the places where they relax. The variety of suburbs is bewildering. In this respect Chicago is far less standardized than most other American cities. The styles of architecture, layout of the suburb, and density of population per acre vary from the spacious, quiet beauty of Glen Ellyn, Hinsdale, Winnetka, Riverside, Evanston, and Highland Park to the greater uniformity and compactness of Oak Park, Rogers Park, and the South Side, with its more frequent apartment blocks, and then to the still more densely settled communities nearer the Loop. No greater luxury, spaciousness, elegance, and beauty could be found than in the old homes and modern apartments of the wealthy on the near North Side—the "Gold Coast"—or the great homes and estates of Lake Forest, Wheaton, or Barrington. Farther out, too, beyond the thirty-mile limit, are the big estates, summer homes, "farms," or week-end cabins of many of the better-off Chicagoans. But the homes of the great majority of Chicagoans, of the German workers on the nearer Northwest Side and of those of all national origins in separate wood-frame or brick and clapboard houses or in brick, stone, and concrete apartment blocks, are homes indeed. For ten miles around, the terrible grime of the soft coal from the many railyards blackens the windows and the outside, and the drapes or curtains inside; but the interiors are generally kept clean, full of those intimate belongings and that informal atmosphere which make a place a home. Chicago is not mainly an apartment city, like most of New York; nor does it live and eat in public places. It is a city of separate homes to which the visitor or client is immediately made welcome. It is a city of home-proud, city-proud citizens whose fathers and grandfathers came there to "make a home"—and made both a home and a city. And in that it is typically midwestern. It is the product of the South, New England, and central Europe. It is even more of a cosmopolitan city than New York.

This has one interesting by-product. Chicago has little of its own to offer the mere visitor or tourist. It is not a center of entertainment or diversion like New York or Los Angeles, or a national historical center like Boston or Philadelphia, or an old and quaint city of non-American origins like New Orleans or San Francisco. There are beautiful things to see in Chicago; but few tourists want to go to the remarkable Art Institute or the wonderful museums. Children and students flock to them. Few businessmen go, and the life of the Midwest is business. They want relaxation or "fun." The "fun" of the Rush Street or North Clark Street night spots and other such places, many run by questionable persons, is ordinary, vulgar, and raw. For those reasons, these places are well patronized—but not regularly by Chicagoans. The theaters are average; and despite or perhaps because of Mr. Sam Insull's colossal barn of an opera-house, with its indifferent acoustics, Chicago has no permanent opera and for an adequate performance has to depend on New York. The smaller and more congenial Orchestra Hall, hallowed with memories of Thomas and Stock, provides music and a home for a good symphony orchestra. The movie-houses are vast, numerous, comfortable, and always full—day and night. The big hotels put on the best "entertainment" in Chicago; but because there is so much to see and do on the street and because, as in the early days, taverns and night spots are extraordinarily numerous, the visitor for a few days and nights gets the impression that there is much liquor, "fun," relaxation, and diversion in Chicago and that Chicagoans are always indulging in them. Again that is grotesquely inaccurate.

Chicagoans will put themselves to no end of trouble and expense to take a visitor or client round the night spots, the floor shows, to the theater, or on a round of a few of the many taverns. But that is not how the Chicagoan lives when the visitor has departed. The Chicagoan is like the Parisian in this respect: a very devoted home-lover, judged by visitors who hardly ever see him at or inside his home. He is judged by what he provides for alien palates. For this, the Chicagoans are not responsible, though America may be. Much of the less attractive, noisy, blatant, neon-signed, liquor-smelling aspect of Chicago is there for the millions of visitors, businessmen, and passers-by who have to traverse this vast crossroads city between transcontinental or other trains. (The greatest railroad hub in the world still has no central terminal, no through connection for passengers; you have to change stations, to the perpetual profit of the men who own taxis and hotels.) True, many of the 20 per cent of Chicagoans who live in mean streets and poor housing areas and work very hard at the rougher jobs regularly patronize the taverns; as the small minority of unimaginative and unwise businessmen, condemned by their fellows as unreliable or unstable, regularly patronize the places on Rush Street and elsewhere. That is because both these groups lack imagination, have poorly stocked minds, and have not acquired, or been able to acquire, any other ideas of relaxation. That occurs with the same groups in every big city. Drowning one's sorrows, or giving them bromide, is not unique to Chicago; nor are the sorrows of humanity. But the vast majority of

Chicagoans lead quiet, domestic lives in their own homes and with their neighbors, who are friends.

One feature in which Chicago is very like big British cities is in the size of its suburbs. That is scarcely surprising, since the city has grown by absorbing small outlying villages and converting them to suburbs. These are now the home of the middle class, the clerical workers and the professional men. Being the Midwest capital and metropolis, Chicago has a very big middle class—or perhaps, as "classes" are not supposed to exist in America, I had better say, as Americans do, "a great concentration in the middle income brackets." But these Chicago suburbs of the well-to-do and the "middle income brackets," unlike the suburbs of European cities, are very beautiful; they have also far more variety than those of British cities. They have more of a community sense and community life of their own, centered round their community houses, libraries, forums, clubs, societies, or high schools. Places like Oak Park with 70,000 souls—"biggest village in the world"—Winnetka, Riverside, and Hinsdale set a high standard for suburban community life, and though they are not satisfied, they have already outdistanced most suburbs in overcoming the problems of life in a big city. They have community sense and community achievement to their credit, where the suburbs of cities in the Old World have only apathy and bleak failure. Indeed, the suburbs of most of the big cities in the Midwest are way ahead of others, both in and out of America, in this respect; and that is scarcely surprising, because the sense of community is, and always was, so strong in this new region. But, in making these communities, the community sense has been taken away from the city's center. The problems of Chicago, as of the other big cities and towns in the Midwest and everywhere else, are left at or near the center: the "inner ring" of solid and densely settled residential areas where the manual workers live; the areas of slums, dilapidation, or overcrowding; and these are linked with the level of incomes and the grading of jobs. That leaves the problems with the city fathers while the satisfied suburbanites go free. You cannot take the "El" or the Illinois Central out of the Loop and look out of the windows without wondering when and how Chicago is going to clear its slums, its deathtraps, and its breeding-grounds of crime and social problems.

The tempo of life in Chicago has to be experienced to be believed. It is much faster than that of New York. I am sure midwesterners work harder and more furiously than any people. They relax harder, too. One reason for that is the restless curiosity and experience-hunting of the midwesterner, which is greater than that of the more sophisticated easterner, which in turn is greater than that of the European. Another reason is the extraordinary gregariousness of all midwesterners, which is part of their sense of community. The Chicagoan is a home-lover, and there he really relaxes. But when he is "on the job," whether it is work or "fun," he (or she) never relaxes.

. . . .

The oldness of Chicago, the old town, has disappeared with the people who made it. The city is always putting on a new dress—but not always changing its underlinen. It is always on the go, going places, seeking "some new thing." If ever anyone tries to build a bridge out of wedding cake in the shape of the letter S, I am sure it will be a Chicagoan—and I am sure the experiment will succeed.

. . . .

The temporary officials—mayors, governors, and so on—are distrusted, even though they are all elected. They are executives. They may exert too much power. They may put their heads together at the cost of the state, the representative assembly, or the people. The American system of checks and balances against executive power reaches its clearest expression in Midwest politics. The machines of both parties are strong. One may rule the biggest city while the other rules the state. They distribute the spoils and decree appointments and candidates. But, once representatives are elected, they show remarkable independence on many issues. . . .

The great strength of a party machine—the spoils system—is also its greatest weakness. The most powerful boss knows that he cannot continue to be boss without an organization and officers behind him. That means spoils, patronage, and big money. He may buy politicians and he may buy voters. But that is not the problem. It is to make them "stay bought." That necessitates a certain responsiveness to public opinion, or at least to a part of public opinion. The machine must be sure of a majority vote. Even the boss has to compromise, either with his powerful lieutenants who command local votes, or with the public. That is when the weakness appears. To keep his judges in power, he may do a deal with the opposition whereby each party gets an agreed quota of judges. All the judges up for election are then settled beforehand. So neither party goes to an election; the list of judges is approved; and the voters have no say.

. . . .

The great strength of party machines in states or cities was built up because that was the only way a two-party system could function among a people so largely composed of unassimilated racial and national groups but with equal adult suffrage. It was natural, therefore, that the machines should trade with each other, in order to get done a little of what each wanted. Often a lot got done. The machines, however, ended by running all politics and government.

In a period when federal or state governments did nothing for the poor and needy, when the federal government scarcely touched the citizens of a state or city at all, the party machine—generally that of the Democrats—was firmly based on a goodly proportion of charity. This, too, was natural: for the city bosses in the Midwest, as elsewhere, tended always to be on the side of the underdogs—of whom there were so many, all with votes. Many of the bosses had been underdogs. They knew and lived among their people. So did their ward heelers and precinct captains. The machine was thus, and still is, very much a local affair, very much in contact with the people, and more so than many who write and speak about "the people." True, there was a heavy rake-off for party funds, and the principle of "I give that thou mayest give" was strictly enforced at the polling booths. But as the cities grew, especially in the Midwest, there was nothing but private charity to deal with the sorrows, ignorance, and bewilderment of the poor, who were so largely alien immigrants. To the poor, the machine seemed merely governmental. It was paternal: kind but authoritative. It was more democratic than anything to which they had ever been used to in Europe. If "no taxation without representation" were sound, why not "no representation without contributions"—especially as representatives themselves were paid by taxpayers? And, after all, what operates in a ward or precinct to aid or relieve voters and their families is what operates as a lobby at the state or national capital to aid economic groups and interests. The important thing to remember is that machines, bossism, and bipartisan deals supplied a real demand. Within the legal, constitutional, or social setting they were the only way politics could operate. They met a real need, when no one and nothing else met it. Whether they meet that need today, whether they ever ought to have met it, whether they meet it as cheaply and efficiently as state and federal authorities, whether the days of the machines are numbered because of new movements and social agencies—these are other questions.

The power of the boss, of the lobby, and of many city or state machines in the Midwest owes a great deal to the public's deep distrust of government, civil service, executives, and elected officials. Parties in power, like officials, come and go; but the machine and its boss or bosses go on forever. So do lobbies. Both lobbies and machines are therefore like watchdogs—in their own interests, of course—but still they perform an obvious political function. A national party has to respect local machines, as these have to respect their own district bosses. There are a lot of lobbies on behalf of a lot of interests, too. They are constantly increasing. To that extent they also represent many elements of public opinion. They "get things done."

. . . .

Another firsthand impression of busy Chicago is given by the French novelist Simone de Beauvoir, from her book *America Day by Day* (London, 1952). The book was the product of a diary kept during a four-month stay in the United States. Her sojourn in Chicago, unfortunately, lasted less than two days, but her impressions are nonetheless vivid and revealing.

Chicago

SIMONE DE BEAUVOIR

21st February

Thirty-six hours in Chicago, this was little. I took the first morning train, but it was already two o'clock when I arrived at the station. The taxi took me along an avenue that seemed crushed under the heavy structure of an overhead railway. They made me book a room at Palmer House: of all hotels I have seen this one is the biggest. Bar, cafeteria, lunch room, blue room, red room, Victorian room, tzigane orchestra, Mexican orchestra, flowers, sweets, all kinds of magazines, travel agencies, air lines—it is a town with its residential districts, its quiet alleys and its noisy business centre; the heat is terrific and there is a strong smell of dollars. My room was on the sixteenth floor.

As in Washington, first of all I took refuge in the Museum. At the Institute of Modern Art there is a fine collection of impressionist and contemporary paintings; during the two hours which I spent there looking at them the earth felt firm. But back on the terrace again, on the edge of the lake and on Michigan Avenue which trails away out of sight, I was seized with uncertainty that amounted to agony. I liked the hard line of the sky-scrapers; they are more massive than those of New York and purer: there are no Renaissance windows, no Gothic belfries, for they were built at a time when the skyscraper was established and they no longer needed to make excuses for themselves. I went down Michigan Avenue, where an icy wind was blowing, and wandered in the streets downtown, called here The Loop. I was glad to find myself again in a city which looks like a capital and not a big village indefinitely multiplied. But what would I get from it? Chicago. The name fascinated me: I remembered Bancroft in *Chicago Nights* and many more gangster stories; I thought of *Studs Lonigan,* in which Farrell described life in the Irish quarter, and of *Black Metropolis,* that huge study of life in the coloured city; there were also the slaughter yards, the burlesques. . . . But I was leaving to-morrow.

My friends in New York had given me two addresses: that of a writer and that of an old lady. If my evening was not to be wasted one of them would have to come to the rescue. To taste the Chicago night the writer seemed preferable. I unhooked the receiver and asked for Mr. N.A. A sulky voice replied: "You have the wrong number." I checked it in the directory: my pronunciation was wrong. I began all over again. I had hardly opened my mouth when the voice repeated, this time with annoyance: "*Wrong* number." I hung up again. What to do? I tried the old lady: she was not at home. Very well. I dined rather dismally at a drugstore counter. Yet I did not want this night to slip through my fingers. Alone I could do nothing: New York itself had only begun to come alive when I had people to guide me. In the confusion of lights, the labyrinth of streets, I should never find the right places. I must try again. Once more I attacked the writer: but he hung up. I was furious. I asked the operator to make contact. When she heard the phone ringing she said with authority, and in tones that inspired confidence: "Will you be so kind as to hold the line a moment. . . ." After I had mentioned some friends by name the unknown voice grew calmer. He perked up; of course, he would be delighted. In half an hour he would meet me in the hall.

I was beginning to get used to meeting people I did not know in hotel lounges or on station platforms: we recognised each other immediately; it was surprising. But the business of getting through the first few minutes together always makes me anxious. In Washington I hesitated for some time before calling F.; he was a French-

Courtesy of the Illinois State Historical Library

The Chicago Water Tower and the John Hancock Building

man, and I had been asked to take him books and the news from Paris; but did he really want these books and messages? He received me cordially. We spent three hours in a friendly atmosphere, though no doubt we would never see each other again; I forget what he talked about or how he reacted to my conversation: this casual meeting that could have no to-morrow seemed absurd to me, a delusion of travel. Even more absurd than walking at night round and round Times Square. Again, had I not arrived quite empty-handed? And to-night I had disturbed an unknown person in order that he should give me an interesting evening: I was not only indiscreet, I also ran the risk of being bored. I was not in a good temper when I went down to the hall with a book in my hand as a signal for the rally; it was as though I had to drag myself to an interview arranged by a marriage bureau. I consoled myself with the thought that the outcome of it all was no longer in my hands; I had done my best, my conscience was clear.

Each time I met an American I had to start on the language all over again: I wondered whether in my country there were also such differences of pronunciation among individuals. I understood R.W. and A.E. But sitting with N.A. in a quiet little bar I missed half what he was saying, and I felt that his difficulties were not less than mine. He hesitated about what to show me in Chicago. There were no worthwhile bands to listen to, the middle-class nightclubs were no more interesting than those of New York, and the idea of a musical show did not appeal to me. If I liked, he could take me to places where probably I should not have occasion to venture; he could give me a glimpse of the lowest districts in Chicago, for he knew them well. I accepted.

He took me to West Madison Avenue, which is also called the Bowery of Chicago; here are the lodging-houses for men only, *flophouses*, squalid bars. It was very cold, the street was almost deserted; and yet there were a few men with shipwrecked faces who hid themselves in the shadows of the doorways or wandered up and down the frozen sidewalks. We entered a bar that reminded me of Sammy's Follies: but there was neither show nor spectators, and no tourist other than myself. N.A. was not a tourist, for he often came here and knew all the people, hoboes, drunks and faded beauties: no one would turn round even if the Mad Woman of Chaillot came in. At the end of the room there was a little negro band; one read on a placard: "It is forbidden to dance"; but people were dancing. There was a lame man who waddled about like a duck: suddenly he started to dance and his legs obeyed him: he spun round, jumped and capered about with a maniacal smile; it seemed he spent his time here and danced all night. Sitting at the bar was a woman with long, fine hair adorned with a red ribbon; sometimes her hair was blonde, and her doll's face was that of a little girl; sometimes her head seemed covered with white tow; she was a siren well over sixty; she drank one beer after another out of the bottle while talking to herself and shouting defiantly; sometimes she got up and danced, lifting her skirts very high. A drunk asleep at a table woke up and seized a fat floosie in his arms; they capered around and danced deliriously. There was something of madness and ecstasy; so old, so ugly, so miserable, they were lost for a moment and they were happy. I felt bewildered, stared and said: "It's beautiful." N.A. was astounded; it seemed to him very French. "With us," he said, "ugliness and beauty, the grotesque and the tragic, and even good and evil, go their separate ways: Americans do not like to think that such extremes can mingle." And, pleased that this place should fascinate me, he said: "I will show you something better."

In a sense it was better. Here there were only men, West Madison men, reprobates and idiots, and so dirty that even their bones must be grey. There was an appalling stench of squalor. At one o'clock in the morning they were pouring in, looking for shelter from the snow and the icy wind outside: some drew near to the counter, clutching a few nickels, and drank beer. Others tried to sell us a pair of scissors, pencils, begging for fifty cents. A false blonde sat at the cash desk: "All that I know of modern French literature I owe to her," N.A. said. "She is very up to date." And as I hesitated before believing him he asked F. to come over and take a glass with us. "What stage has the latest Malraux novel reached?" she asked at once. "Is there a second volume? and Sartre? Has he finished *Les Chemins de la Liberté*? Is Existentialism still in fashion?" I was dumbfounded. The woman spent all her nights surveying this bar which was also a night refuge; the amusements she most preferred were reading and drugs; she was apparently a great drug-taker and more than once had escaped from a house of correction; as for the hospital, nobody knew how often she had been there; from time to time she also had her romances, but they seldom turned out well.

She explained that on the upper floor there was a big room with mattresses where one could stay till morning for ten cents; but many unfortunates preferred to spend the last ten cents on drink; then she allowed them to stay without payment in the corridor which led to the rest rooms. "Come and see!" she said. I saw. Seated on benches, hunched over tables, shrivelled up in corners, men slept, open-mouthed and covered in filth and vermin; even in sleep they could not really relax; their muscles remained taut, and they would wake with stiffened bodies. Louis XI invented the torture cage, so small that a man could not lie down to sleep. With twisted neck and aching limbs, to what dreams did they escape? As I watched them, a red-headed woman, who was very painted, with curly hair, approached with mincing steps and high-heeled shoes; she said like a shy virgin: "I wanted to go to the rest rooms, but all those men. . . ." The woman of the cash desk shrugged her shoulders: "They are far too sleepy to attend to you!" We returned to the bar, where I swallowed another whisky; and soon the red-head appeared again, evidently disappointed.

Going home through the cold streets and under the blackened vaulting of the overhead railway, I thought that squalor had never seemed quite so horrible as in New York or Chicago. In Madrid I had seen the Vallecas slums, in Lisbon the Grace beach, the swarming streets of Naples, and in Sousse children with feet twisted back to front or blinded by ingrowing eyelashes. Squalor in poor countries is often frightful; but, linked to the barren soil and dried-up streams, it is a kind of animal squalor; folly and injustice loom on the horizon; but in a rich country they appear nearer and yet more cruel!

In Naples, in Lisbon, however poor the people, they are still allowed to have their animal pleasures: fierce sun, fresh oranges, exchanges of love deep in the shadowy bed; you hear them sing and laugh and talk of these things; they are all poor together, and together they nurse their sick, mourn their dead and honour their many saints; and around their afflicted bodies they at least feel some human warmth. But here the poor are cursed: the curse of loneliness. They have neither home, nor friend, nor family, nor any place on earth; they are just rubbish, useless flotsam looked on without pity: and why have they come to this? Optimism makes them suspect—it must be their own fault. The police spy on them, and in fact everything drives them to guilt, they are all potential criminals. This social squalor soon swallows them up and they become less than beasts. They move through a hostile world where their enemies have human faces, and they themselves have no other friend than alcohol, an expensive friendship. In their solitude, their want, their drunkenness, they often lose their heads; and, in addition to hunger, there are strange beasts within them which gnaw at their souls.

22nd February

I was awakened by a telephone call: a Frenchman at the Consulate told me he had arranged a luncheon and a dinner for me. I was sorry, for as yet I had seen nothing of Chicago and time was short. But there was nothing I could do. My host, no doubt, was no more pleased than I, it was his job to greet his countrymen: we were both helpless.

I returned to the Museum, the Loop, Michigan Avenue, and the morning went by like a flash. At midday I found J.L. at the hotel with a rich, cultured American who was also a friend of France: they were very nice; and the old ladies, also friends of France, to whose house I was taken, were also very nice; if only I hadn't had the impression I was losing precious time. We lunched at a club with splendid rooms, at the top of a great building. Through the bay windows I saw the canal and the skyscrapers, and I tried to convince myself that it was indeed Chicago. But I was apart from the city, as though it were under a glass case; or rather it was I who had been put under glass. A blonde Frenchwomen sat opposite me. She had been introduced to me as a baroness and a journalist: she lectured throughout America on "French gaiety during the Resistance", and all through the meal she was making patriotic remarks.

J.L. and his American friend soon took me away. They suggested a drive, which consoled me. We toured the city: the edge of the lake, gardens, superb hotels, luxurious residences—this side of Chicago was all wealth and prosperity. But the American shook his head: "All façade!" he said. And indeed, as we plunged into the Polish district where I had an appointment with N.A., the scene soon changed: warehouses, factories, vacant lots, ramshackle buildings; trains crossing the avenues and holding us up; streets far dirtier than those of New York; everywhere disorder and squalor. The beautiful car with its coachwork seemed out of place on Wabansia Avenue, a broad building site dotted throughout its entire length with wooden shacks.

As we found ourselves back again in the Polish district where N.A. lives, we stopped there. It was too cold for a walk and, besides, this district was a town in itself. There are more Irishmen in Chicago than in Dublin, and more Poles than ever there were in Warsaw. We spent the afternoon walking in these streets and going into bars where we drank vodka: some are also grocery stores smelling of dried fish, while others are restaurants where they sell pink and yellow cakes filled with sour cream; in the one that we chose the waitress did not know English. And the one where we stayed longest was bare, impersonal and neutral like other similar places, yet quite American. For long it had been the meeting-place of a famous gang; I was a little disappointed, as I imagined that gangsters' bars could be recognised by some sign or some mysterious quality in the atmosphere; but gangsters, of course, gathered at street corners like everyone else. I asked N.A., but he told me that unless one was exceptionally lucky one saw nothing strange in the streets; yet one did have a vague feeling of insecurity, and there were districts which one avoided on foot at night. As for prohibition, there was no difference whatever between past and present. The speakeasies of yesterday were the bars of to-day; only one paid a little more for whisky then, and the beer was poorer stuff; in certain places they still took precautions before opening the door.

I liked these bars, and the little streets where the wind was biting; I was not too much of a tourist. I seemed to be living through a real Chicago afternoon in the company of real natives. N.A. had spent his childhood here and most of his existence. I asked him about his life, and it was the classic life of an American writer, like so many accounts I had read; what was astonishing was to discover in a single case the truth of the well-worn stories. He had spent his early days dragging about Chicago. Here the children, like their elders, form themselves into gangs; they dash off in bands to strip some grocer's shop, and the raid is so quick that the shopkeepers defend themselves only with difficulty. By the time they have called the police the pilferers have vanished, and it is difficult to identify them later with certainty. Baseball played on vacant sites also takes up their leisure. N.A. was a youth at the time of the great depression. He looked for work through the length and breadth of America, creeping into goods' trucks, eating and sleeping at the expense of the Salvation Army. At New Orleans he became a pedlar, which didn't bring him in much, and for several weeks he ate only bananas. To improve his salesmanship he pretended to offer a permanent wave at a certain hairdresser's to every woman who bought five dollars worth of goods from him. Soon they were rushing to the hairdresser, angrily claiming their dues. When the cat was out of the bag N.A. left for Mexico, whence he returned to America, trying his hand at a number of odd jobs: hot dog and hamburger seller, masseur, bowling alley boy: he said that this job, which consists of setting up the skittles endlessly knocked down, is one of the most tiring. Having got into a petrol-filling station with a friend, he started to write, at first for pleasure, then in the hope of earning some money in this way. His first novel was a success and he got contracts with a publisher which enabled him to undertake further work. He became the friend of R. Wright and J.T. Farrell, and they are often called "The Chicago School", although there are no great literary affinities between them. During the war he was in Germany and Marseilles; he had passed through New York on the way there and back but did not know it. He never left Chicago and hardly knew any other writers. His friends were people of the

Bowery or neighbours in the Polish quarter. He seemed a striking example of that intellectual solitude in which writers of America live to-day.

When I was together again with J.L. and V. in a big elegant restaurant on the Loop, where Martinis and grilled lobsters are served, I had difficulty in believing that it was still the same town. Before taking me to the station they showed me the illuminated skyline, which is almost as beautiful as that of New York. But I thought (and I feared it on looking back) that if I had not been so insistent last night, I would not have known any more of Chicago than this *décor* made up of lights and stone, this façade at once so opulent, so polished and deceptive. At least I had glanced behind the painted scenes and had a glimpse of a real city, with its tragic daily life, fascinating like all cities where men must live and struggle in their millions. The station where I got into the train for Los Angeles made a strange contrast with the one at which I had arrived only yesterday: it was nothing more than a half-demolished, huge wooden shack. V. filled my arms with magazines and books, and J.L. kindly put me on the train. I was sorry to be leaving. I would have to arrange matters somehow so that I came back to Chicago.

. . . .

Abbott Joseph Liebling, a noted writer for *The New Yorker*, gives a sketch of the state's capital at mid-century. This article was the first in a *New Yorker* series on the Lincoln tradition, and the "tall man" does indeed "cast a long shadow" in this "Southern town." Liebling, who died in 1964, also wrote *Chicago, the Second City* (New York, 1952), *The Earl of Louisiana* (Baton Rouge, 1970), and *The Road Back to Paris* (New York, 1944), among other books.

Abe Lincoln in Springfield

ABBOTT JOSEPH LIEBLING

If you visit Springfield, the capital of Illinois, you are bound to get mixed up with Abraham Lincoln. This is not because Springfield looks as it did in Lincoln's time. It doesn't; not many buildings remain in the city that were standing then. One that does is the old state capitol, now the three-story-plus-a-cupola Sangamon County Courthouse, which seems to have grown up through the middle of the public square, since its lower portion is plainly newer than the rest of it. The upper part is a Greek Revival palace of buff stone, dating from 1837. A practical architect added a new ground floor fifty years ago by hoisting what was already there up into the air and making the original first floor the second and the second the third. How he did it, I do not know, but, whatever his method, he laid a trap for future archeologists, who are likely to assume, as archeologists usually do, that a lower stratum is older than an upper one. This architectural accomplishment was first called to my attention by the taxi driver with whom I rode from the railroad station the day I arrived in Springfield. "Mr. Lincoln used to sit in the legislature there," the driver added. Across from one corner of the Courthouse lawn is a narrow, three-and-about-a-third-story building of brick painted gray, with a shoe store on the ground floor. The driver said, "Mr. Lincoln's law office is up there, over the shoe store." This jumble of past and present made Lincoln seem more alive than would have been the case if everything had been preserved exactly as he left it. I could fancy him walking out the side door of the narrow building, the top of his hat seven feet above the sidewalk. (I have read somewhere that he carried legal documents in the crown.) He might be on his way to Diller's Drugstore to have a sarsaparilla and a look at the newest generation of lobbyists. The Illinois lobbyists of his day were a sociable lot.

From A. J. Liebling, "Our Far-Flung Correspondents: Abe Lincoln in Springfield," *The New Yorker*, June 24, 1950. Reprinted by permission of Russell & Volkening, Inc. Copyright © 1950 by A. J. Liebling.

"We have a regular Lincoln tour," the driver said. "If you'd like to take it after you put your bag in the Abe, I'd be glad to wait for you. It costs twelve dollars, which is a price the drivers have set to stop chiselling. We allow you thirty minutes at the Home, thirty minutes at the Tomb, and then we drive you out to New Salem, twenty miles, and bring you back. Ann Rutledge's grave is extra. I never drove anybody yet on the tour that when he came back he didn't say it was worth it." I didn't take the driver up on his offer. I didn't want to think of Lincoln in his tomb. I preferred to imagine him in his law office, across the square, trying to make up his mind whether or not to go out for that glass of sarsaparilla. Besides, the driver's assumption that I was visiting Springfield because of Lincoln was a mistake, or so I thought at the time. I supposed that I had simply gone there to see a friend of mine who has a job in the state government.

When the driver mentioned the Abe, he meant the Abraham Lincoln, Springfield's largest and newest hotel. After I reached my room there, I picked up the telephone directory to look for my friend's number and right in the front of the book found the A. Lincoln Tourist Court, the Abe Lincoln Baggage Transfer, the Abraham Lincoln Association, the Ann Rutledge Apartment Hotel, and the Ann Rutledge Beauty Salon. After that, instead of looking up my man's name, I made my initial concession to curiosity about Lincoln. I turned to the "L"s and found listings for the Lincoln Advertising Agency, Lincoln Air Lines, Lincoln Automotive Mechanics School, Lincoln Baggage Transfer Company, Lincoln Cab Company, Lincoln Café, Lincoln Candy Company, Lincoln Cash Market, Lincoln College of Law, Lincoln Dental Laboratories, Lincoln Library, Lincoln National Life Insurance Company, Lincoln Park Fieldhouse and Pavilion, Lincoln Radiator and Auto Parts Company, Lincoln School, Lincoln's Home, and Lincoln's Monument. Nothing, apparently, had been named for Mrs. Lincoln. Nor, I found, on turning to the "D"s, was there anything named after Stephen A. Douglas, although in 1860 Springfield's vote was almost evenly divided between the two Illinois Presidential candidates. Cults form around defeated generals and unhappy lovers, but the stature of wives and losing politicians evidently diminishes.

. . . .

Contemporary Springfield's preoccupation with its pre-Civil War self is not a sign of senescence. The city, which bears much the same relationship to Chicago that Albany does to New York, has a population of almost a hundred thousand, as against only nine thousand when Lincoln left for Washington; it also has more politicians and lobbyists than it had in Lincoln's day, because the population of the state has increased five times and there is at least five times as much to lobby for. It has a fairly active industrial life, several good-looking department stores, and a generous quota of pubs. The percentage of visible women who are pretty is higher in Springfield than it is in Chicago; "Springfield's a Southern town," the women you meet there say when you mention this fact to them, as if that were sufficient explanation. Springfield is nearer to St. Louis and southern Indiana than to Chicago, and the eternal whitefish of Chicago restaurant menus loses the place of honor to catfish in Springfield, marking the change from a lacustrine to a river culture. (No great civilization has ever grown up around a lake.) The Springfield countryside is full of fat cattle being made fatter for market, and farmland there sells for more an acre than farmland almost anyplace else in the United States.

Still, the tall man casts a long shadow. With Lincoln as a competitor, it is hard for any present-day politician to make an impression in Springfield. . . .

I stopped in at the bar of the Leland Hotel, which is older and more frequented by politicians than the Abraham Lincoln, for a glimpse of contemporary Springfield. While taking a rather harder drink than Lincoln favored, I listened to a couple of large, hearty men commiserating boisterously with a thin, sallow fellow because he had not succeeded in landing a state contract to build an airport in some downstate town. "You had the wrong bull by the horns," one of the large men said to him. "You should have come to me first." It was a congenial barroom. The two bartenders on duty looked as if their fathers might have poured for Lincoln's last law partner, William H. Herndon, who was a whiskey man and survived his senior partner by twenty-six years. I do not mean that it was the whiskey that made Herndon live longer. It was the brandy John Wilkes Booth drank that killed Lincoln.

. . . .

At dinner at my friend's home that evening, the conversation hovered briefly over contemporary politics (there was a primary election coming up) and then settled on Lincoln. One of the other guests—Mrs. Gertrude Masters, who has white bangs and is the widow of a Springfield physician—said with finality, "I don't know any of these men in the primaries, and three-quarters of them are no good anyway. What *I* want to know is when the state is going to get some decent furniture in the Lincoln house. It's a disgrace." The Lincolns, I learned from her, sold most of their furniture when they moved from Springfield, in 1861. Some of the pieces they took to the White House with them came into the possession of a female relative who lived in Springfield, but she took them with her when she moved to the East a number of decades ago. The Lincoln house, which was visited by three hundred thousand people last year, has in it only a few odds and ends of period furniture, and Mrs. Masters assured me, with obvious authority, that Mrs. Lincoln would have been ashamed to let anybody see them. "It should be furnished with beautiful Victorian pieces," she said. "Why, the man was a leading corporation attorney! And Mrs. Lincoln was a Kentucky aristocrat, and a good neighbor, too!" From the way Mrs. Masters said it, one might have thought that she had lived next door to the Lincolns. Another woman, whose name I didn't catch, nodded briskly and said that it always amused her when people referred to Lincoln as a rail splitter. Her tone implied that if Lincoln split any rails, it was during a summer vacation from Northwestern, to get himself into condition for football.

Later in the evening, Mrs. Masters told me that the late Edgar Lee Masters was a brother-in-law of hers. Her family comes from Petersburg, Illinois, where Ann Rutledge is buried. Mrs. Masters herself was born in Toledo, but, like everybody else in Springfield, she has decided opinions about the Lincolns. Her principal Lincolnistic interest, I gathered, is the preservation of the Benjamin Edwards place, a vast Springfield mansion in which Lincoln must often have been a guest, inasmuch as Benjamin was the brother of Ninian Edwards, who was married to Mrs. Lincoln's sister. The Edwards place now houses the Springfield Art Association, of which Mrs. Masters is a director. A woman descendant of Benjamin Edwards bequeathed the mansion to the Art Association about forty years ago, Mrs. Masters told me, but left no money for its maintenance. "You must come with me to see the house tomorrow afternoon," she said. "It will give you an idea of what life could be in Lincoln's Springfield." I promised to.

I met Mr. Bunn at his bank next morning. He is a former New York *Sun* reporter (1912-14), whose grandfather, Jacob Bunn, was the merchant prince of Springfield in Lincoln's time and founded the bank and helped start the town's library; the intervening generation of Bunns established the local light-and-power company. The present Mr. Bunn, whose attempt at escape ended when he was called back from New York to take a role in the family enterprises, is a compact man with a kind manner, a clipped mustache, and a rectangular profile. He led me to a desk in a corner of the banking room, as if we were going to discuss a small loan, and began to talk about Lincoln. He said he couldn't remember being so young that he hadn't heard about Lincoln. "Of course, there were any number of men and women around when I was a boy who remembered him," he said. I asked him if there had been any who had heard the famous debates and still held Douglas had been right, and he said no, adding, "Douglas was a man who would shift his course to get elected." Mr. Bunn told me that his grandfather had been a Lincoln man, and that he himself is a Republican, but a Lincoln Republican, having, for example, voted for Roosevelt in 1944 because the situation at the time reminded him of the one in 1864, when Lincoln warned against changing horses in the middle of the stream.

. . . .

We went upstairs to the bank cafeteria for a cup of coffee. When we had seated ourselves at a table there, Mr. Bunn said that although Springfield people have always been ready to boast about Lincoln, they hadn't always kept Springfield the kind of city Lincoln would have been proud of. For some years before the election of 1948, he said, it was a wide-open gambling town, and the gamblers had been getting a grip on city and county politics. I consoled him with the reflection that this was nothing new; just the previous night, I had read in Angle's book that in 1834 Springfield had had a bad gambling situation. (I have since learned that Mr. Lincoln himself defended a number of gamblers in court.) "Well, in 1948 we elected a state's attorney [that would be a district attorney in New York] pledged to stop gambling," the banker said, "and he not only stopped the professionals but took the slot machines out of the Country Club and the Elks and the American Legion, and stopped the bingo games for the Catholic church. That may be going a little too far. I never play golf myself without having a small bet on every hole." He added that he had never heard whether or not Lincoln gambled, but that Lincoln had certainly been a cock-fighter, and had wrestled Jack Armstrong to win a side bet for an employer. "It isn't so much the gambling as the bribery that goes with it that's bad," Mr. Bunn said. "I wonder what Lincoln would have thought of legalizing it."

After we had talked for a while about New York, a place in which, Mr. Bunn recalled, a young newcomer can get mighty lonely, he excused himself to keep a luncheon engagement, and I started back to my hotel. On the way, I decided that I might as well stop by to see Mr. Snigg, the Herndon man. His office, like that of the Abraham Lincoln Association, is in the First National Bank Building. I found him, a lean, limber man with the form and face of a determined pedestrian, seated at his desk in a determinedly plain room. "The important thing about Lincoln," he said when I had introduced myself, "is that he was a Springfield lawyer—a plain man. Thirty-five or forty years ago, they used to have a Lincoln Centennial Association here, and it would celebrate Lincoln's Birthday with a banquet in the Armory at twenty-five dollars a plate, and after the speeches everybody would get tight on champagne. Lincoln would have been ill at ease in such surroundings. They might have suited his wife, except that she would have been sore because only men were admitted to the banquet. She was a Todd with two 'd's. Abe used to say, 'One "d" is enough for God but not for the Todds.' Now, on Lincoln's Birthday, we make our pilgrimage wearing old clothes, in memory of his humility and early poverty, and do it walking, in memory of the many times he walked clean from New Salem to Springfield to borrow or return a lawbook of John Stuart's, his first teacher. Out at the cemetery, he lies among the lawyers he knew—Stuart, Stephen T. Logan, and William H. Herndon, the Uncle Billy of beloved memory."

Mr. Snigg asked if I had been to see the Lincolns' home, and I replied that I had passed it but hadn't gone inside. "Bleak-looking place, isn't it?" he said. "Did you ever hear how she had an extra story put on it while he was away in Washington attending Congress?" No, I said, I really hadn't heard much about the domestic life of the Lincolns before I came to Springfield. The lawyer snickered. "Well," he said, "old Abe walked up to where he had left his house and didn't recognize it for a minute. Just then Mrs. Lincoln stuck her head out the window and yelled, 'What's the matter, you old fool? Don't you know your own house when you see it?' "

On leaving Mr. Snigg, I found that I had just about time to get back to the hotel and eat catfish before keeping my date with Mrs. Masters. She lives in a small, new house next to the home of a son and daughter-in-law, in the country-club part of the town. Her living-room walls are hung with vigorous, unacademic paintings, which their author introduced as "genuine Gertrude Masters." Mrs. Masters' painting is representational, but the abstractionists also interest her, she told me. Downstate Illinois as a whole, however, is not prepared for them, she said. Public response to a non-representational show put on by the Art Association a short time before in a one-story studio and gallery it has built onto the Edwards mansion had been unfortunate. "I could have strangled them," Mrs. Masters said. She also expressed a desire to strangle a man named Ivan Elliott, the Attorney General of Illinois, because five thousand dollars that somebody had bequeathed to the Art Association was tied up in such a way that the Association couldn't get the principal to spend on repairs. More than anybody else, however, Mrs. Masters said, she wanted to strangle the newspapermen who, on the occasion of Edgar Lee Masters' death, this spring, had revived in their obituaries the canard that he was destitute in his last years. "They said that he had been found starving in his room at the Hotel Chelsea, in New York, in 1944 and had been taken off to Bellevue Hospital," she told me. "Actually, he had pneumonia, and they took him to Bellevue because he had collapsed, and while he was there, they found he was suffering from malnutrition, too, because he had been too cranky to eat regularly. He had money in the bank at the time and an uncashed check from Hollywood for the moving-picture rights to one of his old books. After he got out of the hospital, he wrote to all the papers and threatened to sue them, and they said they were very sorry for their mistake. And then, as soon as he died, they brought it up again. They just couldn't resist that picture of the starving poet abandoned in an attic."

. . . .

The next morning, before leaving Springfield, I went for a farewell stroll about the town. As I walked toward the square, I bethought myself of the building where Lincoln had had his law office, at the corner of Sixth Street and the square. Above the entrance on the Sixth Street side, leading to the offices over the store, I noticed a plaque stating that the firm of Logan & Lincoln had offices on the third floor from 1841 to 1843. Logan was Lincoln's second partner, I knew by this time. He was an able lawyer and, as the senior of the firm, a demanding partner; among the reasons Lincoln quit him was that instead of preparing cases for someone else, Lincoln wanted to enjoy the luxury of having a junior prepare *his* cases. Lincoln had selected young Herndon for that role.

I walked up two flights of stairs and found myself in front of a door with a plate-glass window on which was inscribed the name of a firm of architects, S. J. Hanes & Son. The door was locked, but, looking through the glass, I could see an office at the far end of which a tall man wearing a green eyeshade was standing at a drawing board beside a window fronting on the square. There was a bell, and I rang it again once or twice, and then, deciding that one so absorbed would resent being disturbed, I was about to go away. Just then the man raised his eyes and looked in my direction. He came to the door and opened it.

I judged that he was in his sixties and only an inch or two under Lincoln's six feet four. He had a long nose and a wide mouth, and his head and neck inclined forward slightly, as if from years spent standing at drawing boards. I introduced myself and told him that I had just walked up from the street to find out if there was anything of Lincoln's to be seen about the office. He didn't seem surprised; instead, he said that this was something that happened once a week, on an average, and that he always liked to chin about Lincoln. "But one thing I don't want you to do is consider me an authority," he said. "I'm no historical authority. All I know is what I've heard around here." I promised not to consider him an authority, and he shook my hand and asked me to be seated. "My name's Murray Hanes," he said. "My father moved into these offices in 1894, and I came along with him." I said I had hesitated to interrupt his work, and he replied, "Oh, I don't do much now—don't want any big jobs. I just came down here this morning to keep out of my wife's way. Didn't want to have breakfast with her. Don't want to see her until dinner." (It came out later that he meant noon dinner.)

I said that I had known other men who felt the same way at times, and that seemed to establish an understanding.

"Two fellows from *Life* magazine came in here a couple years ago to ask some questions, same as you're doing," Mr. Hanes said, "and I told them the same as I'm telling you—I'm no authority. 'What! You no authority?' one of the fellows says. 'Why, show him the books,' he says to the other fellow. He had the other fellow along just to carry books. The fellow puts six books down on the table and says, 'You're quoted as an authority in every one of these books.' 'Well,' I said, 'if they quoted me, they did it on their own responsibility.' *You're* not an authority, are you?" Mr. Hanes asked with sudden suspicion.

I assured him that I wasn't, and he looked relieved.

"One thing I don't like and Springfield don't like," he said, "is somebody to come in from the outside and tell us about Lincoln."

"Not me," I said.

"I'm trained as an architect," Mr. Hanes said, "and an architect don't put in a beam until he has worked out the structural formula of stress. It should be the same way with a historian. But I don't mind telling you what I've heard. My grandfather on my mother's side was old Judge Murray, who was Billy Herndon's last law partner, in the eighteen-eighties. So, naturally, I've heard a good deal. Old Billy and the old Judge used to talk about old Abe together, and then afterward my grandfather used to tell what Billy had told him. Some of the stories wouldn't bear repeating, but they were funny. The ladies didn't like old Abe, because he was always taking the men away to tell them dirty stories. He was a man that could always see the funny side of anything—and he had to, old Billy used to say. He had a cross to bear."

"You mean—"

Mr. Hanes nodded. "She was a wildcat," he said. "One of those

Kentucky aristocrats, and I know how bad they can be. My grandmother was one of them—and oh, my!"

"There are people who think well of Mrs. Lincoln," I said.

"I know," Mr. Hanes conceded. "That was Robert Todd Lincoln's work. My grandfather had a presentation copy of Herndon's 'Lincoln'—the original edition, not the one they got out in 1891, after Robert had told them what to cut. I looked for the book in the old Judge's library after he died, and it was gone—and when my grandmother died, there was sixteen hundred dollars in one of her bankbooks that nobody could account for. What I always thought was Robert Lincoln bought it. He bought up every copy. You can't find a first edition of that book anywhere."

. . . . , ...

Mr. Hanes called my attention to several portrait photographs of Lincoln on the walls of the office, all showing him beardless, as he was until he left Springfield. "That's the picture I like," he said, singling one out. "The Smiling Lincoln. That's the way he must have looked when he was thinking of one of those stories. I made a Lincoln Christmas card last year—make a card every year. I modelled it on the face of the Smiling Lincoln. But mine came out more like a satyr. The quotation I used was this: 'Our reliance is in the love of liberty which God has planted in our bosoms.' "

I said that it was a mighty fine quotation, and added that I must be going, for it was half past twelve.

"My God, is it?" said Mr. Hanes, jumping up and grabbing his hat. "I don't want to be late for dinner, or Mrs. Hanes will be angry."

This, it occurred to me as we walked down the stairs together, was a moment that might have made the Smiling Lincoln laugh.

. . . . , ...

In 1958, the Center for The Republic (currently the Center for the Study of Democratic Institutions) began an investigation into modern American life. One of their staff members, Joseph P. Lyford, moved to Vandalia to see what life was like in a small midwestern town. The regularity of life in that downstate town stands in sharp contrast to the pace of modern Chicago. Lyford, who graduated with honors from Harvard University, was a journalist, assistant editor of *New Republic*, and press secretary to Governor Bowles of Connecticut, before joining the Center in 1953. He has written *Candidate* (New York, 1959), *The Agreeable Autocracies* (New York, 1961), and *The Airtight Cage* (New York, 1966).

The Talk in Vandalia

JOSEPH P. LYFORD

I

Judged by the map, the city of Vandalia (population 5,500) has a fine location. It lies across a junction of the Pennsylvania and the Illinois Central Railroads, appears to be the center of a criss-cross of highways, and is on the edge of the Kaskaskia River, which winds its way diagonally downstate to the Mississippi. But the map reader will be deceived. The Kaskaskia, swollen and icy in winter, subsides by summertime into a winding trail of mud and snags; the new superhighways—Routes 40 and 70—pass by to the north, and the only concession by the Pennsylvania's "Spirit of St. Louis" is a raucous bellow as it hurtles through a cut in the center of town an hour before noon. The Illinois Central is more considerate. Occasionally a freight engine shunts back and forth a few blocks outside of town to pick up some crates from one of the small factories along the tracks. "No trains stop here," the stationmaster says. The indifference of the railroads to Vandalia is paid back in full by the town's oldest practicing Democrat, eighty-eight-year-old Judge James G. Burnside. "We don't pay any attention to the railroads any more," he remarks. "They're just passing acquaintances."

A train traveler from the East can alight at Effingham, thirty miles away, trudge through the snow to the Greyhound Post House, and take the 1:30 p.m. bus, which is always overdue. The driver does not smile when along with a St. Louis ticket he gets a request for a stopover in Vandalia, which means that the express bus has to

From Joseph P. Lyford, *The Talk in Vandalia* (Santa Barbara, 1964), pp. 1-7, 29-35, 98-103. Copyright © 1964 by Joseph P. Lyford. Reprinted by permission. One footnote in the original has been retained.

make a ten-minute detour off the main highway. Route 40 runs straight and flat as a tight ribbon through wide umber plains sheeted with winter rain, past farmhouses four or five to the mile. For a few hundred feet at a time the road will stagger and pitch slightly as the land wrinkles into prairie, creek, and brushwood, then it subsides again to a level as monotonous as the roar of the bus. The see-sawing pump of an occasional oil well is the only motion in the fields on a rainy day. There are a few crossroads villages, then the town of St. Elmo, and, finally, a few miles along Alternate Route 40, the city of Vandalia, once the western terminus of the Cumberland Road, capital of Illinois from 1819 to 1839, seat of Fayette County, and country of Abraham Lincoln of the House of Representatives of the State of Illinois.

· ·

The township of Vandalia is grouped in three economic units. On its outer ring are the farms, the town's main support, ranging from sixty or eighty acres to several hundred, the average being somewhere in the middle. The chief crops are corn, soybeans, and livestock—mainly hogs and cattle. The land is worked with modern machinery by farmers who combine their own land with leased acreage—as much as they can get.

On the western edge of town are four factories, which employ altogether about 850 people. They are the Princess Peggy dress factory; United Wood Heel, manufacturers of heels for women's shoes; the Johnson, Stephens and Shinkle shoe factory (the largest single employer with a work force of 475), and the Crane Packing Company, which turns out mechanical seals for automobiles, machines, appliances, etc.

At the core is the town itself—the stores, the banks, professional offices, churches, schools, filling stations, garages, plus the Elk, Mason, Moose, Odd-Fellow and Legion Halls, the Town Hall and County Courthouse, one movie theatre, restaurants, and nine of the only taverns in a county noted for its religion and its aridity. Vandalia's supermarkets are big and modern; its dry-goods stores range from the antique-looking Fidelity Clothiers to the Hub Department Store which has quality merchandise at New York prices. Only one commercial establishment—Radliff's Pool Parlor—remains open for business seven days a week. The local newspaper plant is built of yellow brick and houses the editorial staff of two weekly papers, the *Union* and the *Leader*. Most of the business district lies south of the Pennsylvania tracks except some hardware and feed stores, the Farm Bureau offices, and a cleaning establishment. On the north side of town the streets are lined with small frame houses, and a few large and attractive Victorian homes. Some blocks further out are the new County Hospital, the million-dollar Vandalia High School which is the community's pride, and a new development of luxurious, ranch-type homes. Beyond the high school is the intersection of Route 51 out of town and Route 40, which has given rise to a cluster of motels, restaurants, and filling stations. To the west lie the factories and on the far side of Shoe Factory Hill, along the Pennsylvania Railroad, are patches of dilapidated wooden dwellings which make up the hopeless part of town. To the east is the Kaskaskia River. The southern part of town peters out rather quickly a few blocks below the Post Office and the white frame house which is the home of Charlie Evans.

When he is not in the front parlor of his home, which he uses as his office, Mr. Evans is in the lobby of the Evans Hotel. He built the hotel in 1924 and, along with a hardware business and various real estate dealings, it made him probably the richest man in Vandalia. Last year, his eighty-first, the $106,000 library he gave to the town opened its doors. "We were a money-saving family, all of us," he says. "We're Welsh by descent. I was never a man to sell, I always bought and added to it. When I sold the hotel I'd been saving all the time. I guess I'd saved too much. I didn't have any use for the money, so I built the library. When I built it, I didn't try to cut corners. I didn't try to save as if I was building for myself."

Mr. Evans leans back, and crosses his arms when he talks about his town. "This is a historic city. When they moved the capital from here to Springfield in 1839, our population was only 400. We've gained a little bit all the time. Population-wise we've never had a setback. We've never had a boom. We held our ground. A big percentage of people own their own homes, including a lot who work at the factory. This makes us a good town for a factory. The companies know our workers are not fly-by-nighters. Their employees are here to stay. They have money invested in our town. Homes today build from $12,000 to $18,000, and we have a good building and loan program. Banks will lend money to anybody here who wants to build a building. We have good, sound, sincere bankers. Back in the late 20's, when people were trying to buy more and more land for their farms, the bankers warned them against it. When the crash came, we weren't so badly off as some. We had hard times in 1932, oh mercy.

"I think the town is going to develop pretty well. Rental housing is pretty scarce. The homes here are good ones, and people have made substantial payments on them. I don't know what we're going to have to do to keep our young people here, though. When they go to the city, they don't come back. They want new people to get acquainted with. Industry might be the answer. We should have more opportunities for skilled workers. The Crane Packing Com-

pany has been very good. They have a training program for employees and they are expanding. The shoe factory is a shoe factory.
Their idea is how much work you can get out of your help. It's as
good a shoe factory as there is. It's a good town, but we have one
bad problem. It's the farmers. The farmers are in trouble."

. . . .

The popularity of the farmer in the abstract has not always
thawed out farmers in particular, some of whom still harbor ancient
resentments against the town. (One farmer says he wants his children to stay in the rural schools because Vandalians think that
"farm kids still piss on stumps and never heard of inside plumb-
ing.") But many of the farmers seem to feel closer to the town than
before the war, partly because of the knowledge that a lot of other
people besides farmers are involved in their economic troubles, and
partly because the farmers' own social life has become more and
more interlaced with the life of the town. As the one-room rural
schoolhouses have dwindled, over the farmers' opposition, from
three dozen in the school district to a half dozen, farm mothers
have become members of the PTA's of the Washington, Lincoln,
and Central elementary schools. There is more talk in the homes of
educational problems jointly shared with the townspeople.

Those farmers who work in the factories—"Saturday farmers," J.
B. Turner, the county farm agent, calls them—have a growing
association with non-farmers, and some even join labor union locals
in the shoe and heel factories. Also, the growing cost of running a
farm because of the new machinery required and the rising prices of
land have increased the extent of the farmer's dependence on local
financial institutions. The farmers buy more and more of their food
locally—most of them have disposed of their dairy cows and buy
their milk at the Tri-City Supermarket and the A&P. The farmer's
machinery is repaired by local mechanics. Feed-dealer Norman
Michel, who carries as many as 21,000 people on his credit rolls, is a
farmer's banker in his own way. Vandalia shapes its commercial
activities to suit the farmers' tastes, and the farmer, his wife and
children, and his trucks are a regular part of the scenery on Gallatin
Street. This is not to say that the town has been taken over by the
farmers: in one sense it is the farmers who have changed their habits
and tastes—even in dress—to fit the town.

The farmer has responded in other ways to the town. He partici-
pates more in local events. He comes more to the city's churches.
One outstanding farmer is chairman of the school district's Board of
Education. Many of the more prosperous farm families contribute
their women's time to fund drives. The high school's football and
basketball teams are getting a little more help from the farm

youngsters who used to shy away from extra-curricular activities after the last school bell. One still hears complaints from the townspeople that the farmer is hard to reach, but he is less and less remote.

Partly as a result of his accumulating difficulties, the political attitudes of the farmer seem to have become less distinct from those of his fellow-citizens in town. If anything, his views on such matters as health insurance, social security, the United Nations, even labor unions, have often become more tentative than those of some of his city brethren. The realization that government may be the only power capable of restraining the technological and political forces gnawing at his economic position has affected the farmer's outlook considerably, and more than he will admit.

. . . .

II

It would be misleading to say that Vandalia takes everything in its stride, because "stride" implies a measured forward movement which has never been a community characteristic. It is also inaccurate to take the community's easygoing manner at face value. Its calm demeanor is sometimes achieved at the cost of suppressing grave internal discontents. Nevertheless, the atmosphere is rarely charged with the type of emotional storms that test the tempers of New York or Chicago suburbanites. The political fracases that periodically rock a Westport, Connecticut, to its foundations, setting commuter against ancient inhabitant, are unknown. Public controversies usually do not get past the stage of fairly low-pressure arguments over personalities or such transient irritations as disintegrating sidewalks and sheriffs. Candidates do not run for municipal office, they file for it, on ballots that do not mention party affiliations. The only lively competition recently was for the job of county sheriff, but the plenitude of aspirants was attributed to a rise in the unemployment rate, adding considerable glamour to the sheriff's $5,000 yearly stipend.* The community blood pressure is unaffected by animosities between Republican and Democrat. County administrations alternate between the two with regularity, and the towns do not even have local political organizations.

. . . .

The columns of the *Leader* and the *Union* mirror the general unconcern with politics. Some of this editorial anaemia comes from

*The only Democratic candidate for sheriff who had a campaign plank was Everett Jarrett, a house painter. ("If I am elected, the jail will get a new coat of paint.") He ran ninth and last.

THE TALK IN VANDALIA

a slightly stuffy sense of responsibility which dates back to when the Democratic *Leader* acquired the Republican opposition, the *Union.* Charles Mills, the tall, white-haired editor of the two papers, and one of the most overworked men in town, says that "ever since the opposition was bought out, we have had to realize that when we say something unpleasant about someone, he has no other place to go. We have to present both sides of everything. We think we've got an obligation to promote good activities and criticize bad ones regardless of the politics."

Mills takes a detached view of local customs. He says that city elections are not supposed to be political. "People run on a non-partisan basis, but sometimes it shapes up political. Mr. Smith, the former mayor, didn't put enough Republicans to work on the streets, so a lot of Republicans supported the Democrat, Mr. Michel. Well, the mayor has done pretty well as far as taking care of Republicans; the Board of Aldermen is Republican, too. Also, the county government is divided. We've had Democratic county officers and Republican Boards of Supervisors, then we've turned right around and had Republican officers with Democratic supervisors. The size of election pluralities varies from around 1,500 in favor of the Republicans to 1,500 in favor of the Democrats. There's a lot of personality voting. We've got our radicals and our rabids, but people as a whole are more interested in the best man for the job, and, as far as the papers go, we don't like to do too much endorsing of candidates and lacing them up and down in elections. We have to work with everybody, and if a man we oppose gets elected, we have to remember that we have to do business with him. We have to work with him for four years. I don't mean that we're afraid of criticizing the administration. We're doing it right now."

Such philosophizing doesn't sit well with some of the town's old-time Democrats. One of them, reporting that Democratic county advertising helped the *Leader* stay alive during the hard days of the depression, says, "Charlie Mills got less Democratic as soon as he got the wrinkles out of his belly." Whatever the situation may be, the GOP still has a spokesman in the *Union,* which as far back as April, 1859, ran up its colors by calling for the election of Republican candidates everywhere.

The other customary sources of small-town disturbances and civic strife are also unpromisingly dry. "People behave pretty well here, considering," says Robert Burnside, a local lawyer who would know better than anyone who was misbehaving, since he defends a large number of them in court.

This is not to say that Vandalia conversation is totally deprived of juicy subject-matter. Last winter the *Leader* printed the details of the foiling, through a tip to the police, of a young man's attempt to stick up a local supermarket; and any citizen, asked to recall examples of irregular or anti-social behavior, will recount the story of two cases of prostitution nipped in the bud by town constables. But, except for a brief flurry of store robberies, a two-man police car has been able to keep Vandalia law-abiding at night. A first impression that Vandalia is unpolluted is confirmed by more detailed investigation.

Its respectability and churchliness do not set Vandalia apart. Most of its neighboring communities, heavily populated by German Lutherans, Baptists, and Methodists, are relatively free from dissension or violence. Whether this is the result of an abundance of Christian virtues, good police work, or simply an elaborate system of civilian intelligence work is not clear. What is clear is that it is impossible to be in Vandalia very long without being noticed. Vandalia's social and moral regularity depends greatly on several thousand pairs of eyes. There is nothing malicious or prying about this sort of surveillance. In a small town one does not peep, one sees, whether one wishes to see or not. When a housewife goes to market, she learns where she has been soon afterwards from an interested friend. Ministers have come to rely heavily on kind-hearted parishioners for information on what members of their flock lie ill at home or in the hospital. In a town where the lives of their neighbors are the yarn of everyone's knitting, it is possible to be immoral, but utterly past imagination that one remain undetected. "It's positively neolithic how things get around here, positively tribal," exclaims a recent arrival from Europe who, it should be added, lives in Vandalia because he likes it.

This kind of atmosphere is a mixed blessing. While many Vandalians appreciate the neighborly sort of mutual assistance in an emergency which is a standard fact of life in a small town, there is also some feeling that sympathy and first aid from one's fellow-citizens are often bought rather dearly—at the sacrifice of individual privacy, for instance. "Nobody could ever die in Vandalia and not be missed right away," says one complainer, "but sometimes I think I'd prefer a big city. At least you can live without being noticed, even if you may decay in your apartment for several days after you're dead." The almost familial social climate also tends to create an illusory sense of security and complacency. The Presbyterian minister, a pipe smoking transplant from Cincinnati named Ralph Smith, has preached more than one sermon on "Peaceful Valley" in the hope of stirring up a little healthy discontent, without noticeable success. "This is a fine community," he says sadly, "but I sometimes wonder if we aren't just an island of the past floating into the present."

One ancient pattern of behavior at which Mr. Smith, almost alone among his fellow-ministers, has publicly aimed his irony has been Vandalia's treatment of the Negro. "We call our town the land of Lincoln but the hotels won't rent a room to a Negro, and no Negro can buy property or rent a home in Vandalia. There is an old saying that people in Vandalia are glad to help a Negro as long as he keeps on going right out of town."

There is some improvement taking place in the situation, he notes. Charles Truitt's Abe Lincoln Motel on St. Louis Avenue and the Riviera Motel on Route 40 take Negroes, and they have been seen eating at the Abe Lincoln Café and the Patio Restaurant. But with the exception of Mr. Smith and a handful of others, the town's anti-Negro habit patterns have not bobbed to the surface in public conversation.

. . . .

VII

. . . .

The talks in Vandalia do not support the American myth that a rural town today is a land-locked island inhabited by people who share an abiding complacency with each other. There are the surface appearances of unity and its concomitant sterility in Vandalia, and the appearances are sometimes overwhelming. But they do not persist in the face of its own citizens' conflicting testimony. Vandalians today are in some ways in a better position to observe and to feel, sometimes most painfully, the consequences of a changing society than the suburbanite who lives in a bedroom town or the city dweller who hears about the world mainly from his newspaper and who enjoys the protective layers afforded him by his corporation, his union, and his various other institutional affiliations. There is also a special urgency in the air of Vandalia. A town on the edge of Chicago, Los Angeles, or New York City is forced to deal with the problems of sudden and uncontrolled growth, but Vandalia is beset by the much more desperate problem of how to hold on to what it has in order to survive.

. . . .

Whereas many Americans live in or around the great cities unwillingly because that is where the jobs are, Vandalians live in their town because they want to. Their reasons are not new, but they have an added poignance because the things these people value are becoming harder to hold on to. They like the freedom of association and personal trust they do not believe can be found in a large city. They hope to maintain a school system in which their children receive a common educational experience in small classes with good teachers. Perhaps, as William Deems says, there is something unhealthy about the way Vandalians meet each local problem with a fund drive; nevertheless, they esteem the relationships with each other that make such solutions practicable.

There are many reasons why a man stays in Vandalia when, as Joe Dees puts it, "he could get the paid vacations and fringe benefits in the city," and most of them recur over and over in the talks. Underlying them all seems to be a desire to be able to know the whole of one's town, to be "some kind of a somebody" in it, to be able to circulate in it freely, and to be part of a social arrangement where there are certain justified assumptions about how people will deal with each other. On a freezing day, Mrs. Mark Miller is operating under one of these assumptions when she asks the postmaster who has just sold her some stamps to call a taxi for her. There is nothing trivial about the transaction.

. . . .

Despite all their advertised contact with their fellow human beings, many Vandalians seem to do much of their thinking in isolation. Perhaps it is because their problems are so closely bound up with personal relationships that many of them are less inclined to speak openly about them. In a community where almost everyone knows everyone else by name and face, and converses with ease and frequency, the citizens for the most part exchange commonplaces. Dan Hockman, a high school history teacher, describes the situation when he says, "People here are interested in what other people are up to, not in what they think." With all their togetherness—the word is not used with disdain—there are many, many isolated people in the community. Sometimes the isolation is by choice. Alenia McCord says apologetically, "We have our standards and we tend to be a little intolerant of other people if they don't agree with us, but we don't try to railroad our standards on others. If somebody doesn't come up to our standards that's all right just as long as they keep a long distance away from us." More often, however, the isolation is neither sought nor enjoyed. Conversations on the most affecting personal and intellectual matters are given freely—to the outsider who asks for them—but when the conversations end, sometimes after many hours of intense exchange, the conclusion is very often a wish that it might happen again and a remark that it almost never happened before.

Perhaps the absence of serious talk with others in their community explains why so many of the townspeople combine their own inner guesses with mixtures of the prevalent myths, and thereby supplement the myths. There are many remarks about the curse of complacency in the town and, taken together, the people who are disturbed about it make up a sizable portion of the population. But, like the Reverend Ralph Smith, they are really annoyed at the nature of the peace, not the peace itself, at the inertia that seems to be responsible for the lack of conflict and motion in the community. If the inertia proceeds from smugness and total satisfaction with the past, anything Mr. Smith has to say in criticism of "Peaceful Valley" seems relatively mild. But if the inertia grows out of confusion and bewilderment, and the clinging to tradition is done in desperation, then Mr. Smith is being harsh, because the peace in the valley is a troubled one.

. . . .

If there is to be a new way for the town, it has many assets which do not appear in Robert Hasler's typewritten town biography. Vandalia is not condemned to become a suburb of anything just yet, and it still has transportation facilities that can serve whatever new industrial establishments it may attract. One advantage of its unhurried history is that no huge defense plants have dropped down on the town to crush its character forever and then move on in a few years. Vandalia has natural beauties that make it a place apart. Few towns to the north have spreading elms and maples of such beauty, and in May there is the wild spring blaze of lilac and dogwood. The Kaskaskia is a navigator's nightmare now, but in a few years flood control dams below and above Vandalia will reclaim much valuable farm land, and, not incidentally, provide fishing and boating for local boys and girls and out-of-state tourists.

Obviously, what happens in Vandalia depends on the people who will have to manage these assets, and what improvements they make in their present arrangements of organizing themselves and communicating with each other. One cannot really tell how they will do, even after talking to them for a long, long time. Affairs move slowly. But there are stirrings and there are contradictions. Judge Burnside says nobody pays any attention to the railroads. On the other hand, in his church by the railroad, Mr. Smith has to stop in the middle of his Sunday sermon when he hears the "Spirit of St. Louis" coming down the tracks.

December 1962

Baker Brownell, who was a professor at Northwestern University and later Director of Area Services at Southern Illinois University, discusses life in "Egypt" in *The Other Illinois* (New York, 1958). Prior to his death in 1965, he had published *Art is Action* (Freeport, New York, 1939), *The College and the Community* (New York, 1952), and *The Human Community* (New York, 1950).

The Other Illinois

BAKER BROWNELL

Off to the south of the big-time Illinois and considerably older is another Illinois not well known even to Illinoisans. Though the main show, of course, is a big one that people who live in the long carrot-shaped state take for granted, the other Illinois is something else again. From this Illinois a black report drifts northward now and then, foggy with rumor of a mine disaster, a massacre, or some other desperate instance of life and death, but that is about all that most people hear of it. This southern Illinois sits on the back doorstep as poor as Job's turkey, as beautiful as redbud trees in spring. It may be more passionate, more violent, stubborn, stringy; still it is a sweeter Illinois with soft southern linguals, magnolia blossoms, and a generous heart.

This other Illinois begins at the 39th parallel or thereabouts, in line with Alton and Vandalia, and extends southward into the crotch of the two great rivers down to the 37th parallel. Here at the tip of Illinois Cairo stands with one foot in the Mississippi River and the other in the Ohio and calls itself, not "Kyro" nor "Kayro," but "Kerro." It has about the same latitude geographically as Norfolk, Virginia, with a moral latitude said to be considerably greater.

Southern Illinois is . . . somewhat south of prosperity. For the main show and the big incomes begin with the black, generous soils, the glacier-tilled prairie, the corn, hog, and soy culture of the central counties, and include, no doubt, McLean County corn, Kane County butter, the Chicago River, the Tribune Tower, along with lesser items such as the greatest railroad network in the world and the southwest corner of Lake Michigan. To all this our southern Illinois seems indifferent, too much so, perhaps, for it rejects sometimes the accepted codes of prosperity. Says young Dr. Striegel, a veterinarian just new-minted from college and professional school, "I could make more money up north, but I can go fishing here." That remark is typical of southern Illinois.

From Baker Brownell, *The Other Illinois* (New York, 1958), pp. 3-5, 14-15, 254-261. Copyright © 1958 by Baker Brownell.

Egypt is the popular name for the region; no one knows why. A whimsical Egyptophile influence had a part, perhaps, in naming little, new places hereabouts: Cairo, Karnak, Thebes, Dongola, and from them the regional name may have followed. But legend does not have it so. Although the legend probably was invented after the fact, it is persistent. There was drought in the northern counties, says the legend; the wheat fields dried up; the streams died in their beds. But in southern Illinois rain fell and there were good crops, and from the north came people seeking corn and wheat as to Egypt of old. Thus the name, Egypt. Neither the name nor the legend is a good one, but people stick to them. Instead of Egypt it might better be called, if we must be historical, Mesopotamia, or between rivers. Or, still better, the river country.

Who are these people of southern Illinois? Where do they come from? They are not all Abraham Lincolns, to be sure, but many of them look it. The name or something similar, such as Linkon, is not uncommon. And the Lincoln trail, a thousand miles and a hundred years long, from the Atlantic seaboard, Virginia, the Carolinas, over the Cumberland Gap into Kentucky, and trickling on in slow stages into Indiana and Illinois in the early nineteenth century, was trodden by thousands of southern Illinoisans. These deep-eyed, thin-lipped people were the first to come of those who still remain. Only later by a decade or so, when the Black Hawk War was finished to the satisfaction of the victors, did the white tide, including my own ancestors, begin to flow from New England and New York over the northern prairies. They were the newcomers then.

. . . .

The mortality of villages and of men and their institutions in southern Illinois is not alone a matter of floods and natural disaster. It is also economic. There is a high mortality of jobs. The land is beautiful and broken—tragic some would call it—as beautiful in its own idiom as anywhere on earth.

Spring is incandescent here; it glows with strange, soft fire. The autumns are golden and still; each tree in its own way is a transfiguration. There are more kinds of trees in these few counties than in all of Europe. The north and south, the east and west of the continent meet here. But the lovely spring and fall and the mild winter between them are not enough, if there are no jobs. "You can't eat them," says the man looking for work. Even southern Illinoisans, impractical as they are, admit that.

The cost of public relief in the area is higher by more than 50 per cent per capita than in the rest of the state. In some communities the largest source of income is relief payments. Farsighted relief workers are saying that the costs of community rehabilitation and education would be more than covered by the reduction in relief payments.

In Eldorado, a town of 4,000 in the Saline Valley, the last of six coal mines has closed down. Men, like ants in a hill that suddenly has become hostile to their interests, scurry out to find jobs. Scores of them commute daily to jobs in Evansville, Indiana, Paducah, Kentucky, Joppa, or elsewhere, 169 miles or more for the round trip in order to support their families. Their cars wear out and the men wear out, but the worried, harried traveling continues.

"But labor nowadays must be mobile," says the economist, looking up from his desk. "Why don't they live near their work?"

"Hell!" says Jess Chandler, the big miner, now a pipe fitter in Evansville. "That's all those damn economists know about it. Many of us own our homes in Eldorado. We can't sell them; we can't rent them; and we can't pay the high prices in the new place. Our children are in school in Eldorado. Our wives may have jobs there. It's not so easy to move as it looks on paper."

. . . .

The folks here differ among themselves as in any other region, and some of them, as elsewhere, are soiled and shiftless. Usually they are silent, too, with a tough, arrogant silence. Their reticence is like the clay-pan soil of the plateau, stubborn, recalcitrant, unresponsive. Though misfortune may be a man's mistress in this country, though he may beat her or rape her, he rarely will seek refuge from her in noisy drink or begging.

Said the Union County subsistence farmer, too poor to clothe his children, to his more prosperous neighbor, "I won't work for you, if you mean for money; but if you want to trade work—I help you and you help me—that's all right with me."

Pride burns in his vitals, a useless fever, no doubt, that neither nourishes nor kills him. "And," says the visitor from Chicago or Saint Louis looking him over with a kind of urbane malice, "without much of anything to be proud of."

The visitor, of course, is right—outwardly. The so proud man may be slow of speech and limited in grasp. He has sometimes a kind of dismal honesty, to be sure, but this seems to arise less from principle than from lack of facility. Men without jobs do not have the full kit of personal resources and stratagems. The graceful things designed to lubricate a more sophisticated life are not part of their equipment. A miner laid off more often than he works, a subsistence farmer on forty acres, a boy in his middle twenties who never had a job is definitely down on the gravel bottom of life. His rages may seem explosive and irrelevant, his honesty corrosive, his lies without friendly purpose.

But he doesn't whine, not in southern Illinois. He may find symbols for his pride and stubbornness in lonely squirrel hunting, in strange, creative profanity, or sometimes in revival "meetings." These meetings come seasonally in southern Illinois and often mark the top of his moral and emotional cycle.

Southern Illinois is socially residual in its way. But taken as it is, there is a good deal that is preferable to many a place more unctuously prosperous. The people here are not little, leftover men. Far from it. They know hard times, violence, the risks of living. From a quality of man like this, but under other conditions and from different premises, statesmanship of considerable significance, industry, and the arts can be derived. In some ways the quality called greatness is already there. After all, Lincoln, Logan, Robert Ingersoll, William Jennings Bryan, William E. Borah, and many another in law, labor, government, and industry came from this Illinois country.

. . . .

The Folk Song of a Ten-Ton Truck

Buncombe village is a little clot of life north of West Vienna where Route 37 soars up in a wide curve toward the pass at Goreville. The embankment is a big one and cuts off all to the east of Buncombe except a sky and hilltop. All day and sometimes into the night trucks roar up above the village heading for the top, or down suddenly out of the sky like noisy messengers from another world. They are—if you will consider the etymology—angels no less, bevies of modern, technological angels traveling up and down this Jacob's ladder of concrete. Sometimes they turn off toward the quarry at the left where twenty-three workers are Buncombe's biggest pay roll.

Under the flapping of these gasoline-powered wings Buncombe—pronounced Bunkum—sleeps uneasily and dreams of its destiny.

"It hasn't much new to look forward to," says Fred Medlin, who retired from the railroad a while ago and bought out the other heirs to his father's old home across from the church, "but it's a good place to live.

"It's a good place to live," he repeats a little pensively, "if you've saved something or have a pension. You can't earn much here."

The little street straggles down from the embankment past the post office and store, past other stores boarded up, eyeless, past a little boxlike church looking south and west over a valley, a house or so, another church, and Main Street ends amid gardens and greenery and long overlooks south, west, north across a lovely land.

About 400 people live there, according to Mr. Medlin. A little to the north a consolidated school sits astride the district line. Pupils flow in, he says, from four directions.

The trucks chant harshly as they go up and down the concrete hill. What does this angel choir sing? Well, their song sits firmly on this hill and belongs in this place fully as much as do the empty, speechless stores and the street straggling down from the embankment. The long, guttural note, the rest, the change of tempo, this, too, is Buncombe. It is the call, or possibly the folk song, of a ten-ton truck.

Sixty years ago, says Mr. Medlin, the village was moved about a mile. That was when the C. and E.I. Railroad came by. But now even that is out of sight behind the big embankment where gasoline-smelling angels travel up and down the concrete ladder.

But Buncombe is just one. There is Edwardsville, an old and lively town under the dark wings of East Saint Louis. There is Highland, with something about it still Alpine. Although the name Helvetia unfortunately is gone, a tradition of order and sound, Swiss intelligence remains. There is Fairfield, clean lines, well-swept and well-content, where you will hear just about the best Rotary singing at luncheon in the Illinois wedge.

There are Centralia and Mount Vernon, good-sized towns looking wistfully northward into the bright land of industrial prosperity. But not too wistfully, says Bill Dougherty of the *Southern Illinoisan,* for Centralia and Mount Vernon as well as Harrisburg, Marion, Carbondale, and probably Herrin seem to be on the upgrade again.

There is Pinkneyville, that capital of basketball. The game has grown like a big tree in the quaint old square. It overarches the entire place. Sparta, Redbud, Tamaroa, Collinsville, Nashville, and a hundred more living places, each one unique, each one with its own infinite value, these communities of people are southern Illinois.

There are the editors wielding their dailies and weeklies, but mostly weeklies, like tennis racquets as they bat the news back and forth across the net. From their mastheads they look out over their respective provinces with friendly possessiveness and with considerable responsibility for the welfare of the domain. A surface irony plays across their work, and they kid their readers, their colleagues on papers across the way, and sometimes themselves. They always travel with a full armament of quips or wisecracks, always keep on shooting. They come together at the meetings of the Southern Illinois Editorial Association with more of the same.

· ·

Ben Franklin lives on. The newspapermen shoot their wads of paper back and forth from river to river. Your editor's first concern is his own locality, of course, but one eye always is cocked ironically on the town and editor nearby, and indeed on all the towns of the region, including the whole damned amusing human race.

On the editors' shoulders rests that universal culture of sport that covers all America. Nowhere but in the papers is it a self-sustaining, articulated whole, for the printed news of sports is to a great extent the only reality of them for millions of people. In southern Illinois basketball, with football, a little baseball, a little track in that order are meshed into the huge sport culture. And there's the Du Quoin fair with its famous Hambletonian. As many as 30,000 fans go to see that $120,000 Grand Circuit race. But hunting and fishing, boats and dogs, not in the newspapers but in the long vistas of the streams and lakes themselves or on the woodland roads, are more native to the taste of this land between the rivers.

· ·

What is this beautiful and tormented land chained here like Andromeda against the rock? Who knows? Rivers, forests, mines, love, murder, grass, winds, game, courage, cowardice, hills, and long vistas across open valleys, these and all the other complex data of the southern Illinois country eventually get down to people. They are both the beauty and torment.

· ·

The final document is by Jerry Klein, a feature writer for the Peoria *Journal Star*. His subject is the unhurried lifestyle of a small town in west-central Illinois in the summer of 1975.

There's No Rush in Rushville

JERRY KLEIN

Rushville—Mid-morning and already hot. The cornfields begin to melt into a watery haze far across the prairie, and the thermometer on the bank blinks into the 80s.

It will reach 90 before this day is past, and the men sitting on the green slat benches in the square will slide backwards toward the shade as the sun burns its way across the sky above and the lawn at their feet.

This is circus day. At the fairgrounds at the edge of town, the big top is going up, and members of the Sells and Grey Three-Ring Circus are going about their chores; the scene is reminiscent of the prelude to "Carnival."

An elephant gouges away at the turf, throwing cool black dirt up on its back. "Hey, get away from that elephant," a man shouts at the youngsters who stand there, solemn and wide-eyed. Yes, they have seen elephants before, at the St. Louis Zoo, but never so close.

The circus is here for one day only. Matinee and evening performances. Then it will pick up and go on again, like some Flying Dutchman forever making the rounds of the small towns and cities. It is the first circus here for as long as almost anyone can remember.

Donald Juett, retired farmer and "retired just about everything," leans on a thick square yardstick that he uses as a cane and watches the proceedings. "Used to be some pretty decent circuses here in the old days," he says. "Barnum and Bailey were here, but never Ringling Brothers." He says that he goes around every day now and "stirs up the neighborhood." He says that he will be 77—if he makes it to fall.

Hoofbeats thudding against the hot white surface, breath coming in quick, rhythmic snorts, a lone trotter pulls a sulky and rider around the long, white oval of the fairgrounds track. Circus people go about their chores, washing and hanging out clothes in the slow, wet wind.

The same wind stirs the flag high above the old bandstand in the town square, a source of considerable pride in Rushville. Justifiably

From Jerry Klein, "There's No Rush in Rushville, But There Is a Sense of Vitality," Peoria *Journal Star*, June 29, 1975. Reprinted by permission.

so. Besides the green benches, there are, along the sidewalks, neat borders of flowers, and, around the bandstand, landscaping that is modern without being intrusive. It all imparts a sense of order and care that is formal, yet liveable.

Cars park in multiple rows around the square—diagonally against the curbings and in the middle of the wide streets. There seem to be flower boxes everywhere. And, in most cases, the Victorian store fronts with their high cornices and other ornamentation have been preserved.

The courthouse has been newly tuckpointed, the old red paint stripped away. From the outside, the building looks much as it must have in the late 1800s, clean and solid—a duplicate, supposedly, of the courthouse at Monroe, Mich. The cornerstone is inscribed, "Laid by the Masonic Fraternity, June 24, A.D. 1885." The second-floor courtroom is a curious and unsettling combination of stunning historic preservation and faceless modern.

There is a huge, leather-upholstered witness chair that looks like some Burgundian throne; nearby, there is a plastic-topped table. The judge's bench is of classic oak design, embroidered with elaborate carving and piecework with a surface rubbed and checkered by almost a century of use.

For the jury there are, by contrast, mass-produced barrel chairs upholstered with vinyl. Overhead are suspended acoustical panels and fluorescent tubes; the embossed tin ceiling is hidden away in the upper darkness. Dark oak floors are spattered with paint, partly covered with chartreuse carpeting.

Up in the clock tower, the bell still bongs out the hours, marked once by a man pulling a rope. The wheeled bell that came from the McShane Bell Foundry in Baltimore in 1883 has been converted now and is rapped, on schedule, by a mechanical mallet. County Clerk James Rebman says that there are times when somebody has to go and shut it off, because it rings and rings.

Not today. Twelve solid, clangorous notes that echo dully in the heat. The sound begins the moment that the noon whistle has ceased its wailing. Remarkable.

The circus tents are all up now. A truck filled with animals maneuvers across the grass, a baboon peering intently from a cage.

At Mary's Diner, nearly full, service is quick, and the conversation that arises amid the clatter carries fragments of history. An elderly man is introduced as the baby of the family. "She married a third time, you know, and she had two more boys. She wasn't no spring chicken even then. . . ." "Well, it's been good to see you, too. . . ." "Don't know about this weather. Looks like it's going to be a long, hot summer. . . ."

A police car goes past, slow. Driving is E. E. VanDeventer, a policeman here for 25 years and retired now. At 73, he is, he says, laughing, "the oldest cop in the country." He works only when needed nowadays. Used to live in Peoria, he says, but doesn't think he'd like it these days. E. N. Woodruff was Peoria's mayor back then. "I s'pose he's dead now," VanDeventer reflects.

VanDeventer stops and talks with the men sitting on the green benches in the square. "Everybody sets out here, from the millionaire to the man on welfare," says one of the men. He is neither.

One of the men, wearing a P.A.G. hat, says that he doesn't know what the initials stand for; the seed man gave it to him. Another wears a yellow Caterpillar hat; there are people in town who make the round trip to work at Cat near Peoria twice a day, a trip of 72 miles or better—one way.

VanDeventer's police cruiser circles the square and heads out past Scripps Park with its swimming pool, golf course, picnic area, tennis courts, lake. The park is at the site of the old Scripps home, a gift of the heirs of James Mogg Scripps in 1923. The youngest of the Scripps, Ed, started the chain of newspapers that eventually grew into the Scripps-Howard empire. A sister, Ellen, left a trust in a Cleveland bank that matches, dollar for dollar, town funds earmarked for the park.

Paul Smith is in the park this noontime with his daughter, Paula. He has been out of work for five months and has no idea when he will be called back to the Dana Foundry in Havana. This month. Next month. Later. Meanwhile, there is the park.

One park such as this for a town of 3,300 would be remarkable, but, just south of town, there is the new Schuy-Rush Park, owned by the city, where a huge lake is being developed.

There is the small-town sense of peace and stability in Rushville, but there is a feeling of vitality, too. There is the Culbertson Memorial Hospital, the Schuyler County Jail Museum, several churches, an airport. The major industry remains Bartlow Bros., whose Korn Top Wieners flow from the plant at the south edge of town in somewhat diminished, but still staggering, numbers. The reason for the slowdown, according to Bill Bartlow, is the high price of hogs.

There are few empty store windows in town, hardly any signs of the urban decay affecting small towns and large cities alike. One of the shops, that of barber Jerry Tyson, is named simply "League." Tyson, who has been here 20 years, works by appointment only and offers a free mustache trim with hair styling; cost, $5. The shop is paneled, its walls bearing pennants from area schools: Bradley University, Illinois Wesleyan University, Western Illinois University,

Southern Illinois University; and the medallions of professional baseball teams: Chicago Cubs, St. Louis Cardinals. Business is good, he says; there is no dead time here.

The men in the square lament that Friday and Saturday nights are not what they used to be, when crowds of people surged along the streets and filled the grassy square, and when there was band music and a sense of the festive life. "Lot of that gone now," says one of the men. "Lot of those people gone, too, planted out in the cemetery. Maybe some of us will be, too, next time you come by. Be a whole new bunch here."

Maybe.

The sun pushes on to the west, and the shade from the trees dapples the grass. The flag uncurls slowly in the hot breeze. Ninety degrees now. Two girls in short skirts climb into an old Oldsmobile and drive away, noisily. The McShane Bell in the courthouse tower clangs again, once, twice.

Almost time for the circus matinee. Barefoot boys with dollar bills crumpled in their jeans pockets begin to head toward the fairgrounds, down the wide street, past the houses with the deep lawns, on sidewalks set far back from the curbs.

Step right up. Time to start the music. Time to start the show. Time to start the summer that has, in Rushville, the gentle and easy flow of cool water through a meadow creek, a cloud drifting across a hot sky, the talk of old men beneath the trees in the square, or that of the women on the benches along the sidewalk or in the cafe.

Tomorrow, the circus will be gone. For the young, summer will stretch away endlessly, like the great shimmering prairie. Fall, for the older ones, comes far too soon.

Index of Parallel Readings

Note: This collateral index is provided to assist teachers and students of Illinois history who are using Robert P. Howard's *Illinois: A History of the Prairie State* (Grand Rapids: Eerdmans, 1972) as a standard textbook. The lefthand column lists the chapter titles of Howard's history since the Civil War period; the righthand column lists the pages in this documentary history which cover the historical material corresponding to each of those chapters.

Index